THE BICYCLIST'S SOURCEBOOK

WOODBINE HOUSE • 1991

For information regarding sales of this book, please contact:
Woodbine House, 5615 Fishers Lane, Rockville, MD 20852, 800/843–7323.

Cover design: Supon Design Group

Library of Congress Cataloging-in-Publication Data

Leccese, Michael.
    The bicyclist's sourcebook : the ultimate directory of cycling information / by Michael Leccese and Arlene Plevin.
        p.   cm.
    Includes index.
    ISBN 0-933149-41-7 (pbk.) : $16.95
    1. Cycling—United States—Directories. 2. Bicycles—United States—Directories.
I. Plevin, Arlene. II. Title.
GV1043.7.L43   1991
796.6'0973—dc20   90–50508
                                                                                              CIP

Manufactured in the United States of America

1 2 3 4 5 6 7 8 9 10

Table of Contents

# Introduction

. . . .

*"Vive le velo! C'est un
ami de l'homme, comme le cheval."
(Long live the bicycle! It is a friend
to man, like the horse.)*

—Henry Miller

. . . .

Your bicycle is as versatile a tool as you want. On my bicycles, I have explored national forests, traveled from Austria to England, carried home a fifty–pound bag of cement, delivered a pizza, gone to visit my sister down the street, toured Ireland, gone scouting for bald eagles, raced a ten–mile loop at 30 mph, traveled 3,000 miles by myself, and ridden a hundred miles in a day in the company of several hundred other cyclists. I commute to work by bicycle and pick up groceries on the way home. I courted my wife, Kathleen, on a bicycle.

This book should help you get to know your bicycle, to acquire the necessary accessories, and to avoid the unnecessary. Maybe cycling will not become your way of life, as it has mine. But at least you might reclaim the 10–speed from the attic, buy a new bike, discover a new trail in your area, join a cycling club, or learn how to pack your bike for travel. Or realize that your bike can help you lose weight, lower your blood pressure, or relieve your community's traffic and smog problems. Think of it as your second car (or your first!). Load it up with baguettes and library books.

—Michael Leccese

....

If there's a better way to see the world, it hasn't been found yet. That's what I believe and you can almost deduce this from the semi-permanent chain mark on my right leg and my penchant for dreaming about the next tour. So, I might as well confess from the beginning, whatever I'm doing—if it's not bicycling—well, I'd rather be pedaling.

Ever since I was five and portaged my next-door neighbor Denise around on the back of my red tricycle, I've loved cycling. Back then, my bike was a new and shiny way of getting around faster. It was also a tool of rebellion and discovery: at nine I used my trusty blue Schwinn to run away from home for silly reasons, childish misperceptions of parental injustice. What I determined, however, was that I could change my scenery—I could go wherever I wanted my wheels to.

I agree with Michael: the bicycle is an incredibly versatile piece of equipment. Only our imagination limits us. I've waddled home with a five-pound watermelon bulging from my panniers, commuted to work down tree-lined boulevards, and reveled in unexpected summer rain. From Melbourne to Sydney, Australia; Berkeley, California, to Port Townsend, Washington; Tecate to Cabo San Lucas, Baja Mexico; and throughout some forty states, I've shared adventures, friendship, and miles—all on my bicycle.

When you open up your world by traveling, commuting, or recreating by bicycle, you bring in a great deal. Literally. A whole community of folks flock to the bicycle, attracted by its simple virtues. **The Bicyclist's Sourcebook** is our effort to share the incredible diversity of bicycling; to let you get a feel for its variety and its possibility in your life. Read this book on a rainy day and let it help you plan for future rides and dream about excursions and exotic destinations.

—Arlene Plevin

From Both of Us:
....

Whatever you seek from cycling—this is the place to start looking for encouragement and information. Herein is listed the name and address of every club, nonprofit organization, tour operator, cycling event, manufacturer, and supplier we could find in months of looking.

There's a lot of subjects covered and some cross-pollination, as it were. Use the table of contents and the subject index to discover where you can find everything on your area of interest. Off-road cyclists may, for example, find frame builders in the sections on frames, appropriate book and magazine titles in the book section, and information on legal off-road riding in the section on mountain bike manufacturers.

To acquaint you with the wonderful diversity of cycling, we've included some useful articles on such subjects as racing, advocacy, alternative bikes, and fitness. These articles were contributed by experts who have hundreds of years of cycling experience among them. Some have written books of their own that are worth checking out for more in-depth information.

Now, a few caveats.

First, this sourcebook is expansive; however, bicycling is a diverse and rich field. We'll admit right here: this book doesn't include everything. But if you decide to explore further, you'll find that the many cycling publications and organizations listed can provide excellent leads. At this moment, all information we've included is up-to-date. However, companies move, prices go up—in other words, the world changes. Please double check on prices and do let us know about material you've uncovered so that we may include it in future editions.

We've made every effort to survey the companies who provide cycling goods and services and to present informally the more interesting results. In some cases we quote directly from their promotional material, using, of course, quote marks. Take these statements for what they are worth.

Second, if you read about an intriguing product, say a thermal water bottle, don't call Bic's Bike Bottle Works directly. Their 800 numbers notwithstanding, Bic's and other companies prefer dealing with retail bike shops or their distributors. Find a bike shop (or catalog) you like and order through them. (Beware: Some racing-oriented bike shops only deal with ectomorphic technoids who ride 9–pound, $3,000 bikes. They make the average customer feel like a crasher at a coronation.) The exception to this rule is for custom services, bike tours, publishers, and catalogs. They welcome your calls.

Third, we do not endorse any particular product, company, or organization. This is no consumer testing guide, although it does provide some basic wisdom that will help you make sound choices. The only mandatory equipment, in our view, is a well-maintained bicycle and a helmet. Everything else is strictly for pleasure, comfort, or looks.

The point is, bicycling is for individualists. What works for you won't necessarily work for somebody else. But whether you're a beginning, occasional, casual, dedicated, or fanatical cyclist, you should be able to discover or fine tune your style with the help of **The Bicyclist's Sourcebook.**

one

AIRLINES, TRAINS, BUSES, AND UPS: TRAVELING WITH A BIKE?

*I*n the United States, traveling with your bicycle is not as simple as you might hope. Whether you go by plane, train, or bus, or ship it ahead separately, a certain amount of planning is essential. Transporting a tandem bicycle is a challenge few enjoy: many airlines will not accept one as baggage no matter how well it is boxed, and often it won't fit into the size box required by Greyhound or Amtrak. A single bicycle, carefully packed in a bike box (see "Ten Steps to Painless Packing"), is accepted by most airlines and can withstand the rigors of travel. Sturdy plastic bags are not the container of choice, but some cyclists find them adequate. If you portage your bicycle frequently, a hardshell container, costing $250–400, may be the best investment for you. These are designed to take all the knocks baggage handlers might give . . . and more.

Many Americans fly to their destinations, trundling a boxed bike with them. On many airlines, it can cost as much as $90 round trip, and you need to set aside time and materials to pack your bicycle safely. Getting to and from the airport can be a challenge with a boxed bicycle; however, if you choose to pack it up at the airport, you should check that the airline has a box for you and that you've packed all the necessary tools. This cardboard container may cost $15, or it may be free. Some airlines offer a reasonably priced plastic bag.

Travel by train with a bicycle can be less traumatic, but with this mode you must carefully check your destination. Not all trains have a baggage car or handler, and it may not be possible to take a boxed bike where you want to go.

On Greyhound, the bicycle must fit in a box that is no more than 24" x 53" x 74" and weigh no more than 100 pounds. If you are a passenger, it can be one of your two pieces of free, checked luggage. You may choose to ship it separately by packet express. For example, a boxed bike weighing 35 pounds and shipped from New York to Los Angeles would cost approximately $95.

Bike shops often receive their bicycles and other equipment via UPS (United Parcel Service). Now some traveling cyclists are looking to this service for safe and reasonable bike transport. UPS accepts boxed bikes if they weigh seventy pounds or less and their length and girth combined is 130" or less. If your boxed bicycle weighs 35 pounds, shipping it from New York to Los Angeles can cost $17 for regular ground service. Two-day air would cost $38.50, while overnight air service would be $53. Your bike is automatically insured for $100, but you might consider increasing that amount by paying an additional $.30 for each extra $100 of insurance.

If you choose to rent a car and put your bicycle inside, common sense should be your guide. It is smart to avoid leaving a trail of chain lube on the seats or punching holes in the ceiling with the handlebars. A salesperson at Avis echoed most companies' philosophy, proclaiming, "You can do pretty much what you want as long as you don't damage the car."

AIRLINES

North American

Air Canada, 800/422–6232 * Accepts one bicycle per passenger, single- or tandem-seat touring bicycle or one racing bicycle, provided the handlebars are fixed sideways, the pedals are removed, and bike is enclosed in an official Air Canada Plastic Bicycle Bag or equivalent. Plastic bags are $3. Passengers should prepare bicycle before arrival at the airport. Check-in agents do not have tools to remove pedals and handlebars. On international flights, bikes travel free unless you have excess luggage. On North American flights, bikes travel for $19 (US) each.

America West, 800/247–5692 * Single-seat bikes only; you'll have to cut your tandem in half or find alternative transport for it. Bikes can go boxed or unboxed; however, if they are unboxed, the handlebars must be turned and fastened securely, and the pedals must be removed or covered in plastic. Fee for one-way domestic or international travel is $30. Each bike is insured up to $1250. Additional insurance is $1 more for each additional $100 of value. Until December 15, 1991, the fee is waived for athletes participating in a triathlon when they present proof of membership in an athletic organization.

American Airlines, 800/433–7300 * Passenger must arrive one hour before flight time. One bicycle accepted as checked baggage. Handlebars should be turned sideways and secured to frame. If the bicycle is not in a shipping crate, it must be placed in a standard bicycle bag or box. You can buy these from American at $10 plus tax for the bag, $15 plus tax for the box. The bags are 40" x 22" x 86" and made of thick plastic. The boxes are 40" x 9" x 69". Hand holes are provided for ease of handling. The bicycle will be checked on a limited release tag if not in the original sealed factory carton. Cost of flying: $30 per bike. On most international flights, the bicycle flies free, if it is one of two pieces and goes in place of a 62" bag (length, width, height).

Continental Airlines, 800/525–0280 * Bikes fly for $30 each if the flight is within the domestic U.S.; outside the U.S., the fee is $35. Handlebars must be fixed sideways and pedals removed or placed in a cardboard container. Bikes protected by liability if carried in "hardshell" cases. Otherwise, bicycles are not subject to the same consideration as normal baggage in instances of damage. Bicycle boxes are available for $10.

Delta Airlines, 800/221–1212 * Will accept touring or racing bicycles with single seats. Bicycles must have handlebars turned sideways and pedals removed and be packed in cardboard boxes; or the pedals and handlebars must be encased in plastic foam or similar material. Some Delta aircraft are not large enough to hold bicycles in their luggage compartments. When booking a flight, advise the reservations staff or travel agent that you will be traveling with a bicycle. They will try to accommodate you. Bikes fly for $30 in Northern Hemisphere, $70–$150 for transatlantic and transpacific flights. Properly packed bikes are covered under normal baggage insurance. Domestic checked baggage is covered to $1250 per ticketed passenger. International liability is $9.07 per pound. Additional coverage available for one dollar for each $100.

Northwest Airlines, (800) 225–2525 * Touring, racing, or tandem bicycles accepted except on smaller planes (ask when booking). Bikes fly for $45. Handlebars must be fixed sideways and the pedals must be removed, or the handlebars and pedals must be encased in a cardboard box, plastic foam, or similar material. Northwest accepts no liability for damage. Bike boxes are available for $15. On international flights, the bicycle goes for free when it is properly boxed and one of two pieces of checked luggage.

Pan Am, 800/221–1111 * Box or hardshell container accepted as one of two checked bags on international routes. On flights within the U.S. and the Virgin Islands, one-way transport costs $20. Boxes are free but must be requested in advance.

TWA (Trans World Airlines), 800/221–2000 * One bicycle in TWA's box (available for $7 at all airports or their ticket stores in Manhattan) costs $45 one way, including the Caribbean. International: free if in lieu of one of two allowed pieces of luggage.

United Airlines, 800/241–6522 * Bicycles and other sporting equipment OK if properly packaged. While skis travel free (if within the baggage allowance), bicycles do not and cost $45 for one way. United sells boxes for $10. Maximum liability is $1250 per ticketed passenger—not per bag. Extra insurance available for $1 per $100 value declared. If you take United abroad, in most cases a bike goes for free as part of your baggage.

USAIR, 800/428–4322 * Accepted on most flights. Provides free bicycle boxes at most airports. Check before you go, however. Cost for one-way transport is $45, whether it's domestic or international.

Foreign

For information on carriers that also serve the U.S., check listings under "North American."

Aer Lingus (Ireland's national airline), 800/223–6537 * Box, bag, or hardshell container accepted as one of 2 checked bags.

Aeromexico, 800/237–6639 * Box your bike and it goes for free, if it's one of two pieces of checked luggage.

Air France, 800/237–2747 * One suitably packed bike (single seat, touring, or racing) may be considered as one piece of baggage regardless of its dimensions, so long as handlebars are turned sideways and pedals removed. Groups of cyclists traveling together need prior permission to transport their bikes.

Air Jamaica, 800/523–5585 * Single seat or tandems permitted provided the handlebars are moved sideways and the pedals removed.

Air New Zealand, 800/262–1234 * Bicycles go for free as long as they are one of two pieces of checked luggage and are packed in a bike box. If three pieces of luggage are checked, the boxed bike cannot exceed 70 pounds and will cost $80–$100 to transport one way.

Alitalia, 800/223–5730 * One bicycle is accepted as luggage when it is one of two checked pieces. If not boxed, the bike must have its handlebars turned and fastened and the pedals removed.

All Nippon, 800/235–9262 * If your bicycle is packed in a bike box, and it's the second piece of checked luggage, it is free. Handlebars must be turned and the pedals removed.

Avianca, the Airline of Colombia, 800/284–2622 * Bikes permitted if handlebars are moved sideways and pedals are removed.

Balair, 212/581–3411 * Box or hardshell container accepted as one of 2 checked bags. Box available for $10.

British Airways, 800/247–9297 * Box or hardshell container accepted as one of 2 checked bags.

Finnair, 800/950–5000 * Bikes fly free when included in the free baggage allowance. Handlebars should be fixed sideways, tire pressure reduced, and pedals removed.

Iberia Airlines, 800/772–4642 * One packed single-seat touring or racing bicycle will fly free if handlebars are moved sideways and pedals removed.

Japan Airlines, 800/525–3663 * Boxes are available for free, and the bike flies free if it is boxed and one of two pieces of checked luggage. If you have three pieces of checked luggage, it costs $86 from the East Coast to Tokyo.

KLM, Royal Dutch Airways, 800/777–5553 * Box, bag, or hardshell container accepted as one of 2 checked bags.

Lufthansa, 800/645–3880 * One single-seat bicycle equals one checked piece of baggage. Sum of three dimensions cannot exceed 62 inches. Bikes fly free in place of one piece of checked baggage. Handlebars must be moved sideways and the pedals must be removed when carried as baggage.

Qantas, 800/227–4500 * The friendly koala who flies to Australia and elsewhere is happy to take a boxed bicycle. No box is available from them. The bike flies free when it is one of two checked bags. The second bag's dimensions, however, can't exceed 55 inches.

Sabena World, 800/955–2000 * One bike per person is free, if it is one of two pieces of checked luggage. Must be boxed or in a hardshell container.

Scandinavian Airlines, 800/221–2350 * Box, bag, or hardshell container accepted as one of 2 pieces of checked baggage.

TEN STEPS TO PAINLESS PACKING

....

By Marchant Wentworth

Step One:

Gather together masking tape, heavy strapping tape, lots of old newspapers, a six-inch or larger crescent wrench, Allen wrench, or other wrench suitable for loosening the handlebar stem, a scissors or knife, and an empty bicycle box. The bike box should have originally carried a bike as big as yours or bigger.

Step Two:

Put the chain on the outermost rear cog and the innermost front chainwheel. If you want to protect your bicycle's frame, you may wish to wrap a layer of newspaper around the tubes, forks, and chainstays. Remove the pedals. Remember that they screw on in the direction in which you pedal. That means that the right pedal screws clockwise while the left one screws counterclockwise. They should have a light film of bicycle grease on them, so when you reassemble the bicycle they'll go on and come off again. Wrap the pedals together in newspaper.

Step Three:

Remove the front wheel. Unscrew the front quick release if your bicycle has one and tape it to one of the spokes or put it in a bag with the pedals. Then with the crank arms positioned at nine o'clock and three o'clock, nestle the front wheel across the side of the diamond of the frame. Cushion it where it touches the frame with folds of newspaper, and tape it in place.

Step Four:

Remove the handlebar stem. Place the hooks of the bars over the top tube and fit the stem in between the spokes of the front wheel. You can keep the brake cables attached, but take care not to kink them. Cushion the bars with wads of old newspaper and tape the bars to the frame.

Step Five:

Tilt the seat nose down and remove the seat post from the frame. It, too, should have a light film of grease on it. Wrap the seat in newspaper.

Step Six:

The moment of truth. Drop the bike into your handy bike box. If possible, bribe a friend to help by holding the box open. Your bike should slide in and sit on the box's bottom without the box incurring any nasty bulges or stresses. Cushion everything that sticks out, like the rear derailleur, rear axles, front fork ends. Insert a wad of newspaper or a block of wood in between the front fork ends to brace them.

Step Seven:

Remember to put the wrapped pedals and seat into the box. Make sure you pack appropriate tools to reassemble your trusty steed either in the box or in your carry on luggage. Carry some sort of non-terrorist-looking blade to cut the tape on your box when you need to reassemble it.

Step Eight:

Survey the surroundings to make sure you haven't forgotten anything. Riding a bike without pedals, for example, takes a special talent that not all of us have.

Step Nine:

Tape the box closed with heavy strapping tape. Use serious tape. Don't try to make do with thousands of layers of electrical tape. Reinforce the box's bottom and sides. Also reinforce the hand holes on the side because they tend to rip out. Mark the box liberally with your name and address.

Step Ten:

Relax and have a chilly something. Your steed is resting comfortably in its new cushioned home. Baggage handlers are actually mostly gentle people who have neither the time nor inclination to deliberately wreak havoc on your bicycle. Have faith. Because of your diligence, your bicycle, like thousands before it, will emerge unscathed from its cardboard chrysalis, ready to roll again.

A D.C.-based environmental lobbyist and ex-bike mechanic who massages bicycles in his basement, Marchant Wentworth is the author of *The Clear Creek Bike Book*.

Swissair, 202/296–5380 * Boxed bikes with handlebars turned sideways and pedals removed.

TAP, The Airline of Portugal, 800/221–7370 * Box or hardshell container accepted as one of 2 pieces of checked baggage.

Varig Brazilian Airlines, 800/468–2744 * Bicycles fly free as one regular piece of luggage so long as pedals are removed and handlebars turned sideways.

For More Information

Survey of Airline Baggage Regulations for Bicycles, Baggage Regulations for Bikes, International Bicycle Fund, 4887–Z Columbia Dr. S., Seattle, WA 98108, 206/767–3927 * Rules, regs, and charges for flying with a bike.

See Accessories *section for list of manufacturers of travel cases for bicycles.*

*TRAIN POLICIES**
. . . .

North American

Amtrak, 800/USA–RAIL * Amtrak supplies a roomy box and charges $5 for handling the bike. The boxed bike can only go on trains with a baggage car and can only be checked on and off where baggage is handled. Timetables advise which trains are suitable. When making reservations, be sure to inform your agent or Amtrak that you plan on taking a bike. Amtrak advises passengers with bikes to arrive one hour before departure to box the bike. You must disassemble the bike, which for an Amtrak box means twisting the handlebars and removing the pedals. Most bikes can fit in the box without removing the wheels.

Via Rail, Canada's national rail system, 800/561–3949 for Alaska, D.C., Del., Fla., Ga., Ky., Mass., Md., Me., N.C., N.H., N.J., Penn., R.I., S.C., Tenn., Vt., Va., and W.Va.; 800/361–3677 for Conn. and N.Y.; 800/387–1144 for Ariz., Mich., Minn., Ill., Ind., Mo.,

---

* *All Fees 1990*

Wisc., Ohio, Iowa; 800/665–0200 for everyone else! Via Rail's bike policy mirrors Amtrak's: they supply a box and charge $5 for handling the bike. The boxed bike can only go on and off a train with a baggage car and only at stations that handle baggage.

Note: Various metropolitan light rail systems, such as Washington, D.C.'s Metro and the San Francisco Bay Area's BART, permit bikes during certain hours. Check with local authorities for rules and regulations.

Foreign

Austria * Bikes permitted as free hand baggage. Bike rentals at major train stations for about $3 a day for passengers, $6 a day for everyone else.

Belgium * On most trains bikes may be carried free. Bike rentals at all train stations.

Britain * Bicycles do not need to be boxed, but rules vary from route to route. Some trains accept bicycles, while others don't. A reservation fee of 3 pounds (approximately $5.50) per bike per journey is sometimes required. Check with local stations.

Czechoslovakia * Bikes travel as baggage for small fee. No restrictions on bike travel if visitor has visa.

Denmark * Bikes carried on trains as checked baggage at cost based on length of trip, up to $5.50. Bike rentals at most major train stations.

France * On most trains other than Intercity and high-speed (TGV) trains, bicycles ride free. In timetables, bike symbol indicates which trains accept bikes. Passengers must load and unload bikes; or leave bikes with a baggage handler (about $5 or $6).

Germany * On some trains, indicated in timetable by suitcase symbol (means train has baggage car), bikes ride free with proper receipt obtained from ticket office. Also, bike rentals at 284 train stations.

Hungary * Bikes ride as baggage for small fee.

Italy * Except on InterCity trains, passengers can take bike as checked baggage; cost based on weight and distance. Passengers need claim check from baggage office.

Netherlands * Bikes carried on trains at charge that varies with distance, season, and day of week. Most stations have bikes for rent.

Poland * Bikes checked as baggage for small fee.

Spain * Bikes carried as personal luggage ride free in baggage compartments.

Switzerland * Small fee for trips within Switzerland. Bikes must be checked at baggage office.

 *two*

ACCESSORIES

Despite our repeated advice to keep it simple, we own quite a selection of cycling paraphernalia. There's folding tires for touring; different sets of packs for commuting, touring, and grocery shopping; a (now-antique) solar-powered bike computer and lots of . . . stuff. Stuff hanging on hooks, stuff packed in boxes, stuff bracketed onto the bikes. Stuff we do in fact use regularly. It's easy to spend a couple of hundred annually on bike gear. But heck, that's the cost of one tune-up for a now unnecessary first or second car.

Here's a quick look at who makes gear hardware, racks, trailers, computers, etc. For those of you who haven't got it all or haven't even heard of it, don't worry. It's when you've accumulated five things from each section that you might consider another type of hardware: a storage shed or tree house for all the things you've purchased for that simple bicycle.

BICYCLE CARRIERS AND RACKS

Before shopping for a rack, consider these questions: Where on your car do you want to put the rack? What kind of gutters does your car have? Do you want a rack that goes on and off easily? Are you tall enough to put a bike or two on your car's roof without assistance? (The shorter author of this book must choreograph a running start, bicycle in hand, to get it onto her car's roof.) Do you own a kayak, canoe, skis, or big dog and might, therefore, want the option of carrying other sporting equipment? And, how many bikes do you want to handle at once? Note: whichever brand you do buy, stash bungie cords and soft cloths in your car for additional protection and padding.

Blackburn, 1510 Dell Ave., Campbell, CA 95008, 408/370–1010 * The master designer has just come up with a rack that fits on cars. Check it out. See also "Bike Racks, Panniers, and Packs" below.

Cannondale Corporation, Georgetown, CT 06829, 800/BIKE–USA or in Pennsylvania or outside lower 48, 814/623–2626 * Special rack for pickup truck.

Cyclone Products Corporation, P.O. Box 3182, Lewiston, ME 04243, 800/762–9253 * Designed by an aeronautics engineer, Cyclone's Bi Rap is a stretchy protective cover for bicycles traveling upright on a roof rack.

Graber, 5253 Verona Rd., Madison, WI 53711, 800/542–6644 * Roof and rear-mounted racks for cars and pick-ups. Also, stationary rack for wall storage and parking stands for up to 18 bikes.

Hollywood Engineering, Inc., 5856 Avalon Blvd., Los Angeles, CA 90003, 213/234–0209 * Makes carriers that can handle four bikes. Also features "easily installed" truck rack.

Norco Products USA Inc., 18201 Olympic Ave. S., Tukwila, WA 98188, 206/251–9370 * Rear-mounted bike racks for cars, child carriers, locks, handlebar bags, helmets, pumps, tools, and spare parts.

Slider Corporation, 1488 Railroad St., Glendale, CA 91204, 818/243–4949 * Heavy-duty (13 pounds of steel), rear-mounted auto rack that's supposed to protect the finish of both car and frame.

Staro, 1200 Fisher St., Box 81, Charles City, IA 50616, 515/228–2119 * The "Hitchbiker" is a heavy-duty rear-mounted rack for vans and RVs.

Terzo, 10652 Walker St., Cypress, CA 90630, 800/321–1191 * Roof racks with accessories for luggage, sailboards, etc.

Thule, Eldon Group America, Inc., 175 Clearbrook Rd., Elmsford, NY 10523, 914/592–4812 * Swedish-made roof rack adaptable for everything from mountain bikes to skis. Catalog lists 6 pages of accessories.

TransSporter, Valley Industries, 1313 S. Stockton St., Lodi, CA 95240, 800/423–6726 * A bike carrying system that turns into a floor stand. The TranSporter extends your bike away from the car and prevents each from bashing the other.

Trek, P.O. Box 183B, Waterloo, WI 53594 * Bicycle carriers that can carry up to three bikes.

Yakima, P.O. Drawer 4899, Arcata, CA 95521, 707/826–8133, 707/826–8149 * Made in USA roof racks for bikes, etc. Aerodynamic roof case (weighs 43 pounds) one of many options. 30–page catalog available.

BIKE RACKS, PANNIERS, AND PACKS

Racks enable you to put more stuff on your bicycle. If you're at all serious about commuting, doing errands on your bicycle, or taking a tour, buy a rear rack. If your roads are ragged, bumpy, or rough in general, consider using Locktight™, or a similar product, on the rack's bolts. That way they're less likely to wiggle out.

Panniers or bags fit on the rack, providing a place to carry books, groceries, clothing, or anything else you might desire. Many manufacturers advise purchasers to seal the seams before using the panniers. Definitely do so as this helps keep your possessions dry. Also line your pannier with a large plastic bag to give whatever you're carrying extra protection.

Fanny packs, butt bags, or whatever you label them are quite useful for carrying a few items that don't fit in a jacket or jersey pocket. You might also carry a camera in a pack that's got extra padding.

Advent, Cyclotech, Service Cycle, 48 Mall Dr., Commack, NY 11725 * Panniers, saddles, handlebar bags, fanny packs.

Bike Pro, 3701 W. Roanoke, Suite 3, Phoenix, AZ 85017, 602/272–3588 * Manufactures many things, including a pannier that's more like a shopping basket. In fact, with 2100 cubic inch capacity, these pannier/baskets are perfect for grocery shopping.

Blackburn, 1510 Dell Ave., Campbell, CA 95008, 408/370–1010 * Blackburn made his name designing state-of-the-art bicycle racks, and now *his* company is tackling seat packs, panniers, car racks, and bags.

Bushwacker, 162 Aviador, Camarillo, CA 93010, 805/484–0586 * Handlebars, rack packs, panniers, and travel cases made in the U.S.

Eclipse, Inc., 3771 E. Ellsworth Rd., Ann Arbor, MI 48108, 800/666–1500 * Panniers made of synthetic weaves. The line includes packs for handlebars, saddles, and touring; racks; commuter baskets; and a portable stationary trainer.

5th Wheel Bikerack, 11911 Hamden Place, Santa Fe Springs, CA 91670, 213/948–3181 * A bike rack that converts a rear-mounted spare tire into a bike carrier.

Bruce Gordon Cycles, 613 Second St., Petaluma, CA 94952, 707/762–5601 * Chromoly racks for panniers. See also listing in *Bicycle Manufacturers* section.

Lone Peaks Designs, LTD, Salt Lake City, UT 84109, 800/777–7679 * Packs and panniers for touring, commuting, tools, handlebars, and fannies.

Overland Equipment, 2145 Park Ave. #4, Chico, CA, 916/894–5605 * Bags and panniers for touring, tools, day-trips, cameras, water bottles; also fanny packs.

Rhode Gear, 765 Allens Ave., Providence, RI 02905, 800/456–2800 * Rear-mounted car racks, child seats, racks, helmets, U-locks, pumps, mirrors, panniers, et al, from a veteran New England company.

Specialized, 15130 Concord Circle, Morgan Hill, CA 95037–5037, 408/779–6229 * Colorful, sturdy bags with lots of nooks and crannies for gear and clothes.

Trek, P.O. Box 183B, Waterloo, WI 53594 * Compact seat packs to large duffle bags in assorted bright colors. Free catalog.

COMPUTERS

Avocet, Inc., P.O. Box 120, Palo Alto, CA 94302, 415/321–8501 * Their latest innovation is a bike computer that registers altitude along with speed, pedal RPMs, etc. Most recent catalog lists padded saddles for mountain bikes, tires, touring shoes, socks, gloves, and bottle cages.

Balboa Instruments/Power Pacer, 1611 Babcock St., Newport Beach, CA 92663 * Heart monitors.

Cateye Co., 2–8–25 Kuwaza, Higashi Sumyoshi-ku, Osaka, Japan, 06/719–7781 * Bike computers and lights are what they're best known for, but Cateye also makes toe clips, bottle cages, a wind-trainer, and other accessories.

Ciclo Sport USA/Ciclomaster, 1540 Barclay Blvd, Buffalo Grove, IL 60089 * Bike computers that display speed, trip odometer, average speed, maximum speed, elapsed time and cadence, with accessories for heart-rate and altitude. Available in black and neon colors.

Polar USA, 470 West Ave, Stamford, CT 06902, 203/359–1966 * A computerized heart monitor "for serious cyclists." Straps on to your chest with wristwatch-style monitor.

Professor Speed, Tom Moylan, P.O. Box 7093, Boulder, CO 80306, 303/443–8191 * Professor Speed's "Mathlete" is a simple computation wheel that helps bikers and other athletes figure average speed, heart rate, pace, race goals.

Vitus, 5 rue des Echarneaux, Z.I. du Coin, B.P. 223, 42400 Saint-Chamond, France * See "Cranks, Derailleurs, and Other Components" below.

CRANKS, DERAILLEURS, AND OTHER COMPONENTS

Ah, the choices are staggering. Here's where other cyclists, your local bicycle club, and your trusty bike store come in handy. Just keep what you've got in good repair and try not to lust after every new gee-gaw that comes on the market.

AC International, 11911 Hampden Pl., Santa Fe Springs, CA 90670, 800/BIKE–REP, 213/948–3181 * Manufacturers Tuffy liners, Quik Sticks, and water bottles.

American Cycle Systems, Inc., P.O. Box 2597, 245 8th Ave., City of Industry, CA 91746, 818/961–3942 * Components including hubs, brakes, rims, and tires for everything from racing to BMX.

Armour Mfg. Corporation (North America), 301–8055 Anderson Rd., Richmond, BC V6Y I5Z Canada, 604/270–7867 * Cycling components.

Breeze & Angell, P.O. Box 201–X, Fairfax, CA 94930, 415/454–6536 * For serious mountain bikers, these folks make the Hite-Rite. A handy device, the Hite-Rite allows you to lower and raise your quick release saddle without getting off it. Comes in four models.

Bullseye, 418 South Varney St., Burbank, CA 91502, 800/874–0600; fax: 818/846–0953 * Made in USA hubs, cranks.

Campagnolo Corporation, 43 Fairfield Pl., West Caldwell, NJ 07006, 201/882–8873 * Known on this side of the Atlantic as just "Campy," this is the classic name in Italian components—from brake levers to cranks; basically everything but the frame. Ferrari prices, too.

Dia-Compe, Inc. USA, Cane Creek Rd., P.O. Box 798, Fletcher, NC 28732 * Brake levers, assemblies, cables, blocks, and tools from a company that's been around for a while.

DT-Competition, United Wire Works Ltd. Biel, Division DT-Cycle Parts, Neumarktstrasse 33, CH–2501 Biel, Switzerland, 032/22–99–11 * Double-butted racing spokes made in Switzerland from chromium-nickel stainless steel.

Dynamic Tension Power Grips, P.O. Box 4250, Grand Junction, CO 81502, 303/241–3518 * Elastic straps for mountain bike pedals that replace more cumbersome toe clips and straps.

HuGI-Technik, BikeLab Limited, 1001 Bridgeway, #623, Sausalito, CA 94965, 415/330–5488 * High-tech, Swiss-made hubs.

KEI, 1072 Graham Ave., Kent, OH 44240, 216/673-7656 * Manufactures the Hydra Post, an adjustable shock absorber seat post. For mountain or street bikes.

Look Performance Sports, Inc., 1971 S. 4490 West, Salt Lake City, UT 84104, 801/973–9770 * Manufactures the famous Look pedals, which come in four models. Also check out their shoes.

Mathauser Hydraulic, 101 1st St., Ste. 177, Los Altos, CA 94022, 415/948–0303 * Hydraulic brakes for tandems, touring, racing, ATB.

Mavic, 01990 Saint-Trivier-Sur-Moignans, France. Racing-oriented rims, derailleurs, hubs, cranks, disc wheels, more, for road bikes and ATBs.

Odyssey, Bear Corp., 17101 S. Central Ave., #G, Carson, CA 90746, 213/537–8700; fax: 213/631–1093 * Some interesting design solutions for mountain bikes, such as a pump/seat post combination, a front-fork stabilizer, and a kind of power-assisted brakes. Also: tires, stems, brake cables, and hand-grips.

Ozone Freestyle Co., 1250–E Yard Ct., San Jose, CA 95133, 408/292–5962 * Cycling components.

Paradigm, 3832 148th Ave. NE, Redmond, WA 98052, 800/473–6457 * A transmission system designed to replace the rear derailleur with a sealed system of interlocking sprockets.

Profile for Speed, 6600 W. Armitage Ave. Suite 200, Chicago, IL 60635, 312/237–5782 or 800/852–5952; fax: 312/237–3039 * Aerobars, stems, aerobar shifters, carbon-fiber handlebars, seat posts, leopard-skin handlebar tape, and the "Air Raid," a composite frame that weighs 3.6 pounds and costs in the 4 figures.

Regina USA, 311 Commerce Drive, Easton, MD 21601, 301/820–5556 * Chains, cranks, freewheels, and other components from an Italian manufacturer that just celebrated its 70th anniversary. Racing-oriented.

Rhode Gear, 765 Allens Ave., Providence, RI 02905, 800/456–2800 * Also see "Bike Racks and Panniers" above.

Sachs Bicycle Components, 14526 South Garfield Ave., Paramount, CA 90723, 213/602–0319; fax: 213/602–2145 * Hardware from a veteran European manufacturer. Chains, freewheels, hubs—just about everything for bikes but the frame.

Scott USA, P.O. Box 2030, Dept. B, Sun Valley, ID 83353, 208/622–1000, 800/338–2794 (orders only) * Aerobars, brakes, pedals, and grips for racing and mountain bikes.

Shimano American Corporation, Irvine, CA, 800/833–5540 * One of the larger component companies. Makes indexed shifters, clipless pedals, brake levers, cranks, much more. 31–page catalog available.

SR Sakae USA, 18650 72nd Ave., S. Kent, WA 98032, 206/251–8785; 800/23–SAKAE * Mountain bike components.

SRAM Corporation, 2030 West Carrol Ave., Chicago, IL 60612, 800/346–2928 * Their grip shift is an index shifting system meant to be twisted. To wit, you can shift without moving your hands from the ends of the handlebars. One racer commented, "I'm shifting twice as much and really saving my legs."

Sugino Cycle Industries, 201–1 Karamomo-Cho Nara, Japan, 0742/62–5320 * Aluminum and composite cranks and chain wheels.

Suntour, Maeda Industries Ltd., 75 Digital Dr., Novato, CA 94949, 415/883–1220 * Hardware, including chain rings, cranks, bottom brackets, derailleurs, brakes, and chain cogs. A new system called Grease Guard promises 30–second lube jobs without overhauling the crankset.

Syncros Applied Technology, 15–A W. 2nd Ave., Vancouver, BC V5Y 1B1, Canada, 604/879–4684 * Mountain bike parts and gear, including waterproof grease, mud flaps, handlebars, stems, cranksets, seat posts, forks. Made in Canada.

Time USA, 890 Cowan Rd., Burlingame, CA 94010, 415/692–0272 * Clipless pedals and shoes worn by such pro racers as Greg LeMond, Steve Bauer, and Pedro Delgado. Latest innovation is a clipless pedal designed to be worn with a touring shoe. Instead of a cleated sole, you get a recessed notch. This allows you to walk normally off the bike.

Tioga, P.O. Box 5330, Compton, CA 90224, 213/719–1718 * All manner of software (from tires to toe clips) and hardware (from bottom brackets to seat posts) from this popular Japanese company.

Union Frondenberg USA Co., 1 Union Drive, Olney, IL 62450, 618/395–8471 * German-made pedals, chains, hubs, spokes, and lights. See also listing in *Safety* section.

VF Technology, Inc., P.O. Box 1476, Center Harbor, NH 03226, 603/279–3055 * For all you serious off-road cyclists, the Rock-Ring, a crank cover that allows you to "bike back."

Vitus, 5 rue des Echarneaux, Z.I. du Coin, B.P. 223, 42400 Saint-Chamond, France * Spokes, tires, seat posts, bottom brackets, and cycle computers from the noted French frame-makers.

Winners Products, 2905 Miraloma Ave., Unit 3 & 4, Anaheim, CA 92806, 714/632–9600 * Sealed hubs—meaning no greasing, overhauls, or other maintenance—costing hundreds of dollars a set.

*F*AIRINGS
....

"BreezeCheater," Fairfield Product Engineering Corporation, P.O. Box 1091, Fairfield, CT 06430, 203/371–1901, 800/442–2271 * The BreezeCheater is a wind screen (or "fairing") that promises 20 percent reduction of drag and (if performance doesn't interest you but warmth does) more than 50 percent reduction of wind chill. Weighs 3 pounds.

Zzip Designs, P.O. Box 14, Davenport, CA 95017, 408/425–8650 * Fairings for road, mountain, recumbent, and folding bikes. The manufacturer says it reduces wind drag by 7 percent.

ALL ABOUT ODDBALL GEAR TRAINS

....

By Frank Berto

About a hundred years ago, "the germ of the idea for the lever chain fell on the brain" of an English inventor, W. S. Simpson. I use his own words. Simpson's Lever Chain had triangular links which parted to increase the leverage on the rear sprocket and came together to reduce the leverage on the chainwheel. This "secured much greater speed without any extra exertion." So successful was Simpson's salesmanship that for five years, the major British bicycle manufacturers included Simpson Lever Chains as an extra-cost option. Many early speed records were set with Lever Chains. Simpson started his own bicycle company in 1896 and he listed H. R. H. the Prince of Wales and H. R. H. the Duke of York as users.

Unfortunately the Lever Chain had no mechanical advantage. It cost more and it created extra friction. In 1896, Archibald Sharp, in his splendid Victorian treatise on bicycle engineering, *Bicycles & Tricycles,* wrote the following about the Simpson Lever Chain:

> "It is possible, by using an algebraic fallacy which may easily escape the notice of anyone not sufficiently skilled in mathematics, to prove that 2 x 2 = 5; but though human misunderstanding may be deceived by the mechanical and algebraic paradoxes, in neither case are the laws of Nature altered or suspended. When once the doctrine of 'conservation of energy' is thoroughly appreciated, plausible mechanical devices for creating energy will receive no more attention than they deserve."

I've been attending bicycle shows for two decades and I can say that the spirit of W. S. Simpson is alive and well and germs of ideas for improved bicycle gear trains still fall on the brains of today's inventors. These inventions have common characteristics:

- The inventor believes that current gear trains in which the pedals rotate in a 14–inch diameter circle at 60 to 120 rpm are ergonomically wrong, mechanically inefficient, and probably immoral.

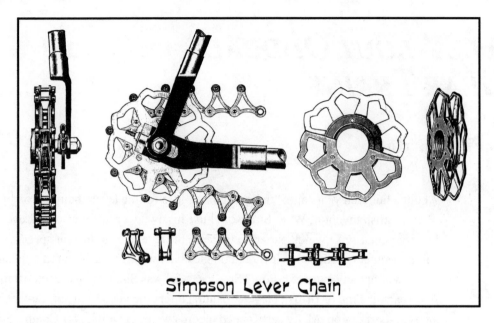

Simpson Lever Chain

- The inventor believes in his invention with true religious fervor. There are testimonials from satisfied users.

- The inventor believes that all he must do is to demonstrate the superiority of his invention. Then financial sponsors and buyers will launch him on the road to fame and fortune.

The real world is hard on bicycle gear train inventors. Only rarely does an invention survive long enough to show up at a second bicycle show. My file titled "Oddball Gear Trains" contained seven inventions from the 1980s. I've arranged them in alphabetical order. Not all of them are "mechanical devices for creating energy." Judge them for yourself.

ALENAX TRANSBAR POWER SYSTEM

I first saw this in 1984. It was invented by a Korean, Byung D. Yim. The transbar pedal levers are about 15 inches long. They move up and down 110 degrees. The levers are connected to rear hub freewheels by chains on either side—much like the old coaster wagons that we called "Irish Mails." The length of the chain lever arm is adjustable to give four "gears." Pushing one pedal down moves the other pedal up. Alenax made a complete line of bicycles for a year or so. They were headquartered in Rochester, New York.

EFROS TRANSMISSION PEDAL SYSTEM

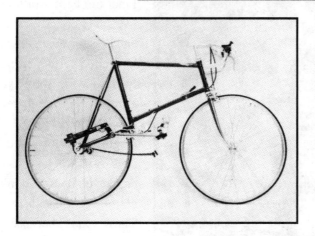

I saw this in 1988 but I didn't pedal it. Boris Efros, the inventor, was from Los Angeles. The Efros has an up-and-down pedal motion similar to the Alenax. Unlike the Alenax, the pedals aren't linked together. With the Efros, one pedal can go up as the other goes down or they can go up and down together. It's possible to vary the "gear."

ERICH SPLIT CRANK

I saw this in 1989. The short outer crank on the end of the long inner crank is geared to turn at the pedal cadence. This converts the pedal motion to a long vertical ellipse "providing the same torque but eliminating inefficient horizontal motion." Richard Erich, the inventor, was from Jackson, California.

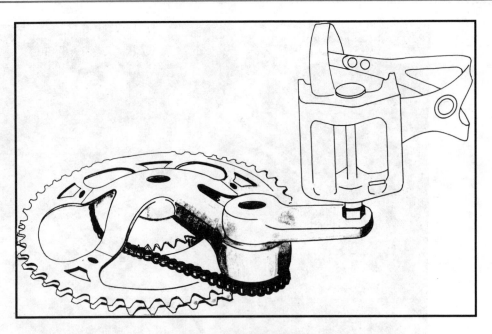

FARNSWORTH FORMULA

I met Jim Farnsworth in 1987. He lives in Laconia, New Hampshire, and he's the evangelist of extra-long cranks. He's been at his lonely crusade for twenty years. The Farnsworth Formula relates the crank length to the rider's leg length. Extra-long is just what it says. A six-footer uses a 225–mm crank. Jim doesn't think that's extra-long. He calls them Full-Throw cranks because they allow a full walking stride. He makes up small batches of extra-long cranks and he can provide custom-built bikes with the necessary high bottom brackets. The basic concept behind Farnsworth, Powercam, and even Shimano's BioPace chainrings is that God intended man to move his legs at a walking cadence, about 60 rpm. Spinning at 100-plus rpm is a skill that must be acquired for optimum performance with conventional gear trains.

HOUDAILLE POWERCAM

Powercam appeared in 1983 and lasted for about five years. There are a fair number in service and I've received testimonials from satisfied users. The pedals go around in conventional circles but the torque delivered to the chainwheel varies with the crank angular position. The action is similar to that of an oval chainring with lots of ovality. I pedaled a Powercam for a few miles, not nearly enough to get used to it. It felt like walking down a staircase. The slow (60 rpm or so) pedaling cadence causes most users to fit and use much higher gears.

Houdaille operated out of Fort Worth, Texas, until they went out of business.

RISIGO

Risigo stands for Rise-Sit-Go. The idea has been around for about three years. The pedals go up and down together in an arc of about 150 degrees. The saddle rises and falls as you alternately stand and sit. Riding is more like working out on an exercise machine than conventional pedaling. George H. C. Hung, the inventor, is headquartered in Hong Kong.

STS POWER PEDAL

Inventor Freder Stuckenbrock of Germany is the worthy successor to W. S. Simpson. The brochure states: "The Power Pedal takes advantage of one of the basic laws of physics: the longer the lever, the more power that lever delivers. The system uses a telescopic crankarm. When you push down on the pedal, the arm extends to 22 cm, 5 cm longer than the standard crankarm length. This 29.4% extension gives greater, more efficient leverage. On the up-stroke, when less power is being applied, the crankarm telescopes back to its normal length." In 1986, the STS Power Pedal Corp. was headquartered in Vancouver, B.C.

Frank Berto, the former Engineering Editor of *Bicycling* magazine, has written numerous technical articles about bicycle components. He's currently writing for *Bicycle USA,* the magazine of the League of American Wheelmen. His book, *Bicycling Magazine's Complete Guide to Upgrading Your Bike,* is available at bookstores.

INDOOR EXERCISERS AND TRAINERS

Don't like to cycle in snow, sleet, rain, or dark? Here's a partial list of manufacturers whose products will terminate your "I can't exercise" excuse. Crank up the music and pedal away in the privacy of your home.

Al Kreitler Custom Rollers, 316 West Wilson, Ottawa, KS 66067, 913/242–1718 * Rollers and wind trainers for stationary workouts on your own bike.

Avita, 7140 180th Ave. NE, Redmond, WA 98052, 206/885–1010, 800/222–9995 * Indoor exercisers.

BCA, 2811 Brodhead Rd., Bethlehem, PA 18017, 215/868–7652, 800/224–2453 * Indoor exercisers.

Cateye Co., 2–8–25 Kuwaza, Higashi Sumyoshi-ku, Osaka, Japan, 06/719–7781 * See listing under "Computers" above.

Eclipse, Inc., 3771 E. Ellsworth Rd., Ann Arbor, MI 48108 800/666–1500 * Makes a portable stationary trainer.

Quickstand, RTS Trainer Corporation, 4334 N.E. 11th Ave., Fort Lauderdale, FL 33334, 305/561–9377 * Folding, portable wind trainer made from anodized aluminum.

Roadmaster Corp., Radio Tower Road, P.O. Box 344, Olney, IL 62450, 618/393–2991 * Indoor exercisers.

Rollfast Bicycle Co., Inc., P.O. Box 430, Waltham, MA 02254 * Indoor exercisers.

Ross Bicycles Ltd., 51 Executive Blvd., Farmingdale, NY 11735, 516/249–6000, 800/669–ROSS * Has the Ross Futura freewheeling air-resistant Ergometer (say that five times fast).

Schwinn Bicycle Co., 217 N. Jefferson St., Chicago, IL 60606, 312/454–7400 * The Aerodyne and other classics head up Schwinn's indoor cycles.

Tunturi, Inc., 1776 136th Pl. NE, Bellevue, WA 98005, 206/643–1000, 800/426–0858 * Indoor exercisers.

Universal Gym Equipment, P.O. Box 1270, Cedar Rapids, IA 52406, 319/365–7561, 800/553–7901 * Manufactures the AerobiCycle.

KICKSTANDS

Greenfield Industries, 99 Doxsee Dr., Freeport, NY 11520, 516/623–9230.

Ross Bicycles USA, 51 Executive Blvd., Farmingdale, NY 11735, 516/249–6000.

Todson, Inc., 14 Connor Ln., Deer Park, NY 11729, 516/586–5300.

LOCKS

Our advice on locks? Whatever you buy, use it!

AC International, 11911 Hampden Pl., Santa Fe Springs, CA 90670, 800/BIKE–REP, 213/948–3181 * Makes "The Hinge," a one-piece, U-shaped lock with a $5000 guarantee. Also cable locks.

Citadel, Rhode Gear, 765 Allens Ave., Providence, RI 02905 * A strong, U-shaped lock.

Cobralinks, J.J Tourek Mfg. Co., 1800–18 Touhy Ave., Elk Grove, IL 60007, 800/323–8172 (outside IL), 800/942–0389 (inside IL) * Billed as "the newest member of America's toughest family of locking systems."

Kryptonite Corporation, 95 Freeport St., Boston, MA 02122, 617/265–4800 * One of the original U-shaped locks to come with an anti-theft guarantee (now scaled back somewhat), Kryptonite rates its manacles according to your neighborhood's "security level" (e.g., "high crime areas," "low crime areas," et al). They've added designer colors to basic black. And they still say the locks beat everything from hack saws to 42–inch bolt cutters.

Life-Link International, Inc., Box 2913, Jackson Hole, WY 83001, 800/443–8620 * Makes the Lock Pocket. See "General" below.

Lionel Enterprises, 776 Avenida Salvador, San Clemente, CA 92672 * Makes very lightweight cable. Good for minor deterrence.

Pacific West Industries, Seal Beach, CA, 213/430–3101 (fax) * Polycarbonate cable lock (6 feet long, 18 oz.) with a built-in alarm.

WJB Industries, 801 West 12th Ave. North, Clear Lake, IA 50428, 515/357–2650 * WJB's "Bike Guard" is a seat tube-mounted alarm that goes off at 110 decibels if anyone messes with your bike. Weighs 86 grams with battery.

LUBRICANTS

Allsop, P.O. Box 23, Bellingham, WA 98227, 800/426–4303 * Portable tool kit, biodegradable "degreaser," cotton T-shirts. See also listing under *Mountain Bikes*.

Bike Elixir, 1132 Mirabella Ave., Novato, CA 94947 * Lubricants for bike parts.

Finish Line, 19 Beech St., Islip, NY 11751, 516/581–2000 * Lubricants for chains and parts; a wax for the paint-job on your frame.

Park Tool Co., 3535 International Dr., St. Paul, MN 55110, 612/490–1074 * Bike lubricants.

Pedro's Racing Grease, P.O. Box 1149, Cambridge, MA 02142, 617/497–4202 * Grease for bike parts.

Phil Wood & Co., 580 N. 6th St., San Jose, CA 95112, 408/298–1540 * Waterproof grease.

R&D Manufacturing, P.O. Box 5449, Fullerton, CA 92635, 714/871–9118 * Lubricants for bike parts.

Super Lube/Syncho Chemical, 24 Da Vinci Ave., Bohemia, NY 11716, 516/567–5300 * Lubricants.

Tri-Flow, 825 Crossover Lane, Memphis, TN 38117, 901/685–7555 * Lubricants.

Ultramax Enterprises, Inc., 6242 Eastland St., Tucson, AZ 85711, 602/790–0544 * Lubricants.

MISCELLANEOUS

AC International, 9115–1 Dice Rd., Sante Fe Springs, CA 90670, 213/948–3181 * Makes Mr. Tuffy Tire Liners, water bottles, Snoopy and Garfield bicycle accessories (those horns, valve caps, bells, streamers, and baskets you can't do without), and Pocket Pro Tools.

BYCUE, Cue Sheet Holder, P.O. Box 14152, Silver Spring, MD 20911, 800/588–2640, 301/588–2640 * Tired of riding with ride sheets clenched in your teeth or dangling precariously from your handlebars? Try the Cue Sheet Holder, a "lightweight, aerodynamic clip for your handlebars that holds your cue sheet in front of you without obstructing your view." This helpful invention comes in light red, ivory, or sky blue.

IMS Enterprises, P.O. Box 16577, Wichita, KS 67216, 800/346–7332 * Manufactures bicycle storage systems in either oak or aluminum which hold one to four bicycles.

ProBikeFit, Premier Cycles, Denver, CO, 303/331–9502 * Computer program developed by Jack Harrier, a former chemical engineer for Amoco, that helps tailor rider to bike using precise measurements. Available for sale to bike shops.

Ultra-Mac, 1800 N.E. 179 St., Miami, FL 33162, 305/949–3434 * 6–speed hand-pedal conversion kit to add arm-driven oomph to your legs. See also *Bicycle Manufacturers.*

Zefal Christophe, 25 Rue de al Courneuve, 93300 Aubervilliers, France, 33/1–48–33–01–90 * Everything about air, from pumps to pressure gauges, plus fenders, toe clips, other accessories, and even classic Gallic cycling posters.

MOUNTAIN BIKE ACCESSORIES

Dynamic Tension Power Grips, P.O. Box 4250, Grand Junction, CO 81502, 303/241–3518 * Elastic straps for mountain bike pedals that replace more cumbersome toe clips and straps.

Hite-Rite, Breeze & Angell, 18 Meadow Way, Fairfax, CA 94930, 415/454–9601 * For mountain bikes only. Enables cyclist to change seat height without getting off.

Kona/Brodie, The Bicycle Group, 1122 Fir St., Blaine, WA 98230, 206/332–5384 * In addition to mountain bikes, Brodie makes forks, toe clips, tires, and stems.

Odyssey, Bear Corporation, 17101 S. Central Ave. #G, Carson, CA 90746, 213/537–8700; fax: 213/631–1093 * Some interesting design solutions for mountain bikes, such as a pump/seat post combination, a front-fork stabilizer, and a kind of power-assisted brakes. Also: tires, stems, brake cables, and hand-grips.

Onza, 6960 Aragon Circle, Ste. 3, Buena Park, CA 90620 * Mountain-bike racing components, including bar ends, chain rings, tires, seat posts.

Scott USA, P.O. Box 2030, Dept. B, Sun Valley, ID 83353, 208/726–7267, 800/338–2794 (orders only) * Aerobars, brakes, pedals, and grips for racing and mountain bikes.

Specialized, 15130 Concord Circle, Morgan Hill, CA 95037–5037, 408/779–6229 * This mountain-bike company says it's gotten tough. Its latest catalog features a three-spoke wheel capable of withstanding 850 pounds of pressure and a Kevlar tire that they suggest is literally bullet-proof. Also, handlebars, rims, cranksets, tires, racks, panniers; all readily available at bike shops or through catalogs.

SR Sakae USA, 18650 72nd Ave., S. Kent, WA 98032, 206/251–8785 800/23–SAKAE * Mountain bike components.

Syncros Applied Technology, 15 A W. 2nd Ave., Vancouver, BC V5Y 1B1, Canada, 604/879–4684 * Mountain bike parts and gear, including waterproof grease, mud flaps, handlebars, stems, cranksets, seat posts, and forks. Made in Canada.

T-Gear, 6824 N.W. 77th St. Ct., Miami, FL 33166, 800/688–4327 * Racing-oriented aerobars, pads, shifters, mountain-bike accessories.

Wilderness Trail Bikes, 134 Redwood Ave., Corte Madera, CA 94925, 415/924–9632 * Mountain bike components from brake pads to chromoly frames. Send for brochure.

SADDLES

. . . .

What a tender subject! Few things discourage cyclists more than an uncomfortable derriere. Take heart (or should we say something else?), for there's a plethora of solutions to this problem. First check to see that your saddle is the proper height and that you are the right distance from the handlebars. If either of these things is off, you'll put undue pressure on . . . guess what. Next try any number of these saddle solutions. Saddles with gel in them or gel-like covers are popular, although friends say the "smushiness" is comparable to sitting on someone else's backside.

If you're a martyr or interested in creating your own legend, buy a Brooks leather saddle. Conservative estimates suggest that a thousand hours of riding will break that saddle in. Do we suggest that? Ah, 'tis up for you to decide. Many cyclists swear by their broken-in Brooks. Would they do it again? Good question.

Advent, Cyclotech, Service Cycle, 48 Mall Dr., Commack, NY 11725 * See "Bike Racks and Panniers" above.

Avocet, Inc., P.O. Box 120, Palo Alto, CA 94302, 415/321–8501 * Sweet saddles, built for all shapes and styles.

Cinelli S.P.A., Via Egidio Follio, 45, 20134 Milano, Italy, 022/215–1578 (fax) * Distributed by numerous American companies, including Mel Pinto Improts and Cycle Imports. Makes racing saddles and a whole host of other types.

G.T. Bicycles, Inc., 17800 Gothard St., Huntington Beach, CA 92647, 714/841–1169 * Has mountain bike, gel, and racing saddles especially designed for their bicycles.

Persons Majestic Mfg. Co., 21 Hamilton St., Monroeville, OH 44847, 419/465–2508 * "America's most experienced saddle makers." Manufactures the cruiser saddle.

Mel Pinto Imports, P.O. Box 2198, Falls Church, VA 22042, 703/237–4686 * Distributes the famous Brookes saddle, which is in great demand, despite its reputation for torture.

Selle San Marco, 36028 Rossano Veneto (Vi), Italy (Imported by Italian Bicycle Products Corporation, P.O. Box 91321, Austin, TX 78709, 512/288–7600) * Racing-oriented saddles; their latest innovations include a seat-mounted brake light and a saddle made of natural, biodegradable materials.

Specialized, 15130 Concord Circle, Morgan Hill, CA 95037–5037, 408/779–6229 * Manufactures a "blob" saddle. Joe Blob is the men's version, while Betty is the women's. What! No kid blob?

Spenco Medical Corporation, P.O. Box 2501, Waco, TX 76702–2501, 800/433–3334 * Padded and gel-filled saddles, gloves, gel saddles, and other products to either prevent or treat aches, pains, and scrapes.

Terry Precision, 1704 Wayneport Rd., Macedon, NY 14502, 315/986–2103 * Georgena Terry has designed and will manufacture a bicycle saddle. Look for these soon. Given the popularity and comfort of Terry bikes and other accessories, Terry's saddles are bound to be an improvement.

Todson, Inc., 14 Connor Ln , Deer Park, NY 11729, 516/586–5300 * Imports Selle Royal, a saddle made in Italy.

"Waveflo," Alden Labs, Inc., Box 9012, Boulder, CO 80301–9012 * 800/356–2668 * A form-fitting, gel-filled saddle pad. Made for mountain, road, racing, and exercise bicycle saddles.

WRS SportMed, Division of WRS Group, Inc., Waco, TX 76702 * Ultra-soft saddle pad made of duraflex gel/polymer.

TIRES

Tires, tires, tires! Are you outfitting a BMX bicycle? Do you want off-road tires that are cozy and quiet on the road? Are you looking for reasonably priced sew-up tires? Are the roads in your area "paved" with glass, necessitating at the very least bullet-proof tires? And finally, what is the width of your rims? Reflect on these questions and your bicycle (or bicycles). Then pick a set of tires. It's time to replace them if the sidewalls are dry, worn through, and ripped. Numerous glass cuts point to replacement tires as well.

American Cycle Systems, Inc., P.O. Box 2597, 245 8th Ave., City of Industry, CA 91746, 818/961–3942 * Components including hubs, brakes, rims, and tires for everything from racing to BMX.

Armour Mfg. Corporation (North America), 301–8055 Anderson Rd., Richmond, BC V6Y I5Z Canada, 604/270–7867 * Cycling components, including tires.

Avocet, Inc., P.O. Box 120, Palo Alto, CA 94302, 415/321–8501 * Manufactures cross tire, "City Tire," smooth tires, in Kevlar or non-Kevlar, makes Freestyle tire and the Fas Grip smooth road tire.

Continental, XL Marketing Group, 3260 N. Colorado St., Chandler, AZ, 800/223–3207, 602/497–2666; fax: 602/497–2888 * German-engineered mountain bike tires. Has high-pressure tires, including one with 150 psi.

Fisher Mountain Bikes, 140 Mitchell Blvd., San Rafael, CA 94943 * Mountain bike tires.

Kenda, Kenstone Corporation, P.O. Box 132 Reynoldsburg, OH 43068, 614/866–9803 * Mountain bike tires.

La Clement, Via C. Cantu' 19, 20092 Cinisello B., (MI) Italy, 026/442–5539; fax: 026/442–2380 * Tubulars from the heart of the bicycle empire. Imported by lots of folks.

Matrix, product of Trek, 801 W. Madison, P.O. Box 183B, Waterloo, WI 53594, 414/478–2191 * Off- and on-road tires. Reputably nice high-end racing tires. Also manufacturers of rims.

Michelin Tire Corporation, P.O. Box 19001, Greenville, SC 29602–9001 * The fat man from France has discovered the mountain bike tire market. The Hi-Lite Hot model promises long life and protection from punctures. Also tires "ridden by some of the best professional racing teams in Europe."

Odyssey, Bear Corporation, 17101 S. Central Ave. #G, Carson, CA 90746, 213/537–8700; fax: 213/631–1093 * Mountain bike tires.

Onza Tires, 6920 Aragon Circle Ste. 3, Buena Park, CA 90620 * Mountain bike tires.

Specialized, 15130 Concord Cir., Morgan Hill, CA 95037, 408/779–6229 * Manufactures 20 or more types of tires, covering youth to adult, both on- and off-road. Known for their touring tires and for Ground Control, a popular off-road tire used by Specialized's racing team.

Tioga, P.O. Box 5330, Compton, CA 90224, 213/719–1718 * Offers wide range of tires. Get out your plow and saddle up your all-terrain bike with Tioga's Farmer Johns.

Troxel, 1333 30th St., San Diego, CA 92154 * Mountain bike tires. See also *Safety* and *BMX and Kids' Bikes*.

Union Rubber Industries, 10577 La Fuente St., Fountain Valley, CA 92708, 714/964–1190. Bicycle tires.

TRAILERS

Because of their low center of gravity, bike trailers are considered by some to be a safer means of carrying kids than a seat mounted above the rear wheel. They can also be used to carry groceries, touring gear, cement bags, etc.

The Bike Farm, Route 1—Box 99, Cushing, WI 54006, 715/648–5519; fax: 612/433–2704 * Industrial-strength trailer.

Blue Sky Cycle Carts, P.O. Box 704, Redmond, OR 97756, 503/548–7753 * Blue Sky says its trailer carries up to 4 rug rats (up to 300–pound capacity). Weighs 22–26 pounds, hooks to seat post, comes with rain canopy, mud guards, reflectors, optional fenders.

Burley Design Cooperative, Inc., 4080 Stewart Rd., Eugene, OR 97402, 503/687–1644; fax: 503/687–0436 * Trailers that take on up to 100 pounds of kids, dogs, gear, etc., with safety and comfort features like tail lights, weather cover, screen door, and splash guards. Weighs 19 pounds. Tourist model (17.5 pounds) is for touring without kids. See also *Bicycle Manufacturers*.

Cannondale, 9 Brookside Pl., Georgetown, CT 06829, 203/833–4488 * Manufactures several varieties of child trailers that attach to the seat post of the bicycle and seat the passenger facing backwards. Their Kiddy Cart is a low budget trailer.

Cycle Trailer Co., 3330 N. Webster Pl., Tucson, AZ 85715, 602/296–6536 * Manufactures the Whiskit, a 13–pound trailer for carrying camping gear, groceries—everything but kids. The Whiskit attaches to the left side of the bicycle's axle.

Equinox Industries, Inc., 1142 Chestnut Ave., Cottage Grove, OR 97424, 503/942–7895 * The Equinox two-wheel trailer can be folded flat or adapted as an auto roof rack. Built from aluminum tubing and synthetic fabric, it weighs 19 pounds and is rated to carry 150 pounds.

Winchester, Cycle Component, 1061 S. Cypress, La Habra, CA 90631, 714/738–4791 * Face your children forward in these lightweight trailers.

TRAVEL CASES

Bike Kase, Box 4770, Mountain View, CA 94040, 415/965–7045. Bike travel case.

Bike Tote, Concarc, Inc., P.O. Box 24, School St., Terryville, CT 06786, 203/589–2957 * Hardshell case with optional casters for air/rail/bus travel with bike as luggage. Room for extra set of wheels. Weighs 45 pounds.

Bike Traveler, Creative Athletic Products & Services, Box 7731, Des Moines, IA 50322, 800/227–4574. Bike travel case.

Bike Traveler, JJM Industries, 4 Piedmont Center, Suite 111, Atlanta, GA 30305, 800/237–5637, 404/266–1043 * A hardshell case with casters for air/rail/bus travel with a bike as luggage. Room for extra set of wheels. Weighs 24 pounds.

Pedal Pack, 24422 South Main St., #504, Carson, CA 90745, 213/830–2312; fax: 213/830–3408, 800/359–3096 * A heavy-duty, hard-shell bicycle "suitcase" complete with casters. Weighs 26 pounds.

Peloton Industries, 9865 Mesa Rim Rd., Suite 214, San Diego, CA 92121, 619/558–8350 * Its "Cycle Safe" is a heavy-duty (25 pounds) travel case for whole bikes with extra room for gear. "Wheel Safe" (for wheels only) weighs 10 pounds.

WHEELS

. . . .

Yes, they do come with most bike purchases; however, you may choose to special order your own separately. If you torque, or stress, the bejeebers out of your wheels, consider having these manufacturers or your local bike store add more spokes for strength.

Specialized, 15130 Concord Circle, Morgan Hill, CA 95037–5037, 408/779–6229 * Tires, handlebars, rims, cranksets, racks, panniers; all readily available at bike shops or through catalogs.

Sun Metal Products, Warsaw, IN 46580, 219/267–3281 * Lightweight, American-made alloy rims.

UNI-USA, 8025 S.W. 185th, Aloha, OR 97007, 503/649–7922; fax: 503/591–9435 * Nylon wheel covers for all types of bikes.

Wheelsmith, 3551 Haven Ave., Suite R, Menlo Park, CA 94025–1009 * Wheels for touring and racing made by brothers Eric and Jon Hjertberg, who run a legendary bike shop in neighboring Palo Alto.

Zipp, Compositech, 8170 Zionsville Rd., Indianapolis, IN 46268, 800/447–8372 *
Another revolutionary new, three-"spoke" wheel costing many hundreds of dollars. Made
from "aircraft-quality" carbon-fiber composites, light, aerodynamic, and strong.

GENERAL

Airlock, Striders, 3855 S. 500 W. Studio S, Salt Lake City, UT 84115, 801/262–7979 *
Combination lock and pump contraption. Has "extra powerful, cut resistant cables" in addition to a pump that works "quickly and efficiently."

L.L. Bean, Inc., Freeport, ME 04033, 800/221–4221 * Bike computers, locks, bike
covers, helmets, mirrors, lights, panniers, seat bags, wind trainers, saddles, tools, and
sunglasses (several brands, including Bean's own) from the venerable sporting goods
company. Call for catalog.

Cinelli S.P.A., Via Egidio Folli, 45, 20134 Milano, Italy, 022/215–1578 (fax) *
Venerable name in racing for handlebars, seat posts, stems, toe clips, and more has
branched out into panniers, clothing, and other gear.

Giant Bicycle, Inc., 475 Apra St., Rancho Dominguez, CA 90220, 213/609–3340 or 800–
US–GIANT * Fanny packs, computers, racks, grips, repair kits, lights, locks, and more ac-
cessories from the fast-growing Taiwanese bicycle manufacturer. See also listings under
Bicycle Manufacturers, Mountain Bikes, and *BMX and Kids' Bikes.*

Italian Bicycle Products Corporation, P.O. Box 91321, Austin, TX 78709, 512/288–
7600 * Wholesale distributor for Casarighi (brake cable, handlebar bags), Cinelli (frames,
hardware, saddles, clothes), Columbus (tubing, bottom brackets, forks, clothing).

Life-Link International, Inc., Box 2913, Jackson, WY 83001, 800/443–8620, 307/733–
2266 * Company started by three guys who spent six years pedaling around the world.
They make the Lock Pocket, a "high security but light weight" lock that comes in a handy
pouch; the Too Tyred Tool Pouch for mountain and road bikes; water bottles; evaporative
cooling covers for water bottles; and Croakies, those sgrungy, neoprene things that keep
your glasses on.

Norco Products USA Inc., 18201 Olympic Ave. S., Tukwila, WA 98188, 206/251–9370
* Rear-mounted bike racks for cars, child carriers, locks, handlebar bags, helmets, pumps,
tools, and spare parts.

Raleigh, Derby Cycle Corporation, Kent, WA 98032, 800/222–5527 * The century-old company also makes gloves, pedals, locks, tools, pumps, helmets, sunglasses, and bottle cages, in addition to replacement parts. Also see listing under *Bicycle Manufacturers*.

Rhode Gear, 765 Allens Ave., Providence, RI 02905, 800/456–2800 * Rear-mounted car racks, child seats, racks, helmets, U-locks, pumps, mirrors, panniers, et al., from a veteran New England company.

Schwinn Bicycle Company, 217 North Jefferson St., Chicago, IL 60606–1111, 312/454–7400; fax: 312/454–7525 * Offers the Paramount line of accessories, including bottle cages, saddles, heart-rate computers, tires, and clothes. Also see listings under *Clothes* and *Safety*.

Specialized, 15130 Concord Circle, Morgan Hill, CA 95037–5037, 408/779–6229 * Tires, handlebars, rims, cranksets, tires, racks, panniers; all readily available at bike shops or through catalogs.

T-Gear, 6824 NW 77th St. Ct., Miami, FL 33166, 800/688–4327 * Racing-oriented aerobars, pads, shifters, mountain-bike accessories.

Tioga, P.O. Box 5330, Compton, CA 90224, 213/719–1718 * All manner of software (from tires to toe clips) and hardware (from bottom brackets to seat posts) from this popular Japanese company.

Vitus, 5 rue des Echarneaux, Z.I. du Coin, B.P. 223, 42400 Saint-Chamond, France * Spokes, tires, seat posts, bottom brackets, and cycle computers from the noted French frame-makers.

WE'VE COME A LONG WAY

By Harold Wooster

In its gleaming mechanical perfection, the bicycle you ride today is the end product of a long line of evolutionary improvements. Let me take you back to the thrilling days of yesteryear and let you in on a bit of the "fun" you've missed.

Tires

Most of us carry a spare inner tube, two tire irons, a pump, and a patch kit. After a flat we're back on the road in ten minutes.

Not so in the old days. The standard bicycle tire in the '20s and into the '30s was the 28–inch, cement-on, single-tube tire. This was the ancestor of the sew-ups or tubular tires still favored by antiquarian masochists. A single tube was irreversibly encased in a fabric casing buried in a treaded rubber carcass. The assembly was glued to the rim with shellac (Fast-Tac™ was yet to be invented, and rubber-based rim cements were unheard of), inflated, and left to dry for twenty-four hours. If a tire punctured, you had choices. One was to call your parents to come get you, and haul you back to the bike shop for a new tire.

If money was tight, you could try to fix the puncture yourself with a rubber-band gun. This was a rod, perhaps ⅛" in diameter, with a longitudinal slot at one end and a trigger/hammer assembly at the other. You stretched as many rubber bands as the slot would hold from the trigger, through the distal slot and back over the hammer, smeared the far end liberally with rubber cement, shoved the band through the hole and pulled the trigger. If you were neat and could borrow mother's scissors, you trimmed off the excess rubber bands and were merrily on your way.

Slits called for a more drastic remedy, costing perhaps as much as 25¢ at the bike shop. For this you got an assembly of two lozenge-shaped, curved-sheet metal plates, connected by a threaded rod. In practice you worried the convex plate, to which the threaded rod was attached, through the slit, made sure it was aligned fore and aft, smeared more rubber cement on the outside, seated the loose, concave plate, tightened the nut, cut off the protruding threaded shaft, inflated the tire (listening for tell-tale hissing noises), and went clicking off down the road.

If you were a husky youth and were careless in shellacking or inflating your back tire, you stood a pretty good chance of pulling out your tire valve—whoosh—and an instant flat tire. When this happened, you bought a replacement valve stem—same arrangement of curved sheet metal plates—but this time the threads and the locking nut were on the valve stem. These replacements seemed to last as long as the original stems, probably because you took better care of them.

These tire problems disappeared by the end of the 1930s. The only problem now is if you are trying to find a pair of tires to restore a vintage bicycle. An undated Schwinn brochure, probably of the late '30s, listed three tire sizes: balloon, at 26 x 2.25 (these are the bikes that became the ancestors of today's mountain bikes); middleweight, at 26 x 1.75; and lightweight, at 26 x 1⅜.

American Bicycles in the Thirties

. . . .

During this time, American bicycle manufacturers aimed their bicycles, and their sales pitches, directly at the juvenile market. Example: a full-page advertisement by the Cycle Trades of America, showing a Western Union messenger and a grocery delivery boy on their bikes, captioned "Ride a Bike and Make Money."

Upon request, the Cycle Trades of America would send you a free booklet, "Cycle-Logical Ways to Happier Days," which was a "handsomely illustrated booklet with pictures of America's greatest athletes and why they think there is nothing like cycling for combining the greatest fun ever with splendid exercise, both interesting and instructive."

My parents bought me an Elgin bicycle from Sears in 1931 as a graduation present from eighth grade. Judging from the catalog description of this bike, Sears was convinced that what I really wanted was a motorcycle. The model was even called the "Elgin Motor-Bike." The frame, with two top tubes, was "patterned after standard motor bike design." It had a "substantial motor-bike stand," "famous De-lux Motor-Bike handlebars," an "approved motor-bike type front fork." It even had a fake gas tank nestled between the top tubes, which held batteries for the headlight. Reflect on this possibility: the motorcycle aspect of this bicycle is still with us. Could it be that the handlebars of contemporary mountain bikes are derived from them?

In retrospect, it wasn't a bad bike. It was heavy, however. The frame was made of one-inch seamless steel tubing welded together, and probably weighed 50 pounds (shipping weight was reported to be 65 pounds!). I rode this bike, and my brother rode it through four years of college, until 1943. Then I gave it to my wife, after first having a Bendix 2–speed rear hub installed, and substituting wheels that would take 26 x 1⅜ tires, which were being made in quantities for war-time civilian transportation.

This was after I'd acquired my first good bike. My brother-in-law left me his Schwinn Continental 3–speed lightweight. It was too small for me, but a bike shop on the south side of Chicago had a Hercules frame nearer to the correct size, so we swapped parts and wound up with a Hercules/Schwinn hybrid. The only time its mixed lineage showed was at tire-change time—it had the infamous Schwinn hooked rim, which would only take Schwinn tires. In 1944 I did my first century, 100 miles from Chicago to Janesville, Wisconsin, and spent a week the next summer touring Door Country, Wisconsin, with heavy canvas panniers made from war surplus musette bags.

I don't know what serious, affluent cyclists did for bicycles during this period. (As an undergraduate, graduate, and post-doc cyclist, I was not of that genre.) The sensible thing to have done would be to import one from England, which—between wars—was a hotbed of quality frame builders, builders with names like Freddy Grubb, Hetchins, Hurlow, and Witcomb. There were, as far as I can find out, only two custom frame builders in the States at that time—Oscar Watsyn in Chicago and Alvin Drysdale in New York and New Jersey. Both of these primarily served the professional bike racers of the local velodromes, but could be persuaded to build road frames.

Most of the rank and file bought heavy coaster-brake clunkers made by Columbia, Huffy, Murray of Ohio, and Rollfast. Mead in Chicago was experimenting with aluminum frames. I briefly owned a Mead track bike, fixed gear converted to road use with a front brake, which didn't slow it down at all. The one point of light in this dreary picture was the Schwinn Paramount, which Watsyn was instrumental in designing. It was possible to go to your local Schwinn dealer, cross his or her palm with silver—$200 sticks in my mind—and wind up with a good bike. The specification sheet still reads good today; frame made of Eccles & Pollack or Reynolds 531 tubing, rear hub fixed or free-wheeling or Sturmey-Archer, 1¼ or tubular tires.

Where Do We Stand Today?

. . . .

As I survey the cycling scene from the perspective of sixty years involvement with the sport and serial monogamous/polygamous cohabitation with perhaps some forty bicycles, I see the following changes and improvements.

Frames

You can now buy frames made of steel, aluminum, composite plastics, carbon fiber, magnesium, and titanium. Most recently Derby, the parent company for Raleigh, has been negotiating with the Russians, who have lots of titanium, to build titanium frames for them. You can buy frames that weigh less than four pounds, and with careful selection of components, bring a completed bike in under twenty pounds. Unfortunately, to my way of thinking, every year frames get shorter, with steeper angles. It has been said that today's road bike is last year's track bike. I miss the long wheelbase, laid-back touring bike of the 1950s, which could carry sixty properly distributed pounds and not shake you to pieces over a long day of touring.

Gears

I think they are wonderful! I have owned bikes with as few as one fixed gear and as many as 45, the result of a 5–speed cluster welded to a 3–speed hub, with a triple crank up front. My current bikes have 21 speeds, with a 7–speed cluster in the back. When 10–speed bikes hit the market in the 1950s, the standard set-up was a 52/42 crank in the front and a 14/28 freewheel in the back, giving you a low gear of 40.5 gear inches. I still have vivid (and horrible) memories of tackling the hills between Frederick and Point of Rocks, Maryland, on a Raleigh Professional with this set-up. The fact that it was all-Campy and had tubular tires didn't keep me from wishing for at least one more gear.

Two wonderful things happened in the '60s. Suntour introduced a freewheel with a range of 14 to 34 teeth (ah, low gears) and a long-arm changer, the VGT that could handle this range. TA and Stronglight made triple chainwheels available, say with 52 (or even 54), 36, 38, and 28 teeth. This can give you a low of 22 gear inches, low enough so that it is moot whether you can push a bike up a hill faster than you can climb it in your lowest gears. I like having the choice.

Tubular Tires (a.k.a Sew-Ups)

Goodbye and good riddance. There was a time when every serious cyclist had to have at least two sets of wheels with tubular tires mounted—heavy duty for normal use and silks for time trials, racing, or centuries. Tubular tires bred their own arcane body of knowledge, in aging, stretching, and mounting with particularly nasty rim cement. Heaven help you if you had to repair them on the road. When I heard that the 7–Eleven team had competed in the Tour de France on wired-on clincher tires, I got rid of my tubulars. Let someone else enjoy the ritual of gluing on tires, thank you.

Rims

We now take alloy rims for granted. It was not always thus. The standard rim once was chrome-plated steel. These worked, after a fashion, until a little grit got on the brake blocks. Voila, rust instead of chrome. They also didn't stop so well when wet. The coefficient of friction of rubber on wet aluminum is much higher than on steel, even rusty steel.

Helmets

They're wonderful. (I know I've said this before.) I had my most serious bike crash in August, 1972. I broke my arm just below the shoulder joint and was knocked unconscious for about forty-five minutes. I was wearing what was then state-of-the-art head covering, a leather "hair net" helmet, which did nothing to protect my head. I was working at the National Library of Medicine at the time and took advantage of my convalescence to do a literature search on head injuries in cycling accidents. Before I got back on my bike, I looked around for a helmet that might offer some head protection. We tried white-water kayaking helmets and hockey helmets and finally wound up with a Mountain Safety Research (MSR) rock-climbing helmet. Bell was, I believe, the first to make a helmet specifically for bicycle use. The May 1991 issue of *Bicycling* lists 59 new helmets. Yes, indeed, we have come a long way.

Harold Wooster is a fallen chemist and administrative bio-medical communicator. He has not, however, fallen off his new recumbent.

 *three*

BMX AND KIDS' BIKES

Kids zipping around a track on 20–inch wheels. Cushioned by thick gloves, pads, a helmet, and other appropriate clothing, they circle the track in one minute or less. The track, sometimes equipped with dirt mounds and other obstacles, makes the participants cycle in short spurts, a distance that's perfect for young athletes who are developing their handling skills. This is BMX racing (bicycle motocross racing), off-road racing for kids. It's performed on a bike that is lighter and more durable than most bikes for young folks. While its popularity is waning a bit in the East, it's still going strong in the Midwest and West, especially in Arizona and California.

From BMX, another form of cycling, freestyle, was born. Freestyle is more performance-oriented: if you see a cyclist "dancing" on a short bike, spinning it gracefully and balancing, you are probably witnessing a freestyle performance. The braking system of freestyle bikes enables the handlebars to turn 360 degrees without tangling the brake cables. Freestyle bikes also have pegs, often on the front and rear forks, to enable the cyclist to perch and balance.

(Arlene Plevin)

There are opportunities for both freestyle and BMX competition throughout the country. Two special events are sponsored by the National Bicycle League and the American Bicycle Association.

The Grand National, a big event for all BMX and freestyle enthusiasts, happens in Louisville, Kentucky, each August 30–September 1. A final national race to see who gets national standing, the Grand National is sponsored by the National Bicycle League (211 Bradenton Ave., Suite 100, Dublin, OH 43017, 614/766–1625). The American Bicycle Association (P.O. Box 718, Chandler, AZ 85244, 714/891–7592) holds its ABA Grand Nationals of BMX every Thanksgiving weekend. Cyclists participate in other series of races throughout the year and accumulate points. Then they take those scores into the Grand Nationals, where the points are quadrupled.

BMX and freestyle are popular, and some of the companies listed below tour the country doing shows and promoting their products. Watch for them in major urban centers and larger bike shops. For those who still believe that childhood is an innocent time, we also offer listings of trikes, scooters, and other so-called "juvenile" bicycles.

Auburn, 17800 Gothard St., Huntington Beach, CA 92647, 714/841–1169 * Specializes in a two-piece, front end chromoly, rear end aluminum bike called the Auburn CR20X. Auburn claims its advantage is lightweight rear end and "unique styling."

Diamond Back, WSI, 4030 Via Pescador, Camarillo, CA 93010–9864, 805/484–4450 * 9 models, from the Lil One (training wheels) to the Viper (ATB with chromoly tubing) to the Recoil (Junior's first mountain bike).

Dyno Bicycles, 17800 Gothard St., Huntington Beach, CA 92647, 714/841–1169 * Freestyle and dirt bikes made in USA with chromoly frames; also helmets, gloves, visors, elbow/knee pads, pants.

Giant Bicycle, Inc., 475 Apra St., Rancho Dominguez, CA 90220, 213/609–3340, 800/US–GIANT * The "Youth Adventure Series" starts with training wheels and keeps going to an 18–speed mountain bike.

GT Bicycles, Inc., 17800 Gothard St., Huntington Beach, CA 92647, 714/841–1169 * BMX, freestyle, and kids' mountain bikes. Manufactures the GT power series, a three-piece chromoly crank with a sealed bearing bottom bracket. This hollow tubular crank is called the "strongest and stiffest crank in BMX." GT also makes other BMX accessories, clothes, and components, and supports several teams.

Haro Designs, Inc., 2225 Faraday Ave., Suite A, Carlsbad, CA 92009 * 12 models for "serious" racing and ramping. Also shirts, knee-pads, elbow-guards, mouth-guards, gloves, racing pants, tires, sprockets, frame/forksets, handlebars, stems, cranks, stems, seat posts.

Huffy Corporation, P.O. Box 1204, Dayton, OH 45401 * 16" "sidewalk" bikes for toddlers, 20" BMX-style for boys and girls, 10–speeds for teens, entry-level mountain bikes, tandems, crossovers, and replicas of beach cruisers—these are cradle-to-grave bicycles, so long as you never get too serious about it.

Mongoose Bicycles, 23879 Madison Ave., Torrance, CA 90505 * "Juvenile" line from this ATB-oriented company features a 12–speed mountain bike, BMX and freestyle competition bikes, pre-BMXers with training wheels and 12" wheels, and a white-wheeled scooter with a side-pull hand brake.

Monty Bicycles, 301 Jacksonville Road, Hatboro, PA 19040, 215–672–9013 * Made in Spain competition-oriented models ($479–$549, 1989).

Powerlite, 17800 Gothard St., Huntington Beach, CA 92647, 714/841–1169 * One of the oldest BMX companies, Powerlite began in Southern California. Famous for handlebars which have a unique geometry.

Rand International Ltd., 51 Executive Blvd., Farmington, NY 11735, 516/249–6000; fax: 516/249–6015 * Scooters, wagons, trikes, training wheels, BMX-style, teen-size (24" wheels) mountain bikes, more.

Robinson Bicycles, 17800 Gothard St., Huntington Beach, CA 92647, 714/841–1169 * The Robinson team is led by Greg Hill, who is old enough to wear a beard and wears one. 4 competition-oriented models with chromoly frames.

Ross Bicycles, 51 Executive Blvd., Farmington, NY 11735, 516/249–600, 800/338–ROSS; fax: 516/249–6015 * The Ross come-on is "Children's Bicycles . . . an investment in your child's safety." A bit different from the other companies who show Junior dressed like Evel Knievel and coming off a tsunami-sized ramp at 50 mph. Trikes, BMX-style bikes, 12–speeds with 26" wheels for kids, beach cruisers, crossover bikes.

Saint Tropez, Aerolite, 51–B Mercedes Way, Edgewood, NY 11717, 516/254–0075 * 13 models, from BMX down to training wheels.

Schwinn Bicycle Company, 217 North Jefferson St., Chicago, IL 60606–1111, 312/454–7400; fax: 312/454–7525 * Bikes for all kids from age 3 to BMX-ed teens. One of the last refuges for the banana seat and chrome fenders.

Sekai, Norco Products, USA, 18201 Olympic Ave. South, Tukwila, WA 98188 * "Mini" and "Micro" models for younger off-roaders. Also adult mountain bikes.

Univega/Sterling, Lawee Inc., 3030 Walnut Ave., Long Beach, CA 90807, 213/426–0474 * Sterling makes kids' and casual bikes; Univega, adult road bikes with chromoly tubing.

ABA BMX Track Directory

Alaska

Fairbanks
Far North BMX/Bon Rohl * 907/456–1698

Arizona

Chandler
Chandler BMX/Hotline * 602/496–6940

Phoenix
Black Mountain * BMX 602/582–0114
Thrasherland BMX * 602/942–3724

San Manual
Coppertown BMX * 602/385–2038

Tucson
Sportspark BMX * 602/797–1268

Yuma
Yuma BMX * 602/726–1024

Arkansas

Fort Smith
Ben Geren Hog Wild BMX * 501/646–9056

California

Bakersfield
Bakersfield BMX * 805/845–3081

Desert Hot Springs
D.H.S. BMX * 619/327–7071

Lakeport
Lake County BMX * 707/994–9783

Lemoore
Lemoore Action Park BMX * 209/924–7950

Marysville
Riverfront Park BMX * 916/673–0600

Modesto
Modesto BMX * 209/461–6056

Moreno Valley
Moreno Valley Action Track * 714/485–0220

Mountain View
Orion Park BMX * 415/965–2716

Napa
Napa Valley BMX * 707/263–2342

Orange
Orange Y BMX * 714/738–7195

Orangevale
Pecan Park BMX * 916/673–0600

Redding-Summit City
NORCAL Boomtown BMX * 916/365–4208

Roseville
Oak Creek BMX * 916/7848–BMX

San Diego
Kearny Moto Park * 619/270–1515

Santa Clara
Santa Clara P.A.L. BMX * 408/727–3448

Simi Valley
Simi Valley BMX * 805/581–2692

South El Monte
Whittier Narrows BMX * 818/448–4040

Stockton
Stockton Fairgrounds BMX * 209/461–6056

Sunol
Sunol BMX * 415/862–1077

Temecula
Rancho BMX * 714/674–6234

Ukiah
Rusty Bowl BMX * 707/462–0249

Woodland
Yolo BMX * 916/666–3461

Yorba Linda
Coast Canyon BMX * 714/998–3142

Colorado

Alamosa
Red River Raceway * 719/589–4131

Arvada
Sky High BMX * 303/424–7733 or 421–3346

Colorado Springs
Pikes Peak BMX * 719/596–4470

Craig
High Desert BMX * 303/824–8453

Elizabeth
Colorado Outback Track * 303/646–0711

Fort Collins
Boothill BMX * 303/569–9415

Grand Junction
Grand Mesa BMX * 303/434–5393 or 241–3425

Greeley
Greeley BMX * 303/454–3889 or 352–8417

Longmont
Pikes Peak Indoor BMX * 719/596–4470

Trinidad
Trinidad Optimist BMX * 719/846–2015

Florida

Panama City
Panama City BMX * 904/872–9261

Pensacola
Brosnaham BMX * 904/453–4822

Hawaii

Hickam AFB
Hickam BMX * 808/422–5429

Kahului, Maui
Maui BMX * 808/878–6158

Lihue, Kauai
Nawilliwilli BMX * 808/828–1091

Idaho

Boise
Boise Valley BMX * 208/888–9391 or 362–4251 or 382–1530

Caldwell
Caldwell BMX Raceway * 208/722–7509 or 467–3293

Idaho Falls
Snake River BMX * 208/522–5863 or 208/523–4788

Montpelier
Bear Lake BMX Raceway * 208/847–1134

Pocatello
Pine Ridge BMX * 208/237–6958

Post Falls
Panhandle BMX * 208/683–2083 or 509/922–4662

Illinois

Elgin
The Hill * 708/980–3136

Rockford
Rockford BMX * 815/877–3168

Indiana

Indianapolis
Lake Sullivan BMX * 317/926–8356 or 923–3485

Iowa

Cedar Rapids
Indian Creek BMX * 319/366–1382 or 373–0474

Mason City
North Iowa BMX * 515/423–9407

Newton
Good Times BMX Raceway * 515/792–4266

Kansas

Dodge City
Dodge City Ambucs BMX * 316/227–6737

Kansas City
Lakeside BMX * 316/459–7151

Topeka
Heartland BMX * 913/267–1361

Wichita
Emery Park BMX * 316/788–5473

Louisiana

Baton Rouge
BREC BMX Raceway * 504/273–6400

Shreveport
Cargill Park BMX * 318/635–6297 or 742–8174

Maryland

Columbia
Columbia BMX Supertrack * 301/489–7095

Glen Burnie
Friendship Park BMX * 301/268–0726

Monrovia
Green Valley BMX * 301/540–4600

Michigan

Escanaba
Superior BMX * 906/786–0006

Marquette
North State Raceway * 906/228–7583

Minnesota

Barnesville
Peterson Park BMX * 218/354–7160

Brainerd
Brainerd Lakes BMX * 218/829–7105

Dilworth
Dilworth BMX * 701/235–9892

Hibbing
Hull Rust BMX * 218/263–8194

Luverne
Luverne Riverside BMX * 507/283–8154

Mankato
Mankato Area BMX * 507/387–2202 or 345–6283

Maple Plain
West Hennepin BMX * 612/479–2874

Shakopee
Shakopee BMX * 612/544–3994

Virginia
North Country BMX * 218/749–5830

Waseca
Waseca County BMX * 507/835–4036

Missippi

Clinton
Clinton Optimist BMX * 601/924–2574

Missouri

Blue Springs
Blue Springs BMX * 816/229–1389

Bridgeton
Renegade BMX * 314/343–9431

Clinton
Sunset Optimist BMX Park * 816/885–5852

Lee's Summit
PBMA Berm Busters BMX * 816/356–3972

Springfield
Spokes BMX Raceway * 417/882–8536 or 883–8041

St. Peters
St. Peters BMX * 314/426–4885

Montana

Bozeman
Bozeman BMX * 406/284–6841

Columbia Falls
Glacier BMX * 406/752–1300 or 752–0811

Great Falls
Electric City BMX * 406/427–4711

Nebraska

Lincoln
Starr City BMX * 402/466–1233

Papillion
Papillion BMX * 402/593–4065

Nevada

Las Vegas
Sundancer BMX * 702/646–RACE

Reno
Washoe County BMX * 702/827–5842

New Mexico

Albuquerque
Alameda BMX * 505/897–3787

Aztec
Boogie Downs BMX * 505/326–3407 or 335–2214

Las Cruces
P.A.L. Roadrunner BMX * 505/526–3267

New York

Ellery Center
Sunrise BMX * 716/484–8146

North Carolina

Fayetteville
Cumberland County BMX * 919/425–6060

North Dakota

Bismarck
Century BMX * 701/222–2655

West Fargo
West Fargo BMX * 701/235–9892

Oklahoma

Jenks
Jenks Riverview BMX * 918/298–1111

Oklahoma City
Sooner Pearl BMX * 405/235–3602

Sand Springs
Cimarron BMX * 918/227–0734

Oregon

Albany
Timber-Linn BMX * 503/928–9575

Bend
High Desert Raceway BMX * 503/388–2408

Clackamas
Rose City BMX * 503/654–0776

Corvallis
Mid-Valley Indoor BMX * 503/485–5623 or 343–7121
Willamette Valley BMX * 503/929–3968

Cottage Grove

Todd Kephart Memorial BMX Park * 503/946–1036

Eugene

Emerald Valley BMX * 503/484–8379

Florence

Waterford Points Park BMX * 503/268–4155

Grants Pass

Grants Pass Boys & Girls Club BMX * 503/471–1328

Roseburg

Roseburg BMX * 503/672–7984

Pennsylvania

Athens

Valley BMX * 717/888–1850

Bensalem

Bensalem BMX Raceway * 215/757–5544 or 639–9539

Honesdale

Hickory Ridge BMX Park * 717/654–0310

Luzerne

Mountain View Park BMX * 717/829–0924

Mammoth

Mammoth Park BMX * 412/837–0155

Newton

Clark Summit Cedar BMX * 717/824–8848

Pine Grove

Sweet Arrow BMX * 717/647–2730

York

Bumps 'n' Berms BMX * 717/757–5313

South Dakota

Aberdeen
Aberdeen BMX * 605/229–5390

Rapid City
Cacius Falls BMX * 605/341–3843

Texas

Austin
Capitol City BMX * 512/244–0933

Baytown
San Jacinio Supercross * 713/326–2431

Cleburne
Cleburne BMX * 817/641–0941

Conroe
Armadillo Downs BMX * 713/431–2761 or 409/588–4523

Corpus Christi
Gulf Coast BMX * 512/241–0806

El Paso
Desert Downs * 915/751–3390

Ft. Worth
Cowtown BMX Racing * 817/338–2269 or 335–1269

Longview
East Texas BMX Raceway * 903/297–1480

Mesquite
Dallas County Cycle Park * 214/495–2299 or 216–1295

Midland-Odessa
Twin Cities BMX * 915/697–3375

Nacogdoches
Tall Timbers BMX * 409/634–2045

Pasadena
Pasadena Supercross * 713/326–2431 or 998–7887

Red Oak
Ellis County BMX * 214/576–8505

Richwood
McDowell Downs BMX * 409/297–9777

San Antonio
Lone Star BMX * 512/656–9630

Schertz
Buffalo Valley BMX * 512/659–6190

Utah

Murray
Twin Peaks Supercross * 801/969–0737 or 250–1606

Ogden
Thunder Hill Raceway * 801/479–8896

Price
Terrace Hills BMX * 801/637–0066 or 637–5762

Washington

Port Orchard
Peninsula Indoor BMX * 206/246–2661
South Kilsap Park BMX * 206/246–2661 or 696–1343

Ridgefield
Clark County BMX * 206/253–9271

Seattle-Tacoma
North Sea-Tax BMX * 206/228–5139

Sumner
River Valley BMX * 206/246–2661

Yakima
Yakima BMX * 509/453–8622 or 248–9414

Wisconsin

Elkhorn
Walworth County Indoor BMX * 815/232–6642 or 758–5672

Oskosh
Winnebagoland BMX * 414/231–0494

Wisconsin Rapids
Central Wisconsin BMX * 715/689–4145 or 325–5127 or 886–4420

Wyoming

Casper
Casper BMX * 307/265–5524

Green River
Sweetwater BMX * 307/382–6642

Thermopolis
Thermopolis BMX * 307/864–5484

four

BOOKS, PERIODICALS, MAPS, VIDEOS, POSTERS, ET AL.

*T*here's an amazing amount of material on bicycling out there. You can cuddle up with a fat book in the winter, slide a tape into the VCR while you spin away a wet evening on the rollers, or just poke through any number of magazines. If you're interested in mountain bike touring, the lives of European bicycle racers, or even how to cook on a tour, there's a title for you. Some distributors and publishers specialize in bicycle books, so contact them directly if your local book or bike store cannot obtain any of the following.

Magazines on every aspect of bicycling abound. Many are available on the newsstands. Others are regional and are distributed at local bike stores. In many cases, organizations of enthusiasts publish a newsletter directed toward their particular interest.

The selection below is just that—a selection. It should give you an excellent sense of the variety of materials. Some of those listed are considered classics, books which cyclists continually read, savor, and recommend. Others are well-known, tried and true fonts of information or a particular viewpoint. We've tried to include a selection large enough to cover the field, but not too large that it would swamp the book. Consider calling or writing the state tourism agencies listed in the *Bicycle Organizations* section. Many stock excellent maps that are free and are happy to help bicyclists.

BOOKS, BROCHURES, AND MAPS

General

Bicycling Magazine's Cycling for Women, 96 pp., $4.95, Rodale Press, 33 E. Minor St., Emmaus, PA 18098, 215/967–5171.

Bicycling Magazine's New Bike Owner Guide, 128 pp., $6.95, Rodale Press, 33 E. Minor St., Emmaus, PA 18098, 215/967–5171.

Bicycling Magazines's 600 Tips for Better Bicycling, 128 pp., $6.95, Rodale Press, 33 E. Minor St., Emmaus, PA 18098, 215/967–5171.

Bicycling Reference Book, 52 pp., $5, Bicycle Institute of America, 1818 R St. NW, Washington, DC 20009, 202/332–6986 * A reference guide from the Bicycle Institute of America for the press and others—contains articles on trends, how-to, safety, history, general info, popular bike rides and events. Updated regularly.

Bike Tripping, by Tom Cuthbertson, 272 pp., $7.95, Ten Speed Press, P.O. Box 7123, Berkeley, CA 94707, 800/841–2665 * Covers commuting, short joy rides, and touring.

Cycle Sport: Equipment, Technique and Training, by Peter Konopka, 160 pp., $19.95, Vitesse Press, Box 1886, Brattleboro, VT 05302–1886 * The basics on gear, riding skills, training, diet, competition, health.

The Cyclists' Yellow Pages, Bikecentennial, P.O. Box 8308, Missoula, MT 59807 * Listings from the national, nonprofit touring organization. Includes worldwide bicycle associations and book and map resources. Available to members only.

Effective Cycling, by John Forester, 350 pp., $15.00, MIT Press, 55 Hayward St., Cambridge, MA 02142 * Covers mechanics and maintenance, physiology of the rider, technique, traffic laws. Considered the definitive guide "to the proper techniques of bicycling."

Keep on Pedaling: The Complete Guide to Adult Bicycling, by Norman D. Ford, 225 pp., $12.95, Backcountry Publications, P.O. Box 175, Woodstock, VT 05091 * Covers the basics for adults in any stage of bicycle enthusiasm.

Living on Two Wheels, by Dennis Coello, 194 pp., $5.95, Ross Books, P.O. Box 4340, Berkeley, CA 94704 * Complete guide to buying a bike, commuting, and touring.

The New Bike Book: How to Make the Most of Your New Bicycle, by Jim Langley, 125 pp., $4.95, Bicycle Books, P.O. Box 2038, Mill Valley, CA 94941 * Pocket-size basics.

Share the Trail, International Bicycle Fund, 4887 Columbia Drive S., Seattle, WA 98108–1919, 206/628–9314 * Free brochure with self-addressed, stamped envelope (SASE).

Street Smarts: Bicycling's Traffic Survival Guide, by John S. Allen, 45 pp., Rodale Press, Rodale Press, 33 E. Minor St., Emmaus, PA 18098, 215/967–5171 * Useful, smart booklet that covers getting across non-standard intersections and cycling in traffic. Cost is $.25 each plus shipping for orders of 50 or more; $1 for one copy. Contact Michelle Gisolfi at Rodale Press for more information.

Survey of Airline Baggage Regulations for Bicycles, Baggage Regulations for Bikes, International Bicycle Fund, 4887–Z Columbia Dr. S., Seattle, WA 98108, 206/767–3927 * Rules, regulations, and charges for flying with a bike.

Tales from the Bike Shop, by Maynard Hershon, 184 pp., $13.95, Vitesse Press, Box 1886, Brattleboro, VT 05302–1886, 800/848–3747 * Humorous essays.

The Woman Cyclist, by Elaine Mariolle and Michael Shermer, 378 pp., $9.95, Contemporary Books, 180 N. Michigan Ave., Chicago, IL 60601 * A book that's not just for women. Includes profiles of all types of bicycle riders.

A Woman's Guide to Cycling, by Susan Weaver, 250 pp., $13.95, Ten Speed Press, Box 7123, Berkeley, CA 94707 * Comprehensive guide for women, covering riding during pregnancy to getting into shape.

Accommodations and Campgrounds

American Youth Hostels Handbook: A Directory of Hostels in the USA, 224 pp., AYH, P.O. Box 37613, Washington, DC 20013–7613, 202/783–6161 * Annual listing of 200 hostels.

Bed & Breakfast in California, by Kathy Strong, 272 pp., $11.95, Globe Pequot Press, 10 Denlar Dr., P.O. Box Q, Chester, CT 06412, 800/243–0495, 800/962–0973.

Bed & Breakfast in the Mid-Atlantic States, by Bernice Chesler, 512 pp., $13.95, Globe Pequot Press, 10 Denlar Dr., P.O. Box Q, Chester, CT 06412, 800/243–0495, 800/962–0973.

Bed & Breakfast in New England, by Bernice Chesler, 512 pp., $13.95, Globe Pequot Press, 10 Denlar Dr., P.O. Box Q, Chester, CT 06412, 800/243–0495, 800/962–0973.

Bed & Breakfast Traveler: West Coast, by Lewis Green, 287 pp., $11.95, Globe Pequot Press, 10 Denlar Dr., P.O. Box Q, Chester, CT 06412, 800/243–0495, 800/962–0973.

Best B & B in the World: England, Scotland, and Wales, by Sigourney Welles, Jill Darbey, and Joanna Mortimer, 400 pp., $15.95, Globe Pequot Press, 10 Denlar Dr., P.O. Box Q, Chester, CT 06412, 800/243–0495, 800/962–0973.

Bicycle Camping in Canada, $12.95 plus $2 postage, Canadian Cycling Association, 1600 James Naismith Dr., Gloucester, Ontario K1B 5N4, Canada, 613/748–5629.

Bicycle Utah, P.O. Box 738, Park City, UT 84060, 801/649–5806 * Free guide to bicycling in Utah. Lists campgrounds, places to go, hotels, and tour companies.

Budget Travel Source Guide, 24 pp., AYH, P.O. Box 28607, Central Station, Washington, DC 20038–8607 * Guide "filled with travel planning tips and information on lodging, discount air fares, and more." Free with self-addressed envelope with $.58 postage.

The Camper's Companion to Northern Europe, by Dennis and Tina Jaffe, 305 pp., $13.95, Williamson Publishing, available through Bikecentennial, P.O. Box 8308, Missoula, MT 59807.

The Camper's Companion to Southern Europe, by Dennis and Tina Jaffe, 287 pp., $13.95, Williamson Publishing, available through Bikecentennial, P.O. Box 8308, Missoula, MT 59807.

Country Inns British Island, by Norman Simpson, $12.95, Harper & Row, 10 E. 53rd St., New York, NY 10012, 800/242–7737.

Country Inns Europe, by Norman Simpson, $11.95, Harper & Row, 10 E. 53rd St., New York, NY 10012, 800/242–7737.

Country Inns North America, by Norman Simpson, $12.95, Harper & Row, 10 E. 53rd St., New York, NY 10012, 800/242–7737.

Don Wright's Guide to Free Campgrounds, 580 pp., $14.95, Cottage Publications, 24396 Pleasant View Dr., Elkhart, IN 46517, 219/875–8618 * A 1990 guide to more than 6,000 freebies.

Don Wright's Guide to Free Attractions, 640 pp., $14.95, Cottage Publications, 24396 Pleasant View Dr., Elkhart, IN 46517, 219/875–8618 * Free things to see along the way.

Going Dutch: A Visitor's Guide to Pennsylvania Dutch County, by Bill Hoffman, 320 pp., $12.95 plus $1.50 shipping, 624 Candlewyck Rd., Lancaster, PA 17061 * Covers sightseeing attractions, accommodations, and restaurants in an area perfect for cycling.

National Parks Camping Guide, 112 pp., $4, available through Superintendent of Documents, US Government Printing Office, Washington, DC 20402, 202/783–3238.

The Old-House Lover's Guide to Inns and Bed & Breakfast Guest Houses, 463 pp., $15.95, The Stephen Greene Press, published by Penguin Group, Viking Penguin, 40 West 23rd St., New York, NY 10010 * Details more than 300 restored hostelries from coast to coast.

Recommended Country Inns in Arizona, New Mexico, and Texas, by Eleanor Morris, 368 pp., $12.95, Globe Pequot Press, 10 Denlar Dr., P.O. Box Q, Chester, CT 06412, 800/243–0495, 800/962–0973.

Recommended Country Inns in the Rocky Mountain Region, by Doris Kennedy, 352 pp., $12.95, Globe Pequot Press, 10 Denlar Dr., P.O. Box Q, Chester, CT 06412, 800/243–0495, 800/962–0973.

Recommended Country Inns in the West Coast, by Julianne Belote, 448 pp., $12.95, Globe Pequot Press, 10 Denlar Dr., P.O. Box Q, Chester, CT 06412, 800/243–0495, 800/962–0973.

Save-A-Buck Campgrounds, by Don Wright, 460 pp., $14.95, Cottage Publications, 24396 Pleasant View Dr., Elkhart, IN 46517, 219/875–8618 * Thousands of cheap campgrounds.

Woodall's Campground Directory, 1600 pp., $14.95 plus postage, Woodall Publishing Co., 28167 N. Keith Dr., Lake Forest, IL 60045–5000, 800/323–9026 * North American edition covers North America, Canada, and Mexico. It is divided into two sections, which can be bought separately ($12.70/Eastern Section, $10.20/Western Section).

Woodall's Tent Camping Guide: North American Editions, 494 pp., $12.70, Woodall Publishing Co., 28167 N. Keith Dr., Lake Forest, IL 60045–5000, 800/323–9026.

Touring

This section includes narratives about road bicycle touring and resources relevant to road bike cycling in the United States.

Bike Touring: The Sierra Club Guide to Outings on Wheels, by Raymond Bridge, 456 pp., $10.95, Sierra Club, 530 Bush St., San Francisco, CA 94108 * The classic for beginners and touring vets alike.

Changing Gears: Bicycling America's Perimeter, by Jane Schnell, $19.95, Milner Press, Ste. 220, 715 Miami Cir. NE, Atlanta, GA 30324 * A retired CIA woman cycles 12,000 miles around the edges of the contiguous 48 states, celebrates her 56th and 57th birthdays on the road, and reports on it in 400 pages.

Computing Across America, by Steven K. Roberts, 350 pp., $9.95, Nomadic Research Labs, P.O. Box 2390, Santa Cruz, CA 95063 * Account of 10,000–mile trip across U.S. on recumbent bike equipped with solar-driven computer. Roberts writes while pedaling his "Winnebiko."

Hey Mom, Can I Ride My Bike Across America?, by John Seigel Boettner, 440 pp., $14.95, Seigel Boettner Fulton, 570 W. Central, Bldg. 4A, Brea, CA 92621, 714/255–8147 * Five kids pedal 5,000 miles across the U.S.

Miles from Nowhere: A Round-the-World Bicycle Adventure, by Barbara Savage, 340 pp., $12.95, The Mountaineers Books, 306 Second Ave. West, Seattle, WA 98119, 800/553–4453, 206/285–2665; fax: 206/285–8992 * A chilling, thrilling journal of a two-year journey of a woman and her husband. Considered a classic.

Pedaling across America, by Don and Lolly Skillman, 160 pp., $9.95, Vitesse Press, P.O. Box 1886, Brattleboro, VT 05301, 800/848–3747 * Tales of a journey across the U.S. in 56 days.

Rails to Trails Conservancy, 1400 16th St., NW, Washington, DC 20036 * Offers guides to bike paths around the country that follow the course of former railroad beds.

Touring Cyclist Catalogue, compiled by Bonnie Wong, 50 pp., $5 ppd., Touring Exchange, Box 265, Port Townsend, WA 98368 * Catalog detailing routes, maps, and guide books available. Includes itineraries from all around the world, submitted by cyclists.

Touring on Two Wheels, by Dennis Coello, 192 pp., $12.95, Nick Lyons Books, 31 West 21 St., New York, NY 10010 * Information on all aspects of long-distance touring.

Two Wheels & a Taxi, by Virginia Urrutia, 245 pp., $14.95, The Mountaineers Books, 306 Second Ave. West, Seattle, WA 98119, 800/553–4453, 206/285–2665; fax: 206/285–8992 * A "feisty" grandmother pedals through the Andes.

The World Up Close: A Cyclist's Adventures on Five Continents, by Kameel B. Nasr, 210 pp., $9.95, Mills & Sanderson, 442 Marrett Rd., Suite 6, Lexington, MA 02173 * Episodes from a 40,000 mile bicycle journey through 70 countries, including Morocco, Colombia, and India.

State and Regional Books and Guides

Eastern U.S.
....

The Best Bike Rides in New England, by Paul Thomas, 272 pp., $9.95, The Globe Pequot Press, Box Q, Chester, CT 06412 * 40 rides from 20 to 100 miles with maps, directions, photos.

Bicycling Central and Southern Maryland, by Chuck and Gail Helfer, $8.95, Cycleways, P.O. Box 5328, Takoma Park, MD 20912.

Bicycling Dorchester County [Md.], by Chuck and Gail Helfer, $5.95, Cycleways, P.O. Box 5328, Takoma Park, MD 20912 * Maps, photos, narrative.

Bicycling Northern Virginia, by Chuck and Gail Helfer, $9.95, Cycleways, P.O. Box 5328, Takoma Park, MD 20912.

Bicycling Talbot County [Md.], by Chuck and Gail Helfer, $5.95, Cycleways, P.O. Box 5328, Takoma Park, MD 20912.

Bicycling the Antietam Area [Md.- Va.- W.Va.], by Chuck and Gail Helfer, $5.95, Cycleways, P.O. Box 5328, Takoma Park, MD 20912.

Bicycling the Blue Ridge, by Elizabeth and Charlie Skinner, 184 pp., $10.95, Menasha Ridge Press, 3169 Cahaba Heights Rd., Birmingham, AL 35243 * Maps, elevation profiles, and photos for bicycling the Blue Ridge Parkway and Skyline Drive.

Bicycling through New Jersey, by Dan Rapaport, $5.95 a set, Apt. 5M Holly House, Princeton, NJ 08540 * 4 cross-state routes.

Bikecentennial Route Maps, Bikecentennial, P.O. Box 8308, Missoula, MT 59807, 406/721–1776 * Maps designed with cyclists' every need in mind. Lists campgrounds, hostels, bike shops, hotels, motels, post offices, and food stores. Maps provide topographic and climatic information. The prices listed are for non-members.

1. TransAmerica Bicycle Trail (from Astoria, Ore., to Yorktown, Va.), 12 sections ($6.95/one, $64.95/all);

2. The Canada to California Bicycle Route, 2 sections ($6.95/one, $10.95/both);

3. Great Parks Bicycle Route North, 2 sections ($6.95/one, $10.95/both);

4. Great Parks Bicycle Route South, 1 section ($6.95);

5. The Maine to Virginia Bicycle Route, 3 sections ($6.95/one, $16.95/all);

6. The Virginia to Florida Bicycle Route, 4 sections ($6.95/one, $20.95/all);

7. The Washington to Minnesota Bicycle Route, 4 sections ($6.95/one, $20.95/all);

8. The Great River North Bicycle Route, 2 sections ($6.95/one, $10.95/both);

9. The Iowa to Maine Bicycle Route, 4 sections ($6.95/one, $20.95/all);

10. California Coast Bicycle Route, 3 sections,($6.95/one, $16.95/all)

11. California to Florida Bicycle Route (under development: currently from San Diego, Calif., to El Paso, Tex.—950 miles), 2 sections ($6.95/one, $12.90/both);

12. The Northern Tier (from Anacortes, Wash., to Bar Harbor, Maine), 10 sections ($49.95/all);

13. The Pacific Coast Bicycle Route (from Vancouver, British Columbia, to San Diego), 5 sections ($26.95/all); and

14. The Eastern Seaboard Bicycle Route (from Bar Harbor, Maine, to Ft. Meyers Beach, Fla.), $34.95/all.

Cross-State Bicycle Rides and Events, 4 pp., $2, The League of American Wheelmen, Suite 209, 6707 Whitestone Rd., Baltimore, MD 21207.

Florida Atlas & Gazetteer, 128 pp., $14.95, DeLorme Mapping Company, P.O. Box 298, Freeport, ME 04032, 800/227–1656. Topo maps, bike routes, and more.

Greater Washington Area Bicycle Atlas, $10, Washington Area Bicyclist Association, 1819 H St., Suite 640, Washington, DC 20006, 202/872–9830 * 62 rides from 10 to 100 miles with maps, photos, directions.

Life in the Slow Lane: Fifty Backroad Tours of Ohio, by Jeff and Nadean Disabato Traylor, 225 pp., $14.95 plus $2 postage, Backroad Chronicles, P.O. Box 292066, Columbus, OH 43229.

Maine Atlas & Gazetteer, 96 pp., $11.95, DeLorme Mapping Company, P.O. Box 298, Freeport, ME 04032, 800/227–1656, 207/865–4171.

Natchez Parkway Bicycle Route, Bikecentennial, P.O. Box 8308–P, Missoula, MT 59807, 406/721–1776 * Map of 450–mile route should be available in late '91. Bikecentennial sells maps for 17,000 miles of other routes throughout the U.S. See *Bikecentennial Route Maps* above.

New Hampshire Atlas & Gazetteer, 88 pp., $11.95, DeLorme Mapping Company, P.O. Box 298, Freeport, ME 04032, 800/227–1656.

New York State Atlas & Gazetteer, 104 pp., $14.95, DeLorme Mapping Company, P.O. Box 298, Freeport, ME 04032, 800/227–1656.

Ohio Atlas & Gazetteer, 88 pp. $12.95, DeLorme Mapping Company, P.O. Box 298, Freeport, ME 04032, 800/227–1656.

Ohio Bicycle Events Calendar, free with a #10 sized SASE, Clockwork Press, 9611 Lorain Ave., Cleveland, OH 44102 * Lists bicycle tours and races. Published by the Ohio Bicycle Federation.

Pennsylvania Atlas & Gazetteer, 96 pp., $12.95, DeLorme Mapping Company, P.O. Box 298, Freeport, ME 04032, 800/227–1656 * Topographical maps and information on bicycle routes, historic sites, scenic drives, parks, forests, and recreation areas.

Short Bike Rides in and around Washington, D.C., by Michael Leccese, 144 pp., $8.95, The Globe Pequot Press, Box Q, Chester, CT 06412 * 22 rides from 6 to 64 miles with maps, photos, directions, descriptions of history and nature along the way.

Short Bike Rides in Connecticut, by Mullen and Griffith, $7.95, The Globe Pequot Press, Box Q, Chester, CT 06412.

Short Bike Rides in Eastern Pennsylvania, by William Simpson, 144 pp., $7.95, The Globe Pequot Press, Box Q, Chester, CT 06412 * 30 rides with maps from 6 to 66 miles with maps, directions, photos.

Short Bike Rides in Greater Boston and Central Massachusetts, by Howard Stone, $14.95, The Globe Pequot Press, Box Q, Chester, CT 06412.

Short Bike Rides in Rhode Island, by Howard Stone, $8.95, The Globe Pequot Press, Box Q, Chester, CT 06412.

Short Bike Rides on Cape Cod, Nantucket & the Vineyard, by Edwin Mullen and Jane Griffith, 128 pp., $7.95, The Globe Pequot Press, Box Q, Chester, CT 06412 * 30 rides, maps, photos, directions from Falmouth to Provincetown and beyond.

Short Bike Rides on Long Island, by Phil Angelillo, 160 pp., $8.95, The Globe Pequot Press, Box Q, Chester, CT 06412 * 28 rides, maps, photos, directions, description of history, villages, beaches.

Sweet Sixteen—Great South Jersey Shore, by Shore Cycle Club, $6.70, Shore Cycle Club, 510 School House Lane, Tuckahoe, NJ 08250 * Rides, maps, and cue sheets.

Tennessee Atlas & Gazetteer, 72 pp., $12.95, DeLorme Mapping Company, P.O. Box 298, Freeport, ME 04032, 800/227–1656.

20 Bicycle Tours in the Finger Lakes, by Mark Roth and Sally Walters, $7.95, Backcountry Publications, Woodstock, VT 05091.

20 Bicycle Tours in New Hampshire, by Tom and Susan Heavey, $7.95, Backcountry Publications, Woodstock, VT 05091.

20 Bicycle Tours in and around New York City, by Dan Carlinsky and David Helm, $7.95, Backcountry Publications, Woodstock, VT 05091.

25 Bicycle Tours in Eastern Pennsylvania, by Dale Adams and Dale Speicher, $8.95, Backcountry Publications, Woodstock, VT 05091.

25 Bicycle Tours in Vermont, by John Friedin, 175 pp., $8.95, Backcountry Publications, Woodstock, VT 05091 * Written by the founder of Vermont Bicycle Tours.

25 Bicycle Tours on Delmarva [Chesapeake region], by John Wennersten, $10, Backcountry Publications, Woodstock, VT 05091.

Vermont Atlas & Gazetteer, 88 pp., $11.95, DeLorme Mapping Co., P.O. Box 298, Freeport, ME 04032, 800/227–1656.

Virginia Atlas & Gazetteer, 80 pp., $12.95, DeLorme Mapping Company, P.O. Box 298, Freeport, ME 04032, 800/227–1656.

Western U.S.

Alaska Bicycle Touring Guide, by Alys Culhane and Pete Praetorius, 250 pp., $15, The Denali Press, P.O. Box 021535, Juneau, AK 99802–1535 * The most complete (well, the only) bike guide to Alaska.

Around Puget Sound, by Bill and Erin Woods, 206 pp., $10.95, The Mountaineers Books, 306 Second Ave. West, Seattle, WA 98119, 800/553–4453, 206/285–2665; fax: 206/285–8992 * Details on trips from 4 to 132 miles.

Bicycle Touring Arizona, by Dennis Coello, 136 pp., $11.95, Northland, P.O. Box N, Flagstaff, AZ 86002 * Mostly road tours, with a few off-road options.

Bicycle Touring Colorado, by Dennis Coello, 129 pp., $11.95, Northland Publishing, P.O. Box N, Flagstaff, AZ 86002.

Bicycle Touring Utah, by Dennis Coello, 126 pp., $11.95, Northland Publishing, P.O. Box N, Flagstaff, AZ 86002.

Bicycle Utah, P.O. Box 738, Park City, UT 84060, 801/649–5806 * Free tourism publication. Includes touring companies, campgrounds, and bike stores.

Bicycling the Backroads of Northwest Oregon, by Philip N. Jones, 208 pp., $10.95, The Mountaineers Books, 306 Second Ave. West, Seattle, WA 98119, 800/553–4453, 206/285–2665; fax: 206/285–8992 * Details for 40 rides.

Bicycling the Backroads of Northwest Washington, by Bill and Erin Woods, The Mountaineers Books, 306 Second Ave. West, Seattle, WA 98119, 800/553–4453, 206/285–2665; fax: 206/285–8992, 208 pp., $10.95 * Details for 39 tours.

Bicycling the Backroads of Southwest Washington, by Bill and Erin Woods, 208 pp., $12.95, The Mountaineers Books, 306 Second Ave. West, Seattle, WA 98119, 800/553–4453, 206/285–2665; fax: 206/285–8992. Details for 45 tours.

Bicycling the Dallas/Ft. Worth Area, The Texas Bicycle Map Company, P.O. Box 740981, Houston, TX 77274 * 25 rides.

Bicycling the Houston Area, The Texas Bicycle Map Company, P.O. Box 740981, Houston, TX 77274 * 25 rides.

Bicycling the Pacific Coast, by Tom Kirkendall and Vicky Spring, 240 pp., $12.95, The Mountaineers Books, 306 Second Ave. West, Seattle, WA 98119, 800/553–4453, 206/285–2665; fax: 206/285–8992 * A Canada-to-Mexico guide.

Bicycling the Texas Hill Country and West Texas, by Bill Pellerin and Ralph Neidhardt, $9.95, The Texas Bicycle Map Company, P.O. Box 740981, Houston, TX 77274 * 25 rides.

Bikecentennial Route Maps. *See* "Eastern U.S." above.

Bike Rides of the Colorado Front Range, by Vici De Haan, 115 pp., $8.95, Pruett Publishing Company, 2928 Pearl St., Boulder, CO 80301 * 45 rides, maps, difficulty ratings, historical background.

Colorado Cycling Guide, by Jean and Hartley Alley, 376 pp., $16.95, Pruett Publishing Company, 2928 Pearl St., Boulder, CO 80301 * Maps, directions, altitudes, sources of food/lodging, riding tips, appendices.

Illinois Atlas & Gazetteer, 96 pp., $14.95, DeLorme Mapping Company, P.O. Box 298, Freeport, ME 04032, 800/227–1656.

Michigan Atlas & Gazetteer, 120 pp., $14.95, DeLorme Mapping Company, P.O. Box 298, Freeport, ME 04032, 800/227–1656. * Topographical maps and information on bicycle routes, historic sites, scenic drives, and parks, forests, and recreation areas.

Minnesota Atlas & Gazetteer, 96 pp., $14.95, DeLorme Mapping Company, P.O. Box 298, Freeport, ME 04032, 800/227–1656.

Minnesota Bike Atlas, $10.50 (postage included), American Youth Hostels, Minnesota Council, 2395 University Ave. West, Suite 302, St. Paul, MN 55114 * Time-tested rides from the state's largest cycling organization.

Northern California Atlas & Gazetteer, 128 pp., $12.95, DeLorme Mapping Company, P.O. Box 298, Freeport, ME 04032, 800/227–1656.

Oregon Atlas & Gazetteer, 96 pp., $14.95, DeLorme Mapping Company, P.O. Box 298, Freeport, ME 04032, 800/227–1656 * Topo maps and bike routes.

Six Islands on Two Wheels, by Tom Koch, 220 pp., $13.95, Bess Press, P.O. Box 22388, Honolulu, HI 96823, 808/734–7159 * Considered a complete guide for cycling in Hawaii.

Southern & Central California Atlas & Gazetteer, 128 pp., $12.95, DeLorme Mapping Company, P.O. Box 298, Freeport, ME 04032, 800/227–1656. Topo maps, recreation areas, bike routes, etc.

Southwest American Bicycle Route, by Lowell Linday and W.G. Hample, 143 pp., $9.95, Sunbelt Publications, 8622 Argent St., Suite A, Santee, CA 92071, 800/626/6579 * Route from Oceanside, CA, to Larned, KS, goes through the Grand Canyon and connects with Bikecentennial's TransAmerica Trail.

Umbrella Guide to Bicycling the Oregon Coast, by Robin Cody, 112 pp., $10.95 plus $2 shipping, Umbrella Books, P.O. Box 1460, Friday Harbor, WA 98250 * Covers 370 miles of coast.

Washington Atlas & Gazetteer, 120 pp., $14.95, DeLorme Mapping Company, P.O. Box 298, Freeport, ME 04032, 800/227–1656.

Wisconsin Atlas & Gazetteer, 104 pp., $14.95, DeLorme Mapping Company, P.O. Box 298, Freeport, ME 04032, 800/227–1656.

Canada, Mexico, and Overseas Destinations

Backcountry Bicycling in the Canadian Rockies, by Gerhardt Lepp, $9.95 plus $1.50 postage, Rocky Mountain Books, 106 Wimbledon Crescent SW, Calgary, Alberta T3C 3JA, Canada.

Bicycle Touring in Europe, by Karen and Gary Hawkins, Random House, 188 pp., $10.95 * 14 tours and tourist addresses.

Bicycle Tours in Nova Scotia, $5 plus $1.50 postage, Bicycle Nova Scotia, Box 3010 South, Halifax, Nova Scotia B3J 3G6, Canada.

Bicycling Baja, by Bonnie Wong, 248 pp., $12.95, Sunbelt Publications, 8622 Argent St., Suite A, Santee, CA 92071, 800/626–6579 * Information on off-road and on-road cycling in Baja.

Bicycling in Africa, by David Mozer, 192 pp., $14.95, International Bicycle Fund, 4887 Columbia Drive S., Seattle, WA 98108–1919, 206/628–9314.

Bicycling Mexico, by Ericka Weisbroth and Eric Ellman, 300 pp., $16.95 plus $2.50 postage, Photo-graphics, P.O. Box Ridgefield, NJ 07657 * Detailed tour maps, distances, road condition of the Interior, Yucatan, Islands, and Baja coasts.

The Bicyclist's Dilemma in African Cities, 26 pp., $3, International Bicycle Fund, 4887 Columbia Drive S., Seattle, WA 98108–1919, 206/628–9314.

The Big Book of Adventure Travel, by James C. Simmons, 350 pp., $12.95, New American Library, 1633 Broadway, New York, NY 10019 * 500 great escapes, including bicycling, river rafting, and kayak expeditions.

Biking through Europe, by Dennis and Tina Jaffe, 317 pp., $13.95, Williamson Publishing, available through Bikecentennial, P.O. Box 8308, Missoula, MT 59807, 800/933– 1116 * Tours in France, Denmark, England, Holland, Belgium, and Switzerland. Information on bike rentals, accommodations, and food.

The Canadian Bed and Breakfast Book, Canadian Cycling Association, 1600 James Naismith Dr., Gloucester, Ontario K1B 5N4, Canada, 613/748–5629, $14.95 plus $2.50 postage.

Cycle Touring in New Zealand, by Bruce Ringer, 320 pp., $14.95, The Mountaineers Books, 306 Second Ave. West, Seattle, WA 98119, 800/553–4453, 206/285–2665; fax: 206/285–8992 * How-to and where-to for 14 tours.

Cycle Touring in the North Island of New Zealand, $8 postpaid, Southern Cyclist, Inc., P.O. Box 5890, Auckland, New Zealand.

Cycle Touring in the South Island of New Zealand, $8 postpaid, Southern Cyclist, Inc., P.O. Box 5890, Auckland, New Zealand.

Cycling in Europe, by Nicholas Crane, Oxford Illustrated Press, available through Bikecentennial, P.O. Box 8308, Missoula, MT 59807–8308, 800/933–1116.

Cycling the Islands, P.E.I. and the Magdalen Islands, by Campbell Webster, 99 pp., Breakwater Press, St. John's, Newfoundland, Canada * 9 routes that may be mixed and matched for multi-day tours of this maritime area of Canada. Maps, photos, directions.

A Cyclist's Guidebook to the Canadian Rockies, by Larry Barnes, $6.95 plus $1.50 postage, Rocky Mountain Cycle Tours, Box 1978, Canmore, Alberta T0L 0H0, Canada.

Europe by Bike, by Karen and Terry Whitehill, 248 pp., $10.95, The Mountaineers Books, 306 Second Ave. West, Seattle, WA 98119, 800/553–4453, 206/285–2665; fax: 206/285–8992 * Details for point-to-point tours of 11 countries.

European Planning & Rail Guide, Budget Europe Travel Service, 2557 Meade Court, Ann Arbor, MI 48105, 313/668–0529.

Grape Expeditions in France, by Sally Taylor, 128 pp., $9, available through Bikecentennial, P.O. Box 8308, Missoula, MT 59807–8308, 800/ 933–1116.

Round Ireland in Low Gear, by Eric Newby, 308 pp., Viking Penguin, 40 W. 23rd St., New York, NY 10010, 212/337–5200 * The veteran of literary travel writing and his wife tackle Ireland on mountain bikes—in winter.

Food and Fitness

The Athlete's Kitchen, by Nancy Clark, MS, RD, 150 pp., $4.50 plus $1.50 postage, New England Sports Publications, P.O. Box 252, Boston, MA 02113 * "The essential guide for pros and part-time athletes." Includes nutrition tips on high energy snacks.

Bicycling Magazine's Nutrition for Cyclists, 128 pp., $6.95, Rodale Press, 33 E. Minor St., Emmaus, PA 18098, 215/967–5171.

Bicycling Magazine's Training for Fitness and Endurance, 128 pp., $6.95, Rodale Press, 33 E. Minor St., Emmaus, PA 18098, 215/967–5171.

Cycle Food: A Guide to Satisfying Your Inner Tube, by Laura Hefferon, 90 pp., $4.95, Ten Speed Press, P.O. Box 7123, Berkeley, CA 94707 * A cookbook for cyclists. Stuffed with pasta and other appropriate dishes.

Cyclist's Log, 85 pp., $6.95, Jogalite/Bikealite, Box 125, Silver Lake, NH 03875, 800/258–8974 * Intro by Mark Gorski. Includes advice on stretching.

Cyclists Training Diary, $8.95, Vitesse Press, Box 1886, Brattleboro, VT 05302–1886 * You fill in the blanks with speed and miles.

Fit & Fast: How to Be a Better Cyclist, by Karen E. Roy and Thurlow Rogers, 164 pp., $15.95, Vitesse Press, Box 1886, Brattleboro, VT 05302–1886 * How-to tips from two former racers.

Gorp, Glop, and Glue Stew: Favorite Foods from 165 Outdoor Experts, by Yvonne Prater and Ruth Mendenhall, 204 pp., $9.95, The Mountaineers Books, 306 Second Ave. West, Seattle, WA 98119, 800/553–4453, 206/285–2665; fax: 206/285–8992.

Medicine for the Back Country, by Buck Tilton and Frank Hubbell, 160 pp., $9.95, ICS Books, 107 E. 89th Ave., Merrillville, IND 46410, 800/541–7323.

Medicine for the Great Outdoors: A Guide to Emergency Medical Procedures and First Aid, by Paul S. Auerbach, M.D., $14.95, Little, Brown & Co., 34 Beacon St., Boston, MA 02108.

Richard's Cycling for Fitness, by John Schubert, 198 pp., $7.95, Ballantine Books, 201 East 50th St., New York, NY 10022 * A thorough guide to training for health and fitness. Drawings, charts, and other useful information.

The Trekking Chef, by Claudine Martin, 200 pp., $14.95, Lyons & Burford, 31 West 21 St., New York, NY 10010 * Don't read this if you are hungry.

The Two-Wheeled Athlete: Physiology for the Cyclist, by Ed Burke, 140 pp., $10.95, Vitesse Press, Box 1886, Brattleboro, VT 05302–1886 * Tips from a physiologist and former technical director for the U.S. Cycling Federation.

Weight Training for Cyclists, by Fred Matheny and others, 78 pp., $7.95 * Vitesse Press, Box 1886, Brattleboro, VT 05302–1886 * When—and if—to train with weights.

Mountain Bikes

See also "Repairs" and "Periodicals" below for more publications.

America by Mountain Bike, Central Appalachia, by Joe Surkiewitz, forthcoming in winter 1991 from Menasha Ridge Press, 3169 Cahaba Heights Rd., Birmingham, AL 35243.

America by Mountain Bike, Northern New England, by Paul Angiolillo, Jr., forthcoming in winter 1991 from Menasha Ridge Press, 3169 Cahaba Heights Rd., Birmingham, AL 35243.

BIA's Mountain Bike Action Kit, $2, Bicycle Institute of America, 1818 R St. NW, Washington, DC 20009, 202/332–6986 * Information on how to work with land managers, other user groups, and the media.

Bicycling Magazine's Mountain Biking Skills, 128 pages, $6.95, Rodale Press, 33 E. Minor St., Emmaus, PA 18098 * For the new mountain biker.

Bicycling the Backcountry: A Mountain Bike Guide to Colorado, by William L. Stoehr, 158 pp., $10.95, Pruett Publishing Company, 2928 Pearl St., Boulder, CO 80301 * 30 rides with photos, maps, difficulty ratings, appendix.

The Complete Mountain Biker, by Dennis Coello, 170 pp., $12.95, Lyons and Burford, 31 West 21 St., New York, NY 10010 * Technique, equipment, and repair.

Cycling the California Outback with Bodfish, by Chuck "Bodfish" Elliot, 66 pp., $6.50, Bodfish Books, 801 Main St., Chico, CA 95926.

Eugene A. Sloane's Complete Book of All-Terrain Bicycling, by Eugene A. Sloane, 200 pp., $12.95, Simon and Schuster, 2000 Old Tappan Rd., Old Tappan, NJ 07675, 800/223–2348 * Just what the title says.

A Guide to Mountain Bike Riding in Washington, by Carla Black and Angel Rodriquez, 122 pp., $ 8.95, Evergreen Group, 5627 University Way, Seattle, WA 98105.

The Lost Coast in Northern California: A Nine Day Mountain Bike Wilderness Camping Trip, by N.W. Bell, 3 pp., $.45, 1805 Cowper St., Palo Alto, CA 94301.

The Marin Mountain Bike Guide, Where to Go and What to Know, by Armor Todd, 150 pp., $9.95, Wheel Escapes, 1000 Magnolia Ave., Larkspur, CA 94939, 415/461–6903 * 60 fire roads and loops.

Mountain Bicycling around Los Angeles, by Robert Immler, 128 pp., $9.95, Wilderness Press, 2440 Bancroft Way, Berkeley, CA 94704–1676, 415/843–8080.

Mountain Bike Adventures in the Four Corners Region, by Michael McCoy, 240 pp., $12.95, The Mountaineers Books, 306 Second Ave. West, Seattle, WA 98119, 800/553–4453, 206/285–2665; fax: 206/285–8992 * 48 rides in Arizona, Utah, Colorado, New Mexico.

Mountain Bike Adventures in the Northern Rockies, by Michael McCoy, 184 pp., $10.95, The Mountaineers Books, 306 Second Ave. West, Seattle, WA 98119, 800/553–4453, 206/285–2665; fax: 206/285–8992 * 40 tours in Montana, Wyoming, Idaho, South Dakota.

Mountain Bike Adventures in Washington's North Cascades/Olympics, by Tom Kirkendall, 224 pp., $12.95 * The Mountaineers Books, 306 Second Ave. West, Seattle, WA 98119, 800/553–4453, 206/285–2665; fax: 206/285–8992 * 60 rides with details on elevation, terrain, distance, level of skill.

Mountain Bike Adventures in Washington's South Cascades/Puget Sound, by Tom Kirkendall, 224 pp., $10.95, The Mountaineers Books, 306 Second Ave. West, Seattle,

WA 98119, 800/553–4453, 206/285–2665; fax: 206/285–8992 * 60 rides with details on elevation, terrain, distance, level of skill.

The Mountain Bike Book, by Rob Van der Plas, 208 pp., $9.95, Bicycle Books, Inc., P.O. Box 2038, Mill Valley, CA 94941 * Advice on riding techniques, touring, choosing an ATB.

Mountain Bike Guide to Oregon, 109 pp., $5.50, Oregon Parks and Recreation Department, 525 Trade St. SE, Salem, OR 97310 * 65 routes.

Mountain Bike Rides in the Colorado Front Range, by William L. Stoehr, 147 pp., $10.95, Pruett Publishing Company, 2928 Pearl St., Boulder, CO 80301 * 27 rides, maps, difficulty ratings.

Mountain Bike Rides of the West, by Dennis Coello, Northland Publishing, P.O. Box N, Flagstaff, AZ 86002, 125 pp., $12.95 * 20 rides in Arizona, Colorado, Montana, New Mexico, Utah, and Wyoming.

Mountain Biking the Coast Range Series, 96 pages, $7.95 each, Fine Edge Productions, Rt. 2, Box 303, Bishop, CA 93514. Series includes these titles, with maps and descriptions: Guide 4—Ventura County and the Sespe;Guide 5—Santa Barbara and Los Padres; Guide 7—Santa Monica Mountains; Guide 8—Saugus District and Mt. Pinos, Angeles National Forest.

Mountain Biking the High Sierra Series, 96 pages, $7.95 each, Fine Edge Productions, Rt.2, Box 303, Bishop, CA 93514. Series includes these titles, with maps and descriptions: Guide 1—Owens Valley and Inyo Country; Guide 2—Mammoth Lakes and Mono Country; Guide 3A—Lake Tahoe, South, Eldorado National Forest; Guide 3B—Lake Tahoe North, Tahoe National Forest.

Mountain Bike Trail Guide: San Diego, 125 pp., $9.95, Sunbelt Publications, 8622 Argent St., Suite A, Santee, CA 92071, 800/626–6579.

The Mountain Bike Way of Knowledge, by William Nealy, 126 pp., $5.95, Menasha Ridge Press, 3169 Cahaba Heights Rd., Birmingham, AL 35243 * Humorous look at the Zen of mountain biking.

Richard's Mountain Bike Book, by Charles Kelly, 192 pp., $8.95, Ballantine Books, 201 East 50th St., New York, NY 10022.

Technical

Bicycle Gearing: A Practical Guide, by Dick Marr, 136 pp., $6.95, The Mountaineers Books, 306 Second Ave. West, Seattle, WA 98119, 800/553–4453, 206/285–2665; fax: 206/285–8992 * How-to and shifting strategies.

Bicycle Mechanics in Workshop and Competition, by Steve Snowling and Ken Evans, 160 pp., $17.95, Human Kinetics Publishers, Box 5076, Champaign, IL 61825–5076, 800/747–4457, 217/351–5076.

Bicycle Metallurgy for the Cyclist, by Douglas Hayduk, 110 pp., $8.95, Vitesse Press, Box 1886, Brattleboro, VT 05302–1886.

Bicycles and Tricycles: An Elementary Treatise on Their Design and Construction, by Archibald Sharp, 536 pp., $14.95, The MIT Press, 55 Hayward St., Cambridge, MA 02142 * Reprint of an 1896 classic.

Bicycling Magazine's Complete Guide to Bicycle Maintenance and Repair, 320 pp., $16.95/paper, $24.95/hardcover, Rodale Press, 33 E. Minor St., Emmaus, PA 18098.

Bicycling Magazine's Complete Guide to Upgrading Your Bike, by Frank J. Berto, 320 pp., $14.95, Rodale Press, 33 E. Minor St., Emmaus, PA 18098 * Guidelines to whether a bike is worth upgrading. Includes detailed tables of bike component testing.

Bicycling Science, by Frank Rowland Whitt and David Gordon Wilson, 364 pp., $12.50, The MIT Press, 55 Hayward St., Cambridge, MA 02142 * Physics and mechanics of cycling explained.

Medical and Scientific Aspects of Cycling, edited by Edmund R. Burke and Mary Margaret Newson, 272 pp., $32, Human Kinetics, Box 5076, Champaign, IL 61825–5076, 800/747–4457, 217/351–5076 * Experts on the latest advances in cycling.

Paterek's Manual, by Tim Paterek, 446 pp., $75, available through Kermesse Distributors, 658 Eastern Rd., Horsham, PA 19044, 215/672–0230 * Guide to frame building.

The Science of Cycling, by Edmund R. Burke, 215 pp., $12.95, Human Kinetics Books/VeloNews Books, 5595 Arapahoe Ave., Suite G, Boulder, CO 80303, 800/234–VELO * Written by researchers and coaches on the physiological, mechanical, biomechanical, psychological, and medical aspects of cycling.

The Sloane New Bicycling Maintenance Manual, by Eugene A. Sloane, 220 pp., $14.95, Simon and Schuster, 200 Old Tappan Rd., Old Tappan, NJ 07675, 800/223–2348 * New book from the old master.

History and Antiques

Around the World on a Bicycle, by Thomas Stevens, 133 pp., $20 plus $2 postage (hardcover), Seven Palms Press, P.O. Box 3371, Tucson, AZ 85722 * A condensation of Stevens' legendary book about his around-the-world-cycling tour in the 1880s.

1991 Bicycle Blue Book, by T.A. Gordon and Jim Hurd, 150 pp., $9, P.O. Box 1049, Ann Arbor, MI 48106 * The only guide to the blue book value of antique and reproduction bicycles.

Bicycles and Tricycles: An Elementary Treatise on Their Design and Construction, by Archibald Sharp, 536 pp., $14.95, The MIT Press, 55 Hayward St., Cambridge, MA 02142 * Reprint of an 1896 classic.

Collectible Elgin-J.C. Higgins-Hawthorn Bicycles 1930's–1960, 250 pp., $16.95 Antique/Classic Bicycle News, P.O. Box 1049, Ann Arbor, MI 48106 * Reprints from old Sears and Montgomery Ward catalogs featuring bikes, parts, and accessories sought after by collectors.

European Cycling: The 20 Greatest Races, by Noel Henderson, 152 pp., $13.95, Vitesse Press, Box 1886, Brattleboro, VT 05302–1886 * History of races from Amstel Gold to Zurich Championship.

Fifty Years of Schwinn-Built Bicycles, by Frank W. Schwinn, 100 pp., $18.95 plus $3 postage, Schwinn Bicycle Company, 217 N. Jefferson St., Chicago, IL 60606 * Originally published in 1945, this reprinting of a collection of old photos and reminiscences highlights the Schwinn Company's contributions to bicycling. According to Jim Hurd of the Schwinn History Center, an original copy of the book would sell for $150–$200.

Hearts of Lions: The Story of American Bicycle Racing, by Peter Nye, Foreword by Eric Heiden, 317 pp., $10.95, W.W. Norton, 500 5th Ave., New York, NY 10110 * From highwheel races of the 1880s through LeMond. Packed with anecdotes.

Introductory Guide to Collecting the Classics, by James L. Hurd and Don A. Hennings, $11.95, Antique/Classic Bicycle News, P.O. Box 1049, Ann Arbor, MI 48106 * Identifying and restoring collectible bicycles.

Major Taylor: The Extraordinary Career of a Champion Bicycle Racer, 304 pp., $19.95, Bicycle Books Inc., P.O. Box 2038, Mill Valley, CA 94941 * Tales of the first black world champion; hardcover.

Memories of the Peloton, by Bernard Hinault, 156 pp., $14.95, Vitesse Press, Box 1886, Brattleboro, VT 05302–1886 * The inside story from the hardbitten multi-champion of the Tour de France.

The Mighty TOSRV, by Greg and June Siple, 128 pp., $12, Columbus Council/AYH, P.O. Box 14384, Columbus, OH 43214 * Illustrated history of the Tour of the Scioto River Valley.

On Your Bicycle, by James McGurn, 208 pp., $25, Facts on File, 460 Park Ave. South, New York, NY 10016, 212/683–2244 * Covers the prehistory of cycling right up to cycling in the motor age. Also available through L.A.W., 6707 Whitestone Rd., Suite 209, Baltimore, MD 21207.

Railroads Recycled: How Local Initiative and Public Support Launched the Rails-to-Trails Movement, 1965–1990, 100 pp., $12.95, Rails-to-Trails Conservancy, 1400 16th St. NW, Washington, DC 20036 * History of the movement from the Illinois Prairie Path (1965) to 3,100–mile system of today. Rails-to-Trails also publishes a sampler of trails.

A Social History of the Bicycle: Its Early Life and Times in America, by Robert A. Smith, 269 pp., American Heritage Press, 1972 * Published in 1972, this book is now out of print, but worth scrounging up in a library or second-hand bookstore.

When Bikehood Was in Flower, by Irving Leonard, 151 pp., $7.95 plus $1.50 postage, Seven Palms Press, P.O. Box 3371, Tucson, AZ 85722 * Profiles of male and female bicycle pioneers, from 1880 to 1920.

Business

Bicycle Retailers Guide to Getting Rich in the Recession, by Randy W. Kirk, 112 pp., $19.95, Infonet Publishing, P.O. Box 3789, San Clemente, CA 92672, 714/492–7219 * Inspiration from a veteran salesman. Sequel to *Principles of Bicycle Retailing*.

(Bicycling's) Marketing & Merchandising, Rodale Press, 33 East Minor St., Emmaus, PA 18098 * A basic business guide for bike shops.

The Interbike Directory, 150 pp., $40, Infonet Publishing, P.O. Box 3789, San Clemente, CA 92672, 714/492–7219 * Directory with index to bicycle industry distributors and manufacturers.

Principles of Bicycle Retailing, by Randy W. Kirk, 104 pp., $19.95, Infonet Publishing, P.O. Box 3789, San Clemente, CA 92672, 714/492–7219 * Words of inspiration from a veteran salesman.

Sports Market Place, Richard Lipsey, Editor, Sportsguide Inc., P.O. Box 1417, Princeton, NJ 08542 * Focus is on sports publishers, magazines, TV and radio shows, clubs, associations.

Advocacy and Education

Aspects of Bikeway Designation: A Special Report, The Bicycle Federation of America, 1818 R St. NW, Washington, DC 20009, 202/332–6986.

The Basics of Bicycling, by Linda Tracy and John Williams, $49, Bicycle Federation of America, 1818 R St. NW, Washington, DC 20009, 202/332-6986 * Seven-lesson, in-class and on-bike education program designed for upper elementary school students. Includes program manual and videotape.

BIA's Mountain Bike Action Kit, $2, Bicycle Institute of America, 1818 R St. NW, Washington, DC 20009, 202/332–6986 * Information on how to work with land managers, other user groups, and the media.

Bicycle Advocate's Handbook, $14.95, The League of American Wheelmen, Suite 209, 6707 Whitestone Rd., Baltimore, MD 21207.

Bicycle Coordinators: How, Where, Who, When and Why? edited by Andy Clarke, $7.50, Bicycle Federation of America, 1818 R St. NW, Washington, DC 20009, 202/332– 6986 * Information on bicycle coordinators' contribution. Directory of coordinators and other references.

The Bicycle Program Specialist Survey, $5, Bicycle Federation of America, 1818 R St. NW, Washington, DC 20009, 202/332–6986 * Results of a survey of more than 250 engineers, planners, and coordinators.

Bicycle Route Research: Technical Report, The Bicycle Federation of America, 1818 R St. NW, Washington, DC 20009, 202/332–6986.

The Bicycle: Vehicle for a Small Planet, by Marcia D. Lowe, 50 pp., $4, Worldwatch Institute, 1776 Massachusetts Ave. NW, Washington, DC 20036 * Thorough examination of the worldwide use of bicycles.

Bicycling to Work Seminar Information, free with SASE, U.S. Environmental Protection Agency (EPA), 410 M St. S.W., Washington, DC 20460, 202/382–2671.

Bicycling Transportation, by John Forester, 280 pp., $27.50, The MIT Press, 55 Hayward St., Cambridge, MA 02142 * A polemic and guide for advocates of cycling equality on the roads.

Captain Cycle and the Bike Ranger's Coloring Book, 10 pp., Outdoor Empire Publishing, Inc., 511 Eastlake Ave. E., P.O. Box C–19000, Seattle, WA 98109, 206/624–3845 * All right, kids and adults, get out your crayons and go for it!

A Guide to Bicycle Rodeos, 30 pp., $5.75, Bicycle Forum, P.O. Box 8308, Missoula, MT 59807, 406/721–1776 * Rodeos are fun ways to teach children safe cycling skills. This handy book illustrates how to organize a successful rodeo. Safety materials, such as posters and brochures, are also available.

How to Get Police on Bikes, brochure, $2, League of American Wheelmen, 6707 Whitestone Rd. Suite 209, Baltimore, MD 21207.

How to Organize a Bike Day, 17 pp., U.S. Environmental Protection Agency (EPA), 410 M St. S.W., Washington, DC 20460, 202/382–2671 * Free brochure with SASE.

How to Promote Bicycling as a Pollution Solution, brochure, $2, League of American Wheelmen, 6707 Whitestone Rd. Suite 209, Baltimore, MD 21207.

How to Rate the States, brochure, $2, League of American Wheelmen, 6707 Whitestone Rd. Suite 209, Baltimore, MD 21207.

How to Succeed at Bicycle Advocacy, brochure, $2, League of American Wheelmen, 6707 Whitestone Rd. Suite 209, Baltimore, MD 21207.

Mountain Bikes on Public Lands: A Manager's Guide to the State of the Practice, by Kit Keller, 68 pp., $25, Bicycle Federation of America, 1881 R St. NW, Washington, DC 20009, 202/332–6986 * Comprehensive review of issues involved in managing mountain bikes on unpaved trails. Details range of options.

Pro Bike Directory, $15, Bicycle Federation of America, 1818 R St. NW, Washington, DC 20009 * Lists more than 1,000 experts in bicycle safety education, facility development, and event promotion plus government and private agencies and organizations.

Selecting and Designating Bicycle Routes: A Handbook, The Bicycle Federation of America, 1818 R St. NW, Washington, DC 20009, 202/332–6986.

Racing

See also "History and Antiques."

Beginning Bicycle Racing: Fast Riding for Fitness and Competition, by Fred Matheny, 240 pp., $14.95, Vitesse Press, Box 1886, Brattleboro, VT 05302–1886 * How to start and reach potential.

The Bicycle Fitness Book, by Rob Van der Plas, 144 pp., $7.95, Bicycle Books Inc., P.O. Box 2038, Mill Valley, CA 94941 * Using the bike for health and fitness.

The Bicycle Racing Guide, by Rob Van der Plas, 256 pp., $10.95, Bicycle Books Inc., P.O. Box 2038, Mill Valley, CA 94941 * Techniques and training for racers/triathletes.

Bicycling Magazine's Complete Guide to Riding and Racing Techniques, by Fred Matheny, 256 pp., $14.95, Rodale Press, 33 E. Minor St., Emmaus, PA 18098, 215/967–5171.

The Cycling Year 90, by John Wilcockson, 160 pp., $34.95, VeloNews Books, 1830 N. 55th St., Boulder, CO 80301, 800/234–8356 * Color photos. Account of 1990 racing season, featuring road and mountain bike races.

In High Gear: The World of Professional Bicycle Racing, by Samuel Abt, 208 pp., $10.95, Bicycle Books Inc., P.O. Box 2038, Mill Valley, CA 94941 * The inside line from the *New York Times* correspondent on cycling.

In Spite of Us: My Education in the Big and Little Games of Amateur and Olympic Sports in the U.S., by David F. Prouty, 279 pp., $12.95, Vitesse Press, Box 1886, Brattleboro, VT 05302–1886 * Former director of the U.S. Cycling Federation tattles.

Kings of the Road: A Portrait of Racers and Racing, by Robin Magowan and Graham Watson, 208 pp., $24.95, Human Kinetics, Box 5076, Champaign, IL 61825–5076, 800/747–4457, 217/351–5076.

The RAAM Book: A Complete Guide to the Race Across America (RAAM) and Long-Distance Cycling, by John Marino, Lon Haldeman, and others, 229 pp., $9.95, Infonet Publishing, P.O. Box 3789, San Clemente, CA 92672, 714/492–7219 * Stats, riders, diaries, and everything about RAAM from those who ride cross-country in under 9 days.

Road Racing: Technique and Training, by Bernard Hinault and Claude Genzling, 208 pp., $16.95, Vitesse Press, Box 1886, Brattleboro, VT 05302–1886 * Tips from a champ and a veteran cycling journalist.

A Rough Ride, by Paul Kimmage, 199 pp., $21.95, VeloNews Books, 1830 N. 55th St., Boulder, CO 80301, 800/234–8356 * Kimmage's story of life on the pro peloton shows widespread use of drugs and fixed races.

7–11/Bicycling Magazine Grand Prix Training Manual II, edited by Pat Griffith, 144 pp., $7.95, Vitesse Press, Box 1886, Brattleboro, VT 05302–1886 * Tips on training, technique, diet, and psychology.

Solo Cycling: How to Train and Race Bicycle Time Trials, by Fred Matheny, 205 pp., $14.95, Vitesse Press, Box 1886, Brattleboro, VT 05302–1886 * Tips for solo, against-the-clock events.

Sport Cycling: A Guide to Training, Racing and Endurance, by Michael Shermer, 256 pp., $9.95, Contemporary Books, 180 North Michigan Ave., Chicago, IL 60601 * The basics from a RAAM rider.

Ten Years of Championship Bicycle Racing, 1972–1981, editors of VeloNews, 122 pp., $14.95 * Compilation of race results for a decade.

Tour de France and Its Heroes, by Graham Watson, 127 pp., $34.95, VeloNews Books, 1830 N. 55th St., Boulder, CO 80301, 800/234–8356 * Photos and text on ten years of the Tour de France.

Tour of the Forest Bicycle Race, H.E. Thomson, 63 pp., $9.95, Bicycle Books Inc., P.O. Box 2038, Mill Valley, CA 94941 * An illustrated children's book written from the point of view of critters observing the Tour de France.

Velo Annual, 572 pp., $24.95, VeloNews Books, 1830 N. 55th St., Boulder, CO 80301, 800/234–8356 * All the racing stats from the folks who cover the races.

Visions of Cycling, by Graham Watson, 127 pp., $34.95, VeloNews Books, 1830 N. 55th St., Boulder, CO 80301, 800/234–8356 * Coffee table book with photos and text on the peloton scene.

Repairs: Mountain and Road Bicycles

Anybody's Bike Book, revised, by Tom Cuthbertson, 256 pp., $8.95, Ten Speed Press, P.O. Box 7123, Berkeley, CA 94707, 800/841–2665 * The classic bike book that started Ten Speed Press, now in its nineteenth year. Includes sections on mountain bikes.

Barnett's Manual: Analysis and Procedures for Bicycle Mechanics, 528 pp., $95, Vitesse Press, Box 1886, Brattleboro, VT 05302–1886, 800/848–3747 * The binder-book pro mechanics use.

Bicycling Magazine's Complete Guide to Bicycle Maintenance and Repair, 320 pp., $16.95/paper, $24.95/hardcover, Rodale Press, 33 E. Minor St., Emmaus, PA 18098.

The Bike Bag Book, by Tom Cuthbertson, 144 pp., $2.95, Ten Speed Press, P.O. Box 7123, Berkeley, CA 94707, 800/841–2665.

The Bike Repair Book, by Rob Van der Plas, 140 pp., $8.95, Bicycle Books Inc., P.O. Box 2038, Mill Valley, CA 94941 * Complete manual of repair.

Eugene A. Sloane's Complete Book of Bicycle Maintenance, 250 pp., $12.95, Simon and Schuster, 1230 Ave. of the Americas, New York, NY 10020, 800/223–2336, 212/698–7000.

Glenn's New Complete Bicycle Manual: Selection, Maintenance, Repair, by Clarence W. Coles and Harold T. Glenn, updated by John Allen, 416 pp., $21.95. Crown Publishers, Inc., One Park Ave., New York, NY 10016 * One of the standards for gearheads.

Mountain Bike Maintenance: Repairing and Maintaining the Off-road Bicycle, by Rob Van der Plas, 110 pp., $6.95 * Illustrated with diagrams by this prolific writer-engineer.

The Mountain Bike Manual, by Dennis Coello, 127 pp., $7.95, Dream Garden Press, P.O. Box 27076, Salt Lake City, UT 84127 * Repairs, preparation for the trail.

The Mountain Bike Repair Handbook, by Dennis Coello, 148 pp., $12.95, Lyons & Burford, 31 W. 21 St., New York, NY 10010.

Roadside Bicycle Repairs, by Rob Van der Plas, 126 pp., $4.95, Bicycle Books Inc., P.O. Box 2038, Mill Valley, CA 94941 * Stick it in your fanny pack.

The Roadside Guide to Bike Repair, by Dennis Coello, 103 pp., $3.95, Warner Books, 666 Fifth Ave., New York, NY 10103 * Tucks in back pocket for handy repairs.

Sutherland's Handbook for Bicycle Mechanics, by Howard Sutherland, Sutherland Publications, P.O. Box 9061, Berkeley, CA 94709, 800/248–2510 * Comprehensive manual featuring charts and diagrams.

PERIODICALS: MAGAZINES AND NEWSLETTERS

General

Bicycle, The Northern and Shell Building, P.O. Box 381, Mill Harbor, London E14 9TW, England, 01/987–5090 * British magazine for all types of bicyclists.

Bicycle Guide, 711 Boylston St., Boston, MA 02116, 617/236–1885 * *Bicycling* magazine's main competitor in the mainstream cycling magazine market, with similar features, road tests, and departments. Publishes the *Bicycle Guide's Buyers Annual,* which lists manufacturers, specs, and prices.

Bicycling, Rodale Press, Inc., 33 E. Minor St., Emmaus, PA 18098 * The general bike mag with the highest circulation. Product news, tests, features, training tips, nutrition, sports medicine, travel.

Bike Events, Bike Events, Ltd., P.O. Box 75, Bath BA1 1BX, Avon, England, 0225–310859 * British magazine listing events and tours all over the world.

Changing Modes, Bicycle Transportation and Safety Office, Dept. of Public Works, 2000 14th St. NW, Washington, DC 20009, 202/939–8016 * Occasional newsletter from cycling coordinator.

Cycling Science: New Development for the Technical Enthusiast, P.O. Box 1510, Mt. Shasta, CA 96067, 916/938–4411 * Quarterly edited by Chester Kyle and Edmund Burke.

Fitness Cycling, Challenge Publications, Inc., 7950 Deering Ave., Canoga Park, CA 91304, 818/887–0550 * Fitness and bodybuilding-oriented monthly magazine for cyclists. Features on health, nutrition, road tests, weight training.

The Network News, c/o The Bicycle Network, P.O. Box 8194, Philadelphia, PA 19101, 215/222–1253 * What's happening with cycle technology in China? With efforts to promote bike commuting in London? The monthly *Network News,* "an information service on all new development in human powered transit and pedal technology," tells all, reprinting articles from the world over, often in their native tongues, but mostly in English.

Outdoor Woman, P.O. Box 834, Nyack, NY 10960, 914/358–1257 * For women interested in bicycling and other sports. Ten-times-a-year newsletter.

Outside, 1165 N. Clark St., Chicago, IL 60610, 312/951–0990 * Increasingly cycling-oriented magazine with literary features on climbing, adventure travel, skiing, more. March issue focuses on cycling.

Pro Bike News, The Bicycle Federation of America, 1818 R St., NW, Washington, DC 20009, 202/332–6986 * Monthly newsletter for advocates and bicycle enthusiasts. Full of all sorts of tidbits on bike programs, education, and innovations.

Schwinn's Cycling & Fitness, 1509 Seabright Ave., #B–1, Santa Cruz, CA 95062, 408/426–3158 * A free magazine from Schwinn, available at many bike shops. Features on tours, diet, training, gear.

Silent Sports: Mid-America's Aerobic Recreational Sports Magazine, P.O. Box 152, Waupaca, WI 54981 * Monthly magazine of biking, running, kayaking, etc.

Women's Cycling News, P.O. Box 73, Harvard, IL 60003 * Newsletter of the Women's Cycling Network. Features interviews and tips.

Women's Sport and Fitness, 1919 14th St. Suite 421, Boulder, CO 80302, 303/440–5111. Women and sports, especially bicycling.

Yellow Jersey Group Publications, 490 2nd street, Suite 304, San Francisco, CA 94107, 415/546–7291; fax: 415/546–9106 * Publishes two regional tabloids—*California Bicyclist* and *Texas Bicyclist*—with total circ. of about 250,000. Distributed free at bike

CYCLING PRESS?
WHAT CYCLING PRESS?

. . . .

By Florio Marsala

People save bike magazines, for some reason. I know of instances where not-inconse-quential publications (like *Harper's* or the *Atlantic*—hey, even the *PMLA* and *Mad* magazine) were consigned to recycling or the Friends of the Library, but the person chose to keep a dog-eared stack of old bike magazines. Why hang on to these often silly, frequently infuriating and all-but-inconsequential rags? Usually neither half as informative as they pretend to be, nor even a fraction as passionate as they ought to be, it's sometimes hard to fathom why anyone would read them in the first place, much less keep them. I suppose the fact that all that Gee-whiz prose can be hilarious after a few years might be a contributing factor.

If I'm right, then this review of the American cycling press should account for all those early numbers stashed away in basements. Keep an eye out at yard sales and look in used-book stores. Ask your older brother who hung up his bike when he finished college and went to work for The Corporation.

The American cycling press as we know it these days is scarcely twenty years old. *Bicycling,* the longest-running of the popular bike mags, began life back in the mists of antiquity in 1961, right about the same time the first ads for derailleur-geared, "light-weight" Schwinn Varsity models appeared in the pages of *Boys Life.*

Under editor Haxtlee Allee the magazine grew to full size, went to glossy paper, and began sporting color covers. As the '70s began and the great "bike boom" hit, *Bicycling* was positioned to become the leading consumer publication of the two-wheeling fad, and that's exactly what happened. In 1978 the magazine was acquired by Rodale Press. New editor James McCullagh undertook to make *Bicycling* into a mainstream newsstand publication. The magazine now has a paid circulation of over 350,000, and is slick and well-produced. For as long as anyone can remember, *Bicycling* has been the biggest kid on the block, the top player. Still, there have been some notable con-tenders.

Bike World was *Bicycling*'s only significant rival through the '70s. A splendidly inconsistent and shamelessly commercial product of the bike boom, it careened wildly between blatant exploitation of the fad and detailed technical articles. There was a good measure of *Mechanix Illustrated*-style cheesiness about the book, but that may have been part of its appeal. It folded as the decade ended, but a lot of people saved every issue. When you finally see that cardboard box full of old *Bike Worlds* at some garage sale, jump on it.

While *Bike World* was going under, *Bicycling* seemed to lose direction. This was due in part to the bottom falling out of the bike market as inflation peaked and the bike boom petered out, but also in part to an apparent attempt to re-direct the magazine's editorial stance.

It went to nine-times-a-year publication and was printed for a couple of years on open-coat, recycled-looking paper stock. Rough, "natural" line illustrations replaced some of the half-tone photos, and articles about growing alfalfa sprouts while touring began to appear. A (very) small portion of the readership heartily applauded the "new" *Bicycling;* everybody else hung their bikes up and went disco dancing.

Fortunately for the bike industry, these people's children had stayed home and invented bicycle moto-cross. BMX didn't work directly to forestall the decline in *Bicycling*'s fortunes, but it gave the bike trade a desperately needed shot in the arm at a very dark moment. The subsequent resurgence of public cycling interest, by way of beach cruisers and the introduction of good, cheap lightweights from Taiwan and Japan, gave *Bicycling* another chance at a wider readership. They were smart enough to go for it.

At the beginning of the '80s *Bicycling* was again basically the only game in town. During this period the magazine became truly insufferable: pontificating from on high about the distinction between "wired-on" tires and clinchers and how it shall be observed, and declaring that henceforth mountain bikes shall be designated "ATBs," etc. In 1984, not one but two serious challengers were launched.

Bicycle Guide purported to be the technically oriented forum for objective discussion—with a dash of irreverent exuberance—that *Bicycling* had never been. While their irreverence is sometimes somewhat labored and their exuberance can seem contrived, they have managed to develop a style that is at least distinguishable from *Bicycling*'s.

Real sticklers for historical accuracy will recall the brief appearance of *American Cyclist:* It folded after eight issues. A couple of years later came *Bicycle Sport,* another stillborn.

Cyclist magazine, on the other hand, was simply an order of magnitude hipper than *Bicycling*—or *Bicycle Guide,* for that matter. While the latter two (and presumably their readers as well) were yattering on about ATBs and derailleur "showdowns," *Cyclist* was doing concours features on classy old balloon-tire bikes, product-testing pedal-powered lawn mowers, and brazenly plastering sexy California blondes on their covers. They ceased publication in 1989, but for the five years they were on the scene, it was really no contest.

So, what have we got for an outcome in twenty years of general-interest bike magazine development? In a three-way contest over nothing much more substantial than mere style, the book with the most style goes under altogether, and the next best contender loses out to a top dog that has no style to speak of. In any event, a few more specialized cycling publications bear consideration next.

BMX gave rise to several youth-oriented consumer publications in the late '70s. *BMX Plus* is the lone survivor. Now, as then, the magazine is a high-decibel mix of wowie-zowie product promotion, middle-class white-kid hip and Radical Rick sensibilities. Through it all, one detects the unmistakable tone of opportunistic 25–year-olds writing down to impressionable 12–year-olds.

Mountain Bike Action is probably the most influential of the new consumer magazines that have come along with the fat tire fad. The original *Mountain Bike* magazine has merged with *Bicycling,* and the newer *Mountain & City Biking* is still trying to define a market niche.

It's tempting to pass off *MBA* as just a grown-up version of *BMX Plus,* except that the grown-up part would be stretching the truth. For all their considerable influence on mountain biking circles, the "wrecking crew" at *MBA* know bikes the way some people know art—which is to say that while they may not know much, they know what they like.

In all fairness, the mountain bike scene is still evolving rapidly. *MBA* may not be the most objective source of information about mountain biking, but it usually makes for interesting reading. If you can appreciate a good comic book, you can probably get something out of *MBA.* If not, you'll do better to wait for the appearance of the International Technical Journal of All-Terrain Cycling Science, due out any day now.

VeloNews and *Winning*. These, then, are the bike mags of choice for the hard-core competitive cyclist. Racing, racing, and more racing—these are what you read if you're a no-foolin' USCF Cat. 1–2–3–4–NORBA-pro racer guy with serious designs on the finish line.

Yes, these are the books for that stripe of cyclist who disdains triathlons as a bastardization, and who likes to ride so hard he throws up. Once the unofficial house organ of the USCF, *VeloNews* is a biweekly tabloid that's been around almost as long as *Bicycling*. Its coverage has broadened somewhat with triathlon and competitive mountain biking, but at heart it remains a road man's racing sheet.

Despite occasional pieces on equipment and nutrition, to pass the time, the real focus is on tactics, strategy, wins and losses, pain, agony, racing in the rain, busting a gut! road rash! triumph! revenge!—one can't help wondering what might happen if we gave *VN* to the Department of Defense.

Winning is a slick monthly that serves as Foreign Affairs to *VeloNews*'s Washington Post: more of the same, but in a more measured cadence, with a definite sense of historical background and an eye toward anticipated developments. *Winning* is a hybrid import of sorts, first appearing in the early '80s as an English translation of a popular Belgian cycling magazine. This made for some amusing reading at first, even if you didn't care a whit for racing. But the photos have always been good, and the magazine's dedication to European professional cycling is reassuring to old hands and intriguing to neophytes.

A special note is in order as regards the official publication of the League of American Wheelmen, *Bicycle USA*. The League is the oldest, most original of our national bicycling institutions, and everyone who really cares about bikes will sooner or later hook up with them for a season or two, and it's well they should.

As an organization, the L.A.W. has been at it since the turn of the century and before. Back issues of their magazine are always worth looking at. Keep an eye out for copies old and new. The emphasis is usually on "responsible" cycling, with a certain obvious bias toward traditional cycle-touring.

The trades—well, here we go, and won't this be fun. . . . Briefly, there are three bike trade magazines, all slick monthlies: *American Bicyclist and Motorcyclist, Bicycle Dealer Showcase,* and *Bicycle Business Journal.* Each has a fairly distinct editorial personality, with *American Bicyclist* as the traditional stand-by, the long-time (better than a hundred years now) "bible-of-the-industry" publication, as irrelevant as your old dad, but still getting a certain respect. *BDS* is the young, west coast upstart, a shirt-sleeves-and-loose-tie production that stays on top of the trends and runs ads from and copy about anybody and everybody who matters in the trade today.

BBJ was formerly called *Bicycle Journal,* and currently is scrambling to come up with enough pages to justify perfect binding and a spine-printed title. It is essentially a gossip rag, and the last redoubt of such old-line domestic manufacturers as Hunt-Wilde, Ross, Huffy, Sun Metal, Wald Co., Troxel Manufacturing, and Murray-Ohio. These are the people who kept us baby-boom kids supplied with Delta Torpedo Horn-Lites, glitter grips, handlebar streamers, saddle baskets, hub shiners, stamped steel luggage racks, and Camel Brand Self-Vulcanizing patch kits. They were also responsible, variously and in their time, for giving us Ashtabula forged forks and cranks, the first "English racer" lightweight 3–speeds, the Schwinn Paramount and the Schwinn Black Phantom, the Bendix coaster brake hub, and a lot of other solid, reliable cycling equipment that was the standard of its day.

A James Brown postscript—I can't stop—Don't make me stop—I'm too bad—I can't stop—Wow—

It would be nice to conclude, what with *Bicycling* still going strong, and *Velo-News* and the trades grinding away, and regional cycling tabloids starting up, that we have an intelligent and discerning cycling press. Conversely, we could be glad at least that our cycling journalists aren't stuck in the mud, blindered by hidebound tradition and nostalgia the way some of their European counterparts seem to be. If only their subjects weren't lighter than helium and their approach so breathless ("We Review 85 Great New Tires!!"-"Glamorize Your Service Department to Maximize Profits").

The real problem with "bike-writing" is that for all the cross-eyed serious attention lavished on race results, touring attractions, equipment reviews, and marketing angles, there is virtually no copy devoted to the basic human significance of these things; not word one, it seems, about the heart, soul, and spirit of bicycling, of using bikes, and having them in our lives. And no, the occasional limp editorial tucked in beside the masthead will not suffice.

The subjects addressed by our cycling press are in the main crass, ephemeral, and bottom-line, and the style in which they are addressed is resolutely pedestrian. What a bunch of click-shifting Babbitts! Where is our history for starters? Who cares about Suntour's latest derailleur; let's hear about Simplex's first one. Maybe a little hidebound tradition would do us good.

In a world that is learning the need for cooperative values, we have a cycling mindset that is overwhelmingly competitive. In a world that could use more simple solutions and appropriate technology, we have bike magazines gaggling on about carbon fiber framesets and titanium components, hi-tech this and space-age that. In a world where people need more than ever to reflect quietly and get in touch with some truth somewhere, we have a cycling press tricked out in neon Lycra touting the "science" of hard-body fitness and the metaphysical "engineering potentials" of a bone-simple machine we trust children to use. A person can't help thinking that the bicycle should be the key to turning these things around, instead of providing more grist for the mills.

Where, for example, are the we-mean-business discussions of transportation cycling? If we could shame a nation into wearing dopey-looking styrofoam helmets, surely we can convince them to run errands on their bikes.

Florio Marsala has been working at the front lines of the retail bike trade in Southern California for the past seventeen years. He's not so sure he likes everything he sees nowadays.

stores, health clubs, and special events. Coverage of races, calendars of events are high points of editorial calendars. "Our publications target active, urban, affluent, well-educated cycling enthusiasts." 11 issues a year.

Advocacy and Education

Bicycle Forum, P.O. Box 8308, Missoula, MT 59807, 406/721–1776 * For bicycle program specialists and activists.

Bicycle USA, League of American Wheelmen, 6707 Whitestone Rd., Suite 209JF, Baltimore, MD 21207 * Magazine of the national cycling advocacy organization. Touring-oriented; also info on sports medicine, mechanics, government relations. Publishes annual Tourfinder of outfitters and organizations that run bike trips.

League Volunteer, The League of American Wheelmen, 6707 Whitestone Rd. Suite 209, Baltimore, MD 21207 * Newsletter for L.A.W. volunteers.

Pro Bike News, The Bicycle Federation of America, 1818 R St., NW, Washington, DC 20009, 202/332–6986 * Monthly newsletter for advocates and bicycle enthusiasts. Full of all sorts of tidbits on bike programs, education, and innovations.

Ride On! Newsletter of the Washington Area Bicyclist Association, 1818 H St. NW, Suite 640, Washington, DC 20006 * Cycling advocacy in the nation's capital.

BMX and Freestyle

BMX Plus, 10600 Sepulveda Blvd., Mission Hills, CA 91345, 818/365–6831 * Sample stories from "The World's Largest BMX & Freestyle Magazine!": "The Raddest Riders' Freestyle Secrets!" and "New $10,000 BMX Bike: What Makes It So Trick and Expensive?!" This and many more features, tests, and departments for the small-tire set.

Go: The Rider's Manual, Wizard Publications, 3882 Del Amo Blvd. Suite 603, Torrance, CA 90503, 213/371–1454 * Monthly magazine focusing on freestyle and motocross bicycle riding.

Business

American Bicyclist and Motorcyclist, 80 Eighth Ave., New York, NY 10011, 212/206–7230 * Monthly industry publication.

Bicycle Business Journal, P.O. Box 1570, Ft. Worth, TX 76101, 800/331–2526; fax: 817/332–1619 * The business publication of the cycle and fitness industries. 10 issues a year.

Bicycle Dealer Showcase, Edgell Communications, 1700 E. Dyer Rd., Suite 250, Santa Ana, CA 92705, 714/250–8060 * Trade magazine for cycle shops.

Cycle Press International, 15–4 Higashie-Ueno, Taito-ku, Tokyo 110, Japan, 03/833–6036 * International, English language bimonthly trade magazine.

History and Antiques

Antique/Classic Bicycle News, P.O. Box 1049, Ann Arbor, MI 48106 * A newsletter for collectors.

The West Coaster, c/o John McDonald, 7935 S.E. Market, Portland, OR 97215, 503/775–2688 * Newsletter of the Cascade Classic Cycle Club, a group of collectors of antique bikes.

Mountain Bikes

Bicycling Plus Mountain Bike, 33 E. Minor St., Emmaus, PA 18098, 215/967–5171.

Dirt Rag, 460 Maple Ave., Springdale, PA 15144, 412/274–15144 * Seven times a year, covers mountain biking events and rides in the east.

Fat Tracks: The Journal of The Chequamegon Fat Tire Festival, P.O. Box 267, Cable, WI 54821 715/798–3811 * Biannual tabloid of a premier mountain bike race, won by Greg LeMond in 1990.

Houston Mountain Bike News, Houston, TX, 713/965–9442 * Newsletter.

Land Access Alert, Rt. 2, Box 303, Bishop, CA 93514, 619/387–2757 * Newsletter of the International Mountain Bicycling Association (IMBA).

Mountain & City Biking, 7950 Deering Ave., Canoga Park, CA 91304, 818/887–0550; fax: 818/883–3019 * Features, tests, competition reports, new products, and departments in a glossy monthly magazine.

Mountain & City Biking Magazine's Buyer's Guide, 7950 Deering Ave., Canoga Park, CA 91304 * Annual specs and stats.

Mountain Bike Action, Hi-Torque Publications, 10600 Sepulveda Blvd., Mission Hills, CA 91345, 818/365–4512 * Competition and "technical"-oriented monthly magazine.

NORBA News, 1750 E. Boulder St., Colorado Springs, CO 80909, 719/578–4717 * Features mountain bike news. Comes out monthly.

Racing

Capital Sports Focus, Capital Sports Focus, Inc., 1432 Fenwick Lane, Silver Spring, MD 20910, 301/587–9351; fax: 301/587–6347 * Biking, triathlons, and other sports around the nation's capital.

College Cycling, P.O. Box 4083, Newport Beach, CA 92661, 714/631–4106 * Reports on college bike races.

Cycling USA, 1750 E. Boulder St., Colorado Spring, CO 80909, 719/578–4581 * Membership publication of U.S. Cycling Federation, the national amateur racing association.

Triathlete Magazine, 1415 3rd St. #303, Santa Monica, CA 90401 * 10 issues a year on food, fashion, training, and bikes for triathletes.

VeloNews, 1830 N. 55th St., Boulder, CO 80301, 303/440–0601 * 18 times a year, up-to-the-minute reports on racing 'round the world.

Winning: Bicycle Racing Illustrated, 1127 Hamilton, St., Allentown, PA 18101–9959, 215/821–1321; fax: 215/821–1321 * National magazine covering racing. Includes calendar of events.

Yellow Jersey Group Publications, 490 2nd Street, Suite 304, San Francisco, CA 94107, 415/546–7291; fax: 415/546–9106 * Publishes two regional tabloids—*California*

Bicyclist and *Texas Bicyclist*—with total circ. of about 250,000. Distributed free at bike stores, health clubs, and special events. Coverage of races, calendars of events are high points of editorial calendars. "Our publications target active, urban, affluent, well-educated cycling enthusiasts." 11 issues a year.

Regional

The Bicycle Paper, 7901 168th Ave. NE, Suite 103, Redmond, WA 98052, 206/882–0706 * Covers cycling around Puget Sound.

Bike Midwest, 2099 W. 5th Ave. Suite C, Columbus, OH 43212, 614/481–7723.

BikeOhio, Clary Communication, 2099 W. Fifth Ave., Columbus, OH 43212, 614/481–7534 * Ten-times-a-year publication for Ohio bicyclists.

California Bicyclist. *See* Yellow Jersey Group publications under "General."

Capital Sports Focus, Capital Sports Focus, Inc., 1432 Fenwick Lane, Silver Spring, MD 20910, 301/587–9351; fax: 301/587–6347 * Biking, triathlons, and other sports around the Nation's Capital.

City Cyclist, Transportation Alternatives, 494 Broadway, New York, NY 10012, 212/941–4600 * Bimonthly newspaper that reports on current bicycling issues and lists events.

City Sport (New York), 696 Washington St., New York, NY 10014, 212/627–7040 * Weekly publication, includes bicycling.

City Sport (California), P.O. Box 3693, San Francisco, CA 94119, 15/546–6150 * Published weekly.

Cycle South, 2891 Twin Brooks Rd., #4, Atlanta, GA 30319, 404/233–1638 * Guide to rides and races in the Southeast.

Northern California/Nevada Cycling Association Newsletter, 1153 Delaware St., Berkeley, CA 94702, 415/526–5983 * Considered "essential" for the competitive cyclist who lives in the West. Listing of regional races.

Northwest Cyclist, P.O. Box 9272, Seattle, WA 98109, 206/286–8566 * Covers cycling in Washington state.

Southwest Cycling, 301 W. California, Suite 201, Glendale, CA 91203 * Articles, lists of club rides in L.A. and elsewhere. 11 issues a year.

Spokes, 5334 Sovereign Place, Frederick, MD 21701, 301/926–0031 * Monthly tabloid with news of the Mid-Atlantic region. Published nine times a year; circulation of 30,000.

Texas Bicyclist. *See* Yellow Jersey Group Publications under "General."

Tandems

Doubletalk, Tandem Club of America, c/o Malcolm Boyd and Judy Allison, 19 Lakeside Dr. NW, Medford, NJ 08055 * Tandem Club of America's bimonthly newsletter.

Santana Cycles Newsletter, Santana Cycles, Box 1205, Claremont, CA 91711 * For owners of tandems.

The Tandem Racing Scoop, Burley Design Cooperative, 4080 Stewart Rd., Eugene, OR 97404, 503/687–1644 * Newsletter for those interested in tandem racing.

Touring

Bicycle Touring Newsletter, Rodale Press, Inc., 33 East Minor St., Emmaus, PA 18098 * Newsletter from *Bicycling* magazine.

Bicycle USA, League of American Wheelmen, 6707 Whitestone Rd., Suite 209JF, Baltimore, MD 21207 * Eight times a year magazine of the national cycling advocacy organization. Touring-oriented; also info on sports medicine, mechanics, government relations. Publishes annual Tourfinder of outfitters and organizations that run bike trips.

Bike Events, Bike Events, Ltd., P.O. Box 75, Bath BA1 1BX, Avon, England, 0225–310859 * British magazine listing events and tours all over the world.

BikeReport, Bikecentennial, P.O. Box 8308, Missoula, MT 59807 * Nine-times-a-year magazine from the nonprofit association that promotes bike touring. Includes technical column by John Schubert and ads from cyclists seeking touring companions.

Hosteling, Metropolitan New York Council, American Youth Hostels, Inc., 891 Amsterdam Ave., New York, NY 10025 * Newsletter.

Knapsack, American Youth Hostels, P.O. Box 37613, Washington, DC 20013–7613 * "Semi-Annual travel journal" about international travel based on biking, hiking, train, canoe, and other types of trips in international network of youth hostel outings.

Miscellaneous

Going the Distance, The Pedal for Power Newsletter, Box 898, Atkinson, NH 03811 * Newsletter written by participants in Pedal for Power cross-country and north-south rides for charity.

HPV News, International Human Powered Vehicle Association, P.O. Box 51255, Indianapolis, IN 46251 * Newsletter on human-powered vehicles, boats, and planes published 8 times yearly.

Pacelines, 43 Upton St., Boston, MA 02118 * Newsletter for gay and lesbian cyclists and their friends.

The Recumbent Cyclist, 427–3 Amherst St. #305, Nashua, NH 03063 * Quarterly newsletter for recumbent enthusiasts.

VIDEOS

All about Bikes, Step-by-Step Video, 15 Laidley, San Francisco, CA 94131 * 150–minute tape covers frame, repair, maintenance, riding position, sizing, riding tips.

Be Safe on Your Bike, Los Angeles Police Dept., 4125 Crenshaw Blvd., Los Angeles, CA 90008, 213/485–7742.

Bicycle Safety First, Tim Kneeland and Associates, 2603 3rd Ave., Suite 101, Seattle, WA 98121, 800/433–0528, 206/441–1025 * 13–minute video for adolescent and adult cyclists.

Bicycling to Work, U.S. Environmental Protection Agency (EN–397– F), 410 M St. S.W., Washington, DC 20460, 202/382–2671 * 16–minute video covering topics including routes, maps, parking, changing facilities.

Bike Talk, P.O. Box 19056, Portland, OR 97219.

The Cycling Experience, Consumer Vision, 342 E. 53rd St., New York, NY 10022.

Elephants Never Forget, Monroe County Bicycle Helmet Coalition, Dr. Eldredge, 59 B Monroe Ave., Suite B, Pitford, NY 14534 * Helmet and bicycle safety tips.

Famous Cycling Videos, 704 Hennepin Ave., Minneapolis, MN 55403 * Sells these titles: 1987 Tour of Ireland; 1988 Tour of Ireland; 1986 Tour of France; 1988 Tour of

Britain; 23 Days in July; Coors States Classic; A Sunday in Hell; Stars and Watercarriers; La Course En Tete; The Impossible Hour; Cycling for Success; 1989 Tour of Texas.

The Great Mountain Bike Video and Ultimate Mountain Biking: Advanced Techniques & Winning Strategies, New & Unique Videos, 2336 Sumac Dr., San Diego, CA 92105, 800/365–8433 * Adventure and racing-oriented, $29.95 each.

Heads . . . You Win, Chapel Hill League for Safe Bicycling, Box 16513, Chapel Hill, NC 27516, 919/933–4870 * VHS tape available for $50 donation.

Intro to BAP (Bicycle Action Project) and **How to Reach and Teach At-Risk Youth,** $10, BAP, 948 N. Alabama, Indianapolis, IN 46202, 317/631–1362.

101 Trix Part II—Psycho Version, Plus Products, P.O. Box 9501, Mission Hills, CA 91345–9501, 818/365–6831 * More than 50 freestyle and BMX experts demonstrate how it's done. Produced by editors of *BMX Plus* magazine.

TOSRV West 1990, Missoula Bicycle Coordinator, 435 Ryman, Missoula, MT 59802, 406/523–4626 * A video of TOSRV's 20th anniversary ride.

VCA/Cycle Vision Tours Inc., 50 Leyland Dr., Leonia, NJ 07605, 800/822–1105 (operator 84N) * 75–minute video tours that provide scenery for stationary riders. "Ride" through Yellowstone Park, San Francisco, Vermont in autumn, or one of 7 other locales accompanied by paced music. "Competition 1" video runs 54 minutes. Each tape $29.95.

Video Bike Shop, 800/628–1092 * Instruction for road and mountain bike maintenance.

MAIL-ORDER SOURCES OF CYCLING PARAPHENALIA

Antiques

Antique Cycle Supply, Inc., Cedar Springs, MI 49319, 616/636–8200 * Medallions, decals, pedals, balloon tires, etc. for really old and medium-old bikes. Also, repros of old bike catalogs.

Memory Lane Classics, 12551 Jefferson St., Perrysburg, OH 43551, 419/874–4501 * 60–page catalog ($3 postpaid) includes parts for a Rollsfast Hopalong Cassidy bicycle, 28–by-an-inch-and-a-half pneumatic tires for wooden wheels—and lots of other parts for 1930s through 1960s balloon-tire and middleweight bikes.

Bikes and Gear

ACE—American Cycle Express, 213 Vestal Pkwy. East, Vestal, NY 13850, 607/786–SAVE * Everything from complete bikes to shoes for BMX. Catalog available.

Bicycle Parts Pacific, Inc., P.O. Box 4250, 2135 E. Main, Grand Junction, CO 81502, 800/999–8BPP * Wholesale catalog. Inquiries from retailers only.

Bike Nashbar, P.O. Box 3449, Youngstown, OH 44513, 800/NASHBAR; fax: 800/456–1223 * Monthly catalog complete with gear from bags to workstands. Nashbar-brand bikes and gear along with other brand names.

The Bike Rack East, 11 Constance Court, Happauge, NY 11788, 800/645–5477 or (in NY) 800/BIKERACK * Bikes and gear from BMX to racing. Wholesale catalog. Inquiries from retailers only.

The Bike Rack West, 17022 Montanero Ave., Carson, CA 90746, 800/662–7882 * See Bike Rack East above.

Bikecology, P.O. Box 3900, Santa Monica, CA 90408–3900, 800/326–2453 * Sells their line of bicycles by catalog.

Branford Bike, 107 Main St., Branford, CT 06405, 203/488–0482 * Racing-oriented parts, accessories, and clothes. Technical assistance available at 203 number.

California Best, P.O. Box 8890, Chula Vista, CA 92012, 800/438–9327 or (in CA) 800/344–1661 * Men's and women's clothes for cycling, running and other sports. Variety of brands.

Cambria Bicycle Outfitters, 1920 Main St., Cambria, CA 93428, 805/927–5510 or 927–5174. They call themselves "your mountain bike cycletherapist . . . a little, out-of-the-way country bike shop that just happens to specialize in high-end, hard-to-find, techno-zip mountain bikes and components." The mimeographed catalog is full of good humor; the mountain bikes go for up to $2,200. Send them your photo and get a free gift "worth at least 5 bucks, maybe more."

Chronometro, 100 S. Baldwin, Madison, WI 53703, 800/783–AERO * Small, racing-oriented catalog specializing in rims, wheels, discs, aero bars and more.

Colorado Cyclist, 2455 Executive Circle, Colorado Springs, CO 80906, 800/688–8600 * High-end and high-tech gear from frames to derailleurs. Write for color catalog.

Cycle Source, REI, P.O. Box 88125, Seattle, WA 98138–2125, 800/426–4840 * Features Novara bikes and gear (made for REI) along with brand names for full line of products. REI is a co-op and offers yearly dividends for members.

Cyclosource, Bikecentennial, P.O. Box 8308, Missoula, MT 59807, 406/721–8719 or 800/835–2246 x 158 * Catalog of the bicycle travel association features 11 groups of maps for cross-country riding (and routes within), lightweight camping gear, books, tools, clothes, reflective vests, wheels, tires, posters, more.

Denver Spoke, 800/327–8532 * Frames, components, wheels, and accessories ordered by phone and delivered to your home.

Exceed Sports International, 3725 Prairie Ave., Boulder, CO 80301–2507 * Racing-oriented catalog from bike shop in the Land of the Lycra Lizard. Accessories for racing bikes and ATBs to work stands; 30–day money-back guarantee.

First Class BMX, 503/253–8688 * Call for order information.

National Trader Sheets, 602 N. Main, Leitchfield, KY 42754 * Collection of ads for selling bicycles and related items. Send $1 for sample copy.

Outdoor Health, P.O. Box 8395, East Hampstead, NH 03826, 603/382–4293 * Catalog of bicycle-specific first-aid kits and equipment.

Performance Bicycle Shop, P.O. Box 2741, Chapel Hill, NC 27514, 800/727–2453 * Full-service quarterly catalog with everything from accessories to workstands. Technical advice available by phone (800/PBS-AIDE).

Rockville BMX, 817 Hungerford Dr., Rockville, MD 20850, 301/424– 3177 * Mail-order for BMX, mountain bikes, and skateboards.

Select Sales, P.O. Box 521, Clifton, CO 81520 * Ultra no-frill tools and hardware catalog that promises low prices.

Stylin', P.O. Box 233, Osage Beach, MO 65065, 314/348–5189; fax: 314/348–2214 * Gear and clothes for BMX.

Technosport, 1112–B South 8th St., Austin, TX 78704 * 800/544–0989; fax: 512/477–0488 * Racing-oriented gear, clothes, and nutritional aids from a catalog/showroom.

The Third Hand, Box 212, Mt. Shasta, CA 96067, 916/926–2600; fax: 916/926–2663 * 75 pages of "bike tools, books & loose screws."

Trend Bike Source, P.O. Box 201778, Austin, TX 78720–1778, 512/338–4466 * Complete catalog of everything from bikes to clothes for BMX.

Gifts and Prints

Bicycle Postcards, c/o David Schott, 1209 Havenwood Rd., Baltimore, MD 21218, 202/965–1374 * Nifty postcards with a bicycle theme. Send SASE for catalog.

Bicycle Posters and Prints, P.O. Box 7164, Hicksville, NY 11802–7164, 516/333–3545 * Bike art and other gifts including mugs, T-shirts, 1–10th scale models of classic bikes, tie tacs, books.

The Bike Farm, Route 1—Box 99, Cushing, WI 54006, 715/648–5519; fax: 612/433–2704 * Bumper stickers, books, videos, rubber stamps, cards, gifts related to cycling.

Cycle and Recycle, The Bicycle Network, P.O. Box 8194, Philadelphia, PA 19101 * A calendar that shows in words and pictures practical uses of bicycles around the world.

Leisure Cards, 3201 Pelham Rd., Dearborn, MI 48124 * Bicycle greeting cards. Send SASE for brochure.

Pedalphernalia Bicycle Curios, P.O. Box 2566N, Ann Arbor, MI 48106 * Bicycle gift items. Send $.50 for catalog.

Maps and Books

Cyclosource, Bikecentennial, P.O. Box 8308, Missoula, MT 59807, 406/721–8719 or 800/835–2246 x 158 * Catalog of the bicycle travel association features 11 groups of maps for cross-country riding (and routes within), lightweight camping gear, books, tools, clothes, reflective vests, wheels, tires, posters, more.

Touring Cyclist Catalogue, compiled by Bonnie Wong, 50 pp., $5 ppd., Touring Exchange, Box 265, Port Townsend, WA 98368 * Catalog detailing routes, maps, and guide books available. Includes itineraries from all around the world, submitted by cyclists.

Miscellaneous

Access Outdoors, 1509 Queen Anne Ave. N., Ste. 606, Seattle, WA 98109, 206/284–7470 * "Sourcebook for those who enjoy and care about the outdoors." Free. For-profit and not-for-profit services offered by environmentally conscious organizations and companies.

Patches, Decals, and Pins

There are cyclists who collect patches like matchbooks. Although we've seen a few jackets positively festooned with them, we can't quite figure out what anyone would do with hundreds of small, round bits of colored cloth. Some folks claim they make dandy coasters or sturdy coverings for holes. Still, if your bicycle club or you yearn for more, here are some organizations and companies that will churn them out to your heart's content.

Bicycle Institute of New South Wales, GPO Box 272, Sydney, NSW 2001, Australia * Send some International Coupons (available from the post office) down under and increase your patch collection. Benefits an Australian bicycle advocacy group. Send three International Coupons (for one patch and sea mail) or four Coupons (for one patch and air mail).

Eastern Emblems, Box 828, Union City, NJ 07087, 800/344–5112 * Patches, decals, and pins.

Fritz Decals, 920 Trowbridge, Suite 68, E. Lansing, MI 48823 * Has an "I'm a Biker" decal for inside windows.

Hein Specialities, Inc., 7960 SW Manitou Trail, Glen Arbor, MI 49636–9711 * Custom embroidered patches.

The League of American Wheelmen, 6707 Whitestone Rd., Suite 209, Baltimore, MD 21207, 301/944–3399 * Has patches for practically every occasion. Sponsors yearly design contest.

Travel Tex, 32401 Stringtown Rd., Dept. S, Greenwood, MO 64034 * Has USA map patches that you can color in. Custom patches available.

five

CLOTHES

*T*he days are gone when you would be laughed at for wearing a helmet and skin-tight shorts, as was possible in the Pleistocene days of cycling in the early 1980s. (This was particularly true when we traveled abroad. People would ask, "Why do you wear that hard hat? Do you often fall?")

No, it's accepted that cycling wear really is comfortable, and that riding hundreds of miles a week in cut-offs and sneakers does cause chafed thighs, battered palms, and sore feet. Clothing designed specifically for bicycling anticipates a cyclist's needs. Those skin-tight shorts and jerseys made of a mixture of materials, holey gloves, helmet, and stiff shoes help you focus on miles of glorious scenery, not aching body parts.

Cycling clothes come in several different registered trademark, synthetic materials. For summer jerseys there's CoolMax™, a lightweight fabric that's supposed to cool sticky backs. Polypropylene™ is thin winter-wear that keeps you warm even when it gets wet. Gore-Tex™ and Supplex™ are breathable, layered fabrics that keep rain and wind out. Stretchy Lycra™ is comfortable in summer or winter. A cotton T-shirt is as comfortable as ever in good weather, but not so comfy or warm in the rain. And good old wool, which has many of the virtues of the synthetics but doesn't get so, well, *smelly* after repeated wearing, is making a comeback.

Furthermore, the cycling look has become rather chic, a badge of coolness like the ski jacket was in the '60s. Among others, high fashion designer Karl Lagerstom puts bike shorts on his models and makes them an integral part of his collections. It seems like everyone from Sacramento, California, to Saratoga Springs, New York is enamored of tight-fitting bike shorts, whether they ever go near a bicycle seat or not. The April 1991 *Cosmopolitan* evolved a list of things women could carry to meet men. And number nine on the list was . . . a bicycle helmet!

The amount you want to invest—and how much you're willing to look like a popsicle or Robocop crossed with a bumblebee—is up to you. Basically, a hundred bucks can get you a pair of padded shorts, a jersey with pockets in the back, and a pair of shoes with stiff soles. Don't forget the helmet ($40 and up) and some sort of eyewear. Whether you favor sunglasses or clear glass in a frame, protecting your eyes from dirt or high-speed bugs is important. (See the section on *Safety* for more on helmets.)

First, the shorts. Many non-cyclists wonder about the tightness and the material. Snug-fitting shorts stay in place: they keep material between you and the bicycle seat, preventing chafing. Most of the stretchy materials, Lycra for example, that are used in bike shorts wick the moisture away. This too prevents chafing and helps keep the rider dry. The padding, whether thin or thick, is of obvious benefit. Coupled with an anatomically designed seat (preferably not made of plastic), padded shorts can make the ride more pleasant. After all, if where you're sitting pains you, will you pursue the sport? There are other advantages: skin-tight black shorts don't show grease and can be a balm for throbbing thighs during a long day's ride.

A brief note about fit—whether you prefer longer or short length shorts, go for those that have more panels. Shorts that are made of four or more panels are most apt to keep their shape. They tend to be more expensive, but for the most part, will last longer.

Gloves are also helpful, and you can don them for more reasons than the funny tan they provide. First off, gloves pad the palms, where the ulnar nerve resides. Constant pressure on the palms causes some folks to suffer from numbness—gloves help alleviate this. And in case you do happen to take a tumble, gloves can protect your tender palms. Many cyclists use them to prevent flats. When they accidentally cycle over glass, they reach down and let the tire roll under their gloved hands as they bike. That quick action can prevent the glass from embedding itself in the tires. Hence there's one less opportunity to demonstrate roadside repair skills. Note: Only skilled cyclists should do this. Some newcomers to the sport are not able to balance bicycling and leaning forward or aft to catch a wheel and perform this trick.

(Dennis Coello/
Backroads
Bicycle Touring)

Some words about shoes. The main advantage of made-for-cycling shoes is their stiff sole. The stiffness emanates from a hard shank inserted in the sole. The advantage, as one racer put it after eyeing another rider's battered running shoes, is "superior power transfer"—more of your stroke results in forward motion. They also protect your feet from being gouged by the pedal during the 35,000 pedal revolutions required, for example, for a 100–mile ride. The disadvantage: They can be hard to walk in, especially if they are designed for racing. However, numerous companies are addressing that problem. Some offer a cover that fits over cleats, enabling a cyclist to walk without looking like a duck.

Cycling shoes come in several different configurations. There are shoes for ATBs or mountain bikes. These are basically rugged sneakers meant for pushing a bike through a stony ravine as well as riding down a fire road. Touring shoes are also an on-bike/off-bike combination. They are relatively flexible and comfortable for walking as well as riding in toe clips. Cleated racing shoes are impossible to walk in. They are very stiff and feature a screw-in ridge in the sole that fits snugly into the notch in the pedal, improving the efficiency of your pedal stroke by about 20 percent. The cleats have to be fitted to each individual. Bike shops charge about $30 for this service. Don't have cleats properly fitted and you risk grinding your knees into baloney. Finally, a new type of cleated shoe manufactured by the likes of Look actually clips your shoe sole to the pedal, eliminating the need for toe clips. This is effective, efficient, and—expensive. Still another innovation features pedals with a nodule that clicks into a notch in the shoe sole. Voila—all the advantages of a racing cleat matched with the convenience of walking shoes.

Here's a guide to who provides what. There are thousands of clothing designers and manufacturers, hundreds of eyeglass specialists, and loads of companies who produce wearable cycling products. The list below is a good place to begin; it is not an endorsement. As a consumer, your best bet is to frequent local bicycle stores and explore what they have to offer. Most manufacturers prefer to deal with their distributors. If you desire custom jerseys or gloves or wish to purchase large quantities of a product, for example, it may be worth your while to contact the manufacturer directly. If you are unable to locate a particular product, contact the manufacturer for a list of local distributors of what you seek.

CLOTHES AND SHOES

Alitta, Inc., P.O. Box 931, Santa Monica, CA 90406, 213/954–1012 * Specializes in women's clothing: shorts, jerseys, jackets.

Andiamo!, Box 1657, Sun Valley, ID 83353, 208/726–1385 * Sports liners and cycle wear are their specialty.

Avocet, Inc., P.O. Box 120, Palo Alto, CA 94302, 800/227–8346; 415/321–8346 * Renowned for their seats, tires, and computers, Avocet also makes cycling shoes.

Aussie Racing Apparel, 1431 Truman St., #F, San Fernando, CA 91340, 818/362–5555 * Manufactures custom-designed and stock bicycle clothing for teams.

Baleno Inc., 1124 N. 97th St., Seattle, WA 98103, 800/426–7739; 206/524–6960 * Custom designs jerseys, shorts, jackets, and skinsuits for teams.

L.L. Bean, Inc., Freeport, ME 04033, 800/221–4221 * Offers cycling jackets and shorts (designed by Bean, made by Hind, with night riding in mind), touring and mountain bike shoes (Nike-made), Lycra and mesh gloves, rain gear, cotton shirts, and short liners. Call for catalog.

Bellwether, 1161 Mission St., San Francisco, CA 94103, 415/863–0436 * One of the original bike clothing manufacturers, Bellwether makes an assortment of items: jackets, pants for all weather, shorts, and shirts.

Bike-a-Lite Inc., Box 125 High St., Silver Lake, NH 03875, 800/258–8974; 603/367–8273 * Reflective vests, belts, legbands, stick-ons, and most anything to enable you to be visible. Custom designs for groups.

Bike Dress, P.O. Box 374, Woolwich, ME, 207/442–9026 * For the woman who's tired of Lycra. Smartly designed, multi-colored, 7–panel dresses that have deep pockets and a hidden snap to fasten the skirt. A new concept that seems perfect for commuters.

Black Bottoms, Box 7104, Salt Lake City, UT 84107, 801/262–6503 * Since 1974, Black Bottoms has manufactured biking shorts. They now produce an assortment of clothes, including shorts of many colors and styles (bib, mountain biking, and 8–panel, for example), arm and leg warmers, wind pants, tights, jackets, and jerseys. But their classic, circa 1975 wool shorts are remembered fondly.

Branford Bike, 107 Main St., Branford, CT 06405, 203/488–0482 * Racing-oriented clothes by a variety of manufacturers. Also parts and accessories.

DRESSING TO BE SEEN

For this purpose, forget shyness. You want to be visible, which usually means bright. Hot pink, a sort of shocking florescent color that screams for attention, is now being touted as a safe color for daytime riding. Although pink may not be what you'd like to be seen in, do consider the visibility factor of your biking clothing.

Riding at night, dusk, or sunrise requires a good lighting system and smart duds. Obviously, black or dark-colored clothing renders you somewhat invisible in the dark. Pick light-colored clothing; white is an excellent choice. Wear a reflective vest and consider striping your panniers or rack with a bit of reflective tape. If your bicycle or pedals have reflectors on them, so much the better. Your goal is to catch the motorists' eye, clueing them in that they are sharing the road with a cyclist, and the movement of your legs on pedals with reflectors helps alert them to this.

If you live in drizzly climates where gray is a semi-permanent shade, pick bright all-weather gear. Bright, bright yellow rain slickers (of whatever waterproof-ish material you fancy or can afford) help you stand out.

While some cyclists affix an orange triangle, signifying slow vehicle, to their backs or bicycle racks, others attach an orange flag on a slim stick to their bikes. Long-distance cyclists sometimes go this route, "oranging" up their gear so that it, too, is visible. Bikecentennial sells some perfectly horrid orange pannier covers that are beautifully designed for two purposes: they help keep your gear dry and they are so visible that they announce you almost a mile before you arrive.

The goal, obviously, is to stand out. There are hundreds of clothing manufacturers weaving textile magic with tens of fabrics. The colors astonish—and that's as it should be, for fashion and safety.

Burley Design Cooperative, Inc., 4080 Stewart Rd., Eugene, OR 97402, 503/687–1644; fax: 503/687–0436 * Better known for its trailers and tandems, Burley also makes rain jackets and pants, windbreakers, hoods, helmet covers, and shoe covers.

Canari Cycle Wear, 8360 Clairemont Mesa Blvd., #105, San Diego, CA 92111, 800/999–2925, 619/277–3377 * Cycling jerseys, including models with black netting stretched over Coolmax™ and Lycra™ with "colorful sublimated logos on chest." This is their –Italian vented crop top" as modeled by about 20 of Gina Lollabrigida's daughters in their catalog. Canari also makes 6–panel Lycra shorts, bib shorts, tank-tops, tights, rain jackets, polypropylene long-sleeve jerseys, cotton/poly T-shirts with mesh rear pockets, windbreakers, and "Capri tights" (they look like stretchy clamdiggers). These all come in black with neon striping or abstract designs. Can custom design for groups.

Cannondale Corporation, 9 Brookside Place, Georgetown, CT 06829 * Jerseys, seam-less chamois shorts, 6–panel shorts, tank tops, crop tops, gloves for men and women. Also unisex jerseys, anoraks, and shorts for mountain bike.

Criterium Cycling Apparel, P.O. Box 1320, Dolores, CO 81323, 303/882–7633 * Cus-tom jerseys and more.

Dante Sports Apparel, Inc., 4884 Sterling Dr., Boulder, CO 80301, 303/444–2418 * Jackets, shorts, jerseys, and other stuff for cyclists to wear.

Descente America, Inc., 109 Inverness Dr. East, Englewood, CO 80112 * Don't be fooled by the Frenchified name. The expensive, ultra-chic cycling wear with the distinc-tive down-pointing arrow logo is made in Japan. Nothing wrong with that, of course, as racers swear by these widely available skins.

Diadodora, Gita Sporting Goods, P.O. Box 7266, Charlotte, NC 28241–7266 * Cycling shoes for racing (toe clips and clipless), touring, casual riding, and mountain-biking. Made in Italy.

Dyno, 178 Gothard St., Huntington Beach, CA 92647, 714/841–1169 * For the BMX crowd, helmets, jerseys, pants, shin splints, knee guards, elbow guards, adhesion gloves, T-shirts, sweats, and high-top sneakers in wild patterns.

Fiasco! Active Sportswear, P.O. Box 1204, Santa Barbara, CA 93116, 805/964–7075 * Jackets, jerseys, shorts, and tights.

Fila, Westway Sports, Inc., 31878 Camino Capistrano, Ste. 270, San Juan Capistrano, CA 92675, 714/240–1311 * Has complete clothing line, including halter tops, tights, jer-seys, cycling caps, and shorts. Does custom designs.

Giordana, Gita Sporting Goods Ltd., 12600 Steele Creek Rd., Charlotte, NC 28217 * Mickey Mouse goes cyberpunk in this clingy, high-style line of cycle wear made in Italy.

Good Stuff Sportswear, 202 N. Main St., Woodsfield, OH 43973, 800/624–1265; 614/472–1910 * Designs and manufactures jerseys, jackets, and shorts. Create your design or use theirs.

Graphic Jackets, 1230 SW First Ave., 4th Fl., Portland, OR 97204, 503/295–1987 * Makes jackets of Tyvek™ suitable for cycling.

Helly-Hensen Inc., 17275 NE 67 Ct., Redmond, WA 98052, 206/883–8823 * Shorts, rainwear, and the fabric Lifa™, a lightweight material used in socks and other products.

Hind Performance, P.O. Box 12609, San Luis Obispo, CA 93406, 805/544–8555 * Jackets, jerseys, tights, and more.

JOGBRA, P.O. Box 927, Burlington, VT 05402, 802/863–3548 * For bicycling or any other athletic activity, JOGBRA makes bras, of course, and other comfortable tops.

J.T. Actif, 119 Coit St., Irvington, NJ 07111, 201/373–1592 * Jackets, etc.

K Sport International. *See* Sunbuster.

Kaos Bodywear, P.O. Box 8504, Dept. BMXP, Little Rock, AR 72215–8504 * For the BMX-ers, T-shirts and tank-tops with silkscreen designs and sayings such as "Channel Your Aggression."

Emily Kay Sportswear, 25 E. Mason, #301, Santa Barbara, CA 93101 * Everything from jackets to jerseys. Specializes in custom orders.

Kinco International Inc., 927 SE Marion, Portland, OR 97202–0345, 503/238–4588 * Hot gloves designed for comfort and style, summer and winter. Custom designs for large orders.

Kucharik Clothing, 1745 W. 182nd St., Gardena, CA 90248, 213/538–4611 * Shorts, jerseys, jackets for on- and off-road cycling.

Lone Peak Designs Ltd., 3474 South 2300 East, Salt Lake City, UT 84109, 801/272–5217 * Bags and stuff to keep your clothes in.

Look Performance Sports, Inc., 1971 S. 4490 West, Salt Lake City, UT 84104, 801/973–9770 * Cleated cycling shoes that eliminate the need for toeclips.

Louis Garneau U.S.A., 66 Main St., Box 755, Newport, VT 05855, 802/334–5885 * Sharp jerseys and shorts. Custom designs orders for teams.

Nike, Inc., 9000 S.W. Nimbus Dr., Beaverton, OR 97005, 503/644–9000 * Not surprisingly, Nike makes shoes and socks for racing, touring, casual riding, and racing. But the running-shoe company has also hit it big with upper-body clothing, particularly for the women's market. (For example, there's a tank-top jersey with a built-in bra.)

Novara, REI, Dept. 5089, P.O. Box 88127, Seattle, WA 98138–0127, 800/426–4840 * Made expressly for REI, the mail-order outdoor gear co-op, Novara provides everything from jerseys to the bicycles themselves. No-nonsense stuff, well-priced. Call the 800 number for free catalog.

Pace Sportswear, 15422 Assembly Ln., Huntington Beach, CA 92649, 714/891–8716; fax: 714/892–0435 * Shorts, Lycra™ tights, Supplex™ pants, Coolmax™ jerseys, women's crop top, bib shorts, and other high-fiber cycle wear.

Parli-Mannina, 5433 Far Hill Rd., Indianapolis, IN 46226, 317/547–5040 * A small company run by two women, Susan Mannina and Rose Parli, who specialize in custom Lycra™ and spandex outfits for team and club riders. Jerseys, shorts, tights, racing suits with custom silkscreens.

Pearl Izumi, 2300 Central Ave., Suite G, Boulder, CO 80301, 800/328–8488 * This Japanese company makes everything from tights to shoe covers. They've got their own trademarked fabrics, including Durawool (a stretchy wool/synthetic weave) and Acrylon (fleeced cold-weather gear). The colors are neon blues, yellows, and crimson mixed with black, vibrant but a little easier to swallow, to our tastes at least. Pearl Izumi publishes spring/summer and fall/winter catalogs.

Prism, 18650 72nd Ave. S, Kent, WA 98032 * Offers cycling socks reinforced at the heel and toe with Kevlar™ threads.

Rad Stuff, 17029 Devonshire St. #114, Dept. BMXP, Northridge, CA 91325 * T-shirts and tanks that celebrate and commemorate Radical Rick, a comic-book character who's kind of a BMX Rambo.

Raleigh Cycle Company, 22710 72nd Ave. S, Kent, WA 98032, 800/222–5527 * Like other well-known bicycle manufacturers, Raleigh is adding a few accessories to their manufacturing list—100 to be exact. Check out their shorts, jerseys, and gloves which are all, naturally, well imprinted with the Raleigh logo.

Revi, 506–D Edwardia Dr., Greensboro, NC 27409, 800/367–2614 * Cycling socks, neon-striped shorts, mountain-biking gloves and more.

Rhode Gear, 765 Allens Ave., Providence, RI 02905, 401/941–1700; 800/456–2800 * Let's see, what doesn't Rhode Gear manufacture? They have shorts, water bottles, panniers, et al.

RJ Cyclewear, 106 Gay St., Philadelphia, PA 19127, 215/482–3300 * They just make biking shorts, but we have a friend who swears by them.

Saranac Glove Co., 1201 Main St., Green Bay, WI 54305, 414/435–3737 * Manufactures (surprise!) gloves. Can do large, special orders.

Schnaubelt Shorts, Inc., 1128 Fourth Ave., Coraopolis, PA 15108, * Does your whole office ride? These folks will stamp out custom-printed cycling jerseys and shorts with the company name—or whatever you'd like. Made in a wide variety of colors and patterns, the jerseys come in CoolMax™, Lycra™, or polyester. The shorts, bib shorts, helmet covers, and skins are Lycra/polyester or nylon/Lycra. Schnaubelt will even incorporate your own drawings or do custom artwork for about $25 an hour.

Sidi Sport, Via Bassanese, 41, 31010 MASER (Treviso), Italy. * This company's "Genius Micro Lock System" for cleated shoes recalls the lock-into-the-pedal shoes that obviate the need for toe clips and straps. Sidi also makes shoes for touring, mountain bikes, cycle-cross, and casual riders. Also pile jackets, short sleeve and long sleeve jerseys, sweatshirts, T-shirts, bib tights, shorts, shoe covers, winter gloves, socks, head bands, and shower shoes.

Specialized, 15130 Concord Circle, Morgan Hill, CA 95037 * Best known for a highly regarded line of touring, mountain, and hybrid bicycles, Specialized markets complementary helmets, helmet covers, shoes, socks, and shorts. They even make baggy cotton shorts for those who shun the second-skin look.

Spenco, P.O. Box 2501, Waco, TX 76710, 817/772–6000 * Padded gloves for on- and off-road cycling to help those tired and numb hands. Also athletic pads to make those toes and soles comfy.

ST Cyclewear, 1820 John Towers #E, El Cajon, CA 92020, 619/449–4300 * Cycling shorts and jerseys. Can custom design clothing for teams and clubs.

Stylin', P.O. Box 233, Osage Beach, MO 65065, 314/348–5189; fax: 314/348–2214 * Gear and clothes for BMX.

Sunbuster, K Sport International, 9020 B Mendenhall Ct., Columbia, MD 21045, 800/255–5003 * Vividly colored jackets, tights, jerseys, shorts, and more that warrant the Sunbuster name.

Time Sport USA, 890 Cowan Rd., Burlingame, CA 94010, 415–692–0272 * Specializes in cycling shoes for racers and sport and fitness riders that are comfortable to walk in.

Tomamaso, 10–Speed Drive Imports, P.O. Box 9250, Melbourne, FL 32902–9250, 407/777–5777 * "Serious cycling apparel" modeled by Greg LeMond in their latest catalog. T–shirts, jerseys, body suits, bib shorts, panel shorts, gloves, caps, suspenders.

Trek USA, 801 West Madison St., P.O. Box 183, Waterloo, WI 53594 * Probably the Schwinn of the 1980s (i.e., an American-made bike with a good rep), Trek has branched out to include Trek Wear and Trek Gear, including helmets, water bottles, gloves, gear packs, shoes (made by the running shoe company New Balance), shorts, jerseys, and stretchy tank-tops. Widely available at bike shops. See also listings under *Bicycle Manufacturers, Mountain Bikes,* and *Safety.*

Trend Bike Source, P.O. Box 201778, Austin, TX 78720–1778, 512/338–4466 * Complete bikes to clothes for BMX.

Triple Sport, Vicky Kilker, P.O. Box 321, Boulder, CO 80306, 800/338–2794. Silkscreened, all-cotton T-shirts for mountain bikers, racers, and triathletes.

Ultima, distributed by Veltec-Boyer Sports, Inc., 801 California Ave., Sand City, CA 93955, 408/394–7114; fax: 408/394–4721 * A full line of Italian-made goods for cold and cool-weather riding. They include long-sleeve jerseys, Lycra™ "training jackets," winter tights, full gloves, shoe covers, bib tights, and rain jackets, in the usual assortment of neon patterns and black. Also, visor-style sunglasses worn by such professional racers as Raul Alcala and Sean Kelly.

Vittoria, BHP, 2135 East Main, P.O. Box 4250, Grand Junction, CO 81502, 303/241–3518 * Hand-made, leather Italian shoes for racing, mountain-biking, and touring. If you're the type who drives the street version of Richard Petty's stock car, you'd like to know that these shoes "have crossed the finish line first in the Tour de France, Giro d'-Italia," et al.

EYEWEAR

Alpina International Sport, D–8904 Friedberg/Derching, Germany * Visor-style, neon-colored sunglasses such as the Superbike S+L (vented to prevent fogging, adjustable, and including forehead padding), the Cross Bike (removable lenses for cleaning), and the Vario Bike (changeable lenses for different times of day).

AME, 244 Mercury Cir., Pomona, CA 91768, 714/594–1767 * Sport Shades with a "unique air-deflector system," meant to prevent foggy and heat buildup.

Bolle America, Inc., 3890 Elm St., Denver, CO 80207, 303/321–4300 * The company's day-glo logo can be seen on many a garish gym bag. For the cyclist they make sunglasses in 27 colors from black to blaze green to "Graffiti III." Made in Oyonnax, France, these stylish shades promise protection from ultraviolet rays and other points of light that were once filtered by our ozone layer. Bolle also makes helmet covers and fanny packs.

Eye Communications, 1241 W. Ninth St., Upland, CA 91786, 714/949–1494 * Large sun goggles that filter 100 percent of ultraviolet light and 85 percent of blue light. Can fit over glasses or be worn alone.

Gargoyles Performance Eyewear, 19039 62nd Ave. S., Kent, WA 98032, 206/251–5001 * One style-one size fits all sunglasses. Features wrap-around lens that covers the complete eye.

Oakley, Inc., 10 Holland, Irvine, CA 92718, 714/951–0991 * Offers a huge variety of sunglasses with good warranty. You'll notice their thermonuclear sticker practically everywhere.

Raleigh, Derby Cycle Corporation, Kent, WA 98032, 800/222–5527 * In addition to bikes, replacement parts, and accessories, Raleigh makes sunglasses. Also see listing under *Accessories* and *Bicycle Manufacturers*.

Revo Sunglasses, 455 E. Middlefield Rd., Mountain View, CA 94043, 415/962–0906 * Lenses are coated in multiple layers and quite bright. Has a good warranty, fairly complex.

Sport Optics International, 6191 Cornerstone Ct. E, #101, San Diego, CA 92121, 619/546–1221 * Manufactures the Flashport RX, which can convert from ordinary sunglasses to prescription sunglasses by mounting whatever is desirable on a rubber brow bar.

Spotlight Industries, 31635 Blue Meadow, Westlake Village, CA 91361, 818/706–1945 * Makes Visual Eyes with wrap-around styling. Can be worn over regular prescription glasses.

Suspension Eyewear, 8780 Warner Ave., Fountain Valley, CA 92708, 714/841–3665 * Lenses, both prescription and non-prescription, suspended on a thin wire.

Ultima, distributed by Veltec-Boyer Sports, Inc., 801 California Ave., Sand City, CA 93955, 408/394–7114; fax: 408/394–4721 * Visor-style sunglasses worn by such professional racers as Raul Alcala and Sean Kelly.

 *six*

EVENTS

Whether you dawdle out the back door, seeking gentle rides, or zip along side streets, pretending you're Jeannie Longo or Greg LeMond, there's a ride, somewhere, that you can gawk at or be a part of. You can select from a potpourri of rides: short one-day rides; long one-day rides; long two- or more-day rides; on-road races; off-road rides; off-road races; biathlons; and triathlons. The first place to start looking for rides is locally: check your local bike store, American Youth Hostels, athletic club, or bicycle club. Most clubs offer weekend rides; some even structure mid-week sorties.

Clubs occasionally share listings. If you have a regional magazine or listing of area-wide rides, you're again fortunate. Many nonprofit organizations—the Multiple Sclerosis Society, American Youth Hostel, and American Lung Association, for example—combine cycling with fund raising. Often these rides are great opportunities to see the countryside, meet new cyclists, and raise money for worthy causes.

Otherwise, many national magazines list major rides or carry advertisements for them. Browse through *Bicycling, Bicycle Guide, Mountain Bike, Dirt Rag* (off-road publication for the Northeast), *Outside, BikeReport* (Bikecentennial's membership magazine), or

BICYCLE USA (L.A.W.'s membership magazine) for listings. Other regional newspapers, such as *Spokes* (the metropolitan Washington, D.C. area); *California Bicyclist* (has north and south editions); *Southwest Cyclist* (California and Arizona); *The Northwest Cyclist* (Washington and Oregon); or the *Puget Sound Cyclist* (Washington and Oregon) contain lists of rides, long tours, and races. *Winning,* a national magazine for bicycle racers, offers a special section on races throughout the U.S.

There are special rides that you might want to schedule a vacation around. Some of these are classics: TOSRV (the Tour of the Scioto River Valley) and RAGBRAI (the *Des Moines Register*'s Annual Great Bicycle Ride Across Iowa) come to mind immediately. They're extraordinarily fun and attract thousands of cyclists and non-cyclists. Plan on days of great cycling and even better food. Keep your eye out for new cross-state rides, which seem to crop up every year. Cycle Oregon and TRIRI (The Ride In Rural Indiana) are two somewhat recent additions to the family of long rides. Their recent vintage, however, hasn't affected their popularity. Other rides, such as the National Bike Ride promoted and sponsored by the Bicycle Institute of America in Washington, D.C. (May 16–17, 1992), are only as organized as you want them to be. For the National Bike Ride, you just get out on your bicycle and ride! Anywhere.

Most of the year, there's a ride near you or within driving distance. Contact these rides in advance. Some of them, like RAGBRAI, limit the number of participants and select them by a lottery held months ahead of time. Most rides charge a modest fee, which covers a snack, route map, route supervision (sag wagon and medical personnel), water, and other amenities. Many rides offer souvenirs of some type, be they a T-shirt, patch, or water bottle. There is a downside to all of this—enthusiastic cyclists often have a T-shirt and water bottle collection to rival that of the most well-equipped bicycle shop.

The list that follows is a representative sampling of offerings throughout the United States. If you are traveling, hooking up with a local ride is a wonderful way to discover new scenery and more reasons to return.

HOTLINE
....

It had to come, and it makes sense. Now there's a 900 number for something *really* worth while—cycling events! The Hotline Cycling (900/246–2453) offers "the fastest news in cycling." In addition to a line for race news, which is updated weekly, the Hotline offers mountain bike news, ultramarathon results, and news about bicycling all over the world. They have a line for regional events, divided into northwest, southwest, midwest, northeast, and southeast. The Hotline Cycling costs $.95 a minute and is only available to callers with touchtone phones.

ALL YEAR ROUND

The Bud Light U.S. Triathlon Series, CAT Sports, Inc., 5966 La Place Ct., Ste. 100, Carlsbad, CA 92008, 619/438–8080; fax: 619/438–3089 * 1.5–kilometer ocean swim, 40–k bike ride, 10–k run. Write for this year's schedule.

JANUARY

Annual New Year's Day Ride (Boston, MA), Charles River Wheelmen, 19 Chase Ave., West Newton, MA 02165, 617/325–BIKE * 20–mile tour around Boston.

FEBRUARY

Annual Fontana Triathlon, c/o city of Fontana, Recreation Dept., 9460 Sierra Ave., Fontana, CA 92335, 714/350–7635 * Triathlon: 5–k run/15–k bike/75–yd swim.

Iditabike (Wasilla, Alaska)—about 40 miles north of Anchorage—907/346–3190 * A 200–mile, 100–person, all-terrain bicycle event that precedes Alaska's Iditarod dog sled race by one week and uses much of the same route.

MARCH

Branders Jeans Tour of Texas, 512/834–8555 * This eight-city, ten-event bicycle stage race and sprint series covers eight Texas cities.

Camellia Festival Races (Sacramento, CA), Sacramento Golden Wheelmen, 1802 Canyon Terrace Ln., Folsom, CA 95630, 916/455–RACE * Two-day series of races, including criterium, circuit race, and more.

Cinderella Classic (Eastern San Francisco Bay area, CA), Valley Spokesmen Touring Club, 415/828–5299 * A 100–kilometer ride for women only.

Easter Hill Country Tour (Kerrville State Park, TX), 512/834–8555 * Nearly 1,500 riders participate in this event sponsored by the Lubbock Club. Rides are from 20 to 100 miles long.

Florence Wildflower Century (Tucson, AZ), Greater Arizona Bicycling Association, P.O. Box 43273, Tucson, AZ 85733.

Gator County Bicycle Stage Race (Gainesville, FL), Team Florida, 1331–A SW 13th St., Gainesville, FL 32608. Criteriums, road races, and a time trial.

Gold Nugget Stage Race, California, Velo Promo, 209/533–4996, 408/425–8688 * A three-day event in northern California for junior racers.

Icicle Century/Half/Quarter (Newark, DE), White Clay Bicycle Club, 321 Indian Town Rd., Landenberg, PA 19350.

Solvang Century (Solvang, CA), SCOR Productions, 12200 E. Washington Blvd. Ste. O, Whittier, CA 90606, 213/945–6366 * 100–mile ride.

Unknown Valley Tandem Rally, Chico, California, 916/343–VELO * A two-day ride with several 1,000–foot climbs.

APRIL

Annual Florida Sunshine Circuit (Gainesville, FL), sponsored by the Florida Council of American Youth Hostels, 904/878–2042 * A 400–mile loop encompassing two Florida coasts.

Bike Around the Buttes, P.O. Box 1088, Yuba City, CA 95992, 916/674–9112 * Sponsored by the Diabetes Society of Yuba-Sutter, BAB takes cyclists through the Sutter Buttes, which are now privately owned. There's a 40–mile and 100–mile option. Send SASE for information.

Catfish Festival Bike Ride (Crescent City, FL), Crescent City Rotary Club, c/o John Fields, Box 483, Crescent City, FL 32112 * Eight 100-mile rides in northeast Florida, culminating with feast of regional food.

Classic Bicycle and Whizzer Club of America Swap Meet, Write Swap Meet, 3744 Robina, Berkley, MI 48072 * Held at Washtenaw Fairgrounds, Ann Arbor, Michigan, on last Sunday in April.

Go Greenbelt!, Greenbelt Alliance, 116 New Montgomery, Ste. 640, San Francisco, CA 94105, 415/543–4291, 408/983–0539 * Challenging seven-day tour traveling through the Bay Area to raise money for the Greenbelt Alliance, which seeks to preserve open space for recreational use.

Grand Prix, La Jolla, CA, 619/296–5165.

Great Greenbrier River Race (Cloverlick to Marlinton, WV), 800/336–7009 * Relay race for bicycles, canoes, and runners.

Los Angeles Times Whittier Hills Bike Challenge (Whittier, CA), SCOR Productions, 12200 E. Washington Blvd. Ste. O, Whittier, CA 90606, 213/945–6366 * 25/50/100 km rides.

Minnesota Ironman, Minnesota Council of AYH, Buffalo, MN, 314/644–4660 * A 200–mile ride for 3,000 cyclists beginning and ending in Buffalo.

Mount Hamilton Ascent and Challenge, P.O. Box 60906, Sunnyvale, CA 94088–0906 * Climb Silicon Valley's highest peak, Mount Hamilton. Its 4,200 feet will get you in shape and benefit CABO, the California Association of Bicycling Organizations. Send SASE for more information.

National Trail Days, League of American Wheelmen, 301/944–3399 * Trail organizations will hold events and forums promoting trails and cooperation between trail users.

Pepsi-Twilight Races, Athens, GA, 404/564–6632.

Primavera Century, Fremont Freewheelers, Box 1089, Fremont, CA 94538 * Pre-registration only for this tough century that attracts more than 1,000 cyclists.

Silver Spring Sixty (Silver Springs, IL), Aurora Bicycle Club, 708/739–6058 * Largest event in Illinois with 1,500 cyclists biking to a spaghetti dinner.

Spring Fling Rail Trail Tour (Whitehall, MI), White Lake Area Footracing Association, Box C, Whitehall, MI 49461–0903, 616/894–8052 * A 25–to–100–kilometer ride on Michigan's first rail-to-trail conversion.

Tour de Moore (Moore County, NC), 919/692–4494 * A 100–mile race around the hills of North Carolina.

MAY

AIDS Bike-A-Thon, Different Spokes, P.O. Box 14711, San Francisco, CA 94114, 415/282–1647 * Yearly bike-a-thon to raise money for a variety of AIDS organizations. Includes 25–, 62–, and 100–mile options.

Annual Cross-Florida Ride, Cocoa Beach, FL, 407/783–1196 * Cyclists pedal 170 miles from Cocoa Beach to Pine Island Beach.

Davis Bike Club Double Century, DBC, 610 3rd St., Davis, CA 95616 * That's right— 200 miles in one day. Pre-registration only.

Five Borough Bike Tour (New York, NY) Metropolitan NY Council of AYH, 212/932– 2300 * 22,000 riders tour 36 miles through New York City.

Great Western Bicycle Rally (Paso Robles, CA), Los Angeles Wheelmen, 213/540– 0521 * 2,000 cyclists participate in rides of five to 100 miles.

Hillier n' Hell Hundred, Shreveport, LA, 318/222–1612 * A choice of 25–, 50–, or 100– mile hilly rides.

Mammoth Cycling Classic Stage Race, Box 24, Mammoth, CA 93546, 619/934–0651 * Formerly Whiskey Creek Stage Race. Held in Big Bear, California.

Mountain Bike Boogaloo, Rough Riders, Box 382, Sacramento, CA 95812 * Two-day event.

National Bike Month. An annual event, now in its 34th year, National Bike Month is coordinated by the Bicycle Federation of America, Bikecentennial, L.A.W., and the Bicy-cling Institute of America. Local clubs hold special rides.

National Bike Ride, Anywhere, U.S.A., May 18–19, 1991 (May 16–17, 1992) * Ride celebrating bicycling. For more information, send a SASE to the Bicycle Federation of America, 1818 R St. NW, Washington, DC 20009.

National Bike to Work Day. Sponsored by League of American Wheelmen, 301/944– 3399.

National Capital MS 150K Bike Tour, (Virginia), National Multiple Sclerosis Society, 2021 K St., NW, Ste. 100, Washington, D.C. 20006–1003, 202/466–6151 * 2–day, 95– mile benefit ride through Virginia countryside.

Annual Northwest Tandem Rally, Salem, OR, Northwest Oregon Cycling Club, 503/742–4355 * A 130–mile ride on country roads through central Oregon.

TOSRV riders punch through a Saturday morning drizzle as they begin a 210–mile round trip from Columbus to Portsmouth, Ohio. (TOSRV photo by Dan Burden)

Annual Santa Fe, New Mexico Century, the Sangre de Cristo Cycle Club, 505/982–1282 * A 25–, 50–, or 100– mile ride along the Turquoise Trail.

Stage Race, Redlands, CA, 714/793–5380.

Thunder Road Bike-a-thon (Dayton, Ohio), Miami Valley Regional Bicycle Committee, Chamber Plaza, 5th and Main St, Dayton, OH 45402 * Considered largest bike-a-thon in U.S. Send SASE for information.

Tour du Pont, Medalist, 1209 E. Cary St., Richmond, VA 23219, 804/649–0034 * Formerly the Tour de Trump. Nine-day stage race on the East Coast; attracts professionals and amateurs from all over the world. May 9–19, 1991; mid-May, 1992.

Tour of the Scioto River Valley (TOSRV), Columbus, Ohio, 614/461–6648 * More than 6,400 cyclists pedal 210 miles from Columbus to Portsmouth, OH. Established in 1962 and considered the oldest mass ride.

Annual Tour of the Swan River Valley (TOSRV-West) (Missoula, MT), Missoula Bicycle Club, 406/543–4889 * 600 cyclists pedal along the Swan and Mission Ranges of Northwestern Montana.

MAY TO JUNE

Autumn in Bonham, Greater Dallas Bicyclists, 214/495–1610 * 25–,50–,62–, and 100–mile rides with professional teams.

Brooklyn Biathlon, 212/289–4113 * A 3–mile run, 20–mile bicycle race.

ConnTour Bicycle Ride, 203/787–0646 * A 110–mile, border-to-border tour across Connecticut.

PEDAL FOR POWER Across America, Box 898–N, Atkinson, NH 03811, 800/762–BIKE * Los Angeles to Boston in 47 days. Riders must have sponsors to raise money for charity.

Rosarito-to-Ensenada 50–mile Fun Ride, Bicycling West, Inc., P.O. Box 15128, San Diego, CA 92115–0128, 619/583–3001 * Annual 50–mile ride along the Pacific Ocean from Rosarito to Ensenada, Mexico, attracts as many as 9,000 cyclists, who ride on a freeway closed to cars. An April event has been added. A popular half-way point stop is for lobster in the fishing village of Puerto Nuevo.

JUNE

Annual Bay to Bay Ride (Betterton, MD) 301/778–4881 * This 72–, 86–, or 107–mile ride includes swimming in the Delaware and Chesapeake Bays.

Bicycle Ride Across Georgia (BRAG), Southern Bicycle League, 404/564–3336 * A 400–mile ride from Atlanta to Savannah usually drawing more than 800 cyclists.

Bicycle Ride Across Nebraska (BRAN), Rotary Club of Northwest Omaha, 402/397–7335 * A 500–person, 488–mile ride from Fort Robinson to Omaha.

Bike Virginia, P.O. Box 203, Williamsburg, VA 23187–0203, 804/253–2985 * 5–day, 250–mile "fun ride" supported by leaders and sag wagons.

CAMP, Cycle Across Missouri's Parks, 314/644–4660 * 450–mile ride across Missouri. Send SASE to Ozark Area Council, AYH, 7187 Manchester Rd., St. Louis, MO 63143.

Chesapeake Bay Bike Tour, American Lung Association of Maryland, 1840 York Rd., Ste. M, Timonium, MD 21093 * A 2–day, 93–mile benefit ride through the Eastern Shore of Chesapeake Bay.

Corestates Championships Preview Races, 203/655–0100 * These races are tentatively scheduled for Freehold, NJ. Call to confirm date and location.

Corestates U.S. Pro Championships (Philadelphia, PA), 203/655–0100 * This professional road race is the only World Cup event outside of Europe.

Dash In/MS 150 Bike Tour, 1055 Taylor Ave., Ste. 201, Towson, MD 21204–8317, 301/821–8626 * A 2–day, 150–k pledge-ride in Annapolis area to benefit Multiple Sclerosis Society.

Denver Post Ride to Rockies, 303/820–1338 * A newspaper-sponsored event for more than 2,000 cyclists.

Escape to Frederick, Wheelbase, 229 N. Market St., Frederick, MD 21701, 301/663–9288 * Non-competitive event, including all-terrain and road rides.

Freewheel, MO, 918/581–8385 * A 400–mile ride for over 2,000 cyclists begins in Ponca City and ends in Southwest City, MO. The event is sponsored by the *Tulsa World* newspaper, Phillips Petroleum, and three bicycle clubs.

The Great Annual Bicycle Adventure Along the Wisconsin River (GRABAAWR), 608/256–2686 * Cyclists ride 500 miles from upper Michigan to the Iowa border.

The Great Ohio Bicycle Adventure, Columbus Council AYH, 614/447–0888 or 800/BUCKEYE * From 1,000 to 5,000 riders will travel 50 miles per day on this circular tour of Ohio. Register early—spaces fill fast!

Hoosier Hills (Bloomington, IN), 812/332–6028 * A two-day event with rides between 15–65 miles.

Kangaroo Baggs' "Cruise the Coast," (Ventura, CA), SCOR Productions, 12200 E. Washington Blvd. Ste. O, Whittier, CA 90606, 213/945–6366 * A 55–mile ride.

La Crosse "Killer Hill," La Crosse Wheelmen, c/o Jim Asfoor, 924½ Caledonia St., La Crosse, WI 54603, 608/782–4630 * Annual 64–mile ride through the Coulee Region.

Le Tour de L'Ile de Montreal, 3575 boul. Saint-Laurent, Bureau 310, Montreal, Quebec, H2X 2T7, Canada, 514/847–8687 * Another good reason to pedal across the border: Le Tour de L'Ile, the biggest bicycle ride in the world with more than 40,000 cyclists. On streets closed to traffic (could the organizers have it any other way?), cyclists ride 35 miles. Pre-registration only.

Ore-Ida Women's Challenge, 208/345–RACE * A women-only race held in Boise, ID.

Paul Bunyan Double Century, Minnesota Council-American Youth Hostels, 2395 University Ave. West, #302, St. Paul, MN 55114, 612/659–0407 * The 200–mile ride starts in Anoka, MN. A tradition since 1967. Riders must have previously completed a 100–mile ride in less than 8 hours.

Annual Pedal Across Lower Michigan (PALM), 313/665–6327 * Beginning at Lake Michigan, 700 riders pedal approximately 250 miles.

PEDAL FOR POWER Associates, P.O. Box 898–F, Atkinson, NH 03811, 800/762–2453 or 603/382–2188 * Ride for charity from Los Angeles to Boston, or Maine to Florida.

The Ride in Rural Indiana (TRIRI) (Bloomington, IN), 812/332–6028 * The Bloomington Bicycle Club sponsors this one-week camping tour ride through southern Indiana.

Rocky Mountain News/Bannock Criterium, 303/388–7829 * A racing event in downtown Denver.

Seattle to Portland (STP), Cascade Bicycle Club, P.O. Box 31299, Seattle, WA 98103 * Legendary 1– or 2–day, 193–mile ride from Seattle to Portland that attracts 9,000 cyclists. Raises funds for the Cascade Bicycle Club's Education Program. Cyclists return to Seattle by train or bus. Send SASE for information.

Show Me Tour, Kansas City Bicycle Club, 816/767–0104 * Three hundred people ride 300 miles across the state.

The Other Bike Ride Across Wisconsin—Mississippi To Michigan Ride (TOBRAW M & M RIDE), 414/383–5563 * This 350–mile tour begins in Fountain City and ends in Mequon. The TOBRAW Bicycle Club sponsors this and three other tours; a 6–day tour of the Door Country Peninsula, a weekend tour on the Elroy-Sparta State Trail, and a weekend tour of Amish Country and the Kickapoo River Valley.

To Hel'en Back/To Hel'en Beyond, R. Humphrey, 2011 Main St., Vancouver, WA 98660 * 1– to 3–day ride around Mt. St. Helens; fundraiser for American Cancer Society. Send SASE for information.

Trek Across Maine, the American Lung Association of Maine, 207/622–6394 * A 180–mile trip from the Sunday River Ski Area to Rockport.

Washington State Sampler (Seattle, WA), 206/353–4548 * This tour of 650 scenic, strenuous miles includes five mountain passes; begins and ends at the Seattle-Tacoma Airport.

Women's International Cycling Criterium, Columbia, MD, 301/929–0677 * Largest purse ever for a women's event.

JUNE TO JULY

Coast to Coast Bicycle Classic™, Tim Kneeland and Associates, 200 Lake Washington Blvd., Ste. 101, Seattle, WA 98122–6540, 206/322–4102, 800/433–0528 * 48–day, fundraising ride across U.S. (from Seattle, W.A, to Asbury Park, NJ). June 3–July 20, 1991 (June 8–July 25, 1992).

JUNE TO AUGUST

Coors Light Biathlon, 1431 Chew St., Allentown, PA 18102, 215/433–3899 * 5–k run, 30–k bike race held in as many as 15 cities.

JULY

Aquatennial Bike Festival (Minnehaha, MN), Minnesota Council-American Youth Hostels, 2395 University Ave. West, #302, St. Paul, MN 55114, 612/659–0407 * 25–mile bike ride attracts 5,000–7,000 riders annually to cruise from Minnehaha Falls north along Mississippi River and back.

Firecracker 100 (Milford, MI), Michigan Council of American Youth Hostels, 3024 Coolidge, Berkeley, MI 48072 * 25–, 50–, or 100–mile ride through farmland around city of Milford.

L.A.W. National Rally and National Congress of Bicyclists, 301/944–3399 * Dozens of rides, workshops, and entertainment for over 1,000 bicyclists. Held in a different site each year.

Montezuma's Revenge, Box 30–B, Montezuma, CO 80435, 303/468–5378 * Off-road, 24–hour, 200–mile event. Ride ten times over the Continental Divide.

NORBA Series, California, Box 24, Mammoth Lakes, CA 93546, 619/934–0651 * Off-road World Cup event.

(Gregory Kovaciny)

Race Across AMerica (RAAM), UMCA, 4790 Irvine Blvd., #105–111, Irvine, CA 92720 * In 1991, RAAM celebrates its 10th year of ultramarathon cyclists riding across the U.S. as fast as they can. Be a part of RAAM: staff a time station or come out and cheer. The route and starting date varies from year to year. In 1991, route is from Irvine, Calif., to Savannah, Ga.

Register's Annual Great Bicycle Ride Across Iowa (RAGBRAI XVIII), sponsored by the Des Moines Register, P.O. Box 622, Des Moines, IA 50303, 515/284–8282 * Approximately 8,000 riders take a week-long trek from the western to the eastern part of the state. Riders chosen by lottery entered by March 1 of each year.

The Shoreline Bicycle Tour (SBT), Sponsored by the League of Michigan Bicyclists, 616/780–2402 * A 500-person event covering 330 miles along the shores of Lake Michigan. A western route from New Buffalo to Traverse City and an eastern route from Au Gras to Traverse City. Ends with a parade.

USCF Masters National Championships, San Diego, California, Nicholson Productions, Box 40289, San Diego, CA 92104, 619/528–9449 * Championships for older cyclists.

U.S. Track Cycling Championship, Marymoor Velodrome, 7901 168th Ave. NE, Ste. 103, Redmond, WA 98052, 206/882–0706 * Trials for the Pan-American Games.

AUGUST

· ·

Atlantic to the Lakes Cycling Adventure™, c/o Tim Kneeland and Associates, 200 Lake Washington Blvd., Ste. 101, Seattle, WA 98122–6540, 206/322–4102, 800/433–0528 * Halifax, Nova Scotia, Canada, to Toronto, Ontario, Canada, August 11–31, 1991 (August 16–September 5, 1992) to benefit Christian Children's Fund of Canada.

Charlotte Observer Moon Ride, Tarheel Cyclists, 704/379–6903 * Three thousand cyclists participate in a 12–mile moonlight ride through downtown Charlotte, NC.

Coors Ride the Range Bicycle Tour, P.O. Box 1740, Denver, CO 80201, 303/278–3818 * Weekend bicycle pledge tour of 150 miles along Colorado's Front Range. Benefits the United Way and public television.

Cycle Across Maryland (CAM-Tour), 800/842–BANK * The First National Bank of Maryland sponsors the 375–mile tour beginning in Hagerstown and ending on the Eastern Shore.

The Dick Allen Lansing to Mackinaw Tour (DALMAC), Sponsored by the Tri-County Bicycle Association, 517/332–5331 * A 350–mile ride for 1,400 riders, the event includes a ride across Mackinac Bridge.

Human Powered Speed Championships, Oregon Human Powered Vehicles, Box 614, Beaverton, OR, 503/644–7038 * All-terrain competition—starting on the road, heading for the dirt, and winding up in water. Attracts "futuristic" entries. Location varies from year to year.

Imperial Beach Championships, 4060 Morena Blvd., No. G–355, San Diego, CA 92117, 619/441–7844 * Annual biathlon and triathlon that benefits the Imperial Beach Chamber of Commerce.

Moonlight Ramble, Ozark Area Council, American Youth Hostels 314/644–4660 * Fourteen thousand cyclists convene at 2:00 a.m. to ride through downtown St. Louis.

MS 150 Bike Tour, Mid-Jersey Chapter, National Multiple Sclerosis Society, 801 Belmar Plaza, Belmar, NJ 07719, 201/681–2322 * Weekend benefit ride from New Jersey across Delaware River to Pennsylvania and back.

The Oregon Bicycle Ride, 503/382–0740 * 225 participants ride nearly 500 miles from Joseph to Lincoln City.

RAAM Kickoff Ride (Irvine, CA), SCOR Productions, 12200 E. Washington Blvd. Ste. O, Whittier, CA 90606, 213/945–6366 * 50–mile ride to celebrate start of cross-country race.

Solvang Prelude (Solvang, CA), SCOR Productions, 12200 E. Washington Blvd. Ste. O, Whittier, CA 90606, 213/945–6366 * 50–mile ride.

Steamboat Road and Mountain Bike Challenge, 2305 Mt. Werner Circle-SSRC, Steamboat Springs, CO 80487 * 7 weekend routes from 10–100 miles to choose from.

Train, Chain & Chili, 11 Columbia St., Cumberland, MD 21502 * Train ride, 13–mile bike ride (all downhill), and picnic held during annual State Chili Championship. Benefits the American Lung Association of Maryland.

West Hollywood Criterium & Tour of West Hollywood, Accord Cycle Group, Box 48464, Los Angeles, CA 90048, 213/871–6959 * A race and an open recreational ride held on same day.

SEPTEMBER
....

Annual Century Bike Tour, Red River Chamber of Commerce, Red River, NM 87558, 800/348–6444 * 2–day, 100–mile bike tour.

Bicycle Across Missouri (BAM), Ozark Area Council of AYH, 314/644–4660 * A 540 mile ride/race from St. Louis to Kansas City and back (or 270 miles one way).

Bicycle Across Tennessee (BRAT), Tennessee Bicycle Federation and the Tennessee Dept. of Conservation, 615/742–6675 * This tour extends from Memphis to Harrison Bay State Park at Chattanooga.

Capitol Motion Bike-a-thon (Washington, D.C.), The Washington Area Bicyclist Association, 202/872–9830 * An annual fund-raiser for WABA.

Chequamegon Fat Tire Festival, Inc., P.O. Box 267, Cable, WI 54821, 715/739–6608 or 715/798–3811 * "The nation's largest off-the-road adventure," the 2–day festival features events ranging from an 18–mile tour to bicycle orienteering to a 40–mile off-road race. Some 1,800 participated in 1989, and Greg LeMond, in his off-road debut, won the main event in '90.

Conference Velo Mondiale Pro Bike Velo City, Velo Quebec, 3575 boul. Saint-Laurent, Bureau 310, Montreal, Quebec H2X 2T7, Canada, 514/847–8356 * An international conference on bicycles co-sponsored by the Bicycle Federation of America and Velo Quebec held in Montreal, Canada, September 13–17, 1992. Write for more information.

Cycle Oregon, 800/547–7842 or 503/323–1270 * A 350–mile, 7–day, north-south tour of Oregon sponsored by Oregon Tourism Department. In 1992, it will be in its fifth year.

The Flattest Century in the East, Narragansett Bay Wheelmen, 401/434–2385 * 1,800 cyclists pedal 25, 50, or 100 miles along the coast and through the forests and marshlands of southeastern Rhode Island and Massachusetts. This ride begins in Tiverton, RI.

Git Outta Town, National Multiple Sclerosis Society, National Capital Chapter, 2021 K St. NW, Ste. 100, Washington, DC 20006–1003, 202/466–6151 * A bike tour in the country.

Harmon Hundred, Wheeling Wheelmen, 708/255–4029 * 1,300 cyclists ride through a suburban and rural area northwest of Chicago.

Harvest Bike Tour, 301/821–8626 * 25– or 50–mile ride through Maryland farmlands.

Lotoja Classic, 138 N. 100 E, Logan, UT 84321, 800/657–5353 * 203–mile, 1–day race from Logan, Utah, through Idaho to Jackson Hole, WY.

MS Fall Bike Tour, NYC MS Society, 30 West 26th St., New York, NY 10010–2094 * A 30– or 60–mile route through Manhattan and Brooklyn. Benefits multiple sclerosis research.

National Off-Road Bicycling World Championships, Durango, CO, 719/578–4717.

NORBA Mountain Bike Championships, Race director, P.O. Box 24, Mammoth Lakes, CA 93546 * Hill climbs, cross-country, "kamikaze" downhill, and other races sanctioned by the National Off-Road Bicycle Association (NORBA).

Old Kentucky Home Tour, 502/491–7120 * A two-day event through the rolling hills and farmland of Kentucky, with rides between 42–100 miles.

PEDAL FOR POWER North-South, Box 898–N, Atkinson, NH 03811, 800/762–BIKE * 23 day ride from Maine to Florida in the fall. Riders must have sponsors to raise money for charity.

San Luis Obispo Bike Club's Lighthouse Ride, SLO Bike Club, Inc., P.O. Box 1585, San Luis Obispo, CA 93406, 805/528–6549 * 103–, 63–, and 35–mile rides.

Six Gap Century, Bicycle Association of North Georgia (BANG), c/o Peach Keller, 18025 Union Hill Rd., Alpharetta, GA 30201, 404/751–1061 * 100–mile ride with 10,300 feet of vertical climbing (more than the assault on Mount Mitchell) through north Georgia mountains. BANG sponsors this ride annually around the 3rd weekend of the month.

Solvang/Santa Maria Century, SCOR, 12200 East Washington Blvd., Ste. O, Whittier, CA 90606, 213/945–6366 * Biggest century on west coast—5,000 riders.

The Storming of Thunder Ridge, Central Region, 725 Church St., 10th floor, Lynchburg, VA 24504, 804/846–1829 * Mid-month, 75–mile ride benefits American Lung Association of Virginia.

Tour Along the South Shore of Lake Erie (TASSLE), 800/432–7447 * More than 1,800 cyclists participate in rides from 50 to 138 miles between Cleveland, Sandusky, and Toledo, Ohio.

Tour of Southern Utah's National Parks, 801/278–9386 * This 230–mile tour begins and ends in Cedar City.

Trident Capital City Bike Festival, American Youth Hostels, Potomac Area Council, 1017 K St. NW, Washington, DC 20001, 202/783–4944 or 202/783–0717 * A 22–mile ride around the national monuments. Rock Creek Parkway in the Nation's Capital is taken over by 4,000 cyclists in this AYH fundraiser.

Tri-State Seacoast Century Weekend, Sponsored by the Granite State Wheelmen, 603/898–9926 * A nearly flat route along the coastlines of Maine, New Hampshire, and Vermont. The ride starts at Hampton Beach, NH.

Whittier Hills Bike Challenge, SCOR, 12200 East Washington Blvd., Ste. O, Whittier, CA 90606, 213/945–6366 * 25–, 50–, or 100–k rides.

Yosemite Bicycling Trek, American Lung Association, 234 N. Broadway, Fresno, CA 93701, 209/266–5864 * Yosemite's auto traffic creates a pollution problem in the wilderness, so the weekend rides in late September and early October promote cycling as an alternative means of seeing the park.

SEPTEMBER TO OCTOBER

Grand Canyon to Mexico Almost across Arizona Bicycle Tour, the Greater Arizona Bicycling Association, 602/628–5313 or 602/325–8114 * 300 riders cycle through 6 national monuments on a ride with more than 16,000 feet of elevation gain and loss.

Indian Summer Bicycle & Wheel Goods Show and Swap Meet, Macungie, PA 18031, 215/285–6180.

West Coast International Bicycle Classic, Tim Kneeland and Associates, 200 Lake Washington Blvd., Ste. 101, Seattle, 98122–6540, 206/322–4102, 800/433–0528 * Fundraiser for charity of choice. Ride from Victoria, British Columbia, Canada, to Tijuana, Mexico. September 22–October 18, 1991 (September 20–October 16, 1992).

OCTOBER

Bike-Aid, 800/827–4480, 415/431–4480 * 2,000 to 3,400 mile tours over five to nine weeks to benefit the Overseas Development Network.

Colorburst, Allen and Sue Brewer, 2021 140th Ave., Dorr, MI 49323 * 25–, 45–, and 62–mile rides in and around Kent County, MI—to benefit Mothers Against Drunk Driving.

Cystic Fibrosis Cycle Tour, Cystic Fibrosis Foundation, 6931 Arlington Rd., Ste. T200, Bethesda, MD 20814, 301/657–8444 * 2–day, 100–mile tour/benefit starts outside Washington, D.C., proceeds to Hume, VA, and back.

Frederick Fall Foliage Frolic (Frederick, Maryland), Potomac Pedalers Touring Club, P.O. Box 23601, L'Enfant Plaza Station, Washington, DC 20024 * Say this weekend's title three times, then plan to go on it. Gorgeous fall colors in Frederick, Maryland, a mere 35 miles from Washington, D.C.

Mt. Dora Bicycling Festival, Mt. Dora Chamber of Commerce, Mt. Dora, FL 32757, 407/649–8761.

Greenbelt Biathlon, Greenbelt Recreation Dept., 25 Crescent Rd., Greenbelt, MD 20770 * 3–mile run, 10–mile ride in suburb of Washington, DC.

Los Angeles Classic, Accord Cycle Group, Box 48464, Los Angeles, CA 90048, 213/871–6959 * Criterium races and open recreational ride.

NEC World Cycling Invitational, c/o Pro Serv Box Office, 1101 Wilson Blvd., Ste. 1800, Arlington, VA 22209, 800/PRO–SERV * 3 days of world-class cycling featuring top international riders. Held at 7–11 Olympic Velodrome, California State University in most recent years.

Tour de St. Croix, LSP 14758 Ostlund Trail N., Marine, MN 55407, 715/648–5519 * 25–, 50–, or 100–mile rides.

NOVEMBER

BMX Grandnational, sponsored by American Bicycle Association, P.O. Box 718, Chandler, AZ 85244, 602/96101903 * Indoor BMX races and BMX Hall of Fame Inductions, held in Oklahoma City in most recent years.

On Trak 'n Cruisin, National Multiple Sclerosis Society, Orange Country Chapter, 2500 Michelson, #475, Irvine, CA 92715, 714/752–1680 * A pair of 2–day rides, 90 and 75 miles, from Anaheim to points south, to benefit fight against MS. Return via train.

Turkey Climb, Accord Cycle Group, Box 48464, Los Angeles, CA 90048, 213/871–6959 * Hill-climb time trials for certified racers, held in Brentwood/Bel Air.

Annual Veteran's Day Bicycling Festival, 318/222–1612 * Two days of riding through Louisiana with distances ranging from 15 miles to 110 miles.

DECEMBER

Annual Fontana Bike Race & Family Ride, c/o city of Fontana, Recreation Dept., 9460 Sierra Ave., Fontana, CA 92335, 714/350–7635 * 13–, 26–, and 52–mile rides.

Death Valley by Moonlight, Vandervogel Bicycle Touring Association, 2364 Mountain Brook Dr., Hacienda Heights, CA 91745, 818/336–5590 * Send SASE for information on this challenging century in the Mojave Desert. Participants must have good set of lights and a taste for the desert at night. This ride is organized by Hugh Murphy, who holds the Ultramarathon Cycling Association's National Points Challenge record for the number of centuries ridden in a single year. That means Mr. Murphy has ridden 100 centuries, (each 100 miles) in 365 days, rain or shine.

STATE-BY-STATE LOCATER

Alaska

Iditabike (Feb.)

Arizona

Florence Wildflower Century (March)
Grand Canyon to Mexico (Sept. to Oct.)

California

The Bud Light U.S. Triathlon Series (throughout year)
Annual Fontana Triathlon (Feb.)
Camellia Festival Races (March)
Cinderella Classic (March)
Gold Nugget Stage Race (March)
Solvang Century (March)
Unknown Valley Tandem Rally (March)
Bike Around the Buttes (April)
Go Greenbelt! (April)

La Jolla, CA, Grand Prix (April)

Los Angeles Times Whittier Hills Bike Challenge (April)

Mount Hamilton Ascent and Challenge (April)

Primavera Century (April)

AIDs Bike-A-Thon (May)

Davis Bike Club Double Century (May)

Great Western Bicycle Rally (May)

Kangaroo Baggs' "Cruise the Coast" (May)

Mammoth Cycling Classic (May)

Mountain Bike Boogaloo (May)

Stage Race (May)

Rosarita-to-Ensenada Fun Ride (May to June)

NORBA Series (July)

Race Across America (July)

USCF Masters National Championships (July)

Imperial Beach Championships (August)

RAAM Kickoff Ride (August)

Solvang Prelude (August)

West Hollywood Criterium & Tour of West Hollywood (August)

NORBA Mountain Bike Championships (Sept.)

San Luis Obispo Bike Club's Lighthouse Ride (Sept.)

Solvang/Santa Maria Century (Sept.)

Whittier Hills Bike Challenge (Sept.)

Yosemite Bicycling Trek (Sept.)

Los Angeles Classic (Oct.)

On Trak 'n Cruisin (Nov.)

Turkey Climb (Nov.)

Annual Fontana Bike Race & Family Ride (Dec.)

Death Valley by Moonlight (Dec.)

Colorado

Denver Post Ride to Rockies (May)

Rocky Mountain News/Bannock Criterium (May)

Montezuma's Revenge (July)

Coors Ride the Range Bicycle Tour (August)

Steamboat Road and Mountain Bike Challenge (August)

National Off-Road Bicycling World Championships (Sept.)

Connecticut

ConnTour Bicycle Ride (May)

Delaware

Icicle Century (March)

Florida

Gator Country Bicycle Stage Race (March)
Annual Florida Sunshine Circuit (April)
Catfish Festival Bike Ride (April)
Annual Cross-Florida Ride (May)
Mt. Dora Bicycling Festival (Oct.)

Georgia

Pepsi-Twilight Races (April)
Bicycle Ride Across Georgia (May)
Six Gap Century (Sept.)

Idaho

Ore-Ida Women's Challenge (May)

Illinois

Silver Spring Sixty (April)
Harmon Hundred (Sept.)

Indiana

The Ride in Rural Indiana (May)
Hoosier Hills (May)

Iowa

Register's Annual Great Bicycle Ride Across Iowa (August)

Kentucky

Old Kentucky Home Tour (Sept.)

Louisiana

Hillier n' Hell Hundred (May)
Veteran's Day Bicycling Festival (Nov.)

Maine

Annual Trek Across Maine (May)
Tri-State Seacoast Century Weekend (Sept.)

Maryland

Annual Bay to Bay Ride (May)
Chesapeake Bay Bike Tour (May)
Dash In/MS 150 Bike Tour (May)
Women's International Cycling Criterium (May)
Escape to Frederick (June)
Cycle Across Maryland (August)
Train, Chain & Chili (August)
Harvest Bike Tour (Sept.)
Frederick Fall Foliage Frolic (Oct.)
Greenbelt Biathlon (Oct.)

Massachusetts

New Year's Day Ride (Jan.)
Flattest Century in the East (Sept.)

Michigan

Classic Bicycle and Whizzer Club of America Swap Meet (April)
Spring Fling Rail Trail Tour (April)
Annual Pedal Across Lower MI (May)
Firecracker 100 (July)
The Shoreline Bicycle Tour (July)
The Dick Allen Lansing to Mackinaw Tour (August)
Colorburst (Oct.)

Minnesota

Minnesota Ironman (April)
Paul Bunyon Double Century (May)
Aquatennial Bike Festival (July)
Tour de St. Croix (Oct.)

Missouri

CAMP (May)
Freewheel, MO (May)
Moonlight Ramble (August)
Bicycle Across Missouri (Sept.)

Montana

TOSRV-West (May)

Nebraska

Bicycle Ride Across Nebraska (May)

New Hampshire

Tri-State Seacoast Century Weekend (Sept.)

New Jersey

Corestates Championships Preview Races (May)
MS 150 Bike Tour (August)

New Mexico

Annual Santa Fe Century (May)
Annual Century Bike Tour (Sept.)

New York

Brooklyn Biathlon (May)
Five Borough Bike Tour (May)
MS Fall Bike Tour (Sept.)

North Carolina

Tour de Moore (April)
Charlotte Observer Moon Ride (August)

Ohio

The Great Ohio Bicycle Adventure (May)
Thunder Road Bike-a-thon (May)
TOSRV (May)
Tour Along the South Shore of Lake Erie (Sept.)

Oklahoma

BMX Grandnational (Nov.)

Oregon

Annual Northwest Tandem Rally (May)
Seattle to Portland (May)
Human Powered Speed Championships (August)

The Oregon Bicycle Ride (August)
Cycle Oregon (Sept.)

Pennsylvania

Corestates U.S. Pro Championships (May)
Coors Light Biathlon (June to August)
MS 150 Bike Tour (August)
Indian Summer Bicycle & Wheel Goods Show and Swap Meet (Sept./Oct.)

Rhode Island

Flattest Century in the East (Sept.)

Tennessee

Bicycle Across Tennessee (Sept.)

Texas

Branders Jeans Tour of Texas (March)
Easter Hill Country Tour (March)
Autumn in Bonham (May)

Utah

Lotoja Classic (Sept.)
Tour of S. Utah's National Parks (Sept.)

Vermont

Tri-State Seacoast Century Weekend (Sept.)

Virginia

Bike Virginia (May)
National Capital MS Bike Tour (May)
Tour du Pont (May)
Storming of Thunder Ridge (Sept.)

Cystic Fibrosis Cycle Tour (Oct.)
NEC World Cycling Invitational (Oct.)

Washington

Seattle to Portland (May)
To Hel'en Back/To Hel'en Beyond (May)
Washington State Sampler (May)
Coast to Coast Bicycle Classic™ (June to July)
U.S. Track Cycling Championship (July)

Washington, D.C.

Capitol Motion (Sept.)
Trident Capital City Bike Festival (Sept.)
Git Outta Town (Sept.)

West Virginia

Great Greenbrier River Race (April)

Wisconsin

The Great Annual Bicycle Adventure Along the Wisconsin River (May)
The Other Bicycle Ride Across Wisconsin (May)
La Crosse "Killer Hill" (May)
Chequamegon Fat Tire Festival (Sept.)

Nationwide

National Trail Days (April)
National Bike Month (May)
National Bike Ride (May)
National Bike to Work Day (May)

Interstate

Lotoja Classic (Sept.)
Pedal for Power (May)

Seattle to Portland (May)
Race Across AMerica (July)
Pedal for Power North-South (Sept.)
Tri-State Seacoast Century (Sept.)
West Coast International Bicycle Classic (Sept. to Oct.)

Canada

Le Tour de L'Ile de Montreal (June)
Atlantic to the Lakes Cycling Adventure (August)
Conference Velo Mondiale (Sept.)
West Coast International Bicycle Classic (Sept. to Oct.)

seven

FOOD AND NUTRITION

*T*he experts say that powdered, high-carbohydrate energy drinks and energy bars help keep you happy and strong over a long, tough day. Furthermore, "real" food in conjunction with exercise makes some athletes nauseous. One of the authors—a die-hard PBJ and banana junkie—tested the theory on a 103–mile ride on the Eastern Shore of the Chesapeake Bay. The organizers had provided vats of powdered energy drink every twenty miles. And since the experts say you should drink about six ounces every fifteen minutes during strenuous exercise, he tanked up at every stop. Sure enough, his speed increased by the hour, creeping up from 16 mph to 21 mph in virtually the same terrain. (The wind was negligible.)

If the commercial stuff seems too expensive, then water, candy bars, and even flat cola (at least one Olympian swore by it) may do the same energy-boosting trick. It also doesn't hurt to have a big plate of spaghetti the night before. And live by the maxim, "Eat before you're hungry, drink before you're thirsty."

BASICS OF CYCLING NUTRITION

By Laura Hefferon

Let's face it—one of the most satisfying payoffs from a good ride, aside from the obvious physical benefits, is the wonderful appetite that results. The problem is that as much as we think we have burned thousands of calories and deserve to pig out on a BLT with the works and a thick chocolate shake, our bodies actually need more discriminate fueling for the next day's ride.

The more you bike and exercise the more you recognize that your body is like a fine-tuned machine. Its efficiency and performance depend on how you choose to fuel it. Experienced cyclists may notice that certain foods affect their level of cycling. Novice cyclists often experience fatigue or even exhaustion because they fail to change their diet according to new demands made on their bodies. Most doctors and nutritionists seem to agree that sports such as running, biking, and cross-country skiing make specific nutritional demands on the body.

For cycling, the basic nutritional concept is simple: 60 to 70 percent of the cyclist's daily caloric intake should come from complex carbohydrates—fruits, vegetables, whole-grain breads, cereals, brown rice.

Why are complex carbohydrates so important? Remember, we're talking about efficiency, and refined carbohydrates—sweets, cookies, candy—are about as inefficient as water in the gas tank. Complex carbohydrates promote greater glycogen synthesis—they store more energy in the blood. In addition, complex carbos have more vitamins and minerals than refined carbos.

Here's how this energy system works. There are basically two kinds of fuels taken from the blood during aerobic exercise: fuels from fatty acids (burned during low-energy activities) and fuels from glucose (burned during high-energy activities). While at rest, the glucose we get from foods is stored in the body as glycogen. The amount of glucose (fuel) in the blood is maintained by the conversion of liver glycogen. A person with a good diet has enough liver glycogen to sustain 1.5 to 2.5 hours of hard cycling. After that, we need to replenish our glucose stores. We're running on empty.

Remember that beginning and recreational cyclists have different dietary needs than competitive cyclists. Riders who cover 5 to 50 miles at speeds of 8 to 15 miles an hour have two main concerns. One: They want to prevent their energy stores from being depleted. This is called "the bonk" or "hitting the wall." It feels like leaden and total exhaustion. Two: They want to avoid dehydration, a loss of body fluids that also leads to sluggishness.

Here are some dietary guidelines.

- Beginning cyclists should eat several high-carb mini-meals throughout a day of cycling. This will continually replenish their glycogen stores.

- Glucose/polymer sports drinks are also good for a long ride. They supply carbos in a liquid form quickly absorbed by the body. But don't rely on these alone. The body needs more liquids than sugar energy. Carry two bottles—one for water and another for a sports drink. Alternate drinks from the two bottles every ten to twenty minutes. You should drink about one bottle of water every hour.

- What about coffee? Avoid it. Caffeine is a diuretic. It causes your body to lose fluids you need during exercise. Also resist fatty foods like pastry, chocolate, cream cheese, or ice cream before a ride. They can cause stomach cramps, take longer to digest, and offer less readily available fuel.

For years, Italian racers have indulged in pasta with tomato sauce as the perfect fuel for an intense workout or race. Now American training tables have rediscovered this simple yet high-energy food. Below are two pasta recipes—perfect for a pre-ride meal.

Spaghetti with Tuna and Spinach

. . . .

1 pound fresh spinach

⅓ cup extra virgin olive oil

1 small onion, finely chopped

¼ cup parsley

one can tuna (dolphin-safe, packed in water)

salt

one pound spaghetti

1) Wash the spinach by soaking in a bowl and cook in boiling water for 3 minutes. Drain.

2) Heat olive oil in saute pan. Cook onion over medium-low heat until softened.

3) Add spinach and parsley and stir.

4) Crumble in tuna fish. Season to taste.

5) Cook spaghetti in 4 quarts boiling water with a touch of olive oil. Drain and combine with sauce.

6) Top each serving with olive oil.

Macaroni with Broccoli

. . . .

About 2 pounds broccoli	salt and pepper
4 garlic cloves, peeled	1 pound ziti, penne, or other macaroni
4 tablespoons extra virgin olive oil	1 cup grated parmesan cheese

1) Trim the flowerlets from the broccoli stems.

2) Peel stems and cut into 2–inch pieces. Steam until bright green.

3) Add flowerlets to pan and cook two more minutes.

4) Drain broccoli and chop into ½–inch pieces.

5) Saute garlic in olive oil until lightly colored. Discard the cloves.

6) Add broccoli to pan with garlic and heat. Season to taste.

7) Cook the pasta in 4 quarts boiling water with olive oil until al dente.

8) Drain and mix with broccoli.

9) Add grated cheese and toss with touch more olive oil.

Laura Hefferon is the author of *Cycle Food: A Guide to Satisfying Your Inner Tube*, available from Ten Speed Press. She is the owner of Ciclismo Classico, a touring company that specializes in bicycle tours in Italy.

Bodyfuel, 1821 East 48th Pl., Los Angeles, CA 90058–1998 * "All-natural" drink mix that purports to improve performance and endurance while inhibiting weight loss.

Champion Nutrition, 2615 Stanwell Dr., Concord, CA 94520, 800/225–4831 * Complex carbohydrate drinks for cyclists and other athletes. Their main product is called "Cytomax Exercise and Recovery Drink."

Exceed Sports Nutritionals, 625 Cleveland Ave., Columbus, OH 43216, 800/543–0281 * Powdered zap of energy popular at biking events.

finHalsa, Inertia Inc., 8055 West Manchester Ave., Suite 550, Playa Del Rey, CA 90293, 213/306–2734, 800/869–7743; fax: 213/306–2072 * Their slogan is "The Legal Advantage" (in races). finHalsa is a food bar consisting of fructose syrup, raisins, wheat germ nuggets, soy, oat bran, peanut butter, and more. Promises quick energy in 20 minutes.

"The Science of Gatorade," 847 West Jackson, 5th floor, Attn: Dept 60, Chicago, IL 60607 * Not satisfied with cornering 90 percent of the market, Gatorade wants respect. Hence this series of brochures that include a "beverage comparison chart" along with sections on "fluid replacement," "gastric emptying," and other topics. In addition to the bottled and canned drinks sold in the soft-drink department, Gatorade markets GatorLode, a high-carbohydrate, powdered drink mix for athletes, and GatorPro, a "sports nutrition supplement" to be taken with meals.

TransAmerica Trail group at breakfast in Idaho. (Bikecentennial photo)

Gookinaid ERG, 4475 University Avenue, San Diego, CA 92105, 800/283–6505 * ERG stands for "electrolyte replacement with glucose."

Gopower, Source, 2540 Main St., Ste. U200, Irvine, CA, 800/76–POWER * From France, a nutritional boost in a tube with about 25 "servings."

Meal on the Go, Provesta Corporation, 800/233–1811 * Fruity energy bars that fit in a bike pocket. Ingredients include wheat flour, dried apples, oats, brown sugar; flavors are apple and pineapple/currant.

Nutriquest, Box 950, Douglas, WY 82633 * The "Official Nutrition" of the storied 7–Eleven cycling team, Nutriquest is a series of powdered drinks and vitamin pills promising quick delivery of carbohydrates. The company also makes various skin creams, liniments, and ointments.

Powerfood, Inc., 1442A Walnut St., Berkeley, CA 94709, 415/843–1330, 800/444–5154 * Their PowerBars come in 3 flavors. The blurb goes, "PowerBars aren't candy, they're a healthful, easy-to-digest energy food made with no fats or oils." Available at many bike shops or in phone-order boxes of 24.

Proline, 1731 W. Rose Garden Lane, Suite 1, Phoenix, AZ 85027, 800/776–5463 * Makes "Second Winds," an endurance-oriented powdered drink.

Shaklee Corporation, Shaklee Terraces, 444 Market St., San Francisco, CA 94111 * "Performance" drink for cyclists claims to boost energy by as much as 30 percent.

Solar Box Cookers, 1724 11th St., Sacramento, CA 95814 * For low-impact bicycle camping, a lightweight stove that relies on little more than a bright afternoon.

Technosport, 1112–B South 8th St., Austin, TX 78704 * 800/544–0989; fax 512/477–0488 * Racing-oriented gear, clothes, and nutritional aids from a catalog/showroom.

Twinlab, Twin Laboratories, Inc., 2120 Smithtown Ave., Ronkonkoma, NY 11779, 516/467–3140; fax: 516/471–2375 * Powdered "Carbo-Fuel" drink, vitamins, and "Ultra-Fuel" drinks in orange, lemon-lime, and fruit punch flavors. Available at health food stores. Publishes catalog, "The Future of Bodybuilding Is Here."

Ultra Energy, 176 University Pkwy., Pomona, CA 91768, 800/54–ULTRA * Billed as a "complete food source"—a "scientific balance of amino acids, electrolytes, carbo-loaders, minerals, and vitamins"—Ultra Energy was the food source of choice of 1990 RAAM winner Bob Fourney.

Exer-Guide

. . . .

Activity	*Calories per Hour*	*Average Calories Used*
Sleeping	65	520 (for 8 hours)
Watching TV	80	80 (for 1 hour)
Eating, reading, writing	90	45 (for ½ hour)
Driving a car	100	50 (for ½ hour)
Dishwashing (by hand)	135	67 (for ½ hour)
Sailing	155	310 (for 2 hours)
Shopping	165	165 (for 1 hour)
Bowling	190	190 (for 1 hour)
Washing, showering, shaving	205	51 (for 15 minutes)
Making beds	210	17 (for 5 minutes)
Yoga ✖	230	230 (for 1 hour)
Washing and polishing car	230	125 (for ½ hour)
Washing windows and floors	250	125 (for ½ hour)
Dancing (waltz, rock, fox trot)	250	105 (for 5 dances; 25 minutes)
Walking, 25 min./mile	255	127 (½ hour)
Baseball (not pitching or catching)	280	560 (for 2 hours)
Weight training ✻	300	150 (for ½ hour)
Canoeing, rowing, 30 min./mile ★✻	300	300 (for 1 hour)
Swimming, 11 min./220 yards ★✖	300	150 (for ½ hour)
Table tennis	300	300 (for 1 hour)
Walking, 15 min./mile ★	345	172 (for ½ hour)
Volleyball, badminton ✖	350	350 (for 1 hour)
Skating, leisure ★✖	350	350 (for 1 hour)
Gardening	390	780 (for 2 hours)
Calisthenics ✖✻	415	207 (for ½ hour)
Bicycling, 6 min./mile ★✻	**415**	**207 (for ½ hour)**
Horseback riding (trot)	415	415 (for 1 hour)
Square dancing	420	840 (for 2 hours)
Tennis ✖	425	425 (for 1 hour)
Aerobic dancing (medium) ★✖	445	222 (for ½ hour)
Running in place or skipping rope (50–60 steps/min.) ★	510	255 (for ½ hour)

Activity	Calories per Hour	Average Calories Used
Downhill skiing ▲✖	595	1,190 (for 2 hours on slope)
Swimming, 5.5 minutes/220 yards ★✖	600	300 (for ½ hour)
Hill climbing ★	600	300 (for ½ hour)
Touch football ✖	600	300 (for ½ hour actual play)
Soccer ▲✖	600	600 (for ½ hour)
Snow shoveling, light	610	305 (for ½ hour)
Jogging, 11 min./mile ★✳	655	327 (for ½ hour)
Cross-country skiing, 12 minute/mile ★✖✳	700	2,800 (for 4 hours)
Basketball, full court ▲✖	750	750 (for 1 hour)
Squash, racquetball ★✖	775	775 (for 1 hour)
Martial arts (judo/karate) ✳	790	395 (for ½ hour)
Running, 7.5 min./mile ★✳	800	400 (for ½ hour)
Ice hockey, lacrosse ★✖	900	900 (for 1 hour)

★ Aerobic exercises

▲ Aerobic only if done continuously

✳ Best strength builders

✖ Good for flexibility

The bigger and more vigorous you are, the more calories your body uses for a given activity. The calories listed here are for the average 158–pound adult. You will lose one pound for every 3,500 calories, as long as you do not change your caloric intake.

The above chart is reprinted through the courtesy of the Center for Science in the Public Interest, 1501 Sixteenth St. NW, Washington, DC 20035.

eight

CUSTOM-BUILT FRAMES AND BICYCLES

*T*hink of a custom-built frame as the bicycle equivalent to a $3,500 Savile Row suit. The framebender takes your measurements, considers the type of riding you do, and forges it in the materials you want. It's much more expensive than the off-the-rack model, but, hey, the shoulders don't droop. (Actually, many framebuilders make their product in standard sizes, but there's still lots of room for customizing.) This is an area in which Italians have always excelled. Americans may be catching up.

Aero Cycles, Inc., 58 North Avenue, Natick, MA 07160, 508/651–3298 * The Trimble Monocoque is an aerodynamic, one-piece carbon fiber/fiberglass enclosed frame that sells for $1,495 (1990).

American Bicycle Manufacturing Corporation, 3102 South Roosevelt Rd., P.O. Box 1245, St. Cloud, MN 56302, 612/251–1641 * Hand-welded, hand-polished aluminum mountain bike frames for the serious racer. They claim that their anodized paint finish is "second in hardness only to diamonds." The company delivers finished bicycles only.

Arctos Machine, P.O. Box 493, Camp Meeker, CA 95419 * Titanium frames for road, mountain, and tandem costing up to $4,000 (1990). Titanium is an alloy of pure titanium, aluminum, and vanadium—durable, light, and expensive. Framebuilder Gary Helfrich says, "I have no stock information. You tell me what you want, and I'll try to come up with a workable design."

Carbonframes, 691 Minna St., San Francisco, CA 94103, 415/431–6315 * Makes the Sapphire™, an all carbon fiber frameset with titanium fittings.

Cicli Masi Inc., P.O. Box 1653, San Marcos, CA 92069 * Steel-alloy racing frames that weigh in at about three-and-a-half pounds.

Color Perfect, Ten Speed Drive Imports, P.O. Box 9250, Melbourne, FL 32902–9250, 407/777–5777 * Custom paint jobs for racing frames.

Columbus, via Dei Pestagalli, 31–20138 Milano, Italy, 011/39–2–504–187 * Fabled steel tubing long used in competition bikes.

Gita Sporting Goods, 12600 Steele Creek Rd., Charlotte, NC 28217 * Gita imports racing-oriented steel frames from such Italian and Europe-based manufacturers as Giordana, Eddy Merckx, Pinarello, and De Rosa. Both road and off-road. Also available as built-up bicycles with Italian components by Cinelli, Vittoria, and Campagnolo.

Hensley Frame Sets, P.O. Box 759, Colstrip, MT 59323, 406/748–4225 * Steel alloy racing frames hand-crafted from $650; tandems from $1,500; complete bicycles from $1,700.

HH Racing Group, 1901 South 13th St., Philadelphia, PA 19148, 215/334–8500 * Hand-brazed steel racing frames for triathlons, track racing, and road racing. Prices range from about $600 to $1,100. Tubebender Harry Havnoonian has been at this since 1976.

Ibis, P.O. Box 275, Sebastopol, CA 95473, 707/829–5686 * Mountain and tandem frames off the shelf or made to order, $375–$2,599 (1990). See also listings under *Mountain Bikes* and *Bicycle Manufacturers*.

Kirk Precision USA, Inc., P.O. Box 866, Menlo Park, CA 94026, 415/329–0622; fax: 415/325–4280 * Not steel, but magnesium frames designed by British engineer Frank Kirk. The promo shows a Cadillac sedan rolling over one of these oddly shaped frames with no damage done. It's not a traditional diamond-shaped frame, but more teardrop-shaped with solid parts instead of tubing. Comes in racing, touring, or mountain-bike styles.

Klein Bicycle Corporation, 118 Klein Rd., Chehalis, WA 98532, 206/262–3305 * Frames-only from aluminum pioneer Gary Klein, who practically invented the form as an MIT grad student project. Mountain and racing frames from $525 to $1,150 (1990).

A BRIEF GUIDE TO BICYCLE FRAME MATERIALS

. . . .

By Douglas Hayduk

Frameset Material Choices: Steel, Aluminum, Titanium, Composites

. . . .

Until this last decade, the cyclist had little choice in selecting a frameset material. With few exceptions, steel was the only tubing on the menu. Now, thanks to a rapid evolution of high-tech developments in the bicycle industry, steel no longer has a monopoly on the market. But consumers may be bewildered about the variety of frame materials now available. The basic categories are alloys of steel, aluminum, titanium, and composites.

Steel: This term describes the iron-based (ferrous) alloys that have reigned over the bicycle industry for a century. Steel is inexpensive, versatile, and easy to fabricate, and is a time-proven metal. There are numerous varieties of steel used for bicycle tubing. Various elements such as carbon, chromium, nickel, manganese, and molybdenum are alloyed with iron to produce different types of steel. Generally, the higher-priced the bicycle, the better the quality and sophistication of steel used. Framesets from steel can cost a hundred dollars up to a thousand dollars. Notable drawbacks to steel are its greater density than the nonferrous metals and composites, and its tendency to corrode if not well coated.

Aluminum: Aluminum is a relatively low-priced metal that is refined from bauxite ore. This lightweight metal (its density is one-third that of steel) is alloyed with other metals such as silicon, magnesium, and zinc to produce alloys that can be drawn into tubing with sufficient mechanical properties and corrosion resistance for bicycles. These tubes are then welded or adhesively bonded together into a frameset. The most apparent feature of aluminum frames is the larger diameter tubing used, as compared to steel. This is necessary to make up for aluminum's lower inherent rigidity. The result is the appearance of a "fat" and heavy frame. However, the frameset will be as light or lighter than a comparable steel frame. Aluminum can be painted similarly to steel or it can be anodized various colors, forming a protective oxide layer in the aluminum. The cost of aluminum framesets is comparable to those of steel.

Titanium: This exotic aerospace metal has recently been used very successfully for bicycle frames. However, it is expensive to refine titanium ore into metal, and production volume of suitable tubing is small. So titanium frames are costly. Tubing used for bicycles is typically an alloy of titanium with aluminum and vanadium for high strength. These titanium alloys have a density only sixty percent that of steel and yet strength equal to or exceeding steel. Framesets costs a thousand dollars or more, and consequently, are found only on "high-end" bicycles. The advantages of this material are its light weight, corrosion resistance, and shock-absorption. Titanium framesets are readily identified by the bare metal appearance. Titanium's excellent corrosion resistance makes painting unnecessary.

Composites: The term "composite" is a general one that describes the combination of two or more materials joined together to make a material with desirable properties. Presently, for bicycles, the term composite usually refers to graphite (carbon) fiber-epoxy resin matrix composites. Most composite framesets are constructed from tubing engineered from these two nonmetals to give adequate strength and yet maintain a lighter weight than steel. Unique to composites is the ability to be tailored into more complex designs than the common diamond-shaped tubular frameset. Graphite epoxy composites can be constructed in nontraditional shapes to put the strength only where needed.

Additionally, composite framesets are well known for their comfort, as they have better shock absorption qualities than all the above-mentioned metals. However, composites are quite expensive. Prices start comparable to those of high-quality steel framesets and run as high or higher than titanium frames.

Composite technology is relatively new and still evolving rapidly. Extensive research and development is being performed to seek new and better composites that may be suitable for bicycle framesets. One example is the metal matrix composite (MMC). These combinations of metals and nonmetals create a superior engineered material.

Douglas Hayduk is a metallurgical product research and development engineer for ASARCO, Inc., in Salt Lake City, Utah. He has been a USCF racer for eleven years and enjoys mountain bike riding and racing. He obtained his B.S. and M.S. degrees in metallurgical engineering from the Colorado School of Mines, Golden, Colorado. He is the author of the book *Bicycle Metallurgy for the Cyclist,* and contributes to various publications on cycling.

Wm. Lewis Imports, Inc., 401 F.M. 685, Suite B203, Pflugerville, TX 78660, 512/251–0088; fax: 512/251–7548 (Order through Colorado Cyclist catalog, 800/688–8600) * Importer of Italian-made frames and forks by Tommasini ($695 to $1,180 in 1990). Hand built in Grosseto, Italy, by Irio Tommasini. Only 1,500 a year are made.

Litespeed, P.O. Box 22666, Chattanooga, TN 37422, 615/238–4999 (fax) * Titanium frames and components for road and mountain bikes.

Marinoni USA Inc., P.O. Box 374, Montgomery Center, VT 05471 * Hand-made goods from a small shop near Montreal that has produced frames for such racers as Steve Bauer and Davis Phinney. Racing frames made from Columbus tubing. Complete bicycles also available.

Medici Bicycle Company, 12465 Mills Rd., Unit B–4, Chino, CA 91710, 714/591–5881; fax: 714/591–6021 * Racing frames that start at $800 for the frame only. Complete bikes begin at $1,050 and go up to $2,700.

Nobilette Cycles, 220 Felch St., Ann Arbor, MI 48104, 313/769–1115 * Framebuilder Mark Nobilette will build either racing (from $675, 1990) or mountain-bike (from $775) to fit your frame.

Peregrine Endurance Racing, P.O. Box 1088, Bend, OR 97709, 503/389–2301 * Titanium frames for racing, off-road, hybrid, and tandem bicycles. Cost: $1,800 to $3,200 (1990).

Phase 3 Cycles, 140 Despatch Dr., East Rochester, NY 14445 716/381–6273 * Chromoly racing frames from $552 to $1,029. Add $125 for custom sizing.

Romani, 43038 Sala Baganza, Parma, Italy (Imported by Iowa Export-Import Trading Company, 601 Locust St., Des Moines, IA 50309, 800/345–0327) * Racing frames forged from Reynolds or Columbus steel-alloy tubing.

Romic Cycle Co. Inc., 4434 Steffani Ln., Houston, TX 77041, 713/466–7806 * Hand-made frames from steel-alloy tubing for road-racing touring, track racing, or mountain biking. Priced from $497 to $1,300 for frame only; $989 to $2,665 for complete bicycles. The craftsman/designer is Ray Gasiorowski, a former racer.

Serotta Sports, Inc., P.O. Box 106, Middle Grove, NY 12850 * Racing frames from $790 to $1,270; custom-sizing $230 extra (1990 prices). Used in Tour de France and other races.

Spectrum Cycles, Inc., Dorney Rd., RD2, Box 59, Breinigsville, PA 18031, 215/398–1986 * Custom-made (using photos, measurements, and descriptions) steel and titanium road frames that weigh as little as 2.9 pounds (but cost $900–$2,500 as of 1990).

Tange USA Corporation, 268–B Lombard St., Thousand Oaks, CA 91362, 805/373–6231 * Chromoly frames and forks used in many expensive factory bikes. Order through bike shops.

Titan Inc., 1784 Crescent, Eugene, OR 97401, 503/683–7163; fax: 503/345–1224 * BMX and mountain-bike frames built from titanium and chromoly.

True Temper Bicycle Tubing, 871 Ridgeway Loop Rd., Memphis, TN 38119, 901/767–9411 * Tubing used in racing frames that have ridden the winning team from the Tour of Italy to the Coors Classic.

Vitus, 5 rue des Echarneaux, Z.I. du Coin, B.P. 223, 42400 Saint-Chamond, France * Racing-oriented chrome-molybdenum steel and composite (carbon manganese/vanadium steel) frames.

J.P. Weigle Cycles, Town St., P.O. Box 265, East Haddam, CT 06423, 203/873–1671 * Racing and mountain bike frames up to $1,350; repairs from $65; painting, $225. The framebuilder, Peter, is a one-man show, "but I still encourage serious phone inquiries."

Zinn, 753 Silverberry Ct., Lafayette, CO 80026 * Framebender Lennard Zinn specializes in tough fits such as 4'11" women and 6'8" men. Uses Columbus, Tange, True Temper, or Reynolds Tubing. Prices start at $549 (1990).

nine

BICYCLE MANUFACTURERS

*O*nly since 1985 or so, mountain bikes have captured more than half the market for new bicycles. That leaves the traditional road bike — the diamond-frame, drop-handlebar, racing-style bike known generically as the "10–speed" for the last two decades — as a fringe occupation for many manufacturers. This is true even for the likes of Raleigh, Peugeot, and Schwinn, who spent the better part of this century cranking out variations of this traditional design.

That said, road bikes still provide a superior ride on anything but the roughest surface. The down-curved handlebars allow for riding in at least four different positions — easier on both the back and the posterior than the bolt-upright, mountain-bike attitude. Intrinsically lighter, and outfitted with high-pressure tires, good road bikes can be a delight for on-road riding through the mountains. (Hill climbing on a mountain bike is more like pushing your bed up a grade.)

Manufacturers seem to have recognized the shortcomings of both the mountain and the road bike and are now producing what they call crossover models. These hybrids combine lightweight frames with tires and rims heavy enough to take a bit of a beating.

Throughout this section we refer to "casual" riders and bikes. In this context, a casual rider is one who occasionally rides five or ten miles on pavement or on a boardwalk. A casual bicycle can generally be recognized by its "safety" brake levers (an extra set bolted on the top of the handlebars that is actually less safe), fake lambswool saddle, and 6–, 10–, or 12–speed gearing. Fine for the casual rider. But don't expect this sort of steed to hold up to frequent long rides, touring, or commutes.

This section also lists manufacturers of recumbent bikes (like pedaling a chaise lounge down the road—many tourists swear by 'em) and other out-of-the-mainstream designs.

HOW TO BUY A BIKE

Venturing into a bicycle store can be intimidating—so many shiny bikes, so much equipment! Do you buy a racing bike with steep angles, one-inch tubulars (also known as sew-ups), and a tiny freewheel? How about a less expensive bike, with steel wheels lacking a quick-release feature? Or there's a fat-tired model that the salespeople point out, detailing its upright handlebars and beefy tubing. Shops also carry what's known as a sport-touring bicycle, one that's touted as appropriate for recreational riding.

The typical bike store is like a candy store—there's an overwhelming selection of bright and colorful goodies. If you think about your needs and what you're interested in spending, when you do finally go into a bicycle store you'll be better able to help them help you. Here are some general guidelines for purchasing a bicycle.

First, remember that most bicycles can last ten or more years, so you may want to spend a little more to ensure you've bought a bicycle that will entice you to pursue bicycling, not discourage you.

Seek out expert advice. It's crucial to find a bicycle store whose staff listens to you and takes time to familiarize you with appropriate models. This is one reason to buy a bicycle in a specialty shop as opposed to a large store that sells everything from toilet paper to fertilizer. The people who staff bicycle stores are knowledgeable; they assemble, maintain, sell, and ride bicycles. They're your best bet for proper fit, and they are eager to have you return. The service you get is an important aspect of bicycle buying. The store you purchase your bicycle from will most likely be the one you return to for other items.

Plan on test riding bicycles. Pedaling a variety of bicycles in various price ranges is one way to see which works best for you. A 21–inch frame in one brand may not fit the same as a 21–inch frame in another. Most stores encourage exploratory rides. So it's best to go bicycle shopping with questions and prepared to ride. Todd Cravens, co-owner of Century Bicycles in Maryland, encourages this approach, saying "You should have an idea of what you want and ask hard questions about fit, warranties, and service after the sale." He supports the idea of taking the bike out for a ride. "You'll get a better feel for how comfortable you can be," he emphasizes.

A store worth its salt will plunk a properly adjusted helmet on your head when you spin out for your ride and offer some cursory instruction on the bike's brakes and handling. (Try getting that level of information from a huge department store.)

Evaluate your cycling interests and needs. Do you plan to ride for recreation? Will you be on trails or roads? Are you hoping to ride on weekends or will you pedal practically every day? Does long-distance cycling interest you? Are you a triathlete who hopes to compete one day? Will you use your bicycle for errands or commuting? Do you live in the city or the country? Do you want to investigate racing? If the bicycle is for a child, will he or she be rough on it? Is it the child's first bicycle? Will he or she be encouraged to ride frequently?

Your answers will help you focus on the most suitable bike for you, and they will help your local bike store address your needs. In general, less expensive bikes (those that are $200 or less) have steel wheels and frames and don't have quick release wheels. Briefly, steel wheels are less forgiving and not as sturdy as aluminum or composite wheels. If you plan on taking the wheels off to store or portage the bike, quick release devices make this easier. You don't need a crescent wrench and the process is less time consuming. Consider, as well, that flat tires are easier to change when they happen on quick release wheels. For many folks, however, inexpensive bikes are adequate if they ride infrequently and don't plan to pursue bicycling as a lifetime activity.

If you're an occasional rider who plans to use dirt roads and city streets, a street bike might be the ticket. A street bike, also known as a hybrid or cross terrain, is a mix between a mountain bike and a touring bike. It offers wider tires than a touring bike and upright handlebars. It can handle the torment most city streets inflict on bicycles and is still lightweight enough to take on longer rides. Its range of gears should help you maintain a good cadence (revolutions per minute—rpm) on the flats and go down low enough to spin smoothly over hills.

Riding offroad is attracting more and more enthusiasts. Throughout the country there are many legal routes, fire roads, and single-tracks to explore. (Refer to "Rules of the Off-Road" in the *Mountain Bike* section for additional pointers.) If off-road riding is your bent, a mountain bike should be your purchase. A mountain bike can make you feel like a kid again. With its fat tires and upright handlebars, it handles gravel, mud, dirt, and all sorts of kid stuff smoothly. It also handles well on city streets, making it popular with cyclists who never take their bicycle offroad. Whether you do or do not plan on hitting the dirt on your mountain bike, enjoy its handling and sturdiness.

Triathletes often choose racing bikes or sport touring models. Racing bikes are designed to help you go faster, although riding one doesn't automatically increase your speed! They have narrow tires and stiffer frames with tighter angles, making them a bit less comfortable for long distances than touring bicycles, for example. The components are generally lighter weight than those found on other models. Some racing bicycles come with tubulars or sew-up tires. These are considered the lightest weight tires, but they are also the most expensive. In general, sew-ups are not as sturdy as other tires. They go flat more readily on gravel or when ridden through glass. Changing a flat tire is a bit trickier too. By the time you get to this stage, however, you'll have undoubtedly mastered the art of changing any tire, whether it be fat or narrow, sew-up or Shrader.

A sport-touring bicycle can answer most recreational cyclists' needs. This style is suitable for commuting, weekend rides, and around town cycling. The sport-touring bicycle has more relaxed angles than a racing bike and at least ten speeds. Most models can easily accommodate a rack and are adaptable for long-distance travel. They are not, however, as comfortable as a true touring bicycle, which is built for miles and miles of touring with panniers, tent, sleeping bag, and other camping equipment.

True touring bikes are becoming rarer and rarer. That's too bad because they offer a great ride and are designed to handle heavy loads and long distances. Touring bikes have relaxed angles and a longer wheelbase. This means that less road shock and fewer bumps are transmitted to the cyclist. The components on touring bikes are supportive of long miles as well. Most touring bikes have what's known as a triple crank. This means that you have three rings up front, which gives you lower gearing options. Most touring bikes have tires of $1\frac{1}{8}$ to $1\frac{1}{2}$ inches wide.

While we've not yet said one word about fit, it's of primary concern. There are some general rules of bicycle fit, but certain types of bikes fit differently than others. The overall recommendation is that you should be able to stand over the top tube of the bicycle and clear it by at least an inch. Note, however, that most experts suggest that you be able to clear the top tube of your mountain bicycle by at least two inches. You should be able to sit comfortably on the bicycle's saddle and reach the handlebars without stretching. And you should be capable of squeezing the brakes, exercising control over the speed of the bicycle. Don't ever buy a bicycle that you think you or your child "will grow into." Someone on a bike that's too big for him or her is an accident waiting to happen. That individual is not as capable of controlling a bicycle and is more likely to flounder than one on a bicycle that fits. For more information on fit, refer to the "Tips on Cycling" in the Appendix and consult salespeople at your local bicycle store. You, too, will become more educated as you test ride several models and brands, discovering for yourself what works best.

Before you leave the store with whatever bicycle you choose, consider upgrading the one or two items that you suspect you might replace soon. Many folks trade up for a better quality saddle, for example. If you do this before you use the standard-issue saddle, you'll get some credit toward the new saddle, which makes it cheaper.

You might also factor into your purchase price a few essential items. Number one, of course, is an approved helmet. (Consult the *Safety* section for more advice.) Other amenities include a water bottle cage, water bottle, pump, and tool kit. The basic tool kit can consist of tire irons, a spare tube, a patch kit, and emergency money. (Note: some cyclists consider a stash of food a permanent component of their "tool" kit.) With a basic tool kit, you'll be able to change a tire easily. Some cyclists prefer cartridges, which are expensive but eliminate the need for a pump.

A bicycle that suits your needs and fits you can last a lifetime. It will provide hours of pleasure, exercise, and fun. As a quick glance on most paths will suggest, warm weather and bicycling are a natural. Maintain your bicycle, and it will be ready for the road or trail whenever you are.

Aero Cycles, Inc., 58 North Ave., Natick, MA 07160, 508/651–3298 * The Trimble Monocoque is an aerodynamic, one-piece carbon fiber/fiberglass enclosed frame that sells for $1,495 (1990).

Bianchi USA Inc., 270 Littlefield, Suite C, South San Francisco, CA 94080, 415/872–1414 * Made in Italy and racing-bred since 1899. Bianchi remains one of the few major manufacturers that still emphasizes road bikes as much as their mountain and crossover models. Also see listing under *Mountain Bike Manufacturers*.

Bike Nashbar, P.O. Box 3449, Youngstown, OH 44513, 800/NASHBAR; fax: 800/456–1223 * Monthly catalog of Nashbar-brand bikes and gear along with other brand names.

Cannondale Corporation, 9 Brookside Place, Georgetown, CT 06829, 800/BIKE–USA or in Pennsylvania or outside lower 48, 814/623–2626 * Pioneer in aluminum-frame "fat tube" bikes. 7 road bikes. See also *Mountain Bike Manufacturers, Clothing,* and *Accessories.*

Cignal, C. Joannou Cycle Co., Inc, 151 Ludlow Ave., Northvale, NJ 07647, 201/768–9050 * Bikes for the "general public," including beach cruisers, a tricycle with a shopping basket, a tandem with a mixte frame for a female stoker, a folding commuter bike, and 18–speed mountain bikes with chromoly frames. Also, stationary bikes.

Cinelli, Italian Bicycle Products Corporation, 10335 Landsbury, Ste. 316, Houston, TX 77099, 713/561–0492 * Laser Rivoluzione Pista is their latest expressionistic road bike made in small numbers in Italy. Like its 7 cousins, built from Columbus tubing, this is a bicycle often seen in races.

Cycle Source, REI, P.O. Box 88125, Seattle, WA 98138–2125, 800/426–4840 * Features Novara bikes and gear (made for REI) along with brand names for a full line of products. REI is a co-op and offers yearly dividends for members.

Diamond Back, WSI, 4030 Via Pescador, Camarillo, CA 93010–9864, 805/484–4450 * 5 models, for criterium racing, fast touring. Also beach cruisers, some with rear derailleurs. Catalog available. See also *Mountain Bike Manufacturers.*

Fila, Westway Sports, Inc., 31878 Camino Capistrano, Ste. 270, San Juan Capistrano, CA 92675, 714/240–1311 * Mountain and racing bikes, including the Torino and the Teton, from a company heretofore known for bike clothes. Tange and chromoly frames. See also *Mountain Bike Manufacturers* and *Clothing.*

Fuji, 118 Bauer Dr., Oakland, NJ 07436, 201/337–1700 * 2 racing, 2 touring, and 3 casual bikes from a manufacturer now more focused (like most) on the mountain/city bike crowd. See also *Mountain Bike Manufacturers.*

Giant Bicycle, Inc., 475 Apra St., Rancho Dominguez, CA 90220, 213/609–3340, 800/US–GIANT * 6 road bikes with carbon fiber or chromoly frames made in Taiwan. See also *Mountain Bike Manufacturers, Accessories,* and *BMX and Kids' Bikes.*

Giordana, Gita Sporting Goods, 12600 Steele Creek Rd., Charlotte, NC 28217 * Italian road, racing, and mountain bikes made from Columbus tubing.

Bruce Gordon Cycles, 613 Second St., Petaluma, CA 94952, 707/762–5601 * Crossover bikes from $1,200–$3,000. Mail-order only. Great reviews in the bike press. See also *Accessories.*

Huffy Corporation, P.O. Box 1204, Dayton, OH 45401, 513/866–6251 * Some casual bikes for adults, but see chapter on *BMX and Kids' Bikes.*

Human Power Research, 600 W. 131st St., New York, NY 10027, 212/505–8276 *
Builds pickup and dump tricycles and pedicabs.

Kestrel, Cycle Composites, Inc., 265 Westridge Drive, Watsonville, CA 95076, 408/724–
9079 * Composite frames and radical geometry in a $1,965 mountain bike. 13 other
models, heavily racing and competition-oriented (e.g, two-time winner in Race Across
America. $1,300–$2,450 (all 1990) includes 5–year frame warranty against everything, including crashes.

Kirk Bicycles USA, Inc., P.O. Box 866, Menlo Park, CA 94026, 415/329–0622; fax:
415/325–4280 * Racing bikes with cast-magnesium alloy frames, $750–$1,100 (1990).

Klein Bicycle Corporation, 118 Klein Rd., Chehalis, WA 98532, 206/262–3305 *
Aluminum pioneer has 2 road bikes, both 19.3 pounds. See also *Mountain Bike Manufacturers* and *Custom-built Frames*.

Miyata Bicycle of America, Inc., 2526 W. Pratt Blvd., Elk Grove Village, IL 60007 * 15
racing, sport, fitness, and touring bikes with chromoly, aluminum, and titanium/carbon
fiber frames from a Japanese manufacturer. Catalog with specs available. See also *Mountain Bike Manufacturers*.

Alex Moulton Bicycles, 20840 Pacific Hwy. South, Seattle, WA 98198–5999, 206/878–
7457 * Hand-built bikes that look straaaange. They combine odd gearing, long seat posts,
suspension, and 20" wheels (BMX size). Mountain, touring, around-town, tandem, recumbent tandem, and performance models, $1,550 to $4,200 (1990). Accessories include a
hand-crank ($750) that augments pedal power. A Moulton bike holds speed record for
conventional riding position: 51.3 mph.

Nishiki, West Coast Cycle, 717 Artesia Blvd., P.O. Box 6224, Carson, CA 90749–6224 *
Company's heart lies in the mountains, but it does make several 14–speed road bikes for
the casual cyclist. Write for catalog.

Peugeot Cycles USA, 555 Gotham Parkway, Carlstadt, NJ 07072 * Medium-priced road
bikes from a company that's been around for a century.

Raleigh Cycle Company, 22710 72nd Ave. South, Kent, WA 98032 * Founded in 1887
by Briton Frank Bowden, the company that made the English racer famous is today most
noted for its Technium bicycles, which combine steel and aluminum tubing in the same
frame. Catalog ($3) lists 9 road bikes, 6 crossovers, and, yes!, a 3–speed with coaster
brakes. See also *Mountain Bike Manufacturers*.

Rand International Ltd., 51 Executive Blvd., Farmington, NY 11735, 516/249–6000;
fax: 516/249–6015 * An adult tricycle, beach cruiser, folding bike, and casual/mountain
bikes among a catalog mostly devoted to kids' bikes. See *BMX and Kids' Bikes*.

Ross Bicycles, 51 Executive Blvd., Farmington, NY 11735, 516/249–600, 800/338–ROSS; fax: 516/249–6015 * Most of line is budget bikes for casual cyclists. See also *Mountain Bike Manufacturers* and *BMX and Kids' Bikes.*

Schwinn Bicycle Company, 217 North Jefferson St., Chicago, IL 60606–1111, 312/454–7400; fax: 312/454–7525 * The 36–page catalog is full of road, mountain, kids', casual, crossover, and beach cruiser bikes with steel, Columbus, aluminum, and oversize framing. The Schwinn Paramount has still won more races than any other bike, but that's mostly from days of old. Latest innovation is a road bike with 26" wheels.

Serotta Sports Inc., P.O. Box 106, Middle Grove, NY 12850, 518/587–9085, 800/338–0998 * Racing models with custom frames from $1,200–$3,350 (1990 prices).

Spectrum Cycles, Inc., Dorney Rd., RD2, Box 59, Breinigsville, PA 18031, 215/398–1986 * Racing-oriented road bikes. 10 steel-frame models ($1,650–$2,650) also available with titanium frames ($3,500–$5,100) (all prices 1990).

Terry Precision Bicycles (for Women), 1704 Wayneport Rd., Macedon, NY 14502, 800/289–8379 * Georgena Terry is an avid cyclist who became frustrated with trying to fit onto men's frames, learned to bend tubes, invented a new design for women, and now mass-produces her designs. The result is 6 road bikes, a touring bike, and a mountain model. The key to comfort for smaller women is a smaller front wheel (24") that allows for different frame geometry.

Trek USA, 801 W. Madison St., P.O. Box 183, Waterloo, WI 53594 * Founded in 1976 in an effort to revive bike manufacturing in the U.S., the company has prospered. 45–page catalog features mountain, road, touring, and crossover bikes with frames made from chromoly, aluminum, and carbon-fiber composite.

Ultra-Mac, 1800 N.E. 179 St., Miami, FL 33162, 305/949–3434 * ULTRA-MAC stands for Ultra Mobile Aerobic Bicycle. 3 models of road bikes ($399–$599, 1990) have 6–speed hand-crank to complement pedal action. Also available in conversion kit—see *Accessories.*

Univega/Sterling, Lawee Inc., 3030 Walnut Ave., Long Beach, CA 90807, 213/426–0474 * Univega offers 7 road bikes with chromoly tubing; Sterling has kids' and casual bikes. See also *Mountain Bike Manufacturers.*

Worksman Cycles, 94–15 100th St., Ozone Park, NY 11416, 718/322–2000 * Designs and manufactures bicycles and tricycles for transporting goods and for urban use.

BUYING A WOMAN'S BIKE

By Suzanne H. Peters

Women often go bicycle shopping with a man because they feel they'll be intimidated by a salesperson and be talked into making the wrong choice. A better strategy is to do your homework. Before you buy a bike, first decide what your needs are, where you plan to ride, and who you might be riding with. Read some magazines and talk to several friends. Most importantly road test any bike before you buy it.

If you want support, you might bring along another woman. What often happens if you go with a man is that the salesperson—usually a man—will talk directly to your male friend, and you'll end up being a third party. If you can find a woman salesperson, she may be more attuned to your sizing needs. Unless you're pretty sure ahead of time what you want, it may be a good idea to resolve not to make a final decision on your first time out.

Choosing the Right Frame

When purchasing a bike, it's essential to get the right size frame. Many people aren't aware that bikes come in sizes. Sometimes women make an incorrect size choice because they insist on a "ladies," frame, which they feel will be easier to mount and dismount. If you plan to install a child carrier, ride during the early months of pregnancy, or wear a dress or skirt, then this may in fact be true. So long as these considerations don't apply and you have no physical limitations (like an arthritic hip), you should probably consider a standard diamond-shaped frame. Aside from offering a greater variety of choices, standard frames typically ride better and the higher bar (or top tube) provides more space for attaching accessories.

Tailoring a Bike to Your Body

No matter which style of bike you choose, be aware that it can be tailored to suit a woman's anatomy. Which differences ought you to be concerned about?

Pelvic structure, of course, is a primary difference. Narrow, long-nosed men's saddles are often uncomfortable for women to ride. Irritation from rubbing against these saddles also seems to increase the chances of getting yeast infections.

It's not just our shape. Our proportions are different too. Our legs tend to be longer and our upper bodies shorter than in men of similar height. You may therefore find that on a bike that allows proper leg extension, you may not be able to reach the handlebars comfortably. This can easily be solved by getting the bike shop to install a handlebar stem with a shorter reach. Hand size is another problem. Many brake levers can be adjusted so they are closer to the handlebar. Otherwise you may want to substitute a set of "compact" levers.

You may need to be firm in getting a shop to agree to make these changes. Be wary of a salesperson who tells you that you will adjust over time to something that doesn't feel right. On the other hand, don't be unreasonable. It will cost the shop something to make these changes and they will likely pass the costs on to you. Until manufacturers begin catering more to women, there doesn't seem to be much of an alternative to getting a shop to make these custom adjustments. In the long run, you'll find the extra expense well worth it.

Suzanne H. Peters lives in Washington, D.C., where she grew up and has ridden bikes all her life. She has toured both the United States and Europe by bike. She began working at Metropolis Bicycles on Capitol Hill in 1986 and is now the store manager.

RECUMBENT BICYCLES
....

Ace Tool & Engineering, P.O. Box 326, 292 West Harrison St., Mooresville, IN 46158, 317/831–8798 * Long wheelbase recumbents.

J. Benditt Co., P.O. Box 589, Feasterville, PA 19047 * Electric recumbent bikes that combine pedaling with volt-driven power to help keep up with traffic. A pollution solution, not a sport bike.

Easy Racers, Inc., 2891 Freedom Blvd., Watsonville, CA 95076, 408/722–9797 * Long wheelbase recumbent.

Participants in Ohio's Tour of the Scioto River Valley (TOSRV). (TOSRVPHOTO by Greg Siple)

FATEBA, Bachmann & Company, Fishmattweg 5, CH–8400 Winterthur, Switzerland * Long wheelbase recumbent.

W.A. Harper, P.O. Box 491871, Redding, CA 96049 * Plans for front wheel drive recumbent.

Wayne Lewis, 10202 E. 206th Street, Arcadia, IN 46030, 317/984–3952 * Recumbent.

Lightning Cycle Dynamics, 1500 E. Chestnut Ct., Lompoc, CA 93436, 805/736–0700 * Short wheelbase recumbent bikes that have been pedalled to speed records and in the Race Across AMerica (relay team covered 2,900 miles in 5 days, 1 hour).

Lightning Cycle, Inc., 3819 Route 295, Swanton, OH 43558 419/826–4056 * Long wheelbase recumbent.

Linear Bicycles, 414 North 4th Street, Guttenberg, IA 52052 * Long wheelbase recumbent.

Tom McGriff, P.O. Box 22444, Indianapolis, IN 46222 * Production tricycle and plans for do-it-yourself version.

Alex Moulton Bicycles, 20840 Pacific Hwy. South, Seattle, WA 98198–5999, 206/878–7457 * See above.

Kurt Pichler Radtechnik, Steinstrasse 23, 7500 Karlsruhe 1, West Germany * Long wheelbase recumbents.

Radius Spezialrader, 16 Frevent Strasser, Muenster 44, West Germany * Long wheelbase recumbent.

Recumbent Vehicle Developments, P.O. Box 589, Featerville, PA 19047 * Recumbents.

Rotator Bicycles, 915 Middle Rincon, Santa Rosa, CA 95409 * Recumbents.

Ryan Recumbents, Inc., 58 Lyle St., Malden, MA 02148, 617/324–1921 * Long wheelbase recumbents.

Thebis International Ltd., 2031 Malaview Ave. #110, Sidney-by-the-Sea, British Columbia, Canada, 604/656–1237 * A 21–speed, recumbent touring tricycle.

University Cyclery, 4007 G. Bellaire Blvd., Houston TX 77025, 713/666–4452 * Recumbent.

Zinn Bicycles, 735 Silverberry Court, Lafayette, CO 80026, 303/666–7749 * Human-powered vehicles and recumbent bikes.

ZZIP Design, P.O. Box 14, Davenport, CA 95017 * Fairings (wind screens) for recumbents.

TANDEMS

. . . .

Burley Design Cooperative, Inc., 4080 Stewart Rd., Eugene, OR 97402, 503/687–1644; fax: 503/687–0436 * 4 models of tandems, including a mountain bike.

Cignal, C. Joannou Cycle Co., Inc, 151 Ludlow Ave., Northvale, NJ 07647, 201/768–9050 * See above.

Fat Chance Cycles, P.O. Box 218, Somerville, MA 02143, 617/625–4922 * Offers a tandem mountain bike with steel frame. See also listing under *Mountain Bike Manufacturers*.

Fisher Mountain Bikes, 140 Mitchell Blvd., San Rafael, CA 94943 * Makes 11 models of mountain bikes, including a tandem.

Ibis Cycles, P.O. Box 275, Sebastopol, CA 95473, 707/829–5615 * Hand-made tandems, $2,500–$3,900 (1990). They'll tailor the production bikes to your wants or custom-make you one from scratch. See also *Mountain Bike Manufacturers* and *Custom-built Frames*.

Lippy Cycles, Inc., 60265 Faugarwee, Bend, OR 97702, 503/389–2503 * 2 models of performance-oriented tandems. Will make to order for $2,800 (1990).

Alex Moulton Bicycles, 20840 Pacific Hwy. South, Seattle, WA 98198–5999, 206/878–7457 * See above.

Mountain Goat Cycles, P.O. Box 3923, Chico, CA 95927, 916/342–4628; fax: 916/342–4647 * $900–plus (1990 prices) singles and tandems that feature Tange tubing. Write for catalog.

Rodriguez Tandems, Evergreen Bicycle Products, 1314 N.E. 56th St., Seattle, WA 98105, 206/527–9145 * Aluminum-frame road and mountain-style tandems. $3,200–$3,700 (1990 prices).

Santana Cycles, Box 1205, Claremont, CA 91771 * 8 models of tandems plus a new single mountain bike built with Nivacrom, a new steel-alloy tubing from Columbus.

KEEPING YOUR BIKE: HOW TO LOCK IT AND PREVENT THIEVERY

You've carefully selected it, maintained it, and enjoyed it. Now, if you're going to keep that bicycle, you've got to lock it properly. One of the more discouraging things for a cyclist is having a bicycle—an extension of that person—stolen.

Locking your bicycle safely is simple, but it's no longer as easy as it once was. Today's thieves are determined and daring. One lock, even the legendary tough U-shaped lock, is no longer sufficient. What you need is a locking system. In brief, plan on buying two good locks and fastening your bicycle to something sturdy.

Most people rely on a combination of locks to achieve their locking system. Shop for a reputable U-shaped lock and add a "collar" or cuff to it. These are usually available at most bike stores and serve to strengthen a weak link that some U-shaped locks possess. Put the U-shaped lock through the main frame of your bicycle and around a fairly immoveable object. Sturdy bike racks are good, as are some types of signs and parking meters. Be certain that whatever object you've chosen as an anchor cannot be moved or lifted. That means avoiding slender trees (thieves have been known to saw down trees) or signs which can be easily yanked from the ground.

The U-shaped lock is part one of your system, the immoveable object is part two, and part three is another sturdy lock. This lock can be a cable fastened by a padlock or combination lock. If you have quick release wheels, thread the cable through one wheel and the frame and then around a post or sign. Your goal is to create a bicycle that is not easy to take. With two obstacles in the way of a quick steal, a potential thief is bound to look elsewhere.

Unfortunately, some scoundrels are determined to whittle away at your bicycle or its accessories. If your bicycle has a quick release saddle, consider removing it. Otherwise, a double-locked bicycle with no saddle will surely await you when you return. If you leave a pump, tool kit, or lighting system attached to your bicycle, these items may not be there when you return. It may be necessary for you to take almost every removable object with you.

One last warning: don't relax your vigilance when you park your bike for the night. While some bicycle owners are able to leave their bicycles out on the lawn overnight, most of us must take more precautions. In general, the first rule is never to leave a locked bicycle out overnight. There's just too much temptation and time to break those locks. Even an unlocked bicycle on a second- or third-floor porch is vulnerable. In some cities, unlocked bicycles in apartment storage units or garages just scream, "Steal me!"

Just remember, if that bicycle is going to remain yours and yours alone, take a few minutes to secure it. That ensures you'll have many miles of pleasure riding it, instead of many miserable moments filing a police report on its theft.

ten

Mountain Bike Manufacturers

*N*ine out of ten mountain-bikers never venture off the road. But that doesn't mean that millions of mountain bikes, like so many 10–speeds in the '70s, are moldering away in garages. Given the appalling condition of many city and suburban roads, the mountain bike is an ideal around-town vehicle. The 18 speeds, oversize brakes, and upright handlebars translate to safety features in traffic.

The 10 percent of mountain-bikers who do go off-road must follow proper off-road etiquette. Ride only where it is legal. (See Jim Hasenauer's "Rules of the Off-Road." Also check out "Mountain Bike Trails and Parks" in the *Tours* section and the books on mountain bikes in the *Books and Periodicals* section for suggestions about where to ride.) Remember other users when you're scooting down a trail. Unless mountain bikers play by the rules today, there won't be any trails to use tomorrow.

MANUFACTURERS
. . . .

Allsop, P.O. Box 23, Bellingham, WA 98227, 800/426–4303 * Frame-mounted suspension system looks like a giant tongue bolted to the top tube.

L.L. Bean, Inc., Freeport, ME 04033, 800/221–4221 * The venerable mail-order sporting goods company offers 4 models of mountain bike by mail (a pair of 21–speeds, a 12–speed "urban cruiser," and an 18–speed "junior" model with a 15–inch frame. ($225–$535, 1991). Also a 21–speed cross-bike ($399, 1991) for city riding. Call for a catalog.

Bianchi USA, 270 Littlefield, Suite C, South San Francisco, CA 94080–2303 * Bianchi has professed concern about environmental damage from mountain bikes; hence in 1990 the Italian company promised to donate money to a conservation group when you buy one of their 8 models with Ritchey components.

Bridgestone Cycle USA Inc., 15003 Wicks Blvd., San Leandro, CA 94577, 800/366–2453 * More than a dozen models with chromoly frames, narrow saddles, toe clips, and presta valves. Available in drab colors only—Bridgestone doesn't think flashy hues and riding in the wilderness go together. Write for their interesting "Mountain Bike Handbook" with tips on riding technique and off-road etiquette.

Cambria Bicycle Outfitters, 1920 Main St., Cambria, CA 93428, 805/927–5510 or 927–5174. They call themselves "your mountain bike cycletherapist. . . . a little, out-of-the-way country bike shop that just happens to specialize in high-end, hard-to-find, techno-zip mountain bikes and components." The mimeographed catalog is full of good humor; the mountain bikes go up to $2,200. Send them your photo and get a free gift "worth at least 5 bucks, maybe more."

Cannondale Corporation, 9 Brookside Place, Georgetown, CT 06829, 800/BIKE–USA or in Pennsylvania or outside lower 48, 814/623–2626 * Pioneer in aluminum-frame "fat tube" bikes and maker of aluminum mountain bikes since 1984. Nine models plus three crossovers. See also *Bicycle Manufacturers, Clothing,* and *Accessories.*

Diamond Back, WSI, 4030 Via Pescador, Camarillo, CA 93010–9864, 805/484–4450 * 9 models from casual to competition-oriented. Some have 21–speed gearing and aluminum alloy frames. Write for catalog ($2).

Fat Chance Cycles, P.O. Box 218, Somerville, MA 02143, 617/625–4922 * 5 basic, made-in-USA mountain models (one tandem) with steel frames. Send for (a very clever) catalog.

Fila, Westway Sports, Inc., 31878 Camino Capistrano, Suite 270, San Juan Capistrano, CA 92675, 714/240–1311 * 3 mountain bikes and 2 crossovers from a clothing company. Ad copy shows *really great* environmental sensitivity: "Ride where there are no others. You are the individual." How about, "Ride off a cliff"? See also *Bicycle Manufacturers* and *Clothes.*

Fisher Mountain Bikes, 140 Mitchell Blvd., San Rafael, CA 94943 * Gary Fisher was a mountain bike pioneer of the 1970s. His company now offers 11 models, including a tandem and a racer with full front and rear suspension.

Fuji, 118 Bauer Dr., Oakland, NJ 07436, 201/337–1700 * The top of the line is titanium; 10 other mountain, city, and all-terrain bikes have conventional diamond frames with chromoly tubing.

A participant on a Bikecentennial group mountain bike tour
(Bikecentennial Photo)

Giant Bicycle, Inc., 475 Apra St., Rancho Domingo, CA 90220, 213/609–3340, 800/US–GIANT * 8 mountain bikes with chromoly frames (1 steel) and 4 crossovers (2 chromoly, 2 steel). See also *Bicycle Manufacturers, Accessories,* and *BMX and Kids' Bikes.*

GT All Terra Bicycles, 17800 Gothard St., Huntington Beach, CA 92647, 714/841–1169 * Frames, mountain bikes, kids' mountain bikes, crossovers in 12 models.

Haro Designs, 2225 Faraday Ave., Suite A, Carlsbad, CA 92009, 619/438–4812 * 12 models for off-road, recreation, and crossover riding; some have oddball frame geometry for maximum clearance when the going gets rough, some have aluminum forks, and some 21–speed gearing.

RULES OF THE OFF-ROAD: WHERE CAN I RIDE THIS THING?

....

By Jim Hasenauer

They say that mountain bikes can go anywhere, and that's technically true. Mountain bicyclists have traveled the world's great mountain ranges, traversed blistering deserts, raced across Alaskan snowpack, explored sandstone wildlands, and returned home to climb the stairs of office buildings in urban canyons.

Yeah, but where can *you* ride? That's a different story. The two main prerequisites for finding routes suitable for you are to know your technical riding abilities and the policies of local land managers. Ignore the former and you're in over your head; tired, cold, out of food and water, and a worry to your loved ones. Ignore the latter and you're busted.

Worse, you'll contribute to the perception that mountain bicyclists are outlaws who won't follow rules. That doesn't help the rest of us who are committed to expanding our riding opportunities, so be aware that you've got responsibilities. As Sergeant Phil Esterhaus used to say, "Hey, hey, hey; let's be careful out there."

Here's how to find the great riding in your own territory or when travelling:

Find the locals. The holy tradition of mountain biking is based on the word-of-mouth sharing of sweet trails, remote beauty and endurance runs. Most mountain bicyclists learned about rideable trails from more experienced riders. These knowledgeable locals are your best source for riding information. Call the local mountain bike club (phone numbers are in the newsletter of the International Mountain Bicycling Association (IMBA), *NORBA News,* and several mountain bike magazines). Tell them what you are looking for—rides for a beginner, intermediate, or expert. Ask them if maps are available or what some of the hazards and points of confusion might be. Give them your itinerary. Heck, they may volunteer to show you the local turf, or if you're really lucky, there will be a club ride and you'll get invited.

Find the pro shops. Retail bicycle dealers are not only a great source of information, they're often the center of riding networks. Many of the best mountain bike shops have regular show-and-rides which expose all comers to local territory. Some of the shops will have a schedule with rides rated for difficulty. To find the pro shops outside of your area, check out retailers in the IMBA newsletter or look for NORBA dealer members. These are committed to mountain bicycling as a sport. They sponsor races and support land access. Promoting responsible riding is in their best interests and they'll help you if they have the time. Buy something from them.

Find the guidebooks. In the last few years, several companies have produced some excellent guidebooks and maps especially for mountain bicyclists. If you live in a popular bicycling area, there's probably one available. Most of these are written by knowledgeable locals so you're buying a hard copy of someone's riding experience. You'll find these in the bike stores or at local backpacking and camping equipment shops. Guidebooks and maps written for hikers are helpful, but may include trails closed to bicyclists. Make sure you check with the proper agencies before assuming you can ride the hiking trails.

Find the land manager. Many mountain bicyclists don't know who owns the wild, undeveloped land they so enjoy. Sometimes it's park land and other times it's privately owned. These look the same, but there's a world of difference. Public land managers will probably have some kind of a policy for bicycle use on their lands. They may have maps, interpretive brochures, decent organized rides with leaders,

(Stephen Simpson Photo/Courtesy Baja Expeditions, Inc.)

and other amenities. Private land owners may tacitly allow mountain bike use (many states give preferred liability status to those who allow recreational trail use), but you're on your own. Some private owners will shoot first and ask questions later. Get to know which ones are which.

Help keep the trails open. Because mountain bicycling is relatively new, policies are still in their early stages and they frequently change. It's the rider's responsibility to know local rules. Don't make excuses.

Every rider represents the sport. If you're prepared, responsible, and in control, you're a credit. If you're riding rudely, illegally, or out of control, you're a detriment. It's that simple. Always follow the IMBA Rules of the Trail:

- Ride on open trails only.
- Control your bicycle.
- Always yield the trail.
- Never spook animals.
- Leave no trace.
- Plan ahead.

Jim Hasenauer is a professor of speech communication at California State University Northridge. He is on the Board of Directors of the International Mountain Bicycling Association (IMBA) and the steering committee of the Concerned Off-Road Bicyclists Association (CORBA) in Los Angeles. He is the author of *Mountain Biking the Coast Range, Guide 7: The Santa Monica Mountains*.

Ibis, P.O. Box 275, Sebastopol, CA 95473, 707/829–5686 * Hand-made and custom-made (in the USA) mountain and tandem models. $1,240–$3,800 (1990). See also *Custom-built Frames* and *Bicycle Manufacturers*.

Jazz Bicycle Company, 108 W. Madison St., P.O. Box 183, Waterloo, WI 53594 * Mountain bikes for the barely post-BMX set, with popsicle colors dashed with a bit of Jackson Pollock and ad lines like: "Radical. With extreme components and a design that never questions your authority. Radical is your ticket to ride—to the wild side." Oddly enough, these 5 models (fairly conventional stuff except for the paint job, $230 and up as of 1990) are made by respectable old Trek. It's like finding out that your father plays bass for the Dead Kennedys.

Klein Bicycle Corporation, 118 Klein Rd., Chehalis, WA 98532, 206/262–3305 * Aluminum pioneer has 5 mountain models that weigh in closer to racing bikes (23.5/24.5 pounds). $995–$2,500 (1990). See also *Bicycle Manufacturers* and *Custom-built Frames*.

Kona/Brodie, The Bicycle Group, 1122 Fir St., Blaine, WA 98230, 206/332–5384 * Their Kona line features 8 models with sloping top tubes ($399–$2,695, 1990). Kona's sister, Brodie, features 5 hand-built and titanium-frame models ($195–$1,850, 1990). Brodie framesets available separately ($795–$1,095, 1990). Brodie (named for Vancouver framebuilder Paul Brodie) also makes forks, toe clips, tires, and stems. The Bicycle Group says its bikes are made with extremes of weather in mind.

Mammoth Mountain Bike, Division of Tracker Designs, P.O. Box 217, Cardiff-by-the-Sea, CA 92007, 800/325–BIKE * Aluminum and steel-frame models with acute-angle, diamond frame geometry, and elevated chainstays for rock clearance.

Marin Mountain Bikes, 999 Andersen Dr., San Rafael, CA 94901, 415/459–7557 * 8 performance-oriented models with a titanium-frame top-of-the-line. Many feature sloping top-tubes and neon paint jobs.

Miyata Bicycle of America, 2526 W. Pratt Blvd., Elk Grove Village, IL 60007, 312/228–5450 * 8 mountain and 3 crossover bikes in chromoly, aluminum, and carbon fiber/titanium from a Japanese manufacturer. Catalog with specs available for $3. See also *Bicycle Manufacturers*.

Mongoose Bicycles, 23879 Madison Ave, Torrance, CA 90505 * A dozen models from a titanium/chromoly racing number to around-town "fitness" bikes with computers built into their upright handlebars. See also *BMX and Kids' Bikes*.

Montague BiFrame, P.O. Box 1118, Cambridge, MA 02238, 617/491–7200 * Invented by a Washington, D.C., architect and manufactured by Schwinn, the "Biframe" is an 18–speed mountain bike that neatly folds in half (thanks to quick releases on the seat tube) to fit into a trunk, closet, carry bag, etc.; thus creating a "real" bike (rather than a dinky, small-wheel folding bike) that happens to fold. (Price: $420, 1990.)

Moots Cycles, 1136 Yampa Ave., P.O. Box 772480, Steamboat Springs, CO 80477, 800/288–0667 * Hand-built mountain bikes from $895 (1990) built for flexibility; e.g., the front fork has double dropouts so you can change the rake of the wheel, and the brake mounts accommodate 2 different types of braking systems so you can switch to skinny racing tires. Framebuilder Kent Erikson also uses varying sizes of tubing for riders of different weights. Their symbol is Mr. Moots, a strange little cartoon alligator astride a mountain bike.

Mount Shasta Bicycle Company, 420 W. Crowther Ave., Placentia, CA 92670 * Race, recreational, and crossover bikes in 12 models with chromoly or high-tensile steel frames.

Mountain Goat Cycles, P.O. Box 3923, Chico, CA 95927, 916/342–4628; fax: 916/342–4647 * $900–plus (1990 prices) singles and tandems that feature Tange tubing. Write for catalog.

Nishiki, West Coast Cycle, 717 Artesia Blvd., P.O. Box 6224, Carson, CA 90749–6224 * Latest models feature aluminum/chromoly frame combos with funky geometry. Current catalog lists 18 models, some made in USA. See also *Bicycle Manufacturers.*

Offroad Bicycles, 115 Front St., Box 1040, Woonsocket, RI 02895 * 6 Pro-Flex models feature 2–piece frames with rear suspension designed for heavy-duty off-road work. Also specialize in small bikes for riders 5'4" and under.

Onza, 6960 Aragon Circle, Ste. 3, Buena Park, CA 90620 * Mountain bike racing components, including bar ends, chain rings, tires, seat posts.

Raleigh Cycle Company, 22710 72nd Ave. South, Kent, WA 98032 * The Mountain Technium combines aluminum and steel tubing in same frame. Latest catalog (44 pp., $3) lists 6 models of mountain bikes.

Reflex Sports Products, 605 North Challenger Road, Salt Lake City, UT 84116, 800/632–8605 * Aluminum, carbon-fiber, and alloy frames on 5 made-in-USA models.

Ritchey USA, 1320 Hancock St., Redwood City, CA 94020, 415/368–4018; fax: 415/368–0840 * Another mountain bike legend in his own time.

Ross Bicycles, 51 Executive Blvd., Farmington, NY 11735, 516/249–600, 800/338–ROSS; fax: 516/249–6015 * 12 models, budget ($199) to expensive ($1,200). See also *Bicycle Manufacturers* and *BMX and Kids' Bikes.*

Saint Tropez, Aerolite, 51–B Mercedes Way, Edgewood, NY 11717, 516/254–0075 * Several beach cruisers, 8 mountain bikes, some with chromoly tubing. See also *BMX and Kids' Bikes.*

Santana Cycles, Box 1205, Claremont, CA 91771 * The tandem specialists now make a mountain-bike tandem plus a single mountain bike with Nivacrom, a new steel-alloy tubing from Columbus.

Scott USA, P.O. Box 2030, Sun Valley, ID 83353, 208/726–7267 * A dozen models in Racing, Sports, Adventure, and Cross Country series. Designed and tested in Idaho's Sawtooth Mountains.

Sekai, Norco Products, USA, 18201 Olympic Ave. South, Tukwila, WA 98188 * 10 models with conventional and funky frame geometry; also "Mini" and "Micro" models for younger off-roaders.

Specialized, 15130 Concord Circle, Morgan Hill, CA 95037–5037, 408/779–6229 * 10 models of mountain bikes. See also *Bicycle Manufacturers* and *Accessories.*

Titan Inc., 1784 Crescent, Eugene, OR 97401, 503/683–7163; fax: 503/345–1224 * BMX and mountain-bike frames built from titanium and chromoly.

Univega Bikes, Lawee Inc., 3030 Walnut Ave., Long Beach, CA 90807, 213/426–0474 * Crossover and all-terrain bikes for off-road, city riding, and general recreation. 7 models.

Wilderness Trail Bikes, 134 Redwood Ave., Corte Madera, CA 94925, 415/924–9632 * Mountain bike components from brake pads to chromoly frames. Send for brochure.

Yeti Cycles Inc., 5330 Derry Ave., Unit Q, Agoura Hills, CA 91301, 818/707–4498; fax: 818/707–4217 * "Racing only" framesets ($1,050–$1,700, 1990) made from carbon fiber. Handmade. The catalog prints this disclaimer: "This vehicle is designed and manufactured for competition only. It does not conform to federal vehicle safety standards and operation on public streets, roads or highways is illegal."

Yokota Cycles, USA, Inc., 1620–D Berryessa Rd., San Jose, CA 95133 * 12 models for competition, off-road, city, and crossover riding. Top models use Tange tubing.

eleven

BICYCLE ORGANIZATIONS

*W*hatever your cycling interest or level of skills, there's an organization or club for you. Recumbent cyclists, off-road bikers, long-distance enthusiasts, and others can all find groups guaranteed to offer support and information. Some organizations are advocacy-oriented, working to improve conditions for all cyclists throughout the country. Others are more regional and may offer information on grassroots events and nearby rides. Many sponsor national races and gatherings, which provide opportunities for like-minded cyclists to get together and have fun. There are also organizations whose sole purpose is to collect data useful for the bicycling industry.

You may find it worthwhile to join one or more of the organizations and clubs listed below. Many offer a newsletter or magazine filled with information on bicycle touring and social events. In addition to finding new bicycling friends, you'll be supporting the sport you love.

NATIONAL ORGANIZATIONS

. . . .

American Association of State Highway and Transportation Officials (AASHTO), 444 N. Capitol St. NW, Ste. 225, Washington, D.C. 20001, 202/624–5800 * The folks that build the roads. Publishes *Guide for the Development of New Bicycle Facilities.*

American Bicycle Association (ABA), P.O. Box 714, Chandler, AZ 85244, 602/961–1903 * Organizes BMX races. See *BMX and Kids' Bikes* section.

American Youth Hostels, Inc., P.O. Box 37613, Washington, D.C. 20013–7613 * Runs tours, accommodations, and events across the continent. See *Tours* section.

A Bicycle Built for One World, P.O. Box 460697, San Francisco, CA 94124, 415/ 378–5973 * Organization of blind and sighted people who promote peace, cycling, and tandems.

Bicycle Federation of America, 1818 R St., NW, Washington, D.C. 20009 * Promotes all aspects of cycling, runs conferences, publishes *Pro Bike News,* conducts research on safety and bike-trail planning.

Bicycle Forum, Box 1776, Missoula, MT 59807 * Advocacy arm of Bikecentennial. See below.

Bicycle Helmet Safety Institute, 4611 Seventh St. South, Arlington, VA 22204, 703/486–0100 * Document center associated with the Washington Area Bicyclist Association. Has consumer brochures.

Bicycle Institute of America, 1818 R St. NW, Washington, D.C. 20009 * Trade and industry supported association that promotes bicycling.

Bicycle Market Research Institute, 1443 Beacon St., Suite 517, Boston, MA 02146 * Compiles and disseminates bicycle industry data and information.

The Bicycle Network, P.O. Box 8194, Philadelphia, PA 19101 * Promotes cycling as a means to improve the environment and promote world peace. Publishes cycling calendar and *The Network News,* a cycling clipping service.

Bicycle Parking Foundation, Box 7342, Philadelphia, PA 19101 * Founded in 1988 to help make communities more "bike-friendly." Designs and builds bike-parking racks, runs seminars and workshops, and works with employers.

Bicycle Ride Directors Association of America, Randy Ice, SCOR Productions, 12200 E. Washington Boulevard, Suite O, Whittier, CA 90606, 213/945–6366 * Organization of

ride (not race) directors concerned with schedules, liability, insurance, safety, sanctioning, promotions, more.

Bicycle Transportation Action, 308 E. 79th St., New York, NY 10021 * Encourages
bicycle transportation.

BikeAid '91, 333 Valencia St., Suite 330, San Francisco, CA 94103, 800/431–4480 or
800/827–4480 * Organizes 5– to 9–week transcontinental rides to benefit Overseas
Development Network, an organization that addresses global poverty. Riders must raise
at least $2,000 each before trips begin.

Bikecentennial, P.O. Box 8398, Missoula, MT 59807 * National nonprofit group
promotes touring, leads extended bike tours, sells cycling goods through catalog. See listing in *Tours* section.

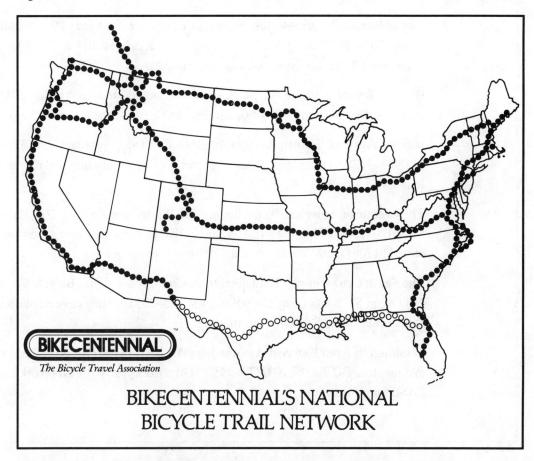

BIKECENTENNIAL
The Bicycle Travel Association

BIKECENTENNIAL'S NATIONAL
BICYCLE TRAIL NETWORK

Canadian Cycling Association, 1600 James Naismith Dr., Gloucester, Ontario K1B
5N4, Canada, 613/748–5629 * Has information on racing and touring, and maps.

BIKE TO WORK DAY

Thinking of organizing a Bike to Work Day? Here are a few resources to get you started. Some of the most successful Bike to Work Days have been planned months in advance, but even if your club or organization can't start early, these pointers should help.

Bicycling to Work Seminar Information, U.S. Environmental Protection Agency (EPA), 410 M St. S.W., Washington, DC 20460, 202/382–2671 * Free information with SASE.

City of Boulder, Attn.: Bicycle Program Coordinator, P.O. Box 791, Boulder, CO 80306, 303/441–3216 * Boulder has organized successful Bike to Work Days for years. Send SASE for information on their manual.

How to Organize a Bike Day, U.S. Environmental Protection Agency (EPA), 410 M St. S.W., Washington, DC 20460, 202/382–2671 * 17–page brochure free with SASE.

Human Powered Transit Association, P.O. Box 1552, Reseda, CA 91337–1552, 818/988–7728 * Organization that promotes bicycle commuting and bicycle safety seminars.

The League of American Wheelmen, 6707 Whitestone Rd., Ste. 209, Baltimore, MD 21207, 301/944–3399 * L.A.W. has a Bike to Work Day promotion kit, which costs $15 for L.A.W. members and $20 for non-members.

The Santa Cruz County Transportation Commission, attn.: Bicycle Coordinator, 701 Ocean St., Santa Cruz, CA 95060, 408/425–2951 * They have a Bike to Work Day manual. Send SASE for information.

Washington Area Bicyclist Association (WABA), 1819 H St. NW, Ste. 640, Washington, DC 20006, 202/872–9830 * Organizes yearly Bike to Work rally. Send SASE for information.

Classic Bicycle & Whizzer Club of America, 35769 Simon, Fraser, MI 48026, 313/791–5594 * A network of bicycle collectors.

Cycle America, P.O. Box 547, Capitola, CA 95010, 408/476–7773 * Committed to building a transcontinental bike path.

Energy Conservation Coalition, 1525 New Hampshire Ave. NW, Washington, DC 20036, 202/745–4874 * Promotes responsible energy use. Organizes the Clean Motion Campaign, which encourages bicycling and carpools.

Environmental Action, 1525 New Hampshire Avenue, NW, Washington, D.C. 20036 * Lobbying group concerned with cycling as environment-friendly transportation.

Family Cycling Club, FCC R.R. 8, Box 319E, Glenwood Dr., Bridgeton, NJ 08302, 609/451–5104 * Promotes cycling together as a family.

Human Powered Transit Association, P.O. Box 1552, Reseda, CA 91337–1552, 818/988–7728 * Organization that promotes bicycle commuting and bicycle safety seminars.

Institute for Transportation and Development Policy, Bikes Not Bombs, 1787 Columbia Rd. NW, Washington, DC 20009, 202/387-1434 * Provides bicycles and other forms of environment-friendly "appropriate technology" to developing nations.

International Bicycle Fund, 4887 Columbia Drive S., Seattle, WA 98108–1919, 206/628–9314 * Promotes bicycles in transportation planning, economic development, and safety education.

International Human Powered Vehicle Association, P.O. Box 51255, Indianapolis, IN 46251 * Nonprofit group that promotes human-powered vehicles, boats, and planes, "as well as encouraging public interest in physical fitness and good health through exercise."

International Mountain Bicycling Association, Rt. 2, Box 303, Bishop, CA 93514, 619/387-2757 * Promotes open trails through responsible and environmentally sound bicycling. Produces *Land Access Alert*.

International Randonneurs, 727 N. Salina St., Syracuse, NY 13224 * Organization for long-distance cycling; sponsors the qualifying rides throughout the U.S. for the Paris-Brest-Paris event.

League of American Wheelmen (L.A.W.), Suite 209, 6707 Whitestone Rd., Baltimore, MD 21207 * Membership organization of cycling enthusiasts; runs events, publishes brochures and magazine.

National Bicycle Center, P.O. Box 3401, Redmond, WA 98073–3401, 206/869–5804 * Working to build an international sporting facility and educational and recreational programs related to bicycling.

BICYCLE COORDINATORS

Many states, cities, and communities employ bicycle coordinators and other staff to promote bicycling in their area by providing information on local resources and routes. The partial list below offers a representative sampling. For a more comprehensive list, contact the Bicycle Federation of America (1818 R St. NW, Washington, DC 20009). The Federation's fifty-four-page publication, *Bicycle Coordinators and Programs: Why, How, and Who,* includes a ten-page list of bicycle coordinators and is available for $7.50.

Boulder Bikeways Coordinator, Boulder County Public Works, P.O. Box 471, Boulder, CO 80306, 303/441–3900.

Colorado Bicycle/Pedestrian Coordinator, Colorado Dept. of Highways, 4201 E. Arkansas Ave., Denver, CO 80222, 303/757–9982.

Eugene Bicycle Coordinator, Traffic Division, 858 Pearl St., Eugene, OR 97401, 503/687–5298.

Florida State Bicycle/Pedestrian Coordinator, Dept. of Transportation, 605 Suwanee St., MS 19, Tallahassee, FL, 32399–0450, 904/488–4640.

Georgia Bicycle Coordinator, Dept. of Transportation, 2 Capitol Square, Rm. 345, Atlanta, GA 30334, 404/656–5351.

Madison Bicycle Coordinator, Madison Dept. of Transportation, Madison Municipal Bldg., Madison, WI 53707, 608/266–6625.

New York Bicycle Program Manager, Governor's Traffic Safety Committee, Empire State Plaza, Swan St. Bldg., Rm. 414, Albany, NY 12228, 518/473–3662.

New York City Bicycle Coordinator, NYC Dept. of Transportation, Bureau of Planning and Research, 40 Worth St., Suite 1035, New York, NY 10012, 212/566–0751.

North Carolina Bicycle Coordinator, P.O. Box 25201, Raleigh, NC 27611, 919/733–2804.

Ohio State Bicycle Coordinator, Ohio Dept. of Transportation, 25 S. Front St., Rm. 418, Columbus, OH 43215, 614/644–8660.

Oregon Bikeway Program Manager, Oregon Dept. of Transportation, Rm. 200, Transportation Bldg., Salem, OR 97310, 503/378–3432.

San Diego Bicycle Coordinator, Engineering and Development Dept., 1222 First Ave., MS 405, San Diego, CA 92101, 619/236–7214.

Seattle Bicycle Coordinator, Engineering Dept., 708 Municipal Bldg., 600 4th Ave., Seattle, WA 98104, 206/684–7583.

Tucson Bicycle Coordinator, Transportation Dept., P.O. Box 27210, Tucson, AZ 85726, 602/791–4641.

National Bicycle Dealers Association, 129 Cabrillo St. #201, Costa Mesa, CA 92627 * Trade organization.

National Bicycle League, 211 Bradenton Ave., Suite 100, Dublin, OH 43017, 614/766–1625 * Sanctioning body for BMX and freestyle racing. See *BMX and Kids' Bikes* section.

NORBA, National Off-Road Bicycling Association, c/o U.S. Cycling Federation, 1750 E. Boulder St., Colorado Springs, CO 80909, 719/578–4717. Governs off-road racing in the U.S. See *Racing* section for more information.

Pacelines, 43 Upton St., Boston, MA 02118 * National cycling network for gay and lesbian cyclists and their friends.

Pedal for Power Associates, P.O. Box 898–F, Atkinson, NH 03811, 800/762–2453 or 603/382–2188 * Ride for charity from Los Angeles to Boston, or Maine to Florida.

Perimeter Bicycle Association, 630 N. Craycroft, Ste. 127, Tucson, AZ 85711, 602/745–2033 * Encourages perimeter bicycling events and sponsors the University Physicians El Tour de Tucson, billed as America's largest perimeter bicycling event. Philosophy is "One learns more by going around than by cutting across."

Rail Riders, P.O. Box 1480, Hillsboro, NH 02118 * Group that rides modified bicycles on abandonned rail tracks.

Rails to Trails Conservancy, 1400 16th St., NW, Washington, DC 20036 * National organization that promotes conversion of disused railroad beds to hiker/biker trails. Sells guides to trails.

Recumbent Bicycle Club of America, 427–3 Amherst St., Suite 305, Nashua, NH 03063 * Organization for recumbent enthusiasts.

Round-the-World Cyclists Registry, P.O. Box 1065, Station A, Toronto, Ontario M5W 1G6, Canada * Gathers information on cyclists who go around the world.

Sport for Understanding, 3501 Newark St. NW, Washington, DC 20016, 202/966–6800 * Sends young athletes, including cyclists, abroad as part of a sports exchange program.

The Tandem Club of America, c/o Jack Goertz, 2220 Vaness Dr., Birmingham, AL 35242 * Sponsors regional events, publishes newsletter.

Triathlon Federation, P.O. Box 1010, Colorado Springs, CO 80901, 719/630–2255 * Sanctions multi-sport races.

Ultra Marathon Cycling Association, 4790 Irvine Blvd., #105–111, Irvine, CA 92720, 714/544–1701 * Organizes the Race Across AMerica (RAAM) and provides information about long-distance cycling events. Publishes newsletter.

U.S. Bicycling Hall of Fame, 1 West Main St., P.O. Box 8535, Somerville, NJ 08876, 908/725-0461 * Honors individuals and other contributors to bicycling. Publishes newsletter.

U.S. Cycling Federation, 1750 E. Boulder St., Colorado Springs, CO 80909, 719/578–4581 * Oversees amateur racing and Olympic training. See *Racing* section for more information.

U.S. National Senior Sports Association, 14323 S. Outer Forty Rd., Ste. N300, Chesterfield, MO 63017, 314/878–4900 * Encourages older athletes and sponsors the U.S. National Senior Sports Classic.

United States Professional Cycling Federation, Rt. 1, Box 1650, New Tripoli, PA 18066, 215/298–3262 * Governing body for professional cycling in the U.S.

Velo Quebec, 3575 boul. Saint-Laurent, Bureau 310, Montreal, Quebec H2X 2T7, Canada, 514/847–8687 * English and French speaking advocacy organization. Sponsors conferences and Le Tour de L'Ile de Montreal, considered the largest bicycle tour in the world.

The Wheelmen, c/o 1708 School House Ln., Ambler, PA 19002 * For antique bicycle aficionados. Sponsors regional and national meets.

Women's Cycling Network, P.O. Box 73, Harvard, IL 60033 * Promotes women's participation in the cycling sport and industry. Organizes conferences.

Women's Sports Foundation, 342 Madison Ave., Ste. 728, New York, NY 10173, 212/972–9170 * Supports women's athletic activities, including bicycle racing.

BICYCLE CLUBS

In almost every state, cyclists have banded together to form a diversity of clubs. Interested novices can encounter clubs with memberships of under twenty or over three thousand. Many clubs print an informal flyer to let prospective cyclists know about rides and events. Other clubs publish professional magazines and newsletters that include cycling tips. Most clubs offer weekend rides appropriate for riders of all skills. Joining up with an area club is a great way to discover routes off the beaten track and those great places to eat that cyclists just seem to know about. Since many of these clubs are staffed by eager and overworked volunteers, when you request information, enclose a self-addressed stamped envelope for their convenience.

Alabama

Birmingham Bicycle Club, P.O. Box 55283, Birmingham, AL 35255, 205/956–0897.

Coastal Coaster Bicycle Club, c/o The Bike Shop, 2417 Ross Clark Circle, Dothan, AL 36301.

Montgomery Bicycle Club, c/o Ted Molnar, P.O. Box 17743, Montgomery, AL 36117.

Spring City Cycle Club, P.O. Box 2231, Huntsville, AL 35804, 204/533–5900.

Alaska

Iditasport, 201 Danner, Ste. 155, Anchorage, AK 99518, 907/344–4505 * Promotes the Iditarod and also Iditasport, which allows racers to choose bicycling, skiing, or walking (or any combination) to cover 200 miles.

Mountain Bikers of Alaska, 2900 Boniface Parkway #657, Anchorage, AK 99504 * Rides, events, newsletter.

Arizona

Arizona Bicycle Bunch, P.O. Box 10583, Scottsdale, AZ 85271.

Arizona Bicycle Sports Association, P.O. Box 30776, Tucson, AZ 85751 * Events, time trials.

Arizona Bicycle Club, c/o Tom Beatson, 6007 N. 10th Way, Phoenix, AZ 85014.

Bicycle Harbor-Tempe, 6316 S. Price, Tempe, AZ 85282 * Sponsors thrice-weekly rides in Phoenix area.

Greater Arizona Bicycling Association (GABA), Phoenix Chapter, P.O. Box 3132, Tempe, AZ 85281 * Sponsors the Grand Canyon to Mexico—Almost Across Arizona Bicycle Tour.

Off-Road Bicyclists of Arizona (ORBA), (formerly Arizona Mountain Bike Racers Association), 9542 E. Duncan, Mesa, AZ 85207 * Rides and races.

Perimeter Bicycling Assn. of America, 630 N. Raycroft St., Suite 127, Tucson, AZ 85711 * See "National Organizations" above.

Scottsdale Bicycle Club, c/o Jim Murphy, 8418 E. Paradise Dr., Scottsdale, AZ 85040.

Team Banzai, c/o Loose Spoke Bicycle Shop, 1529 S. Milton, Flagstaff, AZ 86001 * Sponsors rides.

Arkansas

Arkansas Bicycle Club, P.O. Box 55112, Little Rock, AR 72225.

Fort City Cyclists, P.O. Box 10474, Fort Smith, AR 72917, 501/782–7383.

California

Accord/Quick Release Bicycle Club, Box 48464, Los Angeles, CA 90048, 213/871–6959 * Encourages women racers.

Almaden Cycle Touring Club, c/o 6559 Camden Ave., San Jose, CA 95120.

BGF (Billy Goat Racing, Biking for Good Reasons), P.O. Box 66, San Juan Capistrano, CA 92693 * Mountain bike rides, land-access issues, races, time trials.

Bicycle Center, 1206 S. Pacific Coast Highway, Redondo Beach, CA 90277.

Bicycle Touring Club of Solvang, c/o 1669 Maple Ave. #21, Solvang, CA 93463.

Bicycle Trails Council of Marin, P.O. Box 13842, San Rafael, CA 94913–3842 * Land-access activists for S.F. suburb.

Bicycle Trails Council of the East Bay, P.O. Box 9583, Berkeley, CA 94709–0583 * Land-access activists for mountain bikes.

California Association of Bicycling Organizations (CABO), P.O. Box 2684, Dublin, CA 94568.

Chico Velo Cycling Club, P.O. Box 2285, Chico, CA 95927.

Competition Mountain Riders, Encino, CA, 818/784–3137 * Mountain bike training/racing club.

Concerned Off-Road Bicycle Group (CORBA), 15236 Victory Blvd., Box 149, Van Nuys, CA 91411 * Land-access activists, rides, newsletter.

Davis Bike Club, 610 3rd Ave., Davis, CA 95616, 916/756–3540 * Does the famous (and challenging) Davis Double Century.

Desert Off-Road Bicycle Group, 2150 Deborah, Palm Springs, CA 92262 * Mountain bike club.

Different Spokes, Box 14711, San Francisco, CA 94114, 415/282–1647 * Club for gay and lesbian cyclists and their friends. Sponsors AIDS Bike-a-thon.

Europa Mountain Bikes, 6409 Van Nuys Blvd., Van Nuys, CA 91401, 818/989–BIKE * Organized rides.

Freemont Freewheelers Bicycle Club, Box 1089, Fremont, CA 94538.

Fresno Cycling Club, P.O. Box 11531, Fresno, CA 93773.

Haven Cyclery, 6331 Haven Ave., Suite 13, Alta Loma, CA 91701 * Sponsors rides.

Grizzly Peak Cyclists, P.O. Box 9308, Berkeley, CA 94709.

Laguna Rads, P.O. Box 4283, Laguna Beach, CA 92652, 714/494–8396 * Mountain bike rides.

La Mirada Bike Shop, 14225 E. Imperial Highway, La Mirada, CA 90638, 213/946–3394 * Sponsors mountain bike rides.

Los Angeles Wheelmen, 2212 Charnwood Ave., Alhambra, CA 91803.

Marin Cyclists, P.O. Box 2611, San Rafael, CA 94912.

Mount Wilson Trail Association, P.O. Box 80370, San Marino, CA 91108 * Builds mountain bike trails.

North Ranch Mountain Bikers, 1527 Larkfield Ave., Westlake Village, CA 91362 * Club rides.

Northern California/Nevada Cycling Association, 1153 Delaware St., Berkeley, CA 94702, 415/526–5983 * Publishes complete listing of regional races. Promotes all types of competitive racing.

Orange County Wheelmen, c/o P.O. Box 219, Tustin, CA 92681.

Ortega Mountains Trail Maintenance Association, 29471 Riviera Ct., San Juan Capistrano, CA 92675.

Pasadena Mountain Bike Club, P.O. Box 6101, Altadena, CA 91001 *Rides, events, land-access issues.

Recon Riders, 725 Sunny Manor Way, Santa Rosa, CA 95401 * Mountain bike rides, newsletter, events.

Responsible Organized Mountain Pedalers (ROMP), P.O. Box 1723, Campbell, CA 95009–1723 * Land-access issues, rides, newsletter.

Reyes Peak Mountain Bike Club, 1274 Rubicon Ave., Ventura, CA 95401, 805/647–2585 * Rides, newsletter.

Riverside Bicycle Club, P.O. Box 55160, Riverside, CA 92517–0160.

Rough Riders, Box 382, Sacramento, CA 95812.

Sacramento Rough Riders, c/o Adventure Mountain Bikes, 11282 Pyriles Way, Rancho Cordova, CA 95670 * Rides, land-access issues.

San Diego Bicycle Coalition, P.O. Box 34544, San Diego, CA 92103.

San Diego Wheelmen, c/o 4138 Vermont St., San Diego, CA 92103.

San Fernando Valley Bicycle Club, P.O. Box 4053, Chatsworth, CA 91313.

San Luis Obispo Bicycle Club, Inc., P.O. Box 1585, San Luis Obispo, CA 93401.

Santa Cruz Cycling Club, 414½ Soquel Ave., Santa Cruz, CA 95060.

Scenic Cycling Appreciation Brotherhood (SCAB), c/o Michael's Bicycles, Newbury Park, CA 91320, 805/498–6633 * Sponsors weekend rides.

SCOR Cardiac Cyclists Club, 12200 E. Washington Blvd., Suite O, Whittier, CA 90606.

SDSU Mountain Bike Club, Aztec Center, 5300 Campanile Drive, San Diego, CA 92182.

Section One Trails Club, c/o Bike Doctor, 14141 Imperial Hwy., La Mirada, CA 90638, 213/944–2933.

SHARE, 3535 E. Coast Highway, Suite 226, Corona Del Mar, CA 92625 * Mountain-bike club, land-access issues, rides.

Sierra Club, Angeles Chapter, 3550 W. 6th St. Suite 321, Los Angeles, CA 90020 * Has bicycle touring committee.

Sunnyvale Competitive Cycling Club, c/o Spectrum Cycles, 1683 Hollenbeck Ave., Sunnyvale, CA 94087.

Team Big Bear, P.O. Box 3965, Big Bear Lake, CA 92315, 714/866–4448 * Mountain bike club.

Trail Center, 4898 El Camino Real, #205A, Los Altos, CA 94022, 415/968–7065 * Trail-building, maintenance, info.

Ukiah Wheelers Bike Club, P.O. Box 171, Calpella, CA 95418.

Veloce Santiago, c/o Santiago Cycle Sports, 13762 Newport Ave., Tustin, CA 92680.

Wandervogel Bicycle Touring Association, 2364 Mountain Brook Dr., Hacienda Heights, CA 91745, 818/336–5590 * Sponsors the yearly Death Valley by Moonlight.

Western Wheelers Bicycle Club, P.O. Box 518, Palo Alto, CA 94302.

The Wheelmen, 616 N. Vincent, West Covina, CA 91790.

Women's Mountain Bike & Tea Society (WOMBATS), P.O. Box 757, Fairfax, CA 94930 * Off-road group for women. Publishes newsletter; sponsors events and rides.

Colorado

Aspen Cycling Club, c/o Erik Skarvan, 617 E. Cooper, Aspen, CO 81611, 303/925–4365 * Rides, races, events.

Colorado Heart Cycle Association, P.O. Box 10743, Denver, CO 80210, 303/278–1359.

Denver Bicycle Touring Club, Box 9873, Denver, CO 80201, 303/933–3063.

Strada Bicycle Club, P.O. Box 2513, Colorado Springs, CO 80901, 719/632–0342.

Team Evergreen, P.O. Box 3804, Evergreen, CO 80439.

Telluride Sports, 226 W. Colorado Ave., Telluride, CO 81435, 303/728–3501 * Racing team.

Connecticut

Central Connecticut Cycling Club, 27 Lillian Dr., Trumbull, CT 06611.

Coalition of Connecticut Cyclists, P.O. Box 121, Middletown, CT 06457, 203/434–9864.

Eastern Bloc, c/o Dave Williams and David Lombardi, Simsbury, CT 06070, 203/525–7974 * Racing club.

Farmington Valley Mountain Bikers, c/o The Bicycle Cellar, 532 Hopmeadow St., Simsbury, CT 06070.

Pequot Cyclists, P.O. Box 505, Gales Ferry, CT 06335.

Southern Connecticut Cycle Club, P.O. Box 51, New Haven, CT 06501.

Spokespeople, 37 Canner St., #2–R, New Haven, CT 06511.

Delaware

Delaware Friends of Bikecology, c/o Lou Marino, 802 N. Broom St., Wilmington, DE 19806.

Delmarva Bicycle Club, 1404 Forrest Ave., Dover, DE 19901.

Diamond State Bicycle Club, P.O. Box 1729, Dover, DE 19903.

White Clay Bicycle Club, 4960 S. Raintree Court, Wilmington, DE 19808 * Rides, newsletter, events.

District of Columbia

National Capital Velo Club, Box 14004 Ben Franklin Station, Washington, DC 20024.

Potomac Area Council, American Youth Hostels, 1017 K St. NW, Washington, DC 20001.

Potomac Pedalers, P.O. Box 23601, L'Enfant Plaza Station, Washington, DC 20024, 202/363–8687 * One of the largest clubs in the U.S. Has a plethora of rides in Maryland and Virginia.

Washington Area Bicyclist Association, 1819 H St. NW, #640, Washington, DC 20006, 202/872–9830 * 1,000–member commuter lobbying group for trails, lanes, and commuter rights also sponsors rides and charity events.

The Wayfarers, c/o Tom Pendleton, P.O. Box 73408, Washington, DC 20056.

Florida

Arlington Bicycle Club, 1025 Arlington Rd., Jacksonville, FL 32211.

Bicycle Club of Homestead, P.O. Box 0416, Homestead, FL 33064.

Boca Raton Bicycle Club, c/o 1087 SW 28th Ave., Boynton Beach, FL 33426.

Caloosa Riders, P.O. Box 870, Ft. Myers, FL 33901.

Capital City Cyclists, P.O. Box 4222, Tallahassee, FL 32315.

Everglades Bicycle Club, P.O. Box 430282, Miami, FL 33143.

Fat of the Land, 1208 S. Gadsden St. #1, Tallahassee, FL 32301, 904/561–0662 * Rides, events, newsletter.

Flat Mountain Cycle Club, c/o Benjamin Cyclery, 110 Tamiami Trail South, Naples, FL 33940, 813/649–1661 * Rides, land-access issues.

Florida Bicycle Association, c/o 210 Lake Hollingsworth #1707, Lakeland, FL 33803.

Florida Freewheelers, Inc., P.O. Box 547201, Orlando, FL 32854.

North Florida Bicycle Club, P.O. Box 14294, Jacksonville, FL 32238.

Ocala Cycling Club, P.O. Box 6036, Ocala, FL 32678.

Pedalers of Gainesville, Gainesville, FL, 904/375–5972 * Weekly rides.

Pensacola Freewheelers Bicycling Club, c/o 60 Star Lake Dr., Pensacola, FL 32507.

Sarasota Bicycle Club, 4318 Rockefeller Ave., Sarasota, FL 33481.

South Broward Wheelers, P.O. Box 5022, Hollywood, FL 33083.

Georgia

Chattanooga Bicycle Club, Rt. 1, Box 1319, Flintstone, GA 30725, 615/842–4719.

Emerald City Bicycle Club, c/o 507 Cardinal Dr., Dublin, GA 31021.

Mountain Outdoor Expeditions, P.O. Box 86, Ellijay, GA 30540.

Southern Appalachian Mountain Biker Association, 577 Martina Dr., Atlanta, GA 30305 * Rides, newsletter, events.

Southern Bicycle League, P.O. Box 1360, Roswell, GA 30075, 404/594–8350.

Southern Cyclists, P.O. Box 2554, Statesboro, GA 30458, 912/764–8585.

Southern Off-Road Bicycle Association, P.O. Box 1191, Decatur, GA 30031 * Land-access issues, trail building, rides.

Hawaii

Hawaii Bicycling League, P.O. Box 4403, Honolulu, HI 96812, 808/732–5806.

Mauka Bike Club, 1248 Mokuhano St., Honolulu, HI 96841 * Mountain bike rides, races, newsletter.

Idaho

Holiday Sports, 126 W. Main, Grangeville, ID 83530 * Organizes mountain bike rides.

Illinois

Argonne Bicycle Club, P.O. Box 303, Argonne, IL 60439.

Arlington Road Club, Arlington Heights, IL, 312/253–7700 * Sunday rides.

Aurora Bicycle Club, P.O. Box 972, Aurora, IL 60507.

Bicycle Club of Lake County, P.O. Box 521, Libertyville, IL 60048.

Bike Psychos, P.O. Box 652, Oak Lawn, IL 60454.

Blackhawk Bicycle/Ski, P.O. Box 6443, Rockford, IL 61125.

Central Illinois Cyclists, P.O. Box 892, Mattoon, IL 61938.

Chicagoland Bicycle Federation, P.O. Box 64396, Chicago, IL 60664.

De Kalb Bicycle Club, P.O. Box 192, De Kalb, IL 60115.

Elmhurst Bicycle Club, P.O. Box 902, Elmhurst, IL 60126.

Evanston Bicycle Club, P.O. Box 1981, Evanston, IL 60204.

Folks on Spokes Bicycle Club, Box 824, Homewood, IL 60430.

Illinois Valley Wheelmen, 6518 N. Sheridan Rd., Peoria, IL 61614.

Jacksonville Bicycle Club, P.O. Box 33, Jacksonville, IL 62651.

Joilet Bicycle Club, P.O. Box 2758, Joliet, IL 60436.

McLean County Wheelers, P.O. Box 947, Bloomington, IL 61762.

Mississippi Valley Singletrackers, On Two Wheels Inc., 2018 16th St., Moline, IL 61265, and, 1801 E. Kimberly, Davenport, IA * Mountain bike rides.

Oak Park Cycle Club, Box 2331, Oak Park, IL 60302.

Prairie Bicycle Club, P.O. Box 115, Urbana, IL 61801.

Spoon River Wheelmen, P.O. Box 353, Canton, IL 61520–0353.

Wheeling Wheelmen Bicycle Club, P.O. Box 581–D, Wheeling, IL 60090.

The Wheelmen, Marion Gerling, 2418 Lakeshore Drive, Highland, IL 62249 * For collectors of antique bicycles.

Indiana

Bloomington Bicycle Club, P.O. Box 463, Bloomington, IN 47402 * Sponsors the Hilly Hundred.

Calumet Crank Club, P.O. Box 2202, Valparaiso, IN 46384.

Central Indiana Bicycling Association (CIBA), 4215 S. Eaton Ave., Wanameker, IN 46239.

Maple City Bicycling Club, P.O. Box 55, Laporie, IN 46350.

Michiana Bicycling Association, P.O. Box 182, Granger, IN 46530.

Southern Indiana Wheelmen, 111 W. Highway 131, Jeffersonville, IN 47130.

Terre Haute Touring Cyclists, 2535 N. Ninth, Terre Haute, IN 47804.

Three Rivers Velo Sport, Box 11391, Fort Wayne, IN 46857.

Wabash River Cycle Club, 360 Brown St., West Lafayette, IN 47906.

Wheel People Bicycle Association, R.R. 1, Box 164, Galveston, IN 46932.

Iowa

Another Dam Bike Club, c/o 1302 Robin St., Knoxville, IA 50138.

Bicyclists of Iowa City, P.O. Box 846, Iowa City, IA 52240.

Bike Burlington, P.O. Box 1135, Burlington, IA 52601.

Central Iowa Cyclists, 923 S. 12th Ave. W., Newton, IA 50208.

Des Moines Cycling Club, P.O. Box 2190, Des Moines, IA 50301, 515/255–7638.

Dubuque Bicycle Club, c/o Dept. of Recreation, Bunker Hill Dr., Dubuque, IA 52001.

Grinnell Bicycle Club, P.O. Box 298, Grinnell, IA 50112, 515/236–6128.

Hawkeye Bicycle Club, c/o Secretary, P.O. Box 223, Cedar Rapids, IA 52406, 515/365–6487.

Iowa Valley Bicycle Club, 113 S. 19th St., Marshaltown, IA 50158.

Keokuk Bike Club, P.O. Box 161, Keokuk, IA 52632.

Mississippi Valley Singletrackers, On Two Wheels Inc., 2018 16th St., Moline, IL 61265, and, 1801 E. Kimberly, Davenport, IA * Mountain bike rides.

North Iowa Touring Club, 112 Winnebago Way, Forest City, IA 50436, 515/435–4482.

Quad Cities Bicycle Club, P.O. Box 3575, Davenport, IA 52808.

Rainbow Cyclists, P.O. Box 2463, Waterloo, IA 50704, 319/291–6826.

Riverbend Bicycle Club, P.O. Box 6205, Clinton, IA 52732.

Siouxland Cyclists Inc., P.O. Box 3142, Sioux City, IA 51102.

Kansas

Hutchinson Head Winds, P.O. Box 12, Hutchinson, KS 67504, 316/663–4321.

Johnson County Bicycle Club, Box 2203, Shawnee Mission, KS 66201.

Kaw Valley Bicycle Touring Club, P.O. Box 4474, Topeka, KS 66604.

Leavenworth Bicycle Club, c/o 800 N. 12th St., Leavenworth, KS 66048.

Oz Bicycle Club of Wichita, c/o 2127 N. Sunridge, Wichita, KS 67235.

Kentucky

Bluegrass Wheelmen, P.O. Box 1397, Lexington, KY 40591.

Chain Reaction Cycling Club, c/o Bike World, 830 Joe Clifton Drive, Paducah, KY 42001 * Rides, newsletter, events, races.

Danville Off-Road Cyclists (DORCS), 126 N. Third St., Danville, KY 40422, 606/236–3596 * Mountain bike club.

Kentucky Trail Men, 1103 S. First St., Louisville, KY 40203, 502/581–0336 * Mountain bike club.

Louisville Wheelmen, P.O. Box 35541, Louisville, KY 40232, 502/456–5835.

Louisiana

Baton Rouge Bicycle Club, P.O. Box 253, Baton Rouge, LA 70821.

Bayou Ramblers, c/o P.O. Box 1175, Bastrop, LA 71220.

Cajun Cyclist, Pack and Paddle, 601 Pinhook Rd. East, Lafayette, LA 70503.

Crescent City Cyclists, P.O. Box 6095, Metairie, LA 70009.

Lake City Cyclists, P.O. Box 7303, Lake Charles, LA 70606.

Ped'lin Around, 538 Alamo St., Lake Charles, LA 70601, 318/433–8312 * Breakfast rides, newsletter.

Shreveport Bicycle Club, P.O. Box 1163, Shreveport, LA 71163, 318/861–7067.

Maine

Casco Bay Bicycle Club, c/o 7 Chamers Rd., Cape Elizabeth, ME 04107.

Maine Freewheelers, P.O. Box 2037, Bangor, ME 04401.

Maryland

Baltimore Bicycle Club, P.O. Box 5906, Baltimore, MD 21208.

Capital Cycle Challenge Club, 14 Newberry Ct., Gaithersburg, MD 20879.

Chesapeake Wheelman, P.O. Box 4344, Baltimore, MD 21239.

College Park Area Bicycle Coalition, P.O. Box 1035, College Park, MD 20740 * Lobbies for bicycle transportation routes and trails.

College Park Bicycle Club, Box 468, College Park, MD 20740.

Cumberland Valley Cycling Club, P.O. Box 711, Hagerstown, MD 21740.

Eastern Shore Velo Club, P.O. Box 393, Centerville, MD 21617.

Frederick Pedalers Bicycle Club, P.O Box 1293, Frederick, MD 21701.

Freestate Derailleurs, 4424 Worth Place, Baltimore, MD 21236.

Heartside Bicycle Touring Club, P.O. Box 512, Abingdon, MD 21009.

Maryland Association of Bicycle Organizations, 10353 Maypole Way, Columbia, MD 21044.

National Capital Velo Club, 4021 Wexford Dr., Kensington, MD 20895.

Oxon Hill Bicycle Club, Box 18081, Oxon Hill, MD 20745.

Potomac Pedalers Touring Club, P.O. Box 23601, Washington, DC 20026 * See District of Columbia above.

Salisbury Bicycle Club, c/o 708 Walnut St., Pocomoke City, MD 21851.

Salisbury State Bicycle Club, c/o 1101 Camden Ave., Salisbury, MD 21801.

The Velodrome Project, Inc., 7218 Garland Ave., Takoma Park, MD 20912.

Massachusetts

Boston Area Bicycle Coalition, P.O. Box 1015, Cambridge, MA 02142.

Boston Road Club, 16 Unity Ave., Belmont, MA 02178.

Charles River Wheelmen, 19 Chase Avenue, West Newton, MA 02165 * Large club with annual New Year's Day ride and numerous centuries.

Franklin-Hampshire Freewheelers, RFD 2, Two Mile Rd., Amherst, MA 01002.

Nashoba Valley Pedalers, P.O. Box 2398, Acton, MA 01720.

Seven Hills Wheelmen, Box 24, Greendale Station, Worcester, MA 01606.

Michigan

Albion Bicycle Club, 25031 "D" Dr. S., Homer, MI 49245, 517/629–6002.

Ann Arbor Bicycle Touring Society, P.O. Box 2854, Ann Arbor, MI 48106.

Bicycle Coordination Council, P.O. Box 801, Flint, MI 48501.

Cascades Cycling Club, Box 446, Jackson, MI 49204.

Cherry Capital Cycling Club, c/o 520 Highland Park Dr., Transverse City, MI 49684.

Clinton River Riders, 36558 Moravian, Mount Clemens, MI 48043, 313/792–4040.

Cycling Saddlemen Cycling Club, P.O. Box 2449, Dearborn, MI 48123, 313/928–5253.

Downriver Cycling Club, P.O. Box 488, Flat Rock, MI 48134.

League of Michigan Bicyclists, c/o P.O. Box 16201, Lansing, MI 48901.

Monroe County Cycling, P.O. Box 172, Monroe, MI 48161, 313/242–0876.

Rapid Wheelmen, P.O. Box 1008, Grand Rapids, MI 49501, 616/452–2453.

Team Yogurt Dirt Dogs, c/o The Highwheeler, 76 E. 8th, Holland, MI 49423, 616/396–6084 * Mountain bike club.

Three Oaks Spokes, 110 N. Elm, Three Oaks, MI 49128 * Sponsors Apple Cider Century.

Tri-City Cyclists, P.O. Box 2156, Bay City, MI 48707.

Tri-County Bicycle Association, P.O. Box 13001, Lansing, MI 48901.

West Michigan Spokes Folks, 1790 Roberts St., Muskegon, MI 49442.

White Lake Area Footracing Association, Box C, Whitehall, MI 49461–0903, 616/894–8052 * Organizes charity rides in Michigan.

Minnesota

American Youth Hostels, Minnesota Council, 2395 University Ave. West, Suite 302, St. Paul, MN 55114.

Big River Bicycle Club, P.O. Box 1157, Winona, MN 55987.

Itascatur Club, 101 N. Main, Park Rapids, MN 56470.

Mountain Magic ATB Club, c/o Tim Callen, 27 Northeast 1st Ave., Glenwood, MN 56334 * Rides, education.

Twin Cities' Tandem Club, c/o 5232 Edenmoor St., Edina, MN 55435.

Mississippi

Cycles Plus Cycle Club, 220 Main St., Bay Saint Louis, MS 39520, 601/467–1706.

Golden Triangle Bicycle Club, P.O. Box 9174, Columbus, MS 39705.

Le Fleur's Bluff Bicycle Club, P.O. Box 515, Jackson, MS 39205, 601/956–2106.

Natchez Bicycle Club, c/o 332 Main St., Natchez, MS 39120.

Tupelo Bicycle Club, c/o 1143 W. Main St., Tupelo, MS 38801.

Missouri

Columbia Bicycle Club, 2711 Raintree Ct., Columbia, MO 65201.

Kansas City Bicycle Club, P.O. Box 412163, Kansas City, MO 64141, 816/741–5122.

Kirksville Bicycle Club, 218 W. Clark, La Plata, MO 63549.

Mountain Bike Club, 2728 S. Second St., St. Louis, MO 63118, 314/771–2486 * Rides, racing, tours.

Ozark Area/American Youth Hostels, 7187 Manchester Rd., St. Louis, MO 63143–2441, 314/644–4660.

Springbike Bicycle Club, 609 E. Greenwood, Springfield, MO 65807.

Velo Girardeau, P.O. Box 974, Cape Girardeau, MO 63702.

Montana

Helena Bicycle Club, P.O. Box 4682, Helena, MT 59601.

Missoula Bicycle Club, P.O. Box 8903, Missoula, MT 59807, 406/542–2607.

Nebraska

Omaha Pedalers Bicycle Club, Box 648, Downtown Station, Omaha, NE 68101.

Nevada

Northern California/Nevada Cycling Association, 1153 Delaware St., Berkeley, CA 94702, 415/526–5983 * See California above.

Reno Wheelmen, P.O. Box 12804, Reno, NV 89510.

New Hampshire

Dirty Dog Mud Club, P.O. Box 103, Ashland, NH 03217, 603/536–3655 * Mountain bikers concerned with land access, rides.

Granite State Wheelmen, 16 Clinton St., Salem, NH 03079 * Sponsors Seacoast Century.

The Wheelmen, c/o 2 Charbonneau St., Hudson, NH 03051.

New Jersey

Bicycle Touring Club of North Jersey, c/o 28 Wedgewood Dr. #42, Verona, NJ 07044.

Central Jersey Bicycle Club, P.O. Box 2202, Edison, NJ 08818.

Jersey Shore Touring Society, P.O. Box 8581, Red Bank, NJ 07701.

Morris Area Freewheelers, P.O. Box 331, Lake Hiawatha, NJ 07034.

Outdoor Club of South Jersey, P.O. Box 1508, Riverside, NJ 08075.

The Peddler of Long Branch, 200 Ocean Ave., Long Branch, NJ 07740, 201/229–6623 * Organizes rides.

Princeton Freewheelers, P.O. Box 1205, Princeton, NJ 08542.

Shore Cycle Club, P.O. Box 492, Northfield, NJ 08225.

South Jersey Wheelmen, c/o P.O. Box 2705, Vineland, NJ 08360.

Western Jersey Wheelmen, c/o P.O. Box 230–B, Philhower Rd., Lebanon, NJ 08833.

New Mexico

Cruces Cactus Cyclists, c/o Brad Adam, 700 S. Telshor #1012, Las Cruces, NM 88001, 505/521–1686 * Rides, clinics, newsletter.

Enchanted Circle Wheelers, P.O. Box 868, Red River, NM 87558.

New Mexico Wheelmen, 5705 Royal Oak Place NE, Albuquerque, NM 87111.

New Mexico Touring Society, 3301–6 Monroe NE, Albuquerque, NM 87111.

Roadrunners Cycling Club, 237 Canada Way, Los Alamos, NM 87544.

San Juan Cyclist, 657 Maple St., Farmington, NM 87401 * Club.

Sangre De Cristo Cycling Club, c/o Steve Frothingham, St. John's College, Santa Fe, NM 87501, 505/984–8769 * Ice-cream rides, races, clinics, land-access lobbying for mountain bikes.

New York

Bicycle Commuters of New York, 5 Beekman St., New York, NY 10038.

Country Cycle Club, One Willowbrook Rd., White Plains, NY 10605.

Crystal City Mountain Bike Club, 242 Decatur St., Corning, NY 14830, 607/962–2617 * Rides, newsletter.

Fat Apple, 244 E. 85th St. #1G, New York, NY 10028, 212/439–9016; fax: 212/865–2811 * New York City's mountain bike association.

Huntington Bicycle Club, P.O. Box 322, Huntington Station, NY 11746.

Long Island Bicycle Club, c/o 15 Hemlock Dr., Roslyn, NY 11576.

Mid-Hudson Bicycle Club, P.O. Box 1727, Poughkeepsie, NY 12601.

Mohawk-Hudson Wheelmen, P.O. Box 5230, Albany, NY 12205, 518/393–3475.

New York Bicycle Club, P.O. Box 199, Cooper Station, New York, NY 10276.

Rochester Bicycle Club, P.O. Box 10100, Rochester, NY 14610, 716/473–8041.

Staten Island Bicycling Club, P.O. Box 141016, Staten Island, NY 10314.

Suffolk Bicycle Riders, P.O. Box 404, Saint James, NY 11780.

Transportation Alternatives, 494 Broadway, New York, NY 10012, 212/941–4600.

North Carolina

Blue Ridge Bicycle Club, P.O. Box 309, Asheville, NC 28802.

Cape Fear Cyclists, P.O. Box 3644, Wilmington, NC 28406.

Carolina Tarwheels, P.O. Box 111, Durham, NC 27701, 919/688–3458.

Catawba Valley Cyclists, P.O. Box 4241, Gastonia, NC 28053.

North Carolina Bicycle Club, P.O. Box 32031, Raleigh, NC 27622.

Piedmont Flyers, P.O. Box 5032, Winston-Salem, NC 27143, 919/768–6408.

Piedmont Pedalers, 744 Springdale, Statesville, NC 28677, 704/873–9743.

Tarheel Cyclist, Inc., P.O. Box 35392, Charlotte, NC 28235 * Club.

Triad Wheelers Bicycle Club, P.O. Box 9812, Greensboro, NC 27429, 919/855–5540.

North Dakota

Great Plains Bicycling Club, Box 5085, Fargo, ND 58105.

Ohio

Akron Bicycle Club, P.O. Box 271, Akron, OH 44309.

Cincinnati Cycle Club, 2305 Arrowhead Trails, Loveland, OH 45140.

Cincinnati Off-Road Bicycle Racing Association (COBRA), 710 W. Main St. #101, Cincinnati, OH 45140, 513/677–0576 * Land-access issues, rides.

Cleveland Touring Club, P.O. Box 18189, Cleveland, OH 44118, 216/795–0407.

Columbus Council/American Youth Hostels, P.O. Box 14384, Columbus, OH 43214, 614/294–0338.

Dayton Cycling Club, P.O. Box 94, Dayton, OH 45409, 513/222–1710.

Grand Prix Raceway, 4491 Deerfield Ave., North Lawrence, OH 44666, 216/682–9231, 216/854–2133 * Racing, events.

Greater Miami Bicycle Club, P.O. Box 684, Hamilton, OH 45012, 513/863–6708.

Hancock Handlebars, P.O. Box 232, Findlay, OH 45839.

Licking County Bicycle Club, P.O. Box 593, Newark, OH 43055, 614/344–5683.

Lima Road Runners/American Youth Hostels, P.O. Box 173, Lima, OH 45802, 419/222–7301.

Medina County Bicycle Club, P.O. Box 844, Medina, OH 44258.

Miami Valley Regional Bicycle Council, Chamber Plaza, 5th & Main, Dayton, OH 45402–2400, 513/226–1444.

Mid Ohio Bikers, P.O. Box 844, Mansfield, OH 44901, 419/884–0277.

Ohio Bicycle Federation, 9611 Lorain Ave., Cleveland, OH 44102, 513/226–1444.

Stark County Bicycle Club, P.O. Box 8863, Canton, OH 44711.

Toledo Area Council/American Youth Hostels, 6206 Pembridge Dr., Toledo, OH 43615, 419/243–7680.

Trumbull County Cycling Federation, 3159 B Ivy Circle, Cortland, OH 44410, 216/372–7526.

Western Reserve Wheelers, 7753 Birchmont Dr., Chagrin Falls, OH 44022.

Oklahoma

Bartlesville Pedalers, Inc., P.O. Box 793, Bartlesville, OK 74005, 316/251–6526.

Oklahoma Bicycle Society, 4505 N. Utah, Oklahoma City, OK 73112.

Tulsa Bicycle Club, P.O. Box 471, Tulsa, OK 74101, 918/481–1501.

Tulsa Wheelmen, Utica Square Station, P.O. Box 52242, Tulsa, OK 74152, 918/885–2097.

Oregon

Cascade Classic Cycle Club, 7935 S.E. Market, Portland, OR 97215, 503/775–2688 * A group of collectors of antique bikes. Publishes a newsletter.

Corvallis Racing Club, Peak Sports, 129 NW 2nd, Corvallis, OR 97330 * For mountain bikers.

Disciples of Dirt, (Eugene Off-Road Cyclists), 2848 Greentree Way, Eugene, OR 97405 * Mountain bike club sponsors rides, newsletter.

NW Mountain Bike Racing Association, 503/758–4601, 503/695–5479 * Sponsors racing and events.

Portland United Mountain Bikers (PUMP), 2148 NE Schulyer, Portland, OR 97212 * Rides, land-access issues, newsletter.

Portland Wheelmen, P.O. Box 40753, Portland, OR 97240, 503/282–7982.

Siskiyou Wheelmen, 1729 Siskiyou Blvd., Ashland, OR 97520 * Mountain bike club.

Pennsylvania

Berks County Bicycle Club, P.O. Box 8264, Reading, PA 19601, 215/779–6527.

Bicycle Club of Philadelphia, P.O. Box 30235, Philadelphia, PA 19103, 215/440–9983.

Bicycle Federation of Pennsylvania, 413 Appletree Rd., Camp Hill, PA 17011.

Brandywine Bicycle Club, P.O. Box 3162, West Chester, PA 19381.

Central Bucks Bicycle Club, P.O. Box 295, Buckingham, PA 18912, 215/348–5679.

Cycling Enthusiasts of Delaware Valley, 9325 Marsden St., Philadelphia, PA 19114.

East Coast Ski-n-Cycle, 450 North C.A. Lor Blvd., Pottsville, PA 17901, 717/622–3310 * Organizes rides.

Harrisburg Bicycle Club, P.O. Box 190, New Cumberland, PA 17070, 717/761–4822.

Lakeside Bicycling Association, P.O. Box 10751, Erie, PA, 814/899–7277.

Lancaster Bicycle Club, P.O. Box 535, Lancaster, PA 17603, 717/397–1149.

Lebanon Valley Bicycle Club, 380 Summit Ct., Lebanon, PA 17042.

Lehigh Wheelmen Association, P.O. Box 356, Bethlehem, PA 18016.

Pennsylvania Bicycle Club, 7 Edward Rd., Hatboro, PA 19040.

State College Bicycle Club, P.O. Box 1173, State College, PA 16804.

Susquehanna Valley Bicycle Club, P.O. Box 63, Berwick, PA 18603, 717/784–6856.

Western Pennsylvania Wheelmen, Box 6952, Pittsburgh, PA 15212.

Williamsport Bicycle Club, 327 Adams St., Williamsport, PA 17701, 717/322–7959.

Rhode Island

Narragansett Valley Wheelmen, P.O. Box 1317, Annex Station, Providence, RI 02901.

South Carolina

Aiken Bicycle Club, P.O. Box 2073, Aiken, SC 29802.

Carolina Cyclers, P.O. Box 11163, Columbia, SC 29211.

Greenville Spinners, P.O. Box 2663, Greenville, SC 29602, 803/292/6315.

Spartanburg Freewheelers, P.O. Box 6171, Spartanburg, SC 29304.

South Dakota

Sioux Empire Bicycle Club, 3704 Staten Park Dr., Sioux Falls, SD 57103, 605/332–1446.

Tennessee

Bicycle Federation of Tennessee, P.O. Box 2823, Murfreesboro, TN 37133.

Chattanooga Bicycle Club, 5360 Highway 153, Chattanooga, TN 37343, 615/875–6811.

Highland Runners Bicycle Club, P.O. Box 1022, Tullahoma, TN 37388, 615/455–8729.

Memphis Hightailers, P.O. Box 111195, Memphis, TN 38111.

Nashville Bicycle Club, P.O. Box 158593, Nashville, TN 37215, 615/790–3237.

Rocky Top Riders, P.O. Box 392, Oak Ridge, TN 37830, 615/482–9534 * Weekend mountain bike rides.

Tennessee Cycle Club, P.O. Box 1401, Clarksville, TN 37041.

Texas

Austin Cycling Association, P.O. Box 5993, Austin, TX 78763.

Bell County Bicycle Club, P.O. Box 456, Nolanville, TX 76559.

Dallas Off-Road Bicycle Association (DORBA), 18484 Preston Rd., #102–106, Dallas, TX 75252, 214/424–1066 * Mountain bike club.

El Paso Bicycle Club, c/o 3629 Monroe, El Paso, TX 79930.

Flatlanders Bicycle Association, P.O. Box 1731, Amarillo, TX 79105.

Greater Dallas Bicyclists, P.O. Box 1495, Richardson, TX 75080.

Houston Bicycle Club, P.O. Box 52752, Houston, TX 77052.

Lone Star Cyclists, P.O. Box 532141, Grand Prairie, TX 75053.

Lubbock Bicycle Club, 5409 86th St., Lubbock, TX 79424.

Northwest Cycling Club, 13426 Harpers Bridge Dr., Houston, TX 77041.

Plano Bicycle Association, P.O. Box 860358, Plano, TX 75086.

Possum Pedalers Bicycle Club, Rt. 2, Box 268, Graham, TX 76046.

San Antonio Wheelmen, P.O. Box 34208, San Antonio, TX 78233.

Texarkana Bicycle Club, P.O. Box 7096, Texarkana, TX 75505.

West Elk Road Club, 5427 Blossom St., Houston, TX 77007, 713/861–2271 * Rides, events.

White Rock Cyclists, 10323 Estate Lane, Dallas, TX 75238.

Wichita Falls Bicycle Club, P.O. Box 2096, Wichita Falls, TX 76307.

Utah

Bonneville Bicycle Touring Club, c/o 2175 S. 9th St. E., Salt Lake City, UT 84106.

Peadli of Utah, 925 E. 17800 S., Salt Lake City, UT 84195 * Club.

Timp Velo, 670 S. Main, Payson, UT 84651, 801/465–2484.

Vermont

Three Banana Bicycle Club, c/o 4 Spring St., St. Johnsbury, VT 05819.

Virginia

Arlington County Bike Club, Arlington County Parks Dept., 300 North Park Drive, Arlington, VA 22203–2599.

Bicycle Association of South Side (BOSS), P.O. Box 36458, Richmond, VA 23235.

Blueridge Bicycle Club, 2640 Northview Dr., Roanoake, VA 24015.

Central VA Bicycle Club, P.O. Box 711, Lynchburg, VA 24501.

Emporia Bicycle Club, P.O. Box 631, Emporia, VA 23847, 804/634-2222 * Puts on the famous Great Annual Peanut Rides in early September.

Fredericksburg Cyclists, 608 Hawke St., Fredericksburg, VA 23847.

Old Capital Velo Club, 104 Penniman Rd., Williamsburg, VA 23185.

Potomac Pedalers Touring Club, P.O. Box 23601, Washington, DC 20007, 202/363–8687 * See District of Columbia above.

Prince William Mountain Bikers, P.O. Box 2752, Dale City, VA 22193, 202/223–6767 * Rides, trips, newsletter.

Reston Bicycle Club, P.O. Box 3389, Reston, VA 22209.

Richmond Area Bicycle Club, 409 N. Hamilton St., Richmond, VA 23221.

Rock 'n' Road Riders, P.O. Box 488, Blacksburg, VA 24063, 703/951–0197.

Shenandoah Valley Bicycle Club, P.O. Box 1014, Harrisburg, VA 23221.

Tidewater Area Bicycle Association, P.O. Box 12254, Norfolk, VA 23502, 804/588–7841.

Urban Nomads, P.O. Box 5627, Arlington, VA 22205 * National capital mountain bike club. Publishes newsletter.

Virginia Bike Federation, P.O. Box 255223, Richmond, VA 23260, 804/247–1029.

Virginia Creeper Trail Club, P.O. Box 2382, Abingdon, VA 24210.

Whole Wheel Velo Club, 9514 Main St., Fairfax, VA 22030 * Racing-oriented local club.

Williamsburg Bicycle Association, P.O. Box 713, Williamsburg, VA 23187.

Winchester Wheelman, 1609 Van Couver, Winchester, VA 22601.

Washington

Alki Bicycle Club, 2722 Alki Ave. SW, Seattle, WA 98116 * Mountain bike club rides, tours, newsletter, races.

Boeing Employees' Bicycle Club, c/o The Boeing Co., P.O. Box 3707, M/S 4h–58, Seattle, WA 98124, 206/655–1041.

Broken Spokes Cyclin' Folks, c/o 414 W. Pear St., Centralia, WA 98531.

Capital Bicycling Club, P.O. Box 642, Olympia, WA 98507.

Cascade Bicycle Club, P.O. Box 31299, Seattle, WA 98103, 206/522–2453 * Considered the largest bicycle club in the country. Supports an education person and conducts the Seattle to Portland (STP) ride.

Green River Bicycle Club, P.O. Box 1209, Auburn, WA 98002.

Mountain Bike Specialists, 5625 University Way NE, Seattle, WA 98105 * Rides, racing, touring, land-access issues.

National Bicycle Center, P.O. Box 3401, Redmond, WA 98073–3401.

The Northwest Bicycle Touring Society, 6166 92nd Ave. SE, Mercer Island, WA 98040.

Olympic Peninsula Wheelmen, 222 N. Lincoln, Port Angles, WA 98362.

Puyallup Valley Mountain Bikers, Puyallup Schwinn, P.O. Box 1124, Puyallup, WA 98371 * Rides, events, racing, newsletter.

Spokane Bicycle Club, P.O. Box 62, Spokane, WA 99210, 509/928–7133.

Tacoma Wheelmen's Club, Box 112078, Tacoma, WA 98411.

Tri-City Bicycle Club, P.O. Box 465, Richland, WA 99352, 509/943–9212.

Vancouver Bicycle Club, P.O. Box 1456, Vancouver, WA 98668–1456.

Wheatland Wheelers, P.O. Box 2315, Walla Walla, WA 99362.

West Virginia

Blennerhassett Bicycle Club, P.O. Box 2262, Parkersburg, WV, 26102, 304/485–1611.

Mountain State Wheelers, P.O. Box 8161, S. Charleston, WV 25303.

Wisconsin

Bay Shore Bicycle Club, c/o 1646 Amy St., Green Bay, WI 54302.

Bicycle Federation of Wisconsin, 1315 S. Van Buren St. Green Bay, WI 54301, 414/435–1004.

Bombay Bicycle Club, Inc., P.O. Box 1454, Madison, WI 53701.

Coulee Climbers, 1501 Rose St. #32, La Crosse, WI 54603 * Newsletter, rides.

Cream City Cycle Club, 4880 N. 107th St., Milwaukee, WI 53225 414/527–1779.

Fox Valley Wheelmen, 600 N. Owaissa, Appleton, WI 54911.

La Crosse Wheelmen, P.O. Box 1601, La Crosse, WI 54602.

Spring City Spinners, P.O. Box 2061, Waukesha, WI 53187.

twelve

BICYCLING: THINK GLOBALLY, BIKE LOCALLY

BIKE COMMUTING: HOW TO GET STARTED

Who doesn't love a bargain? Mention half-price sales, double-off coupons, or the like and hordes descend. Using a bicycle to do errands or get to work is another bargain: cyclists get two-for-one, even three-for-one rewards for their efforts. Plus it's fun to enjoy fresh air and travel under your own steam while quickly negotiating traffic-snarled streets. Why reserve bicycling pleasures just for weekend jaunts?

Consider this. When you cycle to work, you not only satisfy a transportation need but you exercise in the process. There's no longer any need to rush home from work and drive to the gym, for example. Jim Hurd, of the Schwinn History Center, loves cycling to work. "It's a great way to begin the day," he claims. Jim can sometimes be seen pedaling his 100-year old Expert, a high wheeler, on the streets of Chicago.

While combining exercise and transportation is appealing, there are even more reasons to switch to pedal power. Bicycling to your nine-to-five job tends to be less expensive than using public transportation or private auto. If parking is a problem where you work, there are no high fees, no parking meters to plug . . . no such worries when you're on a bicycle. Andy Clarke, Project Manager at the Bicycle Federation of America, declares that bicycle commuting is "quicker and cheaper. I'm doing my bit for the environment, keeping fit, and enjoying myself."

Yes, commuting by bicycle is a pollution solution. You can feel great about your fitness and your contribution to clean air. It takes less energy to maintain and propel a bicycle. A bicycle requires a mere 35 calories per passenger mile while a single-occupant automobile guzzles 1,860 calories for the same distance (about a 20th of a gallon of gas). In other words, one apple will power a cyclist two miles! Now, you can't say that about a car.

Since most Americans live within ten miles of work, the bicycle is an ideal means of transportation. Some cyclists combine bicycling with other modes of transport—cycling, for example, to their local light rail or to the bus. Whether you choose to "go all the way" by bicycle or hook up to a form of public transportation, here are some simple steps to help you begin commuting.

1. Scout out where you can park your bicycle at work. Some businesses offer separate parking facilities for their employees' cars. Your bicycle will take up much less space than a car, so your employer may be persuaded to put in a sturdy rack or assign one parking space in a garage to cyclists.

2. Plan a route that works for you. Do this on a weekend when there's less pressure to arrive on time. You may choose to pick up local maps and discover some low traffic routes that parallel your main route. Your local bicycle store or club can help with route suggestions as well. You will be surprised at how many alternates there are to busy main streets. Of course, you may have to ride on main thoroughfares for some portion of your commute. If possible, pick streets where there is a provision for bikes or parked cars, which do not take up an entire lane.

3. Pack clothing that travels well. Many potential bicycle commuters fret about their appearance and wonder how they can both bicycle to work and look professional. There are several solutions to this concern. It's relatively easy to roll most types of clothing and carry it in panniers. Some materials, such as silk, wool, and linen, pack easier than others, but if you wrap the items around a towel, your clothing will emerge relatively wrinkle-free at the other end of your commute. Other cyclists drive or take public transportation

to their place of work once a week, carrying their clothes for that week. While that requires a bit of planning, it does take care of the need to pack clothing on the bicycle.

4. Carry or store supplies with which to clean up. Actually, if you don't cycle as if you're out to win the Tour de France, you won't need to do much to freshen up. A washcloth or towel (that same one around which you wrap your day's clothes) can suffice. Some commuters stash toiletries such as powder in their desks. If you're lucky, your place of work has a shower or there's a gym nearby. Unless it's a broiling summer day, most commuters find that a shower is unnecessary. Besides, bicycle commuters arrive at work alert and refreshed from morning exercise. Often they don't even need that morning cup of coffee.

5. Prepare for riding at dusk or evening. Commuting by bicycle doesn't mean you have to be home before dark. With a good lighting system you can see and be seen. The best systems are lightweight and use halogen lights. They create a beam that enables you to be seen from at least 500 feet in front and maintain a red light in the back that does the same from the rear. Reflective tape on your panniers and clothing helps with nighttime visibility. Equipping your bike with front and rear reflectors is important. Reflectors on the backs of your pedals are also suggested; their movement will help identify you as a bicyclist.

6. Anticipate riding in all types of weather. With the plethora of outdoor clothing offered, there's a lot to choose from, making bicycling an all-weather activity. Raingear that breathes can keep you relatively dry and serve to break the wind as well. How frequently you cycle in wet weather will dictate how much to spend on raingear. Nylon, while less breathable, can do for dry climates. Some cyclists buy fenders to keep themselves and their bikes cleaner.

Riding in cool weather is easy. Dress as you would for most outdoor activities. Wear layers and use materials that wick sweat away from your skin. Some cyclists swear by wool, the old standby.

For hot weather, cotton or some of the new synthetics are good. To cool off, dip a bandanna or headband in water.

7. Get equipment that's commuter-friendly. Here's a great use for that old clunker, the three-speed you wouldn't dream of taking on a longer ride. Some folks refer to their commuter bike as their "beater" bike; they use it to

get around town and aren't particular about dents or scrapes. Many urban cyclists—including the authors—find a mountain bike perfect for city streets. They also enjoy the upright handlebars and oversize brakes.

Your commuting bike should be well maintained. Make sure you inflate tires to the correct pressure. Check the tread for glass cuts and the wall for cracks that indicate drying. A bike that's been hanging in the garage for years may need an overhaul. Dry, cracked, old tires can easily burst.

Wear comfortable clothes. Fasten your pants at the ankles to keep them from the chain. Wear an approved helmet.

Buy a rack and panniers. With panniers, you can carry a change of clothes, books, lunch, and more. You can carry more than with a backpack, and your center of gravity remains low for safety.

These steps will get you started. Many cycling organizations also sponsor a bike-to-work day in April. On such days you can learn routes and pick up tips from experienced commuters. (For more information on bike-to-work days, see the section on *Organizations*.)

And don't stop at commuting to work. Ride to friends' houses or cycle with empty panniers to the grocery store. You'll get your food supply and earn it at the same time.

THE BICYCLE: VEHICLE FOR A SMALL PLANET

By Marcia Lowe

In a world so transformed by the automobile that whole landscapes and lifestyles bear its imprint, a significant fact goes unnoticed. Although societies the world over define transportation in terms of engine power, the greatest share of personal transport needs is met by human power.

From the ten-speeds of Boston to the black roadsters of Beijing, the world's 800 million bicycles outnumber cars by two to one—and each year three times as many bikes as cars are produced. Bicycles in Asia alone transport more people than all the world's autos do.

In developing countries—where urban workers cycle to their jobs and rural dwellers pedal two- and three-wheelers piled high with loads of goods—pedal power is an important part of national economies and the only alternative to walking that many people can afford. In industrial countries, bicycles are a practical supplement to motorized transportation.

Meanwhile, a steady rise in the amount of driving in the world's major urban areas is pushing congestion to intolerable levels. Traffic jams and the byproducts of gasoline combustion—air pollution in cities, acid rain, and global climate change—point to the need for an alternative to the automobile.

A few countries do encourage bicycles in their transportation strategies. Public policy can facilitate cycling in a number of ways. By making ordinary streets safe for bikes and providing a network of cycleways—separate cycle paths, bike lanes on streets, and wide shoulders to accommodate cyclists on major roads—physical improvements can give cyclists and drivers equal access to as many destinations as possible.

A pro-bicycle stance need not be anti-automobile. The Netherlands, the most bicycle-friendly of all industrial countries, has the western world's highest densities of both cycleways and cars, plus a high level of public transit service. Indeed, maximizing the use of bicycling and mass transit could curb the steep growth in driving before urban air becomes unbreathable and rush-hour traffic grinds to a standstill.

The Silent Majority

Most of the world's bicycles are in Asia. China alone has roughly 300 million. And since only one person in 74,000 owns an automobile, Chinese commuters have little choice but to make the most of their bikes. They are also popular because, like cars in industrial countries, they offer the luxury of individual mobility and door-to-door travel without detours or extra stops for other passengers. During the last ten years, rising incomes in China have been matched by rising bicycle purchases, and the country's fleet has nearly tripled. Domestic bike sales in 1987 reached 35 million—meaning that more people bought bikes in China than purchased cars worldwide.

Elsewhere in Asia, bicycles often make up two thirds of the vehicles on city streets during rush hour. Many Asian urban transit systems are enhanced by pedal-powered "paratransit," in which three-wheeled vehicles for hire—variously called rickshaws, trishaws, pedicabs, and becaks—transport one or more passengers. These resourceful adaptations of the bicycle do much the same work cars do elsewhere. Cycle rickshaws are the taxis of Asia; heavy-duty tricycles, hauling up to half-ton loads, are its light trucks. In Bangladesh, trishaws alone transport more tonnage than all motor vehicles combined.

The rest of the developing world lags far behind in bicycle transportation. In much of Africa and even more widely in Latin America, the prestige and power of auto ownership has made governments ignore pedal power and has led people to scorn the bicycle as a

Table 1. Bicycles per Person in Selected Countries, circa 1985

Country	Bicycles Per Person
Netherlands	.79
West Germany	.74
Japan[1]	.49
United States[1]	.42
Australia[1]	.42
China[1]	.27
Mexico	.16
South Korea	.15
India	.06
Malawi	.01

[1] 1988

Sources: Worldwatch Institute, based on United Nations, *Bicycles and Components: A Pilot Survey of Opportunities for Trade Among Developing Countries* (Geneva: International Trade Center UNCTAD/GATT, 1985); and other sources.

vehicle for the poor. Some colonial administrations in Africa built urban bicycle lanes or paths, but most of these have deteriorated or been abandoned in the past three decades. And many African woman do not ride bicycles for reasons of propriety or religion or because of encumbering clothing.

Africa and Latin America lack Asia's widespread domestic bicycle industries. The few bikes available are often of poor quality, spare parts are scarce, and maintenance skills are inadequate. Despite these constraints, the bicycle's utility and the lack of other options have led to more intensive cycling in some African settings—even if it means splicing together worn-out brake cables or filling a punctured inner tube with sand. In parts of Burkina Faso, Ghana, Zimbabwe, and a few other countries, bicycles are widely used.

Latin America also has its cycling pockets, where the vehicle's practicality transcends its low social status. In Bogota, the largest bakery traded in most of its trucks for 900 space-saving delivery trikes that now bring goods to over 60,000 local shops. Nicaragua became perhaps the first Latin American government to promote cycling actively, pledging in 1987 to supplant its war-ravaged transport sector with 50,000 bicycles, some purchased by the government and others donated from outside.

Several heavily polluted areas in Eastern Europe and the Soviet Union have encouraged a revival of bicycling as part of their environmental strategies. The Lithuanian city of Siauliai launched the Soviets' first comprehensive cycling program in 1979; a new bike path system and extensive parking facilities have helped raise bicycle use there. In small Hungarian cities, roughly half the journeys to work are by bike.

Industrial countries have a surprising number of bicycles per person, considering how few are typically found on most city streets. Many industrial nations have two or three times as many bikes per person as their Asian counterparts. But where people have access to automobiles, ownership does not necessarily translate into use. One in four Britons has a bicycle, yet only one transport trip out of thirty-three is made by bike. In the United States, just one in every forty bikes is used for commuting; most of the rest are ridden for fitness, sport, or play—or are collecting dust in basements.

The United States has more than seven times as many bicycles per person as India, but because one in every two Americans owns an automobile—compared with 1 out of 500 Indians—bicycles play a much more modest role in the U.S. transportation system.

West Europeans are the industrial world's heaviest bicycle users. In several countries—among them Denmark, the Netherlands, and West Germany—bike owners outnumber non-owners. Pro-bicycle planning in the last twenty years (rather than conducive climate or flat terrain, as is often assumed) distinguishes Europe's truly "bicycle-friendly"

Table 2. Bicycles and Automobiles in Selected Countries, circa 1985

Country	Bicycles (millions)	Autos (millions)	Cycle/ Auto Ratio
China[1]	300.0	1.2	250.0
India	45.0	1.5	30.0
South Korea	6.0	.3	20.0
Egypt	1.5	.5	3.0
Mexico	12.0	4.8	2.5
Netherlands	11.0	4.9	2.2
Japan[1]	60.0	30.7	2.0
West Germany	45.0	26.0	1.7
Argentina	4.5	3.4	1.3
Tanzania	.5	.5	1.0
Australia[1]	6.8	7.1	1.0
United States[1]	103.0	139.0	.7

[1] 1988

Sources: Worldwatch Institute, based on Motor Vehicle Manufacturers Association, *Facts and Figures* (Detroit, Mich.: various editions); MVMA, various private communications; United Nations, *Bicycles and Components: A Pilot Survey of Opportunities for Trade Among Developing Countries* (Geneva: International Trade Center UNCTAD/GATT, 1985); *Japan Cycle Press International*, various editions; and other sources.

countries. The Netherlands and Denmark lead this group, with bicycle travel making up 20 to 30 percent of all urban trips—up to half in some towns.

In several European countries, from 10 to 55 percent of railway patrons in suburbs and smaller towns arrive at the station by bicycle. Traffic jams and air pollution in the past decade have spurred authorities in Austria, Switzerland, and West Germany to encourage more bicycle use. Riders in Belgium, France, the United Kingdom, and southern European countries, by contrast, still get little support.

Many auto-saturated cities of North America and Australia have all but abandoned the bicycle. The growth of suburbs has sent jobs, homes, and services sprawling over long distances that inhibit both cycling and mass transit. Many major cities are largely bicycle proof, their roadways and parking facilities designed with only motor vehicles in mind. Although several cities explicitly emphasize safety for cycle commuters—including Seattle, Calgary, Melbourne, and several university towns—these are the exceptions.

The world is sufficiently equipped, measured by the number of vehicles, to let bicycles take on a larger share of the transportation burden. Nearly 100 million bicycles are manufactured each year. Backed by strong domestic demand and growing export markets, major producers are sure to keep expanding their capacity, especially in Asia.

Table 3. Production of Bicycles and Automobiles, Selected Countries, 1987

Country	Bicycles	Automobiles
	(millions)	
China	41.0	.00[1]
Taiwan	9.9	.20
Japan	7.8	7.89
United States	5.8	7.10
Soviet Union	5.4[2]	1.33
India	5.3	.15
West Germany	2.9	4.37
South Korea	2.6	.79
Brazil	2.5[2]	.68
Italy	1.6	1.71
Poland	1.3[2]	.30
United Kingdom	1.2	1.14
Canada	1.2	.81
Others	10.5	6.54
WORLD TOTAL	99.0	33.01

[1] In 1987 China produced 4,045 automobiles.
[2] 1986 estimate.

Sources: Worldwatch Institute, based on Motor Vehicle Manufacturers Association, *Facts and Figures '89* (Detroit, Mich.: 1989); *Japan Cycle Press,* various editions; and other sources.

Vehicle for a Small Planet

The automobile—which has brought industrial society a degree of individual mobility and convenience not known before—has long been considered the vehicle of the future. But countries that have become dependent on the car are paying a terrible price: each year brings a heavier toll from road accidents, air pollution, urban congestion, and oil bills. Today people who choose to drive rather than walk or cycle a short distance do so not merely for convenience, but also to insulate themselves from the harshness of a street ruled by the motor vehicle. The broadening of transport options beyond those requiring an engine can help restore the environment and human health—indeed, the very quality of urban life.

Nearly everyone who lives in a large city is exposed to one hazard of the automobile era—air pollution. Cars and other motor vehicles create more air pollution than any other human activity does. Gasoline and diesel engines emit almost half the carbon monoxide, hydrocarbons, and nitrogen oxides that result from all fossil fuel combustion worldwide. Airborne lead, sulfur dioxide, particulate, and many other harmful if not toxic or carcinogenic pollutants also spew out of the tailpipe. On particularly hazy days in the world's most smog-filled cities—Athens, Budapest, Mexico City, and many others—officials must call temporary driving bans to avert public health crises.

Car-induced air pollution does damage far beyond city limits. Vehicles are a major source—indeed, in the United States, the largest source—of the nitrogen oxides and organic compounds that are precursors to ozone. Ground level ozone, believed to reduce soybean, cotton, and other crop yields by 5 to 10 percent, takes an estimated annual toll of $5.4 billion on crops in the United States alone. Nitrogen oxides can be chemically transformed in the atmosphere into acid deposition, known to destroy aquatic life in lakes and streams, and suspected of damaging forests throughout Europe and North America.

As serious as these losses are, they pale in comparison to the disruptions that global warming could inflict on the biosphere. Motor vehicles are thought to be responsible for 17 percent of the worldwide output of carbon dioxide (CO_2), the greenhouse gas that accounts for roughly half the warming effect. And carbon monoxide contributes indirectly to the warming by slowing the removal of methane and ozone, two other greenhouse gases, from the lower atmosphere.

Excessive motorization also deepens the oil dependence that is draining national economies. Many nations' transport sectors account for more than half their petroleum consumption. Even with the recent fall in crude prices, fuel bills are particularly harsh for indebted developing nations that spend large portions of their foreign exchange earnings on imported oil. In 1985, low-income developing countries (excluding China) spent on average 33 percent of the money they earned through merchandise exports on energy imports; many spent more than half.

The oil shocks of the seventies brought home the precarious nature of petroleum as an energy source, exposing the vulnerability of car-dependent countries. Today's stable prices and supply have lulled importers into complacency. But as oil demand continues to rise, another oil crisis looms in the nineties.

The world's largest gridlocked cities may run out of momentum before they run out of oil. Road traffic in many cases moves more slowly than bicycles, with average car speeds during peak times sometimes down to eight kilometers (4.8 miles) per hour. Traffic density in Taiwan's capital is ten times that of congestion-plagued Los Angeles, and work trips take Mexico City commuters up to four hours each day. Some police units in European and North American cities—including London, Los Angeles, and Victoria—use bicycles rather than squad cars for patrolling congested urban centers. The economic and social costs of congestion, such as employee time lost through tardiness and inflated goods prices resulting from higher distribution costs, are bound to multiply if car commuting trends persist.

Decision makers typically seek only technological solutions to auto-induced problems, an approach that, without alternatives to driving, is inadequate. Although exhaust controls such as the catalytic converter have dramatically reduced pollution from U.S. passenger cars since the early sixties, for example, rapid growth in the vehicle fleet and in kilometers traveled have partially offset this progress. Moreover, the catalytic converter has contributed to impressive reductions in hydrocarbon and carbon monoxide emissions in the United States, but actually slightly increases the CO_2 buildup, which contributes to climate change.

Similarly, the quest for petroleum alternatives has focused largely on "clean" fuels such as methanol, made from coal or natural gas, and alcohol substitutes distilled from corn and other crops. But methanol contributes to ozone formation and, if derived from coal, to climate change by emitting twice as much carbon dioxide per unit of energy as gasoline does. Using crop-based feedstocks for alternative fuels carries its own environmental side effects, as well as posing a potential conflict with food production.

Nor is building more roads the answer to congestion. Transport planners are finding that constructing new freeways just attracts more cars, as some public transit riders switch to driving and as new developments spring up along the new roads. Former Federal Highway Administration head Robert Farris concedes: "We can no longer completely build our way out of the congestion crises by laying more concrete and asphalt. Time is too short, money is too scarce, and land is often not available."

For every person who makes a trip by bicycle instead of by car there is less pollution, less fuel used, and less space taken on the road. Bicycle transportation, rather than replacing all motorized trips, would mainly supplant short automobile journeys, precisely those that create the most pollution (because a cold engine does not fire efficiently). A shift to bicycles for such journeys would therefore yield a disproportionately large benefit. Bicycle commuting holds great potential, since more than half of all commutes in the United States and nearly three fourths of those in the United Kingdom are eight kilometers or less.

Unfortunately, dangerously high pollution levels are even more of a health threat to people who are exercising outdoors, including cyclists. Air pollution during such periods becomes, ironically, a deterrent to bicycling. Until air quality improves, cyclists need a workable alternative—ideally, mass transit—on particularly hazy days. Eventually, when more drivers have switched to bicycling, the air is likely to be safer for everyone.

In the rush to run engines on gasoline substitutes such as corn-based ethanol, decision makers have overlooked a technology that converts food directly into fuel. A cyclist can run 5.6 kilometers (about 3.33 miles) on the calories found in an ear of corn—and nothing has to be distilled or refined. Bicycles use less energy per passenger kilometer than any other form of transport, including walking. A sixteen-kilometer commute by bicycle uses 350 calories of energy, the amount in one bowl of rice. The same trip in the average American car uses 18,600 calories, or more than half a gallon of gasoline.

Bicycle transportation also uses space more efficiently than automobile transport. In fact, any other transport mode, especially mass transit, can move more people per hour in a lane of a given size than cars can even at highway speed. Taking into account both space occupied and speed of travel, automobile traffic accommodates roughly 750 persons per meter-width of lane per hour, compared with 1,500 persons traveling by bicycle, 5,200 persons by bus in a separate bus lane, and 9,000 persons by surface rapid rail. Replacing short car trips with bicycling and longer ones with mass transit—especially with cycling as the way to get to the station—would save considerable space on the roads.

Cycling is thus an ever more attractive alternative to the daily grind of traffic congestion. Except when there is no alternative but to ride in the same traffic stream, cycling commuters benefit both themselves and their employers by being less vulnerable than their colleagues to hypertension, heart attacks, and coronary disease, and by arriving at work more alert. The proof that people enjoy cycling to keep fit is in the popularity of stationary exercise bikes; the irony is that so many people drive to a health club to ride them.

Measured by its benefits both to society and the individual, the bicycle is truly a vehicle for a small planet. "Bicycling is human-scale," writes New York cycling activist Charles Komanoff. "Bicycling remains one of New York City's few robust ecological expressions . . . a living, breathing alternative to the city's domination by motor vehicles. There is magic in blending with traffic, feeling the wind in one's face, the sheer fact of traversing the city under one's own power."

Marcia Lowe is on the staff of the Worldwatch Institute in Washington, D.C. This is an excerpt from *The Bicycle: Vehicle for a Small Planet*, reprinted with permission of Worldwatch.

BICYCLING AND AT-RISK KIDS: SUCCESS IN INDIANAPOLIS

By Charles Hammond

For most kids, a bicycle is simply a fun way to get around independent of adults. However, in special programs in Indiana and elsewhere, it's that and more. There the bicycle is the blackboard, chalk, and teacher all rolled into one.

One project where youths and bikes are mixing in a novel way is within cycling distance of the Major Taylor velodrome in Indianapolis. On any given day, eight kids are in and out of a storefront jammed with ten-speeds and BMX bikes. These kids are not on the outside, wishing they had the resources to buy a bicycle. Instead, many of them already own one: they've worked for it themselves, earning theirs through any number of tasks for a set amount of hours. All of this is made possible by the Bicycle Action Project (BAP). Rundown industrial sites, old stores, creeping gentrification, and a thriving liquor store surround BAP, but kids who might turn to mischief or more are finding that their skills and interest can lead to a bicycle.

Check out BAP on Alabama Street between 3 and 6 p.m. on weekdays or during the weekend's daylight hours. There's a steady population of what are labeled "at-risk" youths. At-risk youths are so called because of the crime, drugs, violence, and discouragement they endure on a daily basis. Many are educationally and economically disadvantaged. Things which numerous Americans take for granted—including being able to buy a bicycle and enjoy it for transportation and recreation—are not possible for them. Instead, they encounter discouragement to a far greater extent than their suburban middle-class counterparts.

BAP's at-risk students range in age from nine through sixteen. Instead of hanging out, watching time go by, they can change a bike's flat tire or repack a hub. They might be found bent over a bicycle on a stand, pointing out its innards to other kids. If the weather is passable, a couple of them might strap a helmet on their heads and take a newcomer out for a ride and a lesson in bicycling safely in a group.

 What has gotten them involved? Bikes, and the completely understandable desire to own one. An enterprising group of educators in Indianapolis, who happened to love cycling, formulated an innovative approach to attracting at-risk youths. This approach became the Bicycle Action Project, which is at the forefront of a small grassroots network of educators who are using the bicycle and bicycling to attack some of the educational, economic, and social problems of at-risk youngsters. The heart of BAP is a classroom disguised as a bicycle shop. This bicycle shop provides very appropriate apprenticeship opportunities.

Before BAP was a classroom, it was a bicycle recycling operation. BAP took surplus bikes donated by citizens and reconditioned by volunteer labor and recycled them into the hands of underprivileged youngsters. Before it even got off the ground, however, BAP discarded the bicycle handout plan in favor of a work-incentive arrangement. Kids were required to earn their bicycles by performing twenty-five hours of community service: sweeping up around the shop, teaching another youth how to change a tire, or repairing a bicycle under another young teacher's instruction.

Bicycle Action Project participant Joseph Sowell, 12, is working toward the 25–hour requirement in order to earn a bicycle. (Mary Rose Niemi)

Thus, twenty-five hours of sweat equity evolved into a combined work and learning achievement program: successful completion of the required twenty-five hours of training in bicycle maintenance and safety skills merited the award of a bicycle.

Other organizations around the country are using the bicycle in similar ways. A 4–H program outside of Minneapolis operates the Pedal Power Camp, which teaches bicycle mechanics, riding, and safety skills in a 4–H milieu. The students gain self-esteem and a sense of responsibility, sharpen their cognitive and manual skills, and have fun in a carefully planned and supervised program.

The Bicycle Investment Group (BIG) in St. Louis started independently of BAP in 1988 with an identical mission. In 1990, both BAP and BIG began joint programming, which resulted in the first "Inter-city Bicycle Competition," held at the Children's Museum in Indianapolis. In that event, teams of inner-city youths from the two organizations competed against each other in a contest of bicycle mechanics knowledge and manual skills. The action was unlike anything the museum had every seen: teams identified parts of bicycles correctly and repaired headsets, for example. All the participants won a prize.

BAP continues to refine its methods, constantly testing approaches to urban education and developing new programs. Now there are additional educational possibilities for BAP participants. After completing the initial core training of 25 hours, BAP students who opt to continue in the program have four options, or "program tracks":

  1. Advanced Mechanics Track—occupational skills preparatory to employment as a bicycle mechanic;

  2. Cycling Track—competitive cycling or touring;

  3. Pre-vocational Track—computer skills, inventory skills, advanced customer relations experience; and

  4. Management Track—supervisory experience as a peer instructor and/or a shift coordinator.

Of the twenty-two students currently enrolled at BAP, four are on the Management Track. Those four are all employed as management interns. Their jobs are variously to provide peer instruction, do partially supervised bicycle repair work, assist customers, and help coordinate the educational and retail operations of BAP. They, like the other BAP students, have earned a bicycle, learned how to repair bikes and teach others, acquired skills transferable to other work settings, and learned safe cycling skills. Not too bad a return from the simple bicycle.

Addresses

Bicycle Action Project, 948 N. Alabama, Indianapolis, IN 46202, 317/631–1326.

Bicycle Investment Group (BIG), 3835 A Shaw Blvd., St. Louis, MO 63110, 314/772–6115.

Pedal Power Camp, 4–H Youth Development, Minnesota Extension Service, 340 Coffey Hall, University of Minnesota, St. Paul, MN 55108, 612/625–9719 * Contact Cynthia McArthur for more information about a camp that teaches bicycle mechanics and skills.

Trips for Kids, 138 Sunnyside, Mill Valley, CA 94941, 415/381–2941.

Charles Hammond is the Director and founder of the Bicycle Action Project.

COMPUTER BULLETIN BOARDS: NETWORKING WITH CYCLISTS

What is a bulletin board system? Basically, it consists of someone's personal computer, with appropriate software, hooked to a modem and a dedicated phone line. Typical software allows for multiple message areas, where callers post messages on various subjects. Most systems also have multiple file areas, where public domain and shareware programs can be found.

To join the fun and call a bulletin board, you'll need a personal computer, a modem and cable, and communications software. Then, plug into your phone line, call one of the numbers listed below and—Voila—you're online with the world. Some of the systems are only available during off-hours (e.g. after six p.m. and before eight a.m.), so make sure to call at the appropriate times.

Remember, too, that these boards operate on people's personal computers. The typical system operator (sysop) puts hundreds and thousands of dollars into getting up-and-running and keeping current. In return, they seldom get more than a few donations; clearly, the rewards are of another nature. You'll find most sysops to be friendly and willing to help. But please pay attention to any board rules.

Bikenet Boards

In winter 1987, a small group of bulletin boards in North Carolina formed a cycling network. Each system runs compatible software (OPUS' CBBS or FIDO' BBS) and is part of an international network of FIDO'-compatible systems. As part of the Fidonet network, they can automatically exchange messages in the middle of the night, without sysop intervention. Under the supervision of Mike Talbot of Raleigh, North Carolina, they formed "Bikenet," an ongoing national conference on cycling.

During the summer, Mike learned of a similar network called "Bicycle" that had grown up independently. Bicycle was run by Howard Gerber of Houston, Texas. Mike and Howard got together and combined to form an expanded Bikenet network. The network is always growing and changing. To find out if there's a Bikenet Board in your area, call one of the coordinators' bulletin boards below.

Baltimore Harvester; Baltimore, Maryland; 301/828–4572; 24 hours; 300–2400 bps; Bob Hoffman, Sysop; Fidonet: 261/671.

Bikenet; Missoula, Montana; 406/549–1318; 24 hours; 300–9600 bps; John Williams, Sysop; Fidonet: 17/45; (co-coordinator of Bikenet echo conference).

Dynasoft; Davis, California; 916/753–8788; 24 hours; 300–2400 bps; David Larson, Sysop; Fidonet: 161/955.

The Nervous System; Ann Arbor, Michigan; 313/996–5053; 6 p.m. - 8 a.m./weekdays, 24 hours/weekend; 300–2400 bps; Rich Weinkauf, Sysop; Fidonet: 120/59.

Small Time BBS; Raleigh, North Carolina; 919/781–7047; 24 hours; 300–2400; Mike Talbot, Sysop; Fidonet: 364/701 (co-coordinator of Bikenet echo conference).

Two Wheelers; Houston, Texas; 713/682–6508; 24 hours; 300–2400 bps; Howard Gerber, Sysop; Fidonet: 106/88 (co-coordinator of Bikenet echo conference).

Independent Bulletin Boards

The following boards carry cycling information but are not tied in to the Bikenet network:

The Bikepath; Bloomington, Indiana; 812/332–9926; 24 hours; 300/1200 bps; Nick Gerlich and Pete Beckman, Sysops.

Chicago Metro Net; Chicago, Illinois; 312/231–8223; 24 hours; 300/1200 bps; Jon Jorgenson, Sysop.

Howard's Notebook; Belton, Missouri; 816/331–5868; 300–2400 bps; Jim Howard, Sysop.

Slice of Life; Stanford, Illinois; 309/379–2156; 300/1200 bps; Kevin Wonders, Sysop.

Commercial Systems

Several national commercial networks carry bicycling subjects. Most have local access phone numbers. Write for details.

CIS, P.O. Box 20212, 5000 Arlington Centre Blvd., Columbus, OH 43220, 800/848–8199 * CompuServe; Outdoor Forum (GO OUTDOORS) has information on cycling. For subscription information, call or write. Starter kits available at many computer stores.

Compuserve Information Data Base Company, P.O. Box 1305, McLean, VA 22102, 800/336–3366, 703/821–6666 (Virginia) * The Source; carries cycling discussions. Write for subscription information.

GE Consumer Services, Dept. 02B, 401 N. Washington St., Rockville, MD 20850, 800/638–9636 * Genie; carries Steve Roberts' *Computing across America* stories. To get there, "go CAA." Write for subscription information and check computer magazine ads for online subscription process.

Excerpted with permission from *The Cyclists' Yellow Pages*, Bikecentennial's guide to bicycle trip planning.

thirteen

BICYCLE RACING

By Joe Surkiewicz

*T*he first bicycle race probably went something like this: In the mid-nineteenth century, a French cyclist astride an early boneshaker bicycle rolled up beside another cyclist and thought, "I can beat this guy." A challenge was made, resulting in a sprint to the nearest bistro.

Since then, bicycle racing has evolved into one of the most popular sports in the world. The excitement, drama, and glory of bicycle racing attracts millions of fans, and in increasing numbers in the United States.

But what if you want to do more than watch? If you're intrigued by bicycle racing and want to learn how to get involved, this primer on finding local racing activity, how the sport is organized, and the different kinds of racing will get you started.

First, the awful truth: Bicycle racing is not as popular as bowling — or as organized. In spite of the well-publicized successes of Greg LeMond, the first American to win the Tour de France, finding the local racing community can be frustrating.

A velocipede race in 1887 (Schwinn History Center)

Unlike baseball, football, tennis, or golf, bicycle racing is loosely organized. Nationally, virtually no programs exist to introduce youngsters to the sport, nor are "citizen's" races held to make it available to the public. Bicycle racing, alas, lacks an infrastructure.

As a result, most racing occurs at the local, or grassroots, level. Your best bet for obtaining information on local racing is a "pro" bicycle shop. This is where racers hang out—and frequently work as managers, mechanics, and salespeople. In addition, many shops sponsor racing teams.

Bike clubs are another source of information. Not all clubs are racing-oriented, however, so you may have to call around. A good club will offer regular training rides, coaching, and transportation to races.

The next level after club racing is licensed amateur. The United States Cycling Federation (USCF) administers amateur racing all the way to the Olympics, and sanctions more than 1,000 races a year nationwide.

To allow cyclists the opportunity to race with others on the same level, the USCF organizes competition into age and sex divisions. Each age division is broken down into categories (or "cats") based on experience or performance:

Category IV: novice

Category III: rider completed eight Cat IV events

Category II: rider placed in top three of three Cat III events

Category I: national, international, and Olympic level

Racers compete in a variety of different events. Road racing, the most popular, follows a carefully designed route protected from traffic and suitable for cycling. There are four basic types of road races:

Time trial: The racer rides alone against the clock. Time trials are excellent for novice racers because cyclists can concentrate on building strength, developing good form, and increasing their confidence while free from the anxiety of pack racing. The racer with the fastest time wins.

Criterium: Similar in concept to grand prix auto racing, criteriums follow tight, multi-lap courses that put racers elbow-to-elbow. Criteriums range in length from 10 to 60 miles. Since it features plenty of action for spectators, the criterium is the most popular type of race in the U.S. The first racer to cross the finish line is the winner.

Road race: Longer than criteriums, road races can be point-to-point, several long circuits, or a combination of the two. Road races usually feature long, steep climbs and favor racers with good endurance. Again, the first racer across the finish line is the winner.

Stage race: The ultimate road race, a stage race lasts from three days to three weeks and can include one or more races, or stages, per day. Stages can be time trials, criteriums, or road races. The racer with the lowest accumulated time is the winner.

There is more to bicycle competition, however, than road racing. If you are fortunate enough to live near an indoor bicycle track (called a velodrome), you may want to consider track racing.

In track racing, racers compete on fixed-gear bicycles on a banked, wooden track. In several different events, track racing combines speed, power, handling ability, and tactics in a way that is thrilling for racers and spectators alike.

Off-road, or mountain bike, racing has only been around since 1980, but is now the fastest growing segment of the sport. Its popularity mirrors the success fat-tired bikes have gained in the marketplace.

Mountain bike racing reveals its laid-back, Northern California roots. The race scene is usually friendly and relaxed, without the intensely competitive and serious ambience of road races. At most mountain bike races anyone with a fat-tired bike can pay the fee and race for fun and the chance to beat their own time in previous efforts.

Most races are cross-country (similar to a road race in layout), and usually traverse rough and challenging terrain. Downhill and hill-climbing events test skill, strength, and nerve. Observed trials test a rider's handling skill over a short, obstacle-laden course.

So that racers can compete fairly, mountain bike racing is divided into beginner, sport, and expert classes for each sex. Since the new sport is still evolving, changes in rules and classes occur from year to year.

Before you plunk down your dollars for a racing license, consider this: Whether you race on the road, on the track, or in the dirt, bicycle racing requires commitment and courage. Good racers need physical strength, bike handling skills, and tactical smarts to win a race—formidable goals for the novice racer.

Ned Overend winning the Mountain Bike World Championships in 1990. (Specialized Bicycle Components)

Are you up to it? If the answer is "yes," it's not a challenge you'll meet alone. By training and competing with other cyclists, the novice racer can gain the experience that will lead to a rewarding bicycle racing career.

FOR MORE INFORMATION

There are two sanctioning bodies for bicycle racing: the United States Cycling Federation (USCF) and the American Bicycle Association (ABA). Their standards are similar for licensing—they compete with each other for members. For an amateur license, bikers fill out an application, pay a fee, and join the association. They are then eligible to participate in sanctioned races. (Almost all races are sanctioned.)

To be eligible for a professional license, riders must have earned national ranking as an amateur (points are awarded at each race to top finishers), fill out an application that is reviewed by a board, and pay another fee. Then they can participate in professional races.

Both USCF and ABA have BMX memberships.

The National Off-Road Bicycling Association—NORBA—is affiliated with USCF. NORBA has a licensed membership and sanctions mountain bike races in the U.S. Beginning in 1991, USCF licensed riders must also have a NORBA racing license to compete in NORBA sanctioned events. A USCF license alone is not enough.

Members of ABA and USCF receive a newsletter describing sanctioned events around the country. (Some of these may be found in the *Events* section of this book.)

Amateur Racing

UNITED STATES CYCLING FEDERATION (USCF)
1750 E. Boulder St.
Colorado Springs, CO 80909
Phone: 719/578–4581

AMERICAN BICYCLE ASSOCIATION (ABA)
P.O. Box 718
Chandler, AZ 85244
Phone: 714/891–7592

Off-Road (Mountain Bike) Racing

NATIONAL OFF-ROAD BICYCLE RACING ASSOCIATION (NORBA)
1750 E. Boulder St.
Colorado Springs, CO 80909
Phone: 719/587–4581

Velodromes

Indoor tracks are located in:

- Carson, CA

- Encino, CA

- San Diego, CA

- San Jose, CA

- Colorado Springs, CO

- East Point, GA

- Northbrook, IL

- Indianapolis, IN

- Baton Rouge, LA

- Detroit, MI

- St. Louis, MO

- Flushing, NY

- Portland, OR

- Trexlertown, PA

- Houston, TX

- Redmond, WA

- Kenosha, WI

- Milwaukee, WI

Joe Surkiewicz is a freelance writer living in Baltimore. He is the author of two off-road cycling books forthcoming from Menasha Ridge Press.

fourteen

SAFETY

*E*ach year there are about 1,500 deaths and 600,000 injuries (70,000 debilitating) tied to cycling in the U.S. About 75 percent of the deaths result from head injuries. That should tell you one thing: wear a helmet. There are other reasons. As the Bicycle Helmet Safety Institute puts it, "Road rash and broken bones heal; scrambled brains may not."

The *New England Journal of Medicine* recently reported that helmets are 85 percent effective.

Two organizations test helmets. The tougher standard is set by the Snell Memorial Foundation. Look for the green Snell sticker inside the helmet you're thinking of buying. Even the macho U.S. Cycling Federation, which sanctions races, is requiring that riders wear ANSI-certified helmets, a standard only slightly less tough than Snell.

Early helmets of the 1970s were heavy. Today's helmets look sharp, weigh as little as 6 ounces, and cost $25 to $90. They are colorful, aerodynamic, and cool. Many are well-vented and when properly adjusted are barely noticeable. They are manufactured in sizes to fit infants, children, and adults.

A variety of approved helmets are now available for children six months and older, as well as for adults. (Bikecentennial Photo by Gary MacFadden)

For a helmet to do what it is supposed to, it should fit correctly. Make sure your helmet sits squarely on your head, not towards the back. It's not a beret, either, so it shouldn't favor one side of your head over the other. Your forehead should be covered, and the straps adjusted so that the helmet fits snugly and does not move back and forth. The staff at any bicycle store should help you properly fit your noggin.

For a free copy of a booklet entitled, "Lou and His Friends Have Something to Tell You," which is about how to select, use, and care for a bicycle helmet, write to: National SAFE KIDS Campaign, 111 Michigan Ave. NW, Washington, DC 20010–2970. Include $1 for postage. Another booklet, "Safe Kids Are No Accident," includes games and other activities. It, too, is available for $1.

Here are groups that promote cycling safety with programs and publications.

Accord Cycle Group, Ltd., P.O. Box 48464, Los Angeles, CA 90048, 213/871–6959 * Runs "Smart Moves—Safe Moves," a program of bicycle education and safety for schools and service organizations.

American Automobile Association, Traffic Safety Department, Falls Church, VA 22047 * The AAA publishes 3 brochures: "Bicycling is Great Fun" (stock #3241), "Biking Tips for Kids" (#3278), and "Bike Basics" (#3279). Don't expect the same sort of advice you'd get from L.A.W. from these auto-maniacs.

"Becoming an Effective Cycling Instructor." League of American Wheelmen, 6707 Whitestone Rd., Suite 209, Baltimore, MD 21207, 301/944–3399 * Program to train instructors for LAW conventions, which attract as many as 2,500 cyclists. The idea: "cycling is fun, and it is even more fun if one learns to do it efficiently, safely and confidently."

Bicycle Federation of America, 1818 R St. NW, Washington, DC 20036 * Runs bike education program for grades 4–6.

Bicycle Helmet Safety Institute, 4611 Seventh St. South, Arlington, VA 22204–1419 * A program of the Washington Area Bicyclist Association that promotes the use of helmets. Publishes pamphlet, "A Consumer's Guide to Bicycle Helmets."

"Bicycle Safety First." Tim Kneeland and Associates, 2603 3rd Ave., Suite 101, Seattle, WA 98121, 800/433–0528, 206/441–1025 * 13–minute video for adolescent and adult cyclists.

"Bicycling Magazine Cycling Tips." Rodale Press, 33 E. Minor St., Emmaus, PA 18049, Attn: Ray Lauer * Series of free brochures from Rodale Press.

District of Columbia Department of Public Works, 2000 14th St. NW, Washington, DC 20009 * Publishes pamphlet, "Buckle Up Your Baby: Bicycle Helmets for Children," on riding with infants.

International Bicycle Fund, 4887 Columbia Drive S., Seattle, WA 98108–1919, 206/628–9314 * Promotes safety programs along with overseas travel.

Los Angeles Police Dept., South Traffic Division, c/o Officer Forrest Wilkins, 4125 So. Crenshaw Blvd., Los Angeles, CA 90008 * Has 13–minute video/16 mm film, "Be Safe On Your Bike," available for sale.

Maryland Dept. of Transportation, P.O. Box 8755, BWI Airport, MD 21204, 301/859–7310 * Publishes safety brochures, "Share the Road in Maryland," "A Safety Handbook for Bicycle and Moped Owners," and "Cooperation is the Key."

"Ride Right, Cycle Smart." Rodale Press Inc., 33 E. Minor Drive, Emmaus, PA * Safety tips for the whole family from Plymouth and *Bicycling* magazine.

"Street Smarts—Bicycling's Traffic Survival Guide" by John S. Allen. Rodale Press, Inc., 33 E. Minor Drive, Emmaus, PA 18049 * 40–page pamphlet covers riding through intersections, using brakes and steering, riding in rain and darkness, dealing with rude drivers, and more.

"Teaching Your Child to Ride a Bike." Rodale Press, 33 E. Minor Drive, Emmaus, PA 18049 * Pamphlet by the editors of *Bicycling* magazine.

Westwinds Discovery Center, New York, NY, 212/877–0677 * Sponsors course, "How to Ride a Bicycle," for adults who never learned.

Other Information

Bicycle Safety Camp, Program on The Learning Channel, Underwritten by Triaminic Cough Syrup, a division of Sandoz Pharmaceuticals.

Consumer Reports **magazine,** May 1990 * Rated 34 bicycle helmets and reached some general conclusions about safety, ease of use, and comfort. Precis: Hard-shelled helmets involve a hard plastic fiberglass shell over a polystyrene foam liner that protects users against sharp objects. This type typically weighs about a pound. No-shell helmets are best at absorbing impact. Some models have plastic or nylon reinforcement molded into the foam. Use of a Lycra cover increases protection by holding broken pieces together after impact. Advantages include its light weight, about half a pound. Thin-shelled helmets have a layer of thin plastic that provides more durability and greater resistance to puncture than the no-shell types. They also weigh about one-half to three quarters of a pound.

All helmets should be adjusted for a snug fit, touching the head on top and all sides. Most styles provide sizing pads to fit adjustment. All straps should be equally tight. Five point independently adjustable straps are the most flexible.

SAFETY GEAR

Lights

L.L. Bean, Inc., Freeport, ME 04033, 800/221–4221 * See "Helmets" below.

Brite Lite, P.O. Box 1386, Soquel, CA 95073 * Halogen head and tail lights that plug into a rechargeable battery pack that fits under your seat. Available in 2.4 watts and, for training at night (if you care to), 4.5 watts.

Cateye, Osaka, Japan, 011–81–6/719–7781 * Battery-operated halogen headlamp with clamp that slides on/off handlebars.

GT Roadlight, 4863 F Fulton Rd., NW, Canton, OH 44718, 800/869–6621 * Rechargeable headlight/tail light system rated at 6 watts. Clips on and off.

The Light Company, 2669 Castillo Circle, Thousand Oaks, CA 91360, 805/492–6658 * Rechargeable modifications for standard Cateye® lights that promise to improve the brightness of a $20 light by 300 percent. Not affiliated with the Cateye company.

Nice Lite, Universal Design Technologies, 888 Research Drive, Suite 108, Palm Springs, CA 92262, 619/327–0562; fax: 619/320–6248, 800/654–8366 * Headlights run on 4 AA batteries (recharger optional). An adaptation of a Tekna skin-diving headlight, the handle-bar-mounted Nite Lite claims to be completely waterproof.

Union Frondenberg USA, 1 Union Dr., Olney, IL 62450, 618/395–8471 * Rechargeable and generator lights.

VistaLite, 1830 State Street, East Petersburg, PA 17520, 800/755–9905 * A flashing, tail-mounted light that, its manufacturers say, is visible from 2,000 feet. Runs on AA batteries.

Helmets

Aria Sonics, P.O. Box 684, Orinda, CA 94563 * Hard-shelled, foam lined, teardrop-shaped helmet meets ANSI and Snell standards.

L.L. Bean, Inc., Freeport, ME 04033, 800/221-4221 * Lights, mirrors, and helmets (Bell and Bean's own brand—kids' sizes too). Call for catalog.

Bell, Box 1020, Norwalk, CA 90650 * Helmets that meet Snell and ANSI standards, including the lightweight Bell Quest, which has a reflective cover to increase nighttime visibility.

Brancale, 10–Speed Drive Imports, P.O. Box 9250, Melbourne, FL 32902–9250, 407/777–5777 * Italian-made helmets.

Giro, 2880 Research Park Drive, Soquel, CA 800/969–GIRO * Snell-approved, lightweight helmets.

Mirage Pro-Tech, 19030 62nd Ave. South, Kent, WA 98032, 206/241–5001 * Light (7.5–oz.) helmets made of polystyrene with built-in nylon webbing. Both ANSI and Snell certified.

Schwinn Bicycle Company, 217 North Jefferson St., Chicago, IL 60606–1111, 312/454–7400; fax: 312/454–7525 * Paramount Hard-Core helmets are all-foam with nylon covers.

Simpson Cycling, 12 Winter Sport Ln., Williston, VT 05495, 800/522–2453 * Expensive, lightweight, and aerodynamic helmets that meld the foam liner and plastic shell into a one-piece structure.

Troxel, 1333 30th St., San Diego, CA 92514, 800/288–4280 * Helmets for adults and children in addition to a line of rear-mounted bike racks, seats, and child carriers.

Other Manufacturers

Advent, Cyclotech, Service Cycle, 48 Mall Dr., Commack, NY 11725.

Avenir, Western States Imports, 4030 Via Pescador, Camarillo, CA 93010.

Etto Helmets, 888 Research Drive, Suite 105, Palm Springs, CA 92262, 619/778–1242; fax: 619/778–1245.

Kiwi, Zephyr: (XL Marketing), 3260 N. Colorado St., Chandler, AZ 85225.

Leader, Triple Sport, Box 321, Boulder, CO 80306.

Look Performance Sports, 1971 S. 4490 West, Salt Lake City, UT 84104, 801/973–9770.

Matrix, Trek, Box 183, Waterloo, WI 53594.

Monarch, Box 262369, San Diego, CA 92126.

OGK, NAAD, Inc., Japan. Fax: 011–45–6–945–0006.

Performance, One Performance Way, Chapel Hill, NC 27514.

Spalding, 425 Meadow St., Chicopee, MA 01021.

Specialized, 15130 Concord Circle, Morgan Hill, CA 95037.

Vetta, Orleander USA, 14553 Delano St. Suite 210, Van Nuys, CA 91411.

AN OUNCE OF PREVENTION . . .

By Trudy E. Bell

Ah, bicycling! The sun is shining, your bike is humming along with each turn of the pedals, the road is solitary and winding through a beautiful valley, and your companions relaxed and congenial. What an idyll.

CRASH! an unexpected thunderstorm pours with the fury of Noah's flood, an abusive driver throws garbage at your back, two dogs bound over a fence barking fiercely at your bike, which gets a flat tire out of earshot of your companions, who have the only map . . . and you're starving five miles from the nearest vending machine.

What can you do?

While it's unlikely that all these calamities will befall you at once, if you bicycle a lot, guaranteed, one or another will happen at some point. But take heart: the worst effects of most can be averted by a bit of forethought and preparation. Beyond the good practice of always wearing a helmet and carrying water, here are some further tips for a comfortable and safe ride:

1. Always carry a snack, no matter how short the ride. Even for a one-hour quickie of 5 to 10 miles, I always carry a couple of small boxes of raisins for a quick energy boost. For full-day or multi-day tours, I also carry a stick of jerky or packet of pretzels, to replenish salt lost through sweating. And for an independent bike-camping tour, I carry a full emergency meal that can be reconstituted with just water: good old Kraft dried macaroni and cheese, a tiny can of tuna, and some dried milk. More than once, this habit has rescued me.

Remember, as a cyclist you are the engine as well as the passenger. And even if you ate just an hour before, your body has a strange tendency to hit bottom unpredictably—and all at once.

2. In traffic, never be in a hurry—even if you're in a hurry. Being in a hurry increases the risk of overlooking a driver parked at the right curb opening the

car door in your path, not seeing a pothole or slick oil spot, or not hearing a car approaching from behind pull abruptly ahead of you to make a right turn. Rule of thumb: Obey all the traffic laws yourself, while not trusting drivers to do the same.

3. Be visible. My technique is to look absolutely ridiculous, with international-orange vest and fluorescent stickers all over my helmet and bike frame, and a bright yellow flag bobbing to my left. I'd rather have motorists say, "Look at that weirdo biker" than miss seeing me.

4. With dogs, get off the bike and command: "Go home!" Yes, your instinct is to pedal like hell, but few cyclists can outrun a big dog. Take advantage instead of the doggy psyche: dogs are territorial, setting up a ruckus because you entered their turf. So at the first warning bark of a dog bounding toward you, shout: "Go home!" in an authoritative tone. Get off the bike, put the bike between you and the dog, and walk along the road, continuing to command: "Go home!" The dog is used to obeying a walking figure, and normally will prance barking alongside you until he comes to the edge of his territory. When you've walked past that, he'll just stand and bark, allowing you to safely remount and ride off.

5. In rain, ride extra slowly, avoiding painted lines, puddles, and piles of leaves. The biggest problem with rain is that it wets your rims and seriously reduces your braking, increasing your stopping distance. The only way to compensate for that is decreasing your speed.

The painted lines that separate road surface from shoulder often get dangerously slick in the rain. Puddles can disguise potholes; at the least, the water may be mixed with engine oil from the pavement and make your rims even slicker. Piles of leaves in the fall often congregate over tire-eating drainage grates, and can be extraordinarily slippery when wet. If you're riding in a group, the first rider noting the hazard can point to it to alert the riders behind.

6. Carry a tool kit—and know how to use it. At the very least, you should have a patch kit and pump for repairing a flat tire. A spare tube is even better, in case you get a blow-out that cannot be patched. But once I got stranded twenty miles from home with a rare broken chain—and was saved by the rivet tool and extra links I'd tossed into my tool bag. So if you ride a lot, even exotic mishaps may stop you.

If you don't always cycle with a mechanical genius, the best favor you can do yourself is to take a basic bike maintenance and repair course, often offered by a local bike club, YMCA, American Youth Hostels chapter, or adult education center.

7. Carry a small first-aid kit, especially on a multi-day tour. Many camping and sporting goods stores sell a light nylon pouch with samples of all the basics. While no one plans to be injured, it's nice to know you could clean and soothe the road rash right when it happens.

8. Ignore hostile drivers—don't make the problem worse. Upon seeing cyclists share the road, some drivers get absolutely livid, complete with fist-shaking threats. Maybe they were scared by a freewheel in infancy. Although they are, fortunately, far less common than super courteous drivers, you should be prepared. Absolutely do not throw down your bike and put up your dukes. Their car is bigger than your bike, and they are in the power seat. Instead, ignore them. Teenagers may harass you just for sport, and after their laugh will pass on—unless you give them further ideas by retaliation. Even the hostile ones usually vent enough spleen by shouting.

If they want to pull over and make an issue of it, a solo cyclist's best strategy is not to argue the fine points of vehicle law, but to take advantage of the bike's agility: just turn around right there on the shoulder and begin riding back the way you came, opposing traffic. Since you'll now be on the left side of the road from the car's viewpoint, the motorist can hardly drive up next to you without risking a head-on collision. And if a police officer stops you for riding on the wrong side of the road, you can report the incident, especially if you memorized the license plate.

9. If you get separated from your companions, go back to the place you were last together. That way you can even undo a wrong turn. Better yet, each morning of your trip, set up several prearranged "compression stops" for the day where everyone will wait for the others to make sure there's still perfect attendance. And make sure everyone has a complete map and cue sheet. To cover all bets, you might even arrange one phone number as a central message center for emergencies.

10. If night is overtaking you, hatch an alternate plan. Riding in the dark is dangerous; changing plans is only inconvenient. If you have a tent, you can

set up camp almost anywhere—and, of course, you have extra water and your emergency meal, right? Or check into a roadside motel. Or have a friend come get you. And next time, at the outset, avoid locking yourself into an itinerary so tight or distances so long that you absolutely must make a certain destination each day. Allow slack for weather and mechanical trouble.

11. On a solo tour, let someone responsible know where you are each night. Give a friend at home your general itinerary and a map, and call if you change it along the way. If you're camping out alone, check in with a ranger or the local sheriff. Make sure someone is alerted to potential trouble if you don't call every so often.

12. Go with your gut. If "bad vibes" tell you this is a situation you shouldn't be in, or people who are bad news, don't let your brain override your instinct. Also, use common sense. If the ride takes you through a questionable neighborhood, it's asking for catcalls for women to wear Lycra; I've been known to disguise my sex by bulky GoreTex™ pants and jacket until I'm where I feel more comfortable.

Above all, don't let any of the bad possibilities discourage you from riding. If you're prepared for the worst, you can be free to enjoy the best—with confidence.

Trudy E. Bell is writing a book of original tours around New York City for Menasha Ridge Press, for publication in 1991 or 1992. She also teaches "Bicycle Touring: An Introduction" at the South Orange-Maplewood Adult School in Maplewood, N.J. In 1989 she completed both the intensive two-week course for professional bicycle mechanics at the East Coast Bicycle Academy in Harrisonburg, Va., and the bicycle leadership training course of American Youth Hostels with rank of leader. In her other life, she is senior editor for the engineering magazine *IEEE Spectrum* in New York City.

ARRIVING AT THE ACCIDENT SCENE: EMERGENCY ACTION

. . . .

By David Egan

You're heading down a hill with a 23 percent grade. The winding road is surfaced with loose gravel. As an experienced cyclist, you know that your speed could easily top 40 mph. You control your speed by pumping the brakes, first the rear set, then the front. If you hit the front brake too hard, you could be sent spinning end-over-end.

Then, *whoosh*. Two cyclists, blond surfer guys, pass at twice your speed. All they're wearing is black cycling shorts, socks, and cleated shoes—and they're cranking as hard as possible in top gear.

You turn a corner and there they lie. One lost control, braked too hard, and skidded on his side. The other ran over the first guy's bike and went over his own handlebars. There's some blood, but the two guys are alert, sitting and shaking their heads. Road rash is climbing like rattlesnake skin all up and down their exposed legs and torsos.

What next? When an accident happens, follow these emergency accident principles.

1) Survey the scene: Is it safe for you to care for the victim? Will you be endangering your own life by trying to save someone else's? What steps do you need to take to make the scene safe? For example, if someone has fallen in the road, the first order of business may be to have someone stop traffic.

2) Conduct a primary survey of the victim. Does the victim have an open airway? Is he breathing? Does he have a pulse? Each of these items must be carefully assessed. You can learn how to restore breathing and pulse in a cardiopulmonary resuscitation (CPR) course.

3) Call an ambulance, these days known as the Emergency Medical Services (EMS) system. This isn't always necessary, but you definitely need an ambulance if the victim does not have an open airway, is not breathing, or does not have a pulse. Or if the victim is unconscious or has a damaged helmet. If there's any doubt, call an ambulance.

4) Conduct a secondary survey: Interview the victim and any bystanders. Examine the victim head-to-toe. Measure and record vital signs: pulse, respiration rate, temperature, and wetness or dryness of the skin.

Check for injuries that the victim may not yet see or feel. These include:

Head Injuries. The signs of serious brain injury include disorientation, unusual emotional reactions, obvious skull fracture, and white or clear fluid or blood leaking from the ears. If any of these signs are present, call an ambulance. If the victim has not removed his helmet, leave it on.

Bleeding. The three basic ways to stop bleeding are to apply direct pressure, elevate the bleeding area higher than the heart, and apply pressure to the pressure points of the arms or legs. Try to cover the bleeding areas with sterile dressing.

Note: Don't elevate the legs of someone with a head injury, and don't elevate limbs that may have fractures.

Fractures. If you suspect fractures, don't move the victim. Control the bleeding, but don't elevate a fractured arm or leg. Call an ambulance. If you know how, splint the fracture.

Shock. Any bike accident can cause shock. The signs include confused behavior; very fast or slow pulse; very fast or slow breathing; trembling and weakness in the arms or legs; cool and moist skin; pale or bluish skin, lips, and fingernails; or enlarged pupils.

To treat for shock, lay the victim down, keep him or her calm, elevate feet and legs 8 to 12 inches, and keep the person warm by insulating above and below.

To truly be prepared for accidents, take a hands-on course in first aid, such as the American Red Cross Standard First Aid Course. And carry a first-aid kit you know how to use.

David Egan is an emergency medical technician trained in advanced life support and pre-hospital trauma life support. He is a CPR and first-aid instructor. His company, Outdoor Health, makes first-aid kits for emergency medical service professionals and for outdoor recreation. For more information or a catalog, contact Outdoor Health, P.O. Box 839S, East Hampstead, NH 03826, 603/382–4293.

HELMETS AND KIDS

. . . .

By Sheldon Brown

These days, most serious adult cyclists wear helmets, but few kids do. This situation is changing, but not as rapidly as it should, and it simply makes no sense. Both parents and kids can wear helmets and show each other that they have cycle smarts.

Helmet wearing should start with young children who are passengers in bicycle-mounted child carrier seats. No child should ever be carried in such a seat unless he or she is wearing a properly adjusted and approved helmet. Even experienced cyclists can tip a bike with a child in a seat. The extra weight high up on the rear of a bicycle can make the bike tricky to handle, especially when there is no weight on the front wheel.

Parents cycling bare-headed with helmeted youngsters are sending the wrong message. They should consider wearing a helmet for their own safety and for the message their lack of one sends. A child's perspective will be that it is unfair that he or she has to wear a helmet while their parents do not. Gradually, it may become more and more difficult for a parent to persuade a child to wear a helmet when that parent does not. On the other hand, if the parent wears a helmet, the child can be proud to have a helmet "just like Mommy."

Encouraging a child to wear a helmet is all in the presentation. Saying things like, "We brought you a present—a helmet just like Daddy's" is helpful. Little children might be encouraged to think of a helmet as a toy at first. Eventually, the child should be taught to associate the wearing of the helmet with traveling on the bicycle. All the pleasant sensations of bicycling—the cool breezes, ever-changing scenery, and the company of parents—can be taught to be an extension of the helmet. Without a helmet, there's no bicycling and no fun!

If young children get started right, wearing a helmet while cycling will develop into a lifetime habit. From the time our children were old enough to walk, if they overheard my wife and me talking about going for a ride, they would go and get their helmets without prompting, much as a dog goes for its leash when it hears the word "walk."

Be aware that baby helmets are for babies riding in bicycle-mounted child carrier seats or trailers. They are made for passengers, not riders. They are not ventilated well enough for an active rider, and they often cover the ears, which is dangerous for cycling.

If you want to encourage an older child to get the helmet habit, it can be a bit more challenging. The older the child, and the longer he or she has cycled without a helmet, the tougher it is to introduce its use. If parents want to get their twelve-year-old to start using a helmet, there may be resistance, mainly due to peer pressure.

Sometimes parents in a particular neighborhood can band together and present a united front to get all the neighborhood kids to start wearing helmets. Once a few children start wearing helmets, it is easier to persuade the others that they're missing out on something crucial. Parents can also tie in helmet wearing with a new bicycle purchase, saying "This is your new bicycle, but only if you agree to wear your helmet each time you ride it."

Whatever it takes, whether it's a younger or older cyclist, get that habit established. It just might save your child's life.

Sheldon Brown is technical manager for a chain of bicycle stores in Massachusetts. He is a contributing editor for *American Bicyclist* and is the father of two children, who cycle with their helmets.

POWER BRAKING: PULLING OUT THE STOPS

. . . .

By John Schubert

You should understand braking better than any other aspect of cycling. Otherwise, you can't make a maximum-performance short stop safely. Moreover, the maximum-performance technique allows you to keep going fast until the last second. That's why racers should know this stuff—they can go faster by braking better.

The key is straightforward enough: You get much more force out of your front brake than your rear brake. But you can initiate a pitchover accident if you simply grab the front brake. As you squeeze your brakes, your weight shifts from the rear wheel to the front wheel. That's why you get so little braking power from the rear wheel before it starts to skid. When you're not braking, the rear wheel carries about 60 percent of your weight. But under even modest braking forces, this percentage is greatly reduced. Squeeze the front brake, and you also transfer weight to the front wheel. The more weight you transfer, the more braking you can get without wheel lockup—but only up to a point.

This weight transfer is also the precursor of danger. When the rear wheel is entirely unweighted, it lifts off the ground, and pitchover begins.

Here's how to get maximum braking without any danger of pitchover. Squeeze the front brake twice as hard as you squeeze the rear brake. When the rear wheel is almost entirely unweighted, it will lose traction, lock up, and start to skid. When this happens, let up on the *front* brake. Some of your weight will shift to the rear wheel, and it will stop skidding.

Let me repeat that: When the *rear* wheel starts to skid, you let up on the *front* brake.

You must practice this under controlled conditions to be able to do it in an emergency. You need a bike in *perfect* condition. And you need a smooth, quiet road with no intersections.

When you first practice, you probably won't have the nerve to squeeze hard enough to get rear wheel lockup. That's okay. Even at sub-maximum braking levels, you'll be impressed with how short you stop.

In addition, you can make your bike stop shorter yet by moving your center of gravity rearward. Just shove your rear end out behind the saddle. When you do that, your bike can accept harder braking and you can stop shorter. This is an additional skill to practice. Shove your rear rearward, then make a maximum performance stop as described above. You'll feel awesome stopping power.

John Schubert is Technical Editor of *BikeReport* magazine. This essay was adapted from a previously published *BikeReport* article. Schubert is also author of the books *Cycling for Fitness* (Ballantine, 1988) and *The Tandem Scoop* (Burley, 1991).

fifteen

TOOLS

Bicycles are simple machines, elegant and fairly easy to maintain. While many cyclists derive great satisfaction from tinkering with them, others rush them to the dealer for every squeak and clink. Whether or not you're a natural born "tinkerer," an intensive course in bicycle maintenance at one of the schools below will enable you to do practically any bicycle repair. Although some of the schools listed offer courses designed for folks with sophisticated bike repair experience, others are geared toward the mechanical neophyte. Of course, if you're just interested in learning a few of the basics, many local bicycle clubs, community colleges, and bicycle shops offer courses.

SCHOOLS

Barnett Bicycle Institute, 2755 Ore Mill Dr., #14, Colorado Springs, CO 80904, 719/632–5173 * 1– and 2–week courses in Introduction to Bicycle Mechanics and Advanced Bicycle Mechanics. Evening tutorials on principles of bike position and gearing design. Courses for aspiring mechanics, pro mechanics, and shop owners.

East Coast Bicycle Academy, 40 S. Liberty St., Harrisonburg, VA 22801, 703/433–0323 * Weekend and 1– and 2–week courses. The weekend course is a "tune-up" offered for beginners. Novice and advanced mechanics choose from different 1–week courses, while intermediate folks have a 2–week course. Courses for anyone with a yen for repairing every molecule of their bike.

Flat Tire Weekend, Country Pedal'rs, R.D. 6, Box 249C, Somerset, PA 15501, 800/762–5942, 814/445–6316 * One weekend in May that combines a basic maintenance and repair clinic with cycling.

New England Cycling Academy, 12 Commerce Ave., West Lebanon, NH 03784, 603/298–7784 * Offers a 1–week master mechanics course, their Technicians Course, which demands prior experience, and three-day managers' workshop given in six different locations. (These locations vary, but a course can usually be found in Chicago, Los Angeles, and Texas, for example.)

Paterek Frames, 935 Quarry Rd., River Falls, WI 54022, 715/425–9324 (day), 715/425–9327 (evenings) * Tim Paterek, builder of bicycle frames for 15 years, offers a 5–day frame-building workshop. Cyclists take home a frame they've built.

United Bicycle Institute, P.O. Box 128, 423 Williamson Way, Ashland, OR 97520, 503/488–1121 * Has a 2–week course for beginners and a 1–week course for more advanced mechanics.

The Weekend Workshop, Michigan Bicycle Touring, 3512 Red School Rd., Kingsley, MI 49649, 619/263–5885 * A hands-on weekend course in basic repairs and maintenance of 10–,12–, and 15–speed bicycles. Time is allowed for "biking a well-planned route on scenic backroads." Offered in May.

TOOLS

AC International, 9115–1 Dice Rd., Sante Fe Springs, CA 90670, 213/948–3181 * Makes Pocket Pro Tools, as well as Mr. Tuffy Tire Liners, water bottles, horns, valve caps, bells, streamers, and baskets.

Allsop, P.O. Box 23, Bellingham, WA 98227, 800/426–4303 * Portable tool kit, biodegradable "degreaser."

Bike Elixir, 1132 Mirabela Ave., Novato, CA 94947 * Biodegradable soap for cleaning road and mountain bikes.

Blackburn, 1510 B Dell Avenue, Campbell, CA 95008 * The WorkStand and Bench-Stand models are designed for pro and home mechanics.

Giant Bicycle, Inc., 475 Apra St., Rancho Dominguez, CA 90220, 213/609–3340 or 800–US–GIANT * Offers repair kits, among many other accessories. Also see listings under *Accessories, Manufacturers, Mountain Bikes,* and *BMX/Kids' Bikes.*

Life-Link International, Inc., Box 2913, Jackson, WY 83001, 800/443–8620, 307/733–2266 * Company makes the Too Tyred Tool Pouch for mountain and road bikes. Also see *Accessories* section.

Park Tool Company, 4756 Banning Ave., #208, St. Paul, MN 55110, 612/490–1074; fax: 612/490–0953 * The company started in 1963 by selling a repair stand and has become one of the standard names in bike tools. 17–page catalog available for $2.

Pedro's Racing Grease, Inc., P.O. Box 1149, Cambridge, MA 02142, 401/849–2909 * Synthetic lubricants for mountain and road bikes.

Select Sales, P.O. Box 521, Dept. 2–B, Clifton, CO 81520 * Ultra no-frill tools and hardware catalog that promises low prices.

The Third Hand, Box 212 B, Mt. Shasta, CA 96067, 916/926–2600; fax: 916/926–2663 * 75–page catalog of tools, repair manuals, and instruction videos.

Wheelsmith Fabrications, Inc., 3551 Haven Avenue, Suite R, Menlo Park, CA 94025–1009, 415/364–4930; fax: 415/368–0351 * Tools for building and repairing wheels.

FIXING A FLAT

. . . .

By Les Welch

Flat tire repair is a skill all cyclists should have. But know-how won't do you much good unless you carry the proper tools. The ideal kit would include a spare inner tube of the correct size and valve type (read the size off your tire sidewall), a patch kit, tire levers, and pump. We are assuming the wheel is held to the frame with a quick-release mechanism, removable without tools. If your bike has axle nuts, your emergency bag should also include a wrench that fits them.

The best way to learn how to fix a flat is to observe and practice. Some bike shops offer beginning maintenance classes, or will be willing to coach you through the first time. If you have any doubt about the integrity of your repair, especially the wheel attachment, walk, don't ride, to your local bike shop and have their service department okay your work.

The following step-by-step instructions should get you through a crisis.

STEP ONE: Remove the wheel

Since the tire is flat, removing it from between the brakes should be easy. Now is a good time to take notice of a button or lever, on the brake caliper, cable, or handle, that will cause the brake to open wider than normal. If you have a brake release, use it now to open the brake.

Front Wheel, Quick-release: Pull the lever on the axle and the wheel should loosen. Some bikes have a retention device, which might require unwinding of the release. Count the number of turns (as you face the lever, turning counter-clockwise loosens) to make installation easier.

Front Wheel, Axle Nut: Loosen the axle nuts with the wrench, turning them counter-clockwise as you face them. Grasp the wrench near the end, for improved leverage, and note the effort necessary to break the nuts free; a similar effort, in the reverse direction, will be necessary later to properly tighten the nuts once repairs have been completed. Typically, removing the nuts is not necessary. If a retention device on the fork requires you to remove the nuts, put them on the axle for safe-keeping, along with the washers and retention devices, in sequence of disassembly, to aid in proper reassembly.

Rear Wheel, Quick-release: Before removal, turn the pedals and move the shift levers to engage the chain on the smallest sprockets, front and rear. Pull the lever on the axle, and the wheel should loosen. The trick is to pull the body of the derailleur rearward (it pivots from a point just below the axle), while pushing the wheel forward. With a little practice, the wheel can usually be removed without touching the chain.

Rear Wheel, Axle Nut: Directions are the same as for quick-release rear wheel, except that loosening the axle is done with a wrench, turning the nuts counter-clockwise as you face them. Take note of the effort necessary to break the nuts free, as well as the point where you grip the wrench—this will be helpful when re-installing the wheel.

With the front wheel off, the bike can be leaned, resting on the forks. If you've removed the rear wheel, lay the bike on its side, with the chain side up.

STEP TWO: *Remove the tire*

. . . .

Mark the side of the tire where the valve is (some mechanics install the tire so that its label is next to the valve).

The degree of difficulty in removing a tire from a rim varies from effortless to mind-boggling. Rim width, country of manufacture, type of tire bead, and other factors combine to make this step simple or difficult. Start by verifying that all the air is removed. If you have a slow leak, tire removal may be difficult until all the air escapes.

Shrader valves are the American, or automotive style. With the cap removed, use a fingernail, ballpoint pen, or anything handy to depress the center "core" of the valve, while squeezing the tire to force out all the air.

Presta valves are also called French Valves, and are smaller in diameter than Shrader. Once uncapped, the valve is opened by turning the knurled endpiece (not the miniature threaded stalk) counter-clockwise four or five turns, and depressing it, while squeezing the tire to force out all the air.

With all the air out, you may be able to pull the tire off with your bare hands. Start at the valve, and squeeze both sides of the tire toward the center of the rim. Work around the rim, until you get back to the valve. The trick is to keep the tire edge, or bead, in the center of the rim. You may be able to pull the bead over the edge with your hands. If not, use two tire levers, opposite the valve, about three or four inches apart from each other, and with light pressure, pry one side of the bead over the rim edge. Use your hands to pull off the rest of that side of the tire. Remove the tube. The second side of the tire should be easily removable with the tube out.

STEP THREE: *Determine the cause of the puncture*

. . . .

Merely installing a new tube will not always correct the problem. A tiny sharp object stuck in the tread, a protruding spoke, or rim strip out of place can cause the new tube to have a short life.

Start the process by inflating the old tube, being careful not to overinflate. Large or multiple holes will be obvious, while pin holes may take some searching. Passing the tube near your jaw will allow the sensitive skin of your face to feel the air leak, and also allows your ears to help find the problem. If the problem seems invisible, you can immerse sections of the tube in water, until bubbles appear, or you can put the tube away and focus on getting the bike back together with the spare tube, and continuing the ride. Sometimes, a "high-pressure leak" is impossible to find, as the tube cannot take high pressure outside the tire.

Once the problem area has been located on the tube, focus your attention on the corresponding area of the tire. Check the tread, the inside of the tire, the rim, and the rim strip. If there seems to be nothing sharp, re-examine the tube.

Two small holes on the side of the tube (not the tread area) indicate a pinch, or "snakebite," usually a result of under-inflation and/or impact, with curb, pothole, or even a driveway lip.

A problem near the valve can be a manufacturing defect, or the result of improper assembly, with no tell-tale signs of sharp object in the tread.

Occasionally, an object will self-remove from the tread leaving a mystery and an empty hole. (TIP: A thumb-tack, staple, or small nail might not cause deflation until removed—you may be able to limp home if you avoid high speed down hills.)

Sidewall damage can result from brake shoes touching the tire, especially common on mountain bikes.

Hollow rims should have an adhesive, reinforced tape covering the spoke holes—rubber or plastic liners can allow the tube to bulge through under high pressure or heat.

Slowly, and with light pressure, run your fingertips along the inside of the tire, until you make one full revolution. Some small object will usually be found on the first pass; remove it and continue by running your fingers the opposite direction. When the tire is free of any sharp protruding objects, check the rim, and the rim liner; sharp edges or uncovered spoke ends will cause another flat. Everything clean? Time to put it back together.

STEP THREE-A: Patching and booting

. . . .

If you carry only a patch kit, or have already used your spare tube, it's important to know a few thing about patching:

1. With sandpaper, abrade an area around the puncture that is slightly larger than the patch.

(Dennis Coello)

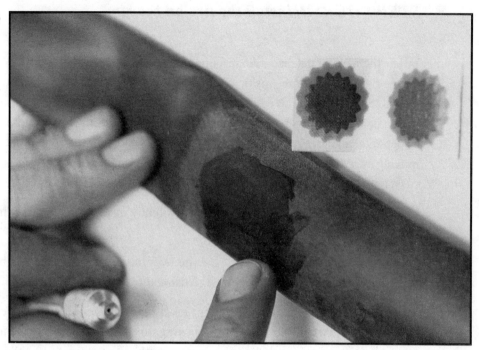

2. Apply a thin, even coat of cement on the abraded area (the unthreaded end of the cap is used to puncture the opening of the tube of cement).

3. Wait until the cement is dry, and then wait one minute longer before applying the patch (Patches stick to dry glue).

4. Peel the foil off the patch, and without touching it, place it on the dry glue of the tube, plastic side up.

5. Use the smooth edge of a key, or a coin, to apply pressure to the patch, and remove the plastic.

Your patch kit will be more useful if you add a dollar bill, and a quarter coin. If the hole in your tire is large enough for a pen to get most of the way through, or if the puncture was caused by the tube blowing through a hole in the tire, a dollar bill, folded to one-quarter size, will usually allow you to get a few more miles out of the tire. By placing the folded bill on top of the hole in the tire, then carefully installing the tube, the paper will act as a reinforcement, or "boot." Off-road enthusiasts often carry duct-tape for the same purpose. Canvas, leather, even cardboard, might help you get home. If nothing works, the quarter is for a phone call.

STEP FOUR: Reinstall the tire on the rim

. . . .

Inflate the new, or patched tube just enough to give it shape. With the tire completely off the rim, place the tube inside the tire, and start the installation process by pushing the valve through the valve hole. We're going to install one side of the tire completely before doing anything to the other side. Hook the bead of the tire as close to the valve as possible, and using only your hands, push the bead over the edge of the rim, moving away from the valve in both directions simultaneously. It's usually pretty easy, until the final few inches. Two tricks can help you here:

First, try to keep the bead of the tire, where already installed, as close to the center of the rim as possible.

Second, instead of trying to muscle the tire over the rim, try coaxing it, a half inch at a time, using both thumbs together. Avoid using tools here if at all possible.

Start the second bead at the valve, after tucking the tube completely inside the tire. A common problem can be avoided by checking this area for signs that the tube is pinched at the valve—push the valve stem slightly into the rim to free the tube from the tire bead. Using only your hands, work the beads over the rim edge, moving away from the valve in both directions. Make sure the tube stays tucked into the tire—it's okay to deflate the tube slightly to ease the bead installation. Once again, the final few inches can be troublesome, but please, avoid using anything but your hands. Just as on the first bead, the tricks are to keep the installed part of the bead centered on the rim, and try to roll a fraction of an inch at a time. With a little practice, this job gets a lot easier.

Occasionally there are impossible combinations, usually extra-narrow rims from one continent, combined with extra-narrow, or folding tires from another continent. There is a tool that can be used when these combinations refuse to be installed. Available at most bike shops, the VAR tire tool works by pulling the tire bead over the rim edge, without endangering the tube, as prying with a lever might.

STEP FIVE: Inflate and seat

. . . .

Before inflating, think back to step one, the part about releasing the brake. If your brakes don't have a release, install the wheel first, then inflate.

Before inflating, squeeze the tire away from the edge of the rim, to verify the tube is not "pinched" between the tire and rim. Inflate lightly, and spin the wheel to check that the tire is "seated" correctly on the rim. Most tires have a stripe, near the bead, which should appear to run evenly with the rim when they're spun.

If the stripe dips under the rim, it can be pulled out with the hands, or it may pop in place when fully inflated. Stubborn beads may need lubricating with soapy water (avoid talc, as it is carcinogenic).

If the stripe jumps away from the rim, a pinched tube is indicated. Deflating immediately, then carefully tucking the tube into the rim, with your hands, should cure this.

With a hand pump, proper pressure should make the tread area firm to a squeeze of the thumb, with a slight "give" to the sidewalls when squeezed. Compare with the other tire, or ideally, educate your thumb by squeezing the tread and sidewalls after gauging your tires at the correct pressure (stamped on the side of the tire).

STEP SIX: Reinstall the wheel

. . . .

Wheels should be installed with the bike upright, the weight of the bike resting on top of the axles.

Front Wheel, Quick-release: The wheel should be self-centering in the fork—swing the release lever from the open position to the closed position, arcing the lever a full 180 degrees. Halfway through this arc, you should encounter resistance, making it difficult, but not impossible, to move the lever the final 90 degrees. If necessary, adjust the tension by holding the lever, and turning the other side (skewer adjusting nut); clockwise tightens, so if you encounter light or no resistance when the lever is thrown, turn the adjusting side clockwise until you hit resistance halfway through the arc. If it's impossible to throw the lever completely, turn the adjusting side counter-clockwise (with the lever loose) until it can be closed securely.

Front Wheel, Axle Nut: Finger tighten the nuts, making sure that any washers are where they were before the axle was loosened. Use the wrench to turn one nut one-quarter turn clockwise, holding the other nut with your fingers, to detect any turning. If the axle turns, move the wrench to the other nut, and try turning it one-quarter turn clockwise. Once the nuts are snug, they can be torqued to the original tension, usually one-eighth to one-quarter turn past the point where the wrench stops turning easily.

Rear Wheel, Quick-release: Reinstall the wheel by pulling the derailleur rearward, and catching the chain on the small rear sprocket. Adjusting the quick-release tension is the same as for the front wheel. Once the tension is adjusted, loosen the release, pull the right side (chain side) of the axle rearward until it hits the stop, and center the wheel between the chainstays by moving the left side of the axle slightly front to back, until the tire appears to be evenly spaced in the rear frame (chainstays and seatstays). When the tire is centered, throw the release lever.

Rear Wheel, Axle Nut: Installation and centering of the wheel is the same as for rear wheels with quick-release. Once in place, finger tighten the axle nuts. Use the wrench to turn one nut one-quarter turn clockwise, holding the other nut with your finger, to sense if the axle turns. Move the wrench from side to side, gradually tightening the nuts until they're snug, then one-eighth to one-quarter turn extra, to the same tightness as before you loosened them.

Before your test ride, make sure you hook up the brakes, if you released them. Start slowly, and after ten or fifteen seconds, stop and double check your work, especially the securing of the wheel. Take no chances here—if something seems awry, get your work checked by a qualified person.

Les Welch has been helping people with their bikes for twenty years in bike shops in the Shenandoah Valley and Tidewater regions of Northern Virginia. Recently he completed a four-year term as instructor for the East Coast Bicycle Academy, and is studying Aviation Maintenance. He says, "I don't see me getting away from bicycles. This new knowledge should make me a better mechanic. I guess it's a Wright brothers phase."

sixteen

TOURING

According to the Bicycle Institute of America, more than 1.3 million Americans take bicycling vacations. While some design their own tours, using the services of organizations such as Bicycle Holidays, the Touring Exchange, or Bikecentennial, others seek out companies that take care of almost every aspect of a touring vacation.

There are as many bicycle tour options, both abroad and in the U.S., as there are types of frames. Bicyclists can spin down single tracks in Idaho, challenge themselves in Nepal, or pedal through Belize. Newcomers can try cycling in the golden California wine country or practice saying "le hydrate de carbone" (carbohydrate in French) for a trip to the Bordeaux region. There are companies that combine activities, offering a mixture of cycling, kayaking, hiking, and other ways of enjoying the outdoors. Some tours are self-sufficient: you carry your gear. Others provide van support, or sag service. All of these companies have detail-packed brochures, and they should be able to supply you with a list of prior customers who can share their impressions. This information can help you decide what features are important to you and who you want to travel with.

We've grouped the following organizations and companies according to the countries and regions in which they specialize. Many are cross-listed. While some companies cater exclusively to off-road enthusiasts, others are on-road touring experts. Many, however, have trips that fit either way of going it by bike.

As part of their regular publications, the League of American Wheelmen and Bikecentennial publish a list of touring companies. Contact both organizations (See *Bicycle Organizations*) for more information.

TOURS

North America

Adrift Cyclery, P.O. Box 577, Moab, UT 84532, 801/259–8594 * Offers off-road adventures in Utah. Has snorkeling trips in Central America.

Alaska Bicycle Tours, P.O. Box 829, Haines, AK 99827, 907/766–2869 * 1– to 9–day off- and on-road tours in Alaska. Has accommodations ranging from B & Bs to camping. Go explore the Yukon and British Columbia too!

All Adventure Travel, P.O. Box 4307, Boulder, CO 80306, 800/537–4025, 303/499–1981; fax: 303/939–8889 * Books on- and off-road tours in practically every state in the U.S. and all over the world. See "Europe" below.

Alps Mountain Bike Tours, P.O. Box 2333, Huntington Beach, CA 92646, 714/962–4180 * Mountain bike tours for every skill level. Traverse the Alps in one or more countries, including Switzerland, Germany, Austria, and Italy.

America by Cycling, Fassitt Mansion, 6051 Old Philadelphia Pike, Gap, PA 17527, 717/442–3139 * A B & B in the midst of excellent Pennsylvania Dutch biking country. The innkeepers provide maps for self-guided tours of 5 to 50 miles.

American Wilderness Experience, P.O. Box 1486, Boulder, CO 80306, 800/444–0099, 303/494–2992; fax: 303/494–2996 * Broker for various on- and off-road bike trips. Goes to Hawaii and Baja by bike.

American Youth Hostels, National Office, P.O. Box 37613, Washington, DC 20013–7613, 202/783–4943 * Some 59 different itineraries from Massachusetts to Australia. Tours for groups age 12–18, 18 and over, 50 and over, and mixed groups; from flat rides of 30 miles a day to more than 60 miles a day in the mountains; from 9 to 80 days. All

On Bike-centennial's Great Parks North route in Glacier National Park. (Bikecentennial Photo by Greg Siple)

combinations of hostels, hotels, and camping. No rentals or sag wagons. Flexible routes according to the whims of the groups; these are trips for independent, democratic-minded bike tourists.

America's Adventure, 23418 Fescue Dr., Golden, CO 80401, 800/222–3595, 303/526–0806 * For teens. Both road and off-road biking in the context of other outdoor adventures.

Arrow to the Sun, P.O. Box 115, Taylorsville, CA 95983, 916/284–6263 * Somewhat budget-oriented tours, up to 12 days, of Oregon coast, Columbia River Gorge, Baja, and Mayan sites. Choice of hotel, camping, or combination. Rentals, meals provided. Video preview available for loan.

Backcountry Bicycle Tours, Inc., P.O. Box 4029, Bozeman, MT 59772, 406/586–3557 * Experts in bike travel in the western states, Backcountry has on- and off-road tours in Utah, Montana, Wyoming, and the western Canadian provinces.

Backroads Bicycle Touring, 1516 5th St., Berkeley, CA 94710–1713, 800/BIKE–TRIP, 415/527–1555; fax: 415/527–1444 * 2– to 17–day tours around the world, year-round, from Italy to Thailand and 50 places in between. Stay in Louisiana plantation mansions, Italian villas, California lodges, New England inns. Offers a mountain bike tour in Idaho and special tours, including those for singles. Definitely luxury touring—they even serve champagne on the camping trips. Sag wagons, mountain bike tours, rentals.

Baja Expeditions, 2625 Garnet Ave., San Diego, CA 92109, 619/581–3311; fax: 619/581–6542 * Five- to eight-day mountain bike tours supported by a van to carry food/gear. Rentals available. The company also runs sea kayaking and whale-watching trips.

Bay Area Biking, P.O. Box 6264, Carmel, CA 93291, 800/348–8878 * Mountain bike tours in Monterey and northern California.

Bicycle Adventures, P.O. Box 7875, Olympia, WA 98507, 206/786–0989 * Bicycle Adventures specializes in the Pacific Northwest. They also go to California, Hawaii, and British Columbia.

Bicycle Holidays, R.D. 3, Box 2394, Middlebury, VT 05753, 802/388–BIKE * Custom-planned self-guided tours of Vermont. You fill out a questionnaire; then the company (founded in 1986) plans the route and provides maps and transports luggage. Camp or stay in inns.

Bicycle Utah, P.O. Box 738, Park City, UT 84060, 801/649–5806 * Free guide to bicycling in Utah. Lists tour companies.

Bike Arizona, 7454 E. Broadway, #102, Tucson, AZ 85710, 602/722–3228 * Guided, vehicle-assisted tours of 3 to 7 days of the Grand Canyon area, Indian ruins, ghost towns, and the White Mountains.

Bike East, R.D. 1, Box 85, Ghent, NY 12075, 518/828–7007 * Bike tours in the Adirondacks and northeastern U.S. Has road, off-road, and combination canoe and bike trips.

Bike Vermont, Inc., P.O. Box 207 LM, Woodstock, VT 05091, 802/457–3553 * Weekend to 5–day Vermont tours from inn-to-inn. Groups of 12 to 20 ride 20–35 miles daily. Meals, sag wagons, rentals of 12–speed bikes. Claims to be the sole company to do just Vermont.

Bike Wisconsin, Ltd., P.O. Box 9309, Madison, WI 53715, 608/251–3020 * Weekend, long weekend, and inn-to-inn tours. Meals, maps, and support van provided. Historic inns and sites featured, rentals available for more than a dozen tour routes.

Bikecentennial Tours, P.O. Box 8308, Missoula, MT 59807, 406/721–1776 * A national nonprofit cycle touring organization that plots routes, sells maps, and leads tour groups of 8 to 14 cyclists across the continent. Their TransAmerica and Northern Tier trips are legendary, a sort of bicyclist's rite-of-passage. Self-contained camping trips, inn-to-inn rides, light touring, and mountain-bike excursions from 3 days to 3 months. Also sells maps for 17,000 miles worth of do-it-yourself tours.

Blackwater Bikes, P.O. Box 190, Davis, WV 26260, 304/259–5286 * Off-road cycling in a national forest and on other public lands. Blackwater also rents bikes and organizes off-road races as well as inn-to-inn tours.

Breakaway Adventure Travel, 93 Cherry St., New Canaan, CT 06840, 800/955–5635, 203/972–6559 * Broker for tours anywhere, from Vermont to Kenya. See also "Europe" below.

Breakaway Vacations, 164 E. 90th St. #2Y, New York, NY 10128, 212/722–4221 * Focuses on the Northeast. Offers road tours in Massachusetts, New York, Pennsylvania, Virginia, and Vermont. Also goes to California, Utah, and Quebec.

Breaking Away, 1142 Manhattan Ave., Ste. 253, Manhattan Beach, CA 90266, 213/545–5118 * Racing-oriented tours held near famous races. See "Europe" below.

Budget Travels West, P.O. Box 476, Salida, CO 81201, 719/539–7102 * Tours include biking, rafting, and hiking in the Rockies and Southwest.

Carolina Cycle Tours, Nantahala Outdoor Center, 41 U.S. 19 West, Bryson City, NC 28713, 704/488–6737 * Offers road and mountain bike tours in the Southeast.

Ciclismo Classico, P.O. Box 2405, Cambridge, MA 02238, 617/628–7314 * The Italian experts now pedal through upstate New York. See also "Europe" below.

Club Adventure, P.O. Box 549, Carpinteria, CA 93014, 800/621–4611, 805/684–7903 * Inn-to-inn tours in California.

Country Cycling Tours, 140 West 83rd St., New York,

The pine covered mountains of the Sierra Juarez in Northern Baja California, Mexico, offer superb cycle touring on mountain bikes. (Baja Expeditions)

NY 10024, 212/874–5151; fax: 212/874–5286 * International tours averaging 25–35 miles daily in France, Ireland, England, Holland, or, in the U.S., the Maine coast, Pennsylvania Dutch country, Cape Cod, Virginia, Vermont, and more. From day trips to several weeks. Equipment rental available.

Country Inns Along the Trail, c/o Churchill House Inn, R.R. #3 Box 3265, Brandon, VT 05733, 800/999–6865, 802/247–3300 * A country inn near both the Champlain Valley and Green Mountains. Innkeepers Roy and Lois Jackson rent 12–speed bicycles and provide maps and directions. They will also arrange inn-to-inn tours.

Country Pedal'rs, R.D. 6, Box 249C, Somerset, PA 15501, 800/762–5942, 814/445–6316 * Off- and on-road biking in the Laurel Highlands.

Covered Bridge Bicycle Tours, P.O. Box 693, Main Post Office, Saint John, New Brunswick, Canada E2L 4B3, 506/849–9028 * Week-long tours of the province of New Brunswick. Groups of 12 average 35 miles a day with meals, sag wagon, and lodging provided. Rentals available.

Cruiser Bob's Downhill Bicycle Tours, 505 Front St., Lahaina, HI 96761. 808/579–8445 * 38 miles downhill on the steepest paved road in the world.

Cycle Inn Vermont, Inc., P.O. Box 243, Ludlow, VT 05149–0243, 802/228–8799 * Self-guided tours from 2 days to 2 weeks. Lodging, meals, luggage transport, emergency assistance, maps.

Cyclepaths Mountain Bike Adventures, Box 887, Tahoe City, CA 95730, 916/581–1171 * Has Tahoe-Sierra day and weekend mountain bike tours.

Easy Rider Tours, P.O. Box 1384, E. Arlington, MA 02174, 800/488–8332, 617/643–8332 * While New England and Canada Maritimes are some of Easy Rider's stomping grounds, they also visit Ireland, Portugal, and the San Juan Islands. See "Europe" below.

Elk River Touring Center, Slatyfork, WV 26291, 304/572–3771 * Mountain bike touring in the Monongahela National Forest or the 75–mile Greenbrier River Trail, a rail-to-trail conversion. Guides, lodging, and lessons on off-road riding available.

Endless Summer Tours, 1101 Franklin, Michigan City, IN 46360, 800/345–3389 * Tours in southwest Michigan and Indiana. Also goes to Utah and Colorado.

Four Seasons Cycling, P.O. Box 145, Waterbury Center, VT 05677–0145, 802/244–8751 * More than a score of weekend to week-long tours across the U.S. and a few international trips. Rentals, meals, inns provided. Group size up to 24.

Free Spirit Adventures, 104 Foster St., Lewisburg, WV 24901, 800/877–4749, 304/645–2093 * Mountain biking tours in Greenboro County, four hours from Washington, D.C. Has rentals.

Hawaiian Experience Inc., P.O. Box 1874, Kihei, HI 96753, 800/344–8496, 808/874–1929 * 1–day to 1–week tours of Maui and the Big Island. Includes lodging, meals, sag wagon, guides, maps, some land transportation. Rentals.

Hawaiian Pedals Ltd., 75–5744 Alii Drive, Kailua-Kona, HI 96740, 808/329–2294, 808/325–6416 * Self-guided tours around the volcanoes and beaches of the Big Island. Stay in hotels or B & Bs or camp. Rentals of bikes, camping gear, car racks, and helmets available.

HeartCycle, P.O. Box 10743, Denver, CO 80210 303/934–5015 * Training rides and tours operated by an all-volunteer, nonprofit organization that has promoted cycling since 1978. Routes include the Front Range and Anasazi regions of southwest Colorado. Tours of 5 to 10 days, 35 miles to 125 miles a day. Provide your own bike. Motels and sag wagons.

Heartland Bicycle Tours, 1 Orchard Cir., Washington, IA 52353, 800/798–2859, 319/653–2277 * Cycles in Iowa, "a place to grow," and Illinois. New trips planned for the Bahamas and Caribbean.

High Desert Adventures, 240 E. Morris Ave., Salt Lake City, UT 84115, 800/345–RAFT, 801/483–6165 * Mountain bike trips in Utah. Also has rafting adventures for those who want a break from the bicycle.

Island Bicycle Adventures, 569 Kapahulu Ave., Honolulu, HI 96815, 800/233–2226, 808/734–0700 * 6–day trips on Maui, Kaui, and Hawaii islands. Stay in hotels, eat in local restaurants. Sagwagons, rental bikes.

Kolowisi Southern Utah Bicycle Tours, 6225 Northborough Cir., West Jordan, UT 84084, 801/967–1161 * Mountain bike tours in Moab and other parts of Utah. Some tours stay at a ranch, hidden away from the world.

Mad River Mountain Biking, Box 65, Waitsfield, VT 05673, 800/777–HYDE, 802/496–2322 * Road and off-road tours. Nearby trails. Rentals available.

Mammouth Adventure Connection, Box 353, Mammouth Lakes, CA 93546, 800/228–4947, 619/934–2581 * Mountain bike park that also has guided tours, rental bikes, and sag wagon.

Michigan Bicycle Touring, Michael and Libby Robold, 3512 Red School Rd., Kingsley, MI 49649, 616/263–5885 * 90 trips from May to October in the Upper Peninsula and elsewhere. Weekend and 5–day tours. Off- and on-road excursions. Rentals. Some hiking/canoe trips. Lodging in inns. Run by Libby and Michael Robold since 1977.

Carrie Murray Outdoor Education Campus, 1901 Ridgetop Rd., Baltimore, MD 21207, 301/396–0808 * A center for the rehabilitation of raptors, Carrie Murray also offers classes in orienteering and wilderness survival. Occasionally, they have weekend trips with a cycling component. Their summer camps for children and adults have a one-week cycling program.

New England Bicycle Tours, P.O. Box D, Randolph, VT 05060, 800/233–2128, 802/728–3261 * Mountain bike tours in Maine and Vermont. Takes to the road on Prince Edward Island, Massachusetts, and the Caribbean.

Nichols Expeditions, 590 North 500 West, Moab, UT 84532, 800/653–1792, 801/259–7882 * Runs mountain bike tours and a B & B in the Moab area.

North Country Adventures, P.O. Box 1731, Traverse City, MI 49685, 616/929–1404 * A quartet of 3–day tours of Northern Michigan by mountain bike or road bike. Motels or camping, meals provided, rentals.

Northwest Bicycle Touring Society, 6166 92nd Ave. SE, Mercer Island, WA 98040, 206/232–2080 * Road tours in Oregon, Washington, and British Columbia.

Northwest Passage Outing Club, 1130 Greenleaf Ave., Wilmette, IL 60091, 800/732–7328, 708/256–4409 * Road tours to Michigan, Wisconsin, Vermont, Iowa, and Colorado. See also "Europe" below.

Northwest Voyageurs, P.O. Box 373, Lucile, ID 83542, 800/727–9977, 208/628–3780 * Hells Canyon, the Snake River, the ghost town of Florence, and the Salmon River area are all mountain bike destinations in Idaho for Northwest Voyageurs.

Okanagan Bike Tours, 2 - 516 Papineau St., Penticton, British Columbia, V2A 4X6, Canada, 604/493–BIKE * Washington State tours, camping.

On the Loose, 1030 Merced St., Berkeley, CA 94707, 415/527–4005 * From the San Juan Islands to the Canyonlands, Utah; weekend to 8–day tours. Sag wagons for both inn tours and camping tours (tents provided). Rentals. 10–day winter tours in Hawaii. New destinations for 1991 are New Mexico and Arizona. Has mountain biking.

Otter Bar Lodge, Forks of Salmon, CA 96031, 916/462–4772 * Week-long mountain-bike retreats in the California mountains just below the Oregon border. Located on 40 acres surrounded by national forest, the lodge is better known for its kayak school but is catching on among the ATB crowd as well. Groups limited to 10, rentals available. Day of rafting, hot tub, sauna included.

Outback with Bodfish, P.O. Box 69, Chester, CA 96020, 916/258–4296 * Chuck "Bodfish" knows his part of California well. Outback has challenging mountain bike tours around Lassen and other parts of northern California.

Outward Bound, Hurricane Island, P.O. Box 429, Rockland, ME 04841, 800/341–1745, 207/594–5548 * Take the Outward Bound philosophy on a bike tour in Maine for 9 or 22 days. Geared for both novice and experienced cyclists. "They will teach you the fundamentals of bike repair and maintenance."

Overland Expeditions, 1773 11th St., Los Osos, CA 03402, 805/528–6381 * Uses double-decker buses to sag cyclists. Goes to California and France. Designs tours for cyclists with disabilities.

PAC Tour, P.O. Box 73, Harvard, IL 60033, 815/943–3171 * The next closest thing to RAAM, the Race Across AMerica. Cycle 100 to 153 miles a day, from California to Georgia or Texas to Calgary, British Columbia, Canada. Led by ultra-marathon cyclists/winners of RAAM, and husband/wife team of Susan Notorangelo and Lon Haldeman. Full support.

Pacific Crest Bicycle Tours, 2722 Alki Ave. SW, Seattle, WA 98116, 206/938–3322 * Tours of Olympic Peninsula, Bainbridge Island, Mount Saint Helens, and other spectacular locales of Washington state. Also mountain bike expeditions. International menu includes a mountain bike tour of Mexican jungles with sag wagon and Spanish-speaking guides. Rentals available.

Pack & Paddle, 601 Pinhook Rd. East, Lafayette, LA 70501, 318/232–5854 * The theme is French: the Acadian-accented Mount Desert Island, Maine, and, mostly, French Louisiana, including the Feliciana region where John James Audubon made more than 75 of his paintings. Weekend to week-long trips. Rentals of bikes, panniers, tents, sleeping bags.

PEDAL FOR POWER, Box 898, Atkinson, NH 03811, 800/762–BIKE * A program of the Bicyclists' Education and Legal Foundation of the League of American Wheelmen. PFP conducts long-distance rides to raise money for charity. Each rider must have sponsors. The funds are divided between the Foundation and a second charity selected by each rider. Eat in restaurants, sleep in motels, ride across America in 47 days or North-South in 23 days.

Pocono Inn-to-Inn Tours, Route 903, HC–1, Box 467, Jim Thorpe, PA 18229, 717/325–3655 * 19 tours from 2 to 7 days. Lodging in inns, meals, rentals.

REI Adventures, P.O. Box 88126, Seattle, WA 98138, 800/622–2236, 206/395–7760 * From the outdoor co-op, moderate to difficult trips to Alaska, Utah, and California. See "Europe" and "Elsewhere" below.

Linda Thorpe and Jim Richardson were the first cyclists to ride Bikecentennial's TransAmerica Bicycle Trail, in the summer of 1974. (Bikecentennial Photo)

Rim Tours, 94 W. 1st North, Moab, UT 84532, 801/259–5233 * Slickrock, Valley of the Gods—any number of Utah and Colorado destinations by mountain bike.

Rivanna Bicycle Touring Company, 6 University Ct., Charlottesville, VA 22903, 804/295–6636 * Has bicycle tours with camping and other excursions. Goes across the country and has shorter trips.

Roads Less Traveled Bicycle Adventures, 1250 Bear Mtn. Ct., Boulder, CO 80303, 303/499–4273 * "Spectacular inn-to-inn adventures in the Colorado/Utah backcountry."

Rocky Mountain Cycle Tours, Box 1978, Canmore, Alberta T0L 0M0, Canada, 800/661–2453 (in the U.S.), 403/678–6770 * Hawaii, San Juan Islands, British Columbia, Alberta, and other destinations.

Scenic Byways Bicycle Touring, 942 East, 7145 Stouh, Ste. A–105, Midvale, UT 84047, 801/566–2662 * Mountain bike touring in Utah's Canyonlands. Has raft/bike combination trips, rentals.

Southwest Cycling Expeditions, P.O. Box 2871, Flagstaff, AZ 86003, 602/526–4882 * Groups of 6 to 14 riding from 3,000 to 8,000 feet. Lodging, food, and support vehicles. Trips through the Canyonlands and monuments of Arizona and Utah.

Suwannee Bicycle Tours, Inc., P.O. Box 247, White Springs, FL 32097, 904/878–2042 * On- and off-road tours of a Florida few people enjoy. Also see "Elsewhere" below.

Timberline Bicycle Tours, 7975 East Harvard, #J, Denver, CO 80231, 303/759–3804 * 84 trips through the best of the West, including 28 National Parks, the San Juan Islands, Jasper and Banff, and the Canyonlands of Utah. On- and off-road rides, sagwagons, rentals, tour leaders. Most tours are 5 days; a 9–day loop in Idaho includes whitewater rafting.

Touring Exchange, Box 265, Port Townsend, WA 98368, 206/385–0667 * See "Elsewhere" below.

Triple T Lone Star, 1057½ Nueces, Austin, TX 78701, 512/474–2714 * Triple T wants you to "saddle up" and join them. They'll show you Texas and New Mexico the way no one else can.

Two Wheel Tours, P.O. Box 1235, Bloomington, IN 47402, 800/688–1214, 812/336–1214 * Official tour provider to Tour Du Pont--brings cyclists and "armchair" fans to the ride. Goes to New Mexico, France, and throughout the eastern seaboard. Plans on having mountain bike rides in New Mexico and Quebec.

Utah Outback, 1149–B Sunnyside Ave., Salt Lake City, Utah 84102 * Off-road riding in Utah.

Valley Chamber of Commerce, Box 3236, Winter Park, CO 80482 * Information on bike touring in Winter Park, Colorado.

VCC Four Seasons Cycling, P.O. Box 145, Waterbury Center, VT 05677–0145, 802/244–8751 * VCC offers dozens of trips in Vermont and across the Mid-Atlantic. Rentals, meals, inns provided. Group size up to 24.

Venture Out Unlimited, Inc., N1497 Southern Rd., Lyndon Station, WI 53944, 608/666–3300 * Lots of options for touring Wisconsin, a.k.a. the Dairy State. Offers "pampered" camping, lodges, off-road trips, custom tours, pedal and paddle combos. Groups of 8–20 riders. Sag wagons. Rentals available.

Vermont Bicycle Touring, Monkton Rd., Box 711, Bristol, VT 05443, 802/453–4811 * One of the original touring outfitters, VBT has hosted more than 66,000 riders since 1972. B & Bs, big dinners, shopping, and sag wagons are featured. Rentals, bike/sail options available. Weekends to 8–day trips. VBT has now branched out to California, England, and New Zealand. Free 17–minute video preview available for loan.

Vermont Mountain Bike Tours, P.O. Box 26, Pittsfield, VT 05762, 802/746–8580 * 1– to 5–day off-road tours, guided and self-guided inn-to-inn tours. Bikes provided.

The Wayfarers, P.O. Box 73408, Washington, DC 20056 * Budget, family-oriented 6–day cycle trips in New Jersey and Pennsylvania. Emphasis on a leisurely pace and exploring local sights. See a part of N.J. few do. (Surprise! It's got a lot to offer cyclists.) Camp with your own gear. Groups prepare their own dinners. Limited sag wagon service. All profits go to bicycle causes such as rail-to-trail conversions. Send SASE for information.

Western Spirit Cycling, 545 Locust Lane, Moab, UT 84532, 800/845–BIKE, 801/259–8732 * Mountain bike tours in Utah, Colorado, Idaho, and Montana. "Civilized tours in uncivilized terrain."

WHY GO BICYCLE TOURING?

As inveterate tourers who fell in love with the way the world unfolds from the seat of a bicycle, we say, "Why not?" Few things rival the pleasures obtained from cycling. Just one or more hours in the saddle and the world changes: you keep a pace that allows trees, rivers, mountains, homes . . . indeed, the whole world to unfold. Details that are too often missed, small flowers by a roadside fence or a child waving from a window, float up. Breathe deeply while you spin away the miles, and you'll inhale the sharp scent of pine needles, moisture on new grass, and the seductive smell of just-cooked food.

Cyclists know this, and like spokes radiating from a central hub, hundreds of them take to the open road every day for weekend, week-long, and even year-long trips. For they discover as you have (or soon will) that cycling for one day is not enough.

Once you decide to explore for longer durations, there's a plethora of resources and options. Look in your own neighborhood first and plan a weekend ride. Most villages and even urban areas have ready-made escape opportunities for cyclists. Local newspapers list campgrounds, B&Bs, and youth hostels. Your region's bicycle club or clubs will often publish or share route collections and likely destinations.

The first question you may have is what kind of bicycle is best suited for long rides. One that's comfortable and has been ridden before is the simplest answer. Of course there are other considerations.

A touring bicycle, or sport bicycle, is appropriate for the recreational rider seeking rides of varying lengths. Unlike a racing, or thin-tire, ultra-lightweight bicycle, the sport bicycle can handle bumps in the roads (its tires are at least ¼" wider) and longer distances comfortably. Typically, it has drop handlebars, lightweight wheels, and a frame designed for longer rides (the wheelbase is actually longer—just as in a luxury car, the greater distance between the hubs translates to a smoother ride). A touring bicycle will be equipped with a one-piece rear rack (and possibly a front rack) with hooks to mount panniers. Look for 18– or 21–speed gearing with very low gears. A bicycle loaded for touring weighs double an unloaded bike. Your knees will thank you for the low gears.

Some tourists now head off on mountain bikes. The tough frames and thick tires come in handy on bumpy, back-country roads, but the upright handlebar position can be wearing (the purpose of drop handlebars is to allow riders to vary their position, relieving pressure on back, neck, and posterior as desired). Mountain bikes are also heavier than touring models.

Others opt for "hybrid" or "crossover" bicycles that combine some of the best features of touring and mountain bikes.

The solution: Choose a bicycle that suits your purpose *and* fits well. Any bike shop worth its spokes will take the time to match you to the right model (this can even be done by feeding your vital measurements into a computer). Whatever bike you choose, ride it several times before embarking on a tour. Experiment with different seats if need be; there's no need to suffer. Leather seats are uncomfortable at first but can break in beautifully, just like a baseball glove. Gel-filled and padded seat covers are also available. Standard touring saddles tend to be wider and softer than racing seats.

Consider augmenting your rear panniers with front panniers and a handlebar bag. A general rule is to distribute 40 percent of the weight you're carrying over the front wheel, as low as you can place it. The other 60 percent should be balanced over the back wheel. Panniers are designed to achieve this; just be sure to pack equal weights in each bag.

Some cyclists out on their first extended trip rely on a credit card, taking a minimum of supplies. Others are happy porting a sleeping bag, lightweight tent, and other supplies required for a night away from home. Whichever way you choose to go, there are several items you should take for a long, one-day ride or a longer two- or more-day outing.

Always carry a rudimentary repair kit and know how to use it. A spare tube, tire irons, patch kit, and bicycle pump (or facsimile of all the preceding) are essential. If your bicycle does not have quick-release wheels, pack a crescent wrench. The best thing to do, however, is to maintain your bicycle: major breakdowns are less likely to happen and ruin a good day of cycling. Some cyclists carry handlebar-bag-size repair books that cover the basics. Changing a flat is fairly simple, but it's best to practice at least once so you can become familiar with the process. (See "Fixing a Flat" in the *Tools* section.)

Carrying an article or two of clothing, even if it is warm out, is advisable. Windbreakers or rain jackets usually tuck into a bag or jersey pocket easily. Regardless of the length of a trip, carry a pocket knife and a stash of food. On overnights add to that and bring matches and a warm jacket. Pack something that can be eaten without preparation. Food bars, dried fruit, granola bars, and cookies are easy to carry and can last for months. Of course, emergency money is necessary; make sure you have a quarter for a phone call. Let people know where you are going—acquaint a friend with your route and ultimate destination, especially if you are going by yourself.

If you want guidance on your first excursion, companionship, or expertise, consider going with your local bicycle club or one of the many professional touring companies that offer a host of exciting options. There are reputable companies in practically every region. Several advertise in the back of national bicycle magazines. The League of American Wheelmen (L.A.W.) offers a special issue of their magazine, *Bicycle USA,* which details more than 160 international and domestic tour operators. That issue, the *TourFinder,* is available for $5 from L.A.W., 2707 Whitestone Rd., Suite 209, Baltimore, MD 21207. Bikecentennial (P.O. Box 8308, Missoula, MT 59807, 406/721–1776) has mapped over 17,000 miles in the U.S. and has maps designed specifically for cyclists. While most routes are ten days or longer, it is possible to take advantage of sections of these maps.

Wheel Escapes, 1000 Magnolia Ave., Larkspur, CA 94939, 800/582–BIKE, ext. 1 * Tours for the Marin Headlands, wine country, and Lake Tahoe. Can design custom tours.

Woodswoman, Inc., 25 W. Diamond Lake Rd., Minneapolis, MN 55419, 612/822–3809 * Bicycling and other sports for women only. Join them in Minnesota, Wisconsin, Mexico, "Europe," and "Elsewhere."

Xest, 1534 Klammath, Sunnyvale, CA 94087, 408/2453372 * Has mountain and road bike rentals in the San Francisco area. Offers custom tours with sag service.

Europe

Adventure Center, 1311 63rd St., Suite 200, Emeryville, CA 94608, 800/227–8747, 415/654–1879 * Goes to New Zealand and France.

All Adventure Travel, P.O. Box 4307, Boulder, CO 80306, 800/537–4025, 303/499–1981; fax: 303/499–1984 * Travel agency that arranges bike tours along the lines of doing an African safari on a mountain bike, combining a week of cycling and cooking classes in Italy, bike and barging (on canal boats) in Burgundy, and mountain biking in Nepal.

Backroads Bicycle Touring, 1516 5th St., Berkeley, CA 94710–1713, 800/BIKE–TRIP, 415/527–1555; fax: 415/527–1444 * 2– to 17–day

Cyclists in France. (Dennis Coello/Backroads Bicycle Touring)

trips all over. In Europe, they will guide you through Ireland, Italy, France, and England. Has special tours for singles and photographers of all levels and interests.

Baumeler Tours, Inc., 10 Grand Ave., Rockville Centre, NY 11570, 800/6–ABROAD, 516/766–6160; fax: 516/766–3750 * Guided and self-guided hiking and biking tours of Switzerland, Holland, France, Austria, Germany, Italy, and England. Meals, lodging, rental bikes provided.

Bike Events, P.O. Box 75, Bath, Avon BA1 1BX, England, 0225/310859 * British-based organization that runs a variety of tours—some are fundraisers for charities such as the British Heart Foundation. Bike Events does the famous London to Brighton bike ride and others, including the London to Amsterdam Bike Ride and the Big Green Bike Ride, which raises funds for the World Wildlife Fund.

Bike the Flat Landscapes of Holland, c/o Bon Voyage Travel, 825 S. Shields St., Fort Collins, CO 80521, 303/493–8511 * A biking and barging vacation in Holland. You can't get much flatter than Holland, unless you cycle the salt flats of Utah.

Blue Marble Travel, 1211 Clarks Valley, Dauphin, PA 17018, 800/544–3216, 717/921–2054 * Small group tours of 18 to 39 days for adults from about 20 to 45. Self-supported. Bike across Europe, Denmark, Austria, or France. Meals, inns, an occasional sleeper berth in a train, touring bike provided.

Blyth & Company, One Rockefeller Plaza, Room 1712 B, New York, NY 10020, 212/265–9600, 800/228–7712 * For "pampered pedalers" (their brochure encourages you to fly the Concorde to their destinations), trips through Italy, France, Austria, Eastern Europe, the Canadian Rockies, and Nova Scotia. Rentals available. Group size up to 22 adults. Van supported, meals provided.

Breakaway Adventure Travel, 93 Cherry St., New Canaan, CT 06840, 800/955–5635, 203/972–6559 * Broker for tours anywhere, including France, Switzerland, Italy.

Breaking Away, 1142 Manhattan Ave., Ste. 253, Manhattan Beach, CA 90266, 213/545–5118 * Looking for an excuse to watch the Tour de France up close? Breaking Away structures cycling vacations around 5 major bicycle races: The Tour Du Pont, Giro d'-Italia, Tour de France, Colorado Rockies World Mountain Bike Championships, and Hawaii "Ironman." Basically you follow the race route in a van loaded with bikes and ride as much or as little as you like. Breaking Away promises bilingual tour leaders, pro mechanics, souvenirs, deluxe hotels, and chances to meet the cycling stars.

Butterfield & Robinson, 70 Bond St., Toronto, Ontario M5B 1X3, 800/387–1147 * Self-proclaimed as the most expensive, sophisticated, and erudite of the high-end biking tour outfitters; the buzz is that Sir Kenneth Clark might show up as your guide. About 23 European biking trips. 120–page brochure available. B & R also does a dog-and-pony (AKC and thoroughbred, of course) slide show in swank downtown hotels across the US; call or write for details.

Chateaux Bike Tours, P.O. Box 5706, Denver, CO 80217, 800/678–BIKE, 303/393–6910 * Group and private tours in Italy, France, and Switzerland.

Ciclismo Classico, P.O. Box 2405, Cambridge, MA 02238, 617/628–7314 * Tour the Umbria and Tuscany regions of Italy with van support and Italian-speaking guides. One route combines a week of cycling with classes at the Cooking School of Umbria. Ciclismo now has a tour in upstate New York.

Classic Bicycle Tours and Treks, P.O. Box 668, Clarkston, NY 14430, 800/777–8090; fax: 716/637–9075 * 1– and 2–week tours of Greece, Ireland, France, Canada, Natchez Trace. Meals, lodging, rentals. Custom tours for groups over 8 riders.

Condor Adventures Ltd., 2044 Bellaire St., Denver, CO 80207, 800/729–1262 * Biking all over Europe.

Peter Costello, Ltd., P.O. Box 23490, Baltimore, MD 21203, 301/685–6918 * 6– and 9–day tours in Scotland. Groups of 8–12 traveling 40–50 miles daily. Visit Scotland's "Poet's Country," the Borders and Lowlands of Dumfries and Galloway. Sag wagon, B & Bs, meals provided.

Country Cycling Tours, 140 West 83rd St., New York, NY 10024, 212/874–5151; fax: 212/874–5286 * Large, New York City–based touring company that goes to Pennsylvania, New York, New Jersey, Maryland, Massachusetts, Florida, Virginia, and Europe.

Cycle Portugal, P.O. Box 877, San Antonio, FL 33576, 800/245–4226, 904/588–4132 * Experienced guides take you road biking in Portugal, France, and Spain.

Cyclorama, The Grange Hotel, Grange-over-Sands, Cumbria LA116EJ, England * Walking and cycling in England's Lake District. Self-guided 7–day trips. Stay in hotels and guest houses. Sag wagon for luggage. Rentals.

Earthventures, 2625 N. Meridian St., Ste. 612, Indianapolis, IN 46208, 800/447–2866, 317/783–9449 * England, France, and Italy on road bicycles. Rentals available. See also "Elsewhere" below.

Easy Rider Tours, P.O. Box 1384, E. Arlington, MA 02174, 800/488–8332, 617/643–8332 * Goes to Portugal and Ireland. Says of Portugal that it is a "relatively unvisited corner of Europe that's kept a lot of its traditional culture and charm alive. Most Americans overlook Portugal, except for beach resorts in the south, but there's a tremendous amount to see." See also "North America" above.

EuroBike Tours, P.O. Box 40, DeKalb, IL 60115, 815/758–8851 * 9– to 14–day tours from England to Eastern Europe. Guide, mechanic, meals, sag wagon, maps, rentals provided.

Europeds, 883 Sinex Ave., Pacific Grove, CA 93950, 408/372–1173; fax: 408/655–4501 * 8– to 17–day trips in Dordogne, Provence, Alsace, and Pyrenees regions of France for road and mountain biking (also hiking and skiing). Maximum of 17 to group. Meals, sag wagons, hotels. Rental bike included in cost.

First American Bicycle Tours, 303 E. Southern, Ste. 108, Mesa, AZ 85210, 800/289–6441, 602/992–2527 * Road tours in Austria, Switzerland, Italy, France, Hungary, Czechoslovakia, Liechtenstein, and Germany. Has a luxury bus for support and can arrange off-road tours.

Forum Travel International, Inc., 91 Gregory Lane, #21, Pleasant Hill, CA 94523, 415/671–2900; fax: 415/946–1500, 671–2993 * Tours of Austria, France, Germany,

DESIGNING YOUR OWN ROUTE

. . . .

By Trudy E. Bell

Creating a bicycle tour involves much more than looking at a state road map for motorists. On a bike tour, you're seldom interested in getting from Point A to Point B as soon as possible, but in pedaling scenic back roads with little traffic—roads often not shown on state road maps. Cyclists are affected by factors irrelevant to cars, such as hills, prevailing winds, road surface, and availability of water. Moreover, paved bike paths are inaccessible to cars, and some bridges and tunnels for auto traffic are forbidden to cyclists.

Not to despair. Here are ten tried-and-true steps for success, learned from experience (read "hard knocks") in creating new routes for friends, classes, and a book:

1. Know the abilities of the riders who will be taking the tour. If the ride is for experienced cyclists in August, don't hesitate to plan 50 to 100 miles for a one-day ride. But even relatively strong riders carrying camping gear may be slowed by the extra weight. At the beginning of a multi-day loaded tour, a comfortable expectation is 40 miles per day, which leaves time for striking and setting up camp.

For novice cyclists on an introductory day tour, plan a basic route of no more than 20 miles. In fact, if you have no "sag" vehicle for picking up weary cyclists, plan a cutoff for a shortened ride of 12 to 13 miles. Short? Yes. But you want novices to end the trip glowing at their accomplishment and wanting more—not feeling like road kill or, worse, being unable to finish.

2. Terrain vastly affects speed and total distance. On flat or rolling terrain, a moderately strong rider easily maintains an unhurried pace of more than 10 miles per hour, including brief stops. But in hill country, such as parts of Connecticut or Vermont or California, that average plummets to about 5 miles per hour—or even less for those carrying gear. In other words, 30 miles could take as short as 2 or 3 hours on the flat or as long as 6 or 8 hours in serious hills. Plan accordingly.

For novices, absolutely make the route as flat as possible. Inexperienced cyclists seldom have the stamina, technique, gears, or sheer desire to handle much up and down. Also, even on the flat, count on novices averaging only about 6 miles per hour.

3. Get a feel for attractive and bike-able areas from existing travel guides. New England, the mid-Atlantic states, and the far West are well-mapped by many bicycling guides. Also, scan guides for the motorized crowd to learn about regional attractions, campgrounds, parks, bed and breakfasts, and country inns. Call the state capital to see if the department of transportation has an official bicycle coordinator, who may distribute maps and other information. A local bike club may have cue sheets for its favorite rides.

4. County maps offer the most convenient scale. County maps show all streets, many parks, some trails, plus creeks, bridges, and other useful features, and are often available in book and stationery stores. If you're lucky enough to be in one of the dozen-plus states already mapped by DeLorme Mapping Co. (P.O. Box 298, Freeport, ME 04032, 207/865–4171), for under $15 you can buy a book of 16" by 22" topographic maps of your entire state, most useful in rural areas. The DeLorme books also list popular bike routes and campgrounds.

Bikecentennial (P.O. Box 8308, Missoula, MT 59807, 406/721–1776) has plotted major cross-country routes in strip maps the perfect size for a handlebar bag, complete with information on services. Rails to Trails Conservancy (1400 16th Street NW, Washington, DC 20036, 202/797–5400) also sells guides to a couple hundred bike paths around the country that follow the course of former railroad beds.

5. If you have no topographic information, get clues from the names of features and shapes of roads. On a bike you discover there's a reason for such names as Parsonage Hill Road, Valley Street, or the town of Summit. Roads following river beds and coastlines are generally winding and flat (although not always—California's Pacific Coast Highway rises from sea level to some 1,000 feet). Curvy roads are often hilly, and dead straight roads tend to be flat or rolling (although in parts of Pennsylvania and Connecticut some ruler-straight roads go right up the side of some real wheezers).

6. Plan around the direction of prevailing winds. Coastal rides may have stiff winds from the ocean in the morning and winds from the land in the afternoon—you don't want to plan even a day ride that gives headwinds in both directions. Especially for novices, it'd be like climbing a hill that never quits.

7. Scout the ride before you take the group. While neither practical nor desirable for a cross-country trip, where part of the purpose is to encounter the unknown, this step is absolutely essential if the ride is for novices or for a large group. Maps are dismayingly full of errors, showing roads that never existed, not showing new construction, and not indicating where streets are one-way or turn to ruts and boulders or sand. Scouting the ride by car is the most efficient, but it should be verified by bike for accurate mileage and options not open to cars.

8. Note local attractions on the route. This is, after all, a tour of the area, so do a little research on other activities, especially for novices. Universal favorites are wildlife sanctuaries, historical villages, canoe rentals, and confectioneries with home-made ice cream. For group tours, pre-select a lunch stop in a secluded picnic ground or in some quaint cafe. For novices, make sure this lunch stop is before the short-route cutoff, so everyone can eat together before the group splits.

9. Choose a starting point that, ideally, has parking, restrooms, snacks, and public transportation. Unless the ride begins from everyone's back yard, the riders must meet somewhere first. Cyclists in major cities may be bringing their bikes by train or bus. If people drive, they'll need someplace to park their cars all day without risking a ticket. Many public parks answer all these needs, plus have picnic tables and barbecue grills for a possible cookout at the end of the ride. You can also try the parking lot of a school, shopping mall, or train station; if in doubt, ask the authorities when you scout the ride. Remember, a sandwich shop is useful only if you reach it *before* the lunch stop.

10. Seek the advice of friendly native guides. Local residents—especially local cyclists—can tell you what the maps don't show: whether a bridge is washed out, or a bike path has just been opened, or a particular deli has all-you-can-eat spaghetti for the end of the ride. Also, when you're scouting,

follow any "Bike Route" signs posted in suburban neighborhoods: you may discover the prettiest and most secluded roads by sheer accident.

Trudy E. Bell has custom-designed several dozen tours for a book of rides around New York City for Menasha Ridge Press (for publication in 1991 or 1992) and for her continuing-education class "Bicycle Touring: An Introduction," at the South Orange-Maplewood Adult School in Maplewood, NJ. In her other life, she is senior editor for the engineering magazine *IEEE Spectrum* in New York City.

Czechoslovakia, Hungary, Poland, East Germany, Ireland, Luxembourg, Italy, Spain, Switzerland, New Zealand, China, southeast Asia. Mountain biking in Peru, Ecuador, Soviet Union, Argentina, Chile, Italy. Self-guided and tour company trips.

Gerhard's Bicycle Odysseys, P.O. Box 756, Portland, OR 97207, 503/223–2402 * 2–week tours of Luxembourg, Germany, France, Switzerland, Norway, Austria. Lodging, meals, no rentals.

Goulash Tours, 1707 Olmstead Rd., P.O. Box 2972, Kalamasee, MI 49008, 312/275–1046 or 616/349–8817 * Czechoslovakia, Poland, Bulgaria and—if its borders open—Albania by bike. Tours of up to 8 weeks. Write the proprietors, Bonnie Jo Campbell and Mary Szpur, "This tour is ideal for independent riders. Group members cycle at their own pace, carry their own luggage, and eat when they're hungry. The leaders provide orientations, language lessons, maps, materials and a sense of style."

International Bicycle Tours, 7 Champlin Square, P.O. Box 754, Essex, CT 06426, 203/767–7005 * England, Holland, Belgium, Cape Cod, and Germany for up to 2 weeks. Meals, lodging provided. Special tours for cyclists over age 50. They will customize trips for groups of more than 16 cyclists and offer tours on tandems for blind and sighted cyclists.

Italian Cycling Center, 2117 Green St., Philadelphia, PA 19130– 3110, 215/232–6772 * "Bicycling in Italy for the serious cyclist," including long-distance tourists, fitness riders, racers, and triathletes. Stay in a modest hotel in the Veneto region, tour leisurely or race twice weekly, attend the Giro d'Italia, buy an Italian racing bike wholesale, eat a lot of pasta.

Joyrides Cycle Holidays, The Old Station, Machynlleth, Powys, Wales SY20 8TN, 0654/3109 * A bike shop that arranges week-long loops around Wales. Stay in farmhouses or hostels. Rentals available.

Kolotour, 12580 Boulder, Boulder Creek, CA 95006, 408/338–2979 * Visit Czechoslovakia on road bikes with these folks.

Le Tour, 1030 Merced St., Berkeley, CA 94707, 800/542–4210, 415/525–4990 * Le Tour's tour of France is different because it isn't really a tour—you stay in a private, 200–year-old inn in the Champagne region and explore the countryside at leisure. They promise gourmet picnics en route. Rentals available. Sample video loaned on request.

Lynott Tours, 350 Fifth Ave., Ste. 2619, New York, NY 10118, 800/221–2474, 212/760–0101 * Takes you on the quiet roads of Ireland "in style."

Northwest Passage Outing Club, 1130 Greenleaf Ave., Wilmette, IL 60091, 800/732–7328, 708/256–4409 * In addition to Midwest destinations, Northwest goes to France and Greece.

Progressive Travels, Inc., 1932 First Ave., Ste. 1110, Seattle, WA 98101, 800/245–2229; fax: 206/443–4228 * 6– to 11–day tours of New Zealand, Puget Sound, Italy, Ireland, or France. Meals, lodging in historic inns (or even castles), sag wagons, rentals.

REI Adventures, P.O. Box 88126, Seattle, WA 98138, 800/622–2236, 206/395–7760 * Cycles in the U.S.S.R. See also "North America" and "Elsewhere."

Scottish Highland Bicycle Tours, The Cottage, Clathy by Crieff, Perthshire, PH7 3PH Scotland, 0738/73310; fax: 0738/73357 * Guess where?

Sinbad Tours, Leenderweg 95, Postbus 2022, 5600 CA Eindhoven, Holland, 040/111444; fax: 040–126851 * Cycle trips in Holland.

Travent International, P.O. Box 305, Waterbury Center, VT 05677–0305, 800/325–3009 * Another company that bills itself as designing luxurious tours to Europe, including Switzerland, England, and Ireland.

Triskell Cycle Tours, Lannuon 56110, Gouring, France, 010/33–9723–5950 * Cycling tours of Brittany that coincide with the Tour de France and other races. Other tours take advantage of owner Paul and Simone Turnbull's knowledge of Brittany.

True Wheel Tours, John and Jackie Mallery, 3 Woolerton St., Delhi, NY 13753, 607/746–2737 * Self-sufficient (e.g., no sag wagon, sometimes no leader) tours of Holland, Ireland, Jamaica, Brittany, and Greece. No rentals. Stay in hotels, B & Bs, or villas.

Wilderness Travel, 801 Allston Way, Berkeley, CA 94710, 800/247–6700, 415/548–0420 * The company is better known for running camel safaris and Kilimanjaro climbs, but it promises "deluxe" 9–day tours of the French regions of Burgundy, the Loire Valley, and Provence. Pedal about 35 miles daily, sleep in chateaux, eat in gourmet restaurants. Bikes provided free, but expect "land costs" alone to exceed $250 daily.

Womantrek, P.O. Box 20643, Seattle, WA 98102, 800/477–TREK, 206/325–4772 * Mountain bike and road trips for women. Includes Nova Scotia, France, and eastern Europe in their destinations. See "Elsewhere" below.

Woodswoman, Inc., 25 W. Diamond Lake Rd., Minneapolis, MN 55419, 612/822–3809 * Bicycling and other sports for women only in Ireland, "Elsewhere," and "North America."

Worldwide Nordic Tours, Box 1129, Maplewood, NJ 07040, 201/378–9170 * Trips of a week or longer through the Alps, Germany, Holland, Denmark, Japan, the Loire Valley of France, and Wisconsin. Stay in hotels, or in Holland, a river barge fitted with beds.

BIKING AND PHOTOGRAPHY

. . . .

By Byron Reed

Through all my years of bicycle adventures, I've found that the best way to remember and cherish those spectacular riding days and superb cycling partners is through photographs. I relish getting together with friends and looking at slides and prints from the most recent outing; we order a pizza and relive the fun times. Photography is the best memory I've got—it doesn't fade away, and I can see it in color.

Thanks to modern technology, practically everyone can take excellent photographs, even if they don't know shutter speeds from focal lengths. Inexpensive cameras that automate everything from loading and rewinding the film to controlling the focus and exposure are now readily available. But what are the needs of the bicyclist who wants to carry a camera along?

The Camera

. . . .

First, the camera must be light and compact. It must be somewhat rugged and able to withstand vibration and a moderate degree of road shock. One that is weather-resistant is a real plus, and the fewer nooks and crannies it has to collect dirt, the better off you'll be. A choice of wide-angle and telephoto lenses also helps you to frame your subject well for the best composition.

I recommend the 35mm film format; the vast majority of cameras on the market today use this type of film, and many kinds of 35mm film are available. Disk cameras and the older 110 film size both yield negatives that are too small to produce good quality enlargements, and any camera that uses a film format larger than 35mm is far too specialized and bulky to handle while bicycling.

There are two basic types of 35mm cameras: 1) the cameras that have come to be called "point & shoot," 2) the more complex and usually more expensive single lens reflex, or SLR cameras. Point & shoot cameras (the palm-sized, rectangular units that you've probably seen) have become quite sophisticated over the last few years. Lenses have improved in quality, and automatic focus and exposure control features have been well designed. It's often hard to distinguish amateur photos produced by these compact wonders from those produced by professionals.

Point & shoot cameras can be carried easily in your pocket or handlebar bag, and many of the models on the market today are not only fully automated but water-resistant as well. You simply whip them out, point at your subject, and shoot—nothing could be simpler! There are, however, two drawbacks to point & shoot cameras: the built-in electronic flashes most of them have are limited in range to about twelve feet; and you're also stuck with a narrow choice of lenses (if there's any choice at all other than the standard moderate-to-wide angle lens).

For someone who is a bit more serious about photography, an SLR is a better choice. An even higher level of automation is available in this category, and the range of options in terms of interchangeable lenses and various accessories like electronic flash is much larger. Essentially, you have more ability to take good pictures under a wider range of conditions with an SLR than with a point & shoot. SLR's are the standard type of camera for the majority of professionals. The only drawback to using an SLR is its weight and bulk. The average SLR weighs between three and five pounds, whereas most point & shoot cameras weigh less than a pound.

In short, if you want simplicity, light weight, and compactness, a point & shoot model is for you. If you're a bit more serious and want interchangeable lenses and more powerful electronic flash, the SLR is the route to take. Either type of camera will bring home your memories.

The Maze of Film

. . . .

Now that you have your camera, you'll need to decide what type of film to use— slides or prints? If you plan on showing your pictures to groups of friends or relatives, slides are the way to go. You can always have prints made from your best shots. On the other hand, if you want your photos in an album and don't want to cart around a projector just to look at pictures, you should buy print film.

The next thing you should understand is how film "sees" and captures light. The ISO rating, also known as film speed, indicates the relative ability of film to capture light. The higher the speed, the more efficient that particular film is at capturing light. Speeds of 64, 100, 200, and 400 are common ISO's for slide and print film.

What does all this mean? Let's look at an example. You're trying to take a picture of a friend at dusk. The ambient light is low, and you have two films to choose from—one with a speed of 400 and another with a speed of 100. Since your camera's light-gathering ability is fixed according to the lens you have, the only variable you can control is the film speed. By choosing the faster ISO 400 film in this instance, you can take an acceptable picture, whereas with the ISO 100 film, the same shot would (with the same camera settings) come out too dark.

A word of caution: don't automatically choose high film speed unless you really need it—the higher speeds produce images that are more "grainy" and less sharp than the slower films. So, you have a tradeoff here between films that don't need as much light to produce a given image but are grainy, and other films that need more light but are very sharp. And remember that sharpness is important when enlarging prints or projecting slides on a screen.

The Secret

. . . .

After you have chosen your camera and your film, you're ready for your first bike ride with your new equipment. The most important concept in photography is one that took me years to understand, and once you grasp this simple axiom, your photography will improve greatly. Stated simply, you are *not* taking pictures of people or things or scenery—you *are* taking pictures of *light!* A few years after buying my first SLR camera, I became frustrated that my photos had not really improved over time. But after comparing my shots with those published in magazines, I began to realize the difference between those photos and mine.

The magazine layouts that most attracted my eye all had one thing in common—dramatic light. Golden sunsets, low angle light filtering through trees, and clearing mountain storms all reached off the page and grabbed my attention. I finally understood that the *subject matter* I had been concentrating on in my photos was secondary to the *light*. At last I had found the key!

When you begin using your camera, keep this in mind. The best photos are where the best light is. This certainly doesn't mean you should only take pictures with dramatic light; some of my most cherished possessions are simple snapshots of friends or relatives. But recognizing good light, even in snapshots, will go a long way toward improving your photos.

Finally, a few words about composition. Remember that your photos will "pop" and be more dynamic if they have a strong subject. Wide-angle shots of mountain scenery will always seem lovely to you because you were there. But with no people or items of interest in the foreground to give life to the picture, other people will probably be bored with your empty landscapes. Remember to choose a clear subject for each shot and try to fill the frame with it—isolate it from background clutter.

If you keep these few pointers in mind, you will have the basic knowledge you need to begin your photographic adventures on two wheels. From now on, be sure to bring your camera along wherever you ride—you never know when the right light, the

(Byron E. Reed III)

right landscape, and the right friends will all converge at the same time to make the photo that becomes a lifetime memory.

Byron (Bud) Reed is the Managing Director of Vermont Bicycle Touring, America's oldest and largest bicycle touring company. His bike touring experience includes most of North America and many countries in western Europe, as well as New Zealand, China, and the Soviet Union. Photography is both a passion and a part-time business for Bud, and his work has been published in many magazines, including *Bicycling, Outside, Sunset,* and *Bicycle Guide,* and also in *Newsday,* the *Miami Herald,* the *Atlanta Constitution,* and other daily newspapers.

Zahn's Glacier Tours, P.O. Box 75, Milford, NH 03055, 603/673–1908; fax: 603/673–8415 * Tours up to 3 weeks of Austrian Alps where you stay for one week in each town and conduct loop tours. 15– to 45–mile days. Run by a couple who have visited the Alps annually for 30 years. "Call for details," the brochure says.

Elsewhere

Above the Clouds Trekking, Inc., P.O. Box 398, Worcester, MA 01602, 800/233–4499, 508/799–4499 * Mountain bike trips to Nepal, Tibet, and Pakistan.

Asian Pacific Adventures, 826 South Sierra Bonita Ave., Los Angeles, CA 90036, 800/825–1680, 213/935–3156 * Mountain bike and road bike tours to Thailand, Nepal, China, Japan, Indonesia, and Malaysia.

Backroads Bicycle Touring, 1516 5th St., Berkeley, CA 94710–1713, 800/BIKE–TRIP, 415/527–1555; fax: 415/527–1444 * 2– to 17–day tours around the world, year-round. Includes Bali, Australia, Tasmania, and Thailand. See also "North America" and "Europe."

Baja Expedition, Inc., 2625 Garnet Ave., San Diego, CA 92109, 800/843–6967, 619/581–3311 * Mountain bike tours in Baja, Tibet, and Patagonia. Camping or hotels.

Bicycle Africa, 4887 Columbia Drive South, Seattle, WA 98108–1919, 206/628–9314 * Run by a former Peace Corps volunteer, the IBF leads treks through Kenya, Tunisia, Zimbabwe, Cameroon, and Sahel. The buzz: "Bicycle Africa tours are for the good-natured realist who appreciates the rewards of self-contained bicycle touring in less-developed countries." No rentals.

Bike Moves, P.O. Box 642, Unley, SA 5061, Australia, 08/271–1584 * Tours in rural South Australia.

Bike Treks, c/o Let's Go Travel, P.O. Box 60342, Nairobi, Kenya, 29539/29530; fax: 336890 * Features two- and seven-day mountain bike tours in Kenya. Bikes available.

Bogong Jack Adventures, P.O. Box 221, Oxley, Victoria 3678, Australia, 057/27–3382 * On- and off-road tours in Victoria.

China Passage, 168 State St., Teaneck, NJ 07666, 201/837–1400 * China and Thailand by road bike.

Condor Adventures, Ltd., 2044 Bellaire St., Denver, CO 80207, 800/729–1262, 303/331–9977 * Mountain bike tours in Peru, Chile, Argentina, Costa Rica, Ecuador, Chile, and Mexico. No rentals.

Crocodile Cycles, P.O. Box 5155, Cairns, Queensland 4870, Australia, 070/31–1527 * Tours in north Queensland.

Earthventures, 2625 N. Meridian St., Ste. 612, Indianapolis, IN 46208, 800/447–2866, 317/783–9449 * Down under: Australia and Tasmania. Rentals available. See also "Europe" above.

Forum Travel International, Inc., 91 Gregory Lane, #21, Pleasant Hill, CA 94523, 415/671–2900; fax: 415/946–1500, 671–2993 * Tours of Europe, New Zealand, China, southeast Asia. Mountain biking in Peru, Ecuador, Soviet Union, Argentina, Chile, Italy. Self-guided and tour company trips.

Gametrackers Ltd., P.O. Box 62042, Nairobi, Kenya, 338927/22703 (after 5:30 p.m.: 504281); fax: 330903 * Has three-day mountain bike adventures in Kenya. Individual tours on request.

Journeys, 4011–B, Jackson Rd., Ann Arbor, MI 48103, 800/255–8735 * Journeys has mostly trekking trips, but does offer a mountain bike trip to Costa Rica in February. Maximum number of 10 in group. Stay at small rural hotels.

Lost World Adventures, 1189 Autumn Ridge Dr., Marietta, GA 30066, 800/999–0558 * Mountain biking in the Andes.

Morris Overseas Tours, 418 Fourth Ave., Melbourne Beach, FL 32951, 800/777–6853 * Specializes in mountain biking in Panama and Costa Rica.

New Zealand Pedal Tours, c/o Allan Blackman (booking agent), 522 29th Ave. S., Seattle, WA 98144, 206/323–2080 * Trips from 7 to 18 days. Rentals, accommodations, meals, sag wagon provided.

Off the Deep End Travels, Box 7511, Jackson, WY 83001, 800/223– 6833 * Bike the South Pacific, the Orient, and the wilds of Wyoming. All levels of experience and luxury, from camping tours to self-contained inn-to-inn travel to sleeping on a square-rigger (mountain bikes stored below decks) sailing for Tahiti. From day trips to several weeks long, on-road or off-road.

Pacific Crest Bicycle Tours, 2722 Alki Ave. SW, Seattle, WA 98116, 206/938–3322 * See "North America" above.

Paradise Bicycle Tours, Inc., P.O. Box 1726, Evergreen, CO 80439, 303/670–1842 * A cycling safari through the game parks of Kenya. Rentals of 21–speed Specialized bicycles available. Call to ask to borrow the video preview.

REI Adventures, P.O. Box 88126, Seattle, WA 98138 * 800/622–2236, 206/395–7760 * Environmentally conscious REI goes all over, including China and New Zealand.

PACKING FOR THE LONG HAUL

. . . .

Travel by bicycle requires special consideration: the smart cyclist will be prepared for all types of weather and circumstances. Proper planning means you can cycle in the rain, or be comfortable in the mountains in summer, even if the temperature drops. So when you head for the open road or trail for a weekend, week, or longer, factor in time for that most dreaded activity of all—packing.

The prudent cyclist carefully evaluates all potential situations and judges the amount of equipment needed accordingly. Consider, for example, whether you plan to go "credit card" touring, carrying a minimal amount of equipment and staying at hotels and the like, or whether you'd rather be more self-contained, portaging camping and cooking essentials. Then, after spreading all that you are considering packing on the floor, halve that amount. Just remember, whatever you place in panniers, no matter how carefully it is positioned, will follow you up and down hills. Taking more than you need can turn a bicycle from a lithe form of transport into a semi.

Experienced cyclists know that less can be more with respect to clothing. All clothing can be layered for additional warmth, and a T-shirt with arm warmers worn with a vest and windbreaker can be a "winter" jacket. Many long-distance tourists regard wool with increasing fondness. It's a material that keeps you warm, even if the predominant weather is drizzle. Good raingear is essential and can often make the difference between being slightly damp while cycling or being miserable.

Use the list below as guidance—take only those items that suit your needs. If you are planning on being totally self-sufficient, you will probably want to pack most of what is listed below. If you are not going to camp out or cook your meals, you can probably forgo the kitchen equipment and might pare down the list of "Bicycle Equipment."

However you are traveling, carry a tool kit, emergency food supplies, and clothing adequate for the weather conditions. Sunscreen is essential: use it if you are just going out for a short ride. Remember to include film for your camera. Touring by bicycle is great fun, and you'll want to have pictures of your experiences to share.

Finally, consider doing a "shakedown" tour. This way you can test your equipment and stamina on a short, one-day ride. This is a useful way to solve equipment and other problems before you are out on the road.

Bicycle Equipment
. . . .

- bungie cords or straps
- lock and cable
- pannier covers
- water bottles
- handlebar bag
- panniers
- rear-view mirror

Camping Equipment
. . . .

- ground cloth
- sleeping bag
- tent
- pad
- stakes, extra

Clothing
. . . .

- arm warmers (to convert T-shirts into long-sleeved shirts)
- bandanna
- dress clothes, one nice outfit that is lightweight and can withstand being mashed
- hat, cycling cap for sun or warmth
- jacket, for rain and wind
- long pants (which can be ridden in)
- shirt, long-sleeved
- socks, wool and cotton
- tights
- underwear
- bathing suit
- cycling shorts (take at least two pairs for long trips)
- gloves, cycling and regular if necessary
- helmet
- leg warmers (to make pants out of bicycling shorts)
- sandals (flip-flops, a.k.a. thongs, work well)
- sweater or vest
- T-shirts

First Aid
. . . .

- aspirin
- bandages

- booklet or card with relevant personal medical information
- first aid cream
- insect repellent
- lip balm
- matches, waterproof or packed in watertight container
- moleskin
- prescription medication
- sunscreen (wear at all times, even for short rides)
- tweezers
- water purification tablets

Kitchen Supplies

. . . .

- aluminum foil
- can opener (if not a part of your pocket knife)
- cup and plate
- food (always have some emergency energy available, preferably something that doesn't need preparation)
- fuel
- matches
- pot
- primer for stove
- scouring pads and soap
- silverware
- snacks
- spices
- stove

Miscellaneous

. . . .

- camera and film
- copy of your prescriptions
- extra glasses or contact lenses
- fanny pack or small backpack
- flashlight and extra batteries
- glasses fastener
- journal and pens
- maps, list of potential accommodations
- passport and other identification
- plastic bags
- pocket knife (the familiar Swiss Army standby or some facsimile)
- stamps
- stuff sacks
- sunglasses
- swimming goggles
- tape (electrical, duct, or some other sturdy kind)
- travelers checks

Personal

. . . .

- razor
- shampoo and cream rinse
- toilet paper
- towel (cut in half to reduce weight)

- sewing kit
- soap
- toothbrush and toothpaste

Tools

. . . . . .

- Allen wrenches
- cables, gear and brakes
- chain tool
- freewheel remover
- needle-nose pliers
- pocket vise
- rag
- spokes, extra
- tire, fold-up
- tire patch kit

- brake pads
- chain lube
- crescent wrench
- hand cleaner (small container or wipes)
- nuts and bolts
- pump
- screwdriver
- spoke wrench
- tire irons
- tube, at least one spare

Rocky Mountain Cycle Tours, Box 1978, Canmore, Alberta T0L 0M0, Canada, 800/661–2453 (in the U.S.), 403/678–6770 * San Juan Islands and other destinations. See "North America" above.

Safaricentre, 310 N. Sepulveda Blvd., Manhattan Beach, CA 90266, 800/223–6046, 800/624–5342 (in Calif.) * Mountain biking in Pakistan, Nepal, and Tibet.

Sense Adventures, Box 216, Kingston 7, Jamaica, 809/927–2097 * Mountain bike routes and on-road routes all around Jamaica.

Shelton-Pacific, Inc., 15th floor, Hoge Building, Seattle, WA 98104, 206/622–1604 or 323–3919 * 23–day tour of China run by same leaders since 1981. Meals, lodging, sag wagon provided. Itinerary includes Beijing, Great Wall, Guilin, and Dali. Group of 11–19 people. The brochure buzz: Short daily mileage, no experience necessary.

Snowy Mountainbike Tours, 26 Ingebyra St., Jindabyne, NSW 2627, Australia, 064/56–2863 * Off-road tours in New South Wales.

Suwannee Bicycle Tours, Inc., P.O. Box 247, White Springs, FL 32097, 904/878–2042 * When Suwannee leaves Florida, they take you cycling in New Zealand and Australia. See "North America" above.

Touring Exchange, Box 265, Port Townsend, WA 98368, 206/385–0667 * Winter tours to Baja, Costa Rica, and Belize. 5 days to 2 weeks. Combines camping and cooking with hotels and restaurants. Road and off-road routes. Specialties: kayak/snorkel/hike/mountain bike combos, all-women bike tour of the 1,000–mile length of Baja.

US China Travel Service, 500 Sutter St., #621, San Francisco, CA 94108, 800/332–2831 * Trips in China using Chinese guides.

Wandering Wheels, Inc., P.O. Box 207, Upland, IN 46989, 317/998–7490 * A non-profit touring operator with a Christian philosophy. Goes to China and the USSR.

Womantrek, P.O. Box 20643, Seattle, WA 98102, 800/477–TREK, 206/325–4772 * Trips for women. Goes to China, Russia, and elsewhere. See "Europe" above.

Woodswoman, Inc., 25 W. Diamond Lake Rd., Minneapolis, MN 55419, 612/822–3809 * Bicycling and other sports for women only. Cycles in Cozumel and New Zealand. Also Minnesota. See "North America" and "Europe."

Worldwide Adventures, Inc., 920 Yonge St., Ste. 747, Toronto, Ontario, Canada, 800/387–1483 * 8– to 22–day camping/adventure bike trips in China and India, along with hiking, camel, and boat tours throughout the world. Emphasis on "ecotourism"—appreciating native cultures and leaving no trace of your travels.

Worldwide Nordic Tours, Box 1129, Maplewood, NJ 07040, 201/378/9170 * See "Europe" above.

Student Trips

America's Adventure, 23418 Fescue Dr., Golden, Colorado 80401, 800/222–3595, 303/526–0806 * For teens. Both road and off-road biking in the context of other outdoor adventures.

American Youth Hostels, National Office, P.O. Box 37613, Washington, DC 20013–7613, 202/783–4943 * See "North America" above.

AUTHORS' CHOICE: BEST PLACES TO TOUR

Okay, where do I like to ride when I'm not writing books or working on other projects? For starters, there's Maryland just slightly north and west of me. The gentle hills around Poolesville feel a zillion miles away from the urban hustle of Washington, D.C., and the Virginia countryside, near the Massanutten Mountains offers tens of options. While these places are my favorite close-to-home jaunts, I've also got my "I can't wait to get back there" cycling destinations.

Given almost any place on the planet to pick from, I'll clamor for Point Reyes, California, or something close to it. I love the proximity of ocean and hills, the feeling of being just over the bridge from San Francisco, a great city, and yet of being quite far from it. When the light is just right—a soft golden glow that makes the sky seem peaceful and otherworldly—cycling over Golden Gate Bridge is practically a mystical experience.

In addition to Point Reyes, I love cycling along the Oregon coast or east of Eugene, Oregon, coming up from northern California. You can't beat silent, foggy mornings in the mountains. If you're not too wet or too chilly, there's a quiet that's hard to replicate. I'm also fond of cycling in Vermont, and western Massachusetts, near Northampton and Amherst, isn't too shabby either. In fall, the foliage is spectacular. It's hard not to fall off your bike oohing and ahhing, and it's fun cycling on country back roads. I get to test my best moos as I greet the cows and other critters.

I wouldn't be upset if my bicycle and I got plunked down right around Taos, New Mexico, or in southern Utah. The painter Georgia O'Keeffe lived in the Southwest for many reasons, and I know that the light was one of them. I, too, love the feeling of seeing forever; the brilliant red sandstone of the Southwest must be cycled through to be experienced.

Believe it or not, Iowa is on my list of must-rides. Yes, I'm a veteran of Iowa's RAGBRAI (*Des Moines Register's* Annual Great Bicycle Ride Across Iowa). While the Iowan food and hospitality are great reasons to do RAGBRAI, there's also the mornings. Ever hear crickets chirp when there's no one around? Or watch the early sun light fields lush with ripening corn? Am I sounding a bit, ahem, corny? Too bad.

Iowa brings it out in me. But seriously, if you get on the road before most of the hordes, you can serenely glide to the first breakfast stop, beginning the day all by yourself.

If you haven't guessed, anywhere is a great place to bicycle. If you've got a special destination, share it with a cycling buddy. Let us know about it too. You can contact us at Woodbine House (5615 Fishers Lane, Rockville, MD 20852).

—Arlene Plevin

✳ ✳ ✳

Faves

Beach Drive in Rock Creek Park, Washington, D.C.
The back roads between Oxford and Cambridge, England
The Po Valley and Umbria, Italy
Northern Vermont
The Eastern Shore of Maryland
Western Montgomery County, Maryland
The Austrian Alps
County Clare, the Burren, Dingle Peninsula, western Ireland
Pennsylvania Dutch country, Lancaster County, Pennsylvania
Foothills of the Shenandoah Mountains, Virginia

Wouldn't Go Back on Two Wheels

Quebec between the Vermont border and Quebec City
Mannheim, Germany
The Rhine river road to Cologne, Germany
London
Cork, Ireland
Cape May County, New Jersey
Finger Lakes, New York

—Michael Leccese

The Biking Expedition, 10 Maple St., PO Box 547, Henniker, NH 03242, 800/245–4649
* Student trips of all levels of difficulty from the Pacific Northwest to Central Europe. Camping and hosteling—carry your own gear.

Butterfield & Robinson, 70 Bond St., Toronto, Ontario M5B 1X3, 800/387–1147 *
Biking for ages 13–18. See "Europe" above.

Castle Rock Centre for Environmental Adventures, 412 Country Rd. 6 NS, Cody,
WY 82414, 307/587–2076 * Has a nine-week western trip for teenagers which includes
traveling by bike, kayak, and raft.

Interlocken, R.R. #2, Box 165, Hillsboro, NH 03244, 603/478–3166 * An international
summer camp that includes bike trips of Rome to Paris, Seattle to San Francisco and
Quebec. Also mountain biking at sleep-away camp in New Hampshire. Carry own gear,
camp, eat group meals.

Longacre Expeditions, R.D. 3, Box 106, Newport, PA 17074, 800/433–0127, 717/567–
6790 * For teens 12–17. Mountain and road bicycling in Maine, Nova Scotia, Maryland,
Virginia, West Virginia, and Colorado that begin and end in a base camp.

Odyssey Adventures, 1211 Clarks Valley, Dauphin, PA 17018, 800/544–3216 * 4–week
trips for teens to Yellowstone, France/Switzerland, Scandinavia/U.S.S.R, Spain/Portugal.
Camping, hostels, hotels. Groups of 12–16, grades 7–12.

Riding High Bicycle Tours, P.O. Box 14848, Portland, OR 97214, 503/293–2143 *
Tours for young folks, ages 10–20, to Oregon, Washington, France, Germany, and British
Columbia.

Student Hosteling Program, Conway, MA 01314, 800/343–6132, 413/369–4275 *
Trips for teens, ages 13–17. Trip length is 2 to 9 weeks, groups of 8 to 12. Groups camp
and prepare own meals. No alcohol, smoking, or drugs. Camp gear included in cost and is
yours to keep afterwards. 30 routes, from 16 days through Vermont to 65 days, London to
Moscow. Goes across the country, Alaska, the West Coast, France, Ireland, and more.

Trailmark, 155 Schyuler Rd., Nyack, NY 10960, 800/229–0262, 914/358–0262. Travel
program for teenagers with a strong biking component.

SUMMER CAMPS
. . . .

The following list of camps might just make you wish you were a teenager again. These
camps have been included because they offer a bicycling component, along with a whole
host of outdoor activities. For a more complete list of camps, consult the *Guide to Ac-
credited Camps,* 260 pp., $10.95, 12 West 31st, 12th Fl., New York, NY 10001, 800/777–
CAMP. Other options for summer bicycling can be found in the listings above.

Adirondack Outdoor Adventures, Box 438, Saratoga Springs, NY 12866, 800/777–8677, 518/587–1111 * Mountain bicycling in the Adirondacks.

Camp Cayuga, Box 452, Washington, NJ 07882, 800/4–CAYUGA * In the Pocono Mts.

Camp Lohikan, Box 234, Kennilworth, NJ 07033, 800/488–4321 * In the Pocono Mts.

Camp Somerhill, Dr. Lynn and Larry Singer, 20 Huntley Rd., Box 295, Eastchester, NY 10709, 800/548–0755, 914/793–1303 * Near Lake George, New York. Has mountain bikes and on-road bikes and takes cyclists out on day trips and overnights.

Longacre Expeditions, R.D. 3, Box 106, Newport, PA 17074, 800/433–0127, 717/567–6790 * For teens 12–17. Mountain and road bicycling in Maine, Nova Scotia, Maryland, Virginia, West Virginia, and Colorado that begin and end in a base camp.

Maine Teen Camp, R.R. 1, Box 39, Kezar Falls, ME 04047, 800/752–CAMP, 207/625–8581 * Mountain biking program on miles and miles of wooded trails. Offers three levels of instruction, for ages 13–16.

Carrie Murray Outdoor Center, 1901 Ridgetop Rd., Baltimore, MD 21207, 301/396–0808 * Has summer camp with bicycling component for adults and youths. See also "North America" above.

Pedal Power Camp, 4–H Youth Development, Minnesota Extension Service, 340 Coffey Hall, University of Minnesota, St. Paul, MN 55108, 612/625–9719 * Contact Cynthia McArthur for more information about a camp that teaches bicycle mechanics and skills in a 4–H environment.

CAMPS AND CLINICS

Looking to improve your racing or mountain bike skills? Try the following camps and clinics. While you won't metamorphose into Pete Pensyres or Elaine Mariolle—two winners of the Race Across AMerica (RAAM)—you can put a polish on your spin and become a more powerful, skilled cyclist.

Joseph Azar Cycling Camps, The Cyclist, 619 King St., #709, Columbia SC 29205, 803/254–8309 * Offers 6–day clinics on speed, endurance, and basic skills.

Connie Carpenter and Dave Phinney Cycling Camp, P.O. Box 3001, Copper Mountain, CO 80443, 303/968–2882 * A camp filled with experts in some of the most beautiful and mountainous territory the U.S. has to offer.

Craftsbury Mountain Bike Center, Box 31, Craftsbury Common, VT 05827, 800/336–2848, 802/586–7767 * Has programs on mountain bike handling that range from one day to one week, or longer. Access to several thousand miles of dirt roads.

Cycle Sutton Bicycle Camp, Cycle Sutton, P.O. Box 743, Sutton, Quebec J0E 2K0, Canada, 514/538–0062 * Specializes in hill-riding. Offers clinics in July and August.

Elk River Touring Center, Slatyfork, WV 26291, 304/572–3771 * Mountain bike camp for adults. Basic skills and more in the mountains of West Virginia.

John Howard Champs Camp, Champs Camps, P.O. Box 310469, New Braunfels, TX 78131, 800/444–6204 * Coaching by legendary marathon cyclist John Howard and former 7–Eleven rider Jeff Pierce. Takes place at John Newcombe's tennis camp.

Italia Velo Sport, 1233 35th St., Sacramento, CA 95816, 800/553–5662, 916/731–7236 * Touring and racing camp based in Treviso, Italy, with categories for ages 10–65. Train during the week, race on weekends. Rentals, trainer, mechanic, and masseur available.

Italian Cycling Center, George Phol, 2117 Green St., Philadelphia, PA 19130–3110, 215/232–6772 * Offers racing and training at a camp in northern Italy.

Betsy King Cycling Camps, P.O. Box 14714, Gainesville, FL 32604, 904/378–2479 * Offers one-week sessions from February through April.

The Mountain Bike School, Mount Snow, VT 05356, 800/451–4211, 802/463–3333 * This is what one ski resort does off-season. Two days or more of lessons at the base of a ski area with 140 miles of trails. Learn technique, safety, repairs; stay at area inns. Rentals available.

Taos Training Camp, 227 Lovera, San Antonio, TX 78212, 512/828–8680 * Taos, New Mexico, is not just for skiing: join coaches such as Deborah Shumway and John Howard for 5–day sessions in August.

USCF Coaching Clinics, 1750 E.Boulder St., Colorado Springs, CO 80909, 719/578–4581 * The United States Cycling Federation's clinics are developed by veteran coaches. These weekend clinics are offered throughout the country in the fall and spring.

USCF Developmental Camps, 1750 E. Boulder St., Colorado Springs, CO 80909, 719/578–4581 * Called "a good opportunity to learn the basics." Three-day sessions at Lake Placid, New York, and Colorado Springs, Colorado. In 1991, they conducted one-day sessions with *Bicycling* magazine.

VeloSport Florida, 307 W. Lambright St., Tampa, FL 33604, 813/237–6361 * Accommodates cyclists of all skills. Offers January classes at St. Leo College.

Walden School of Cycling (Schwinn-Wolverine), P.O. Box 090340, Rochester Hills, MI 48309, 313/652–0511 * Located 20 miles north of Orlando, Florida, the Walden School of Cycling accepts various levels of cyclists. The week-long classes are held in February and March.

Leadership Courses

Both American Youth Hostels and Bikecentennial offer courses designed for cyclists interested in leading their tours. While these week-long courses are primarily for potential leaders, cyclists who are not interested in leading also benefit from the instruction, which covers everything from dealing with emergencies to basic bike repair.

AYH Leadership Training Courses, Attention: Programs and Education, P.O. Box 37613, Washington, DC 20013, 202/783–6161 * Course location varies from year to year. In 1991 it was offered in Boston, Pennsylvania, Ohio, and Washington, DC.

Leadership Training Course, Bikecentennial, P.O. Box 8308, Missoula, MT 59807, 406/721–1776 * One on the East Coast and one on the West Coast. Trains you in camping and interpersonal skills needed to lead a Bikecentennial tour.

MOUNTAIN BIKE TRAILS AND PARKS

Numerous ski resorts are turning their ski trails into mountain bike trails in the summer. Check with your favorite downhill or cross-country center and see if this is a possibility. The following are experienced in offering off-road trails to cyclists. A more complete listing is available from Bikecentennial (P.O. Box 8308, Missoula, MT 59807, 406/721–1776) for $2.

Eldora Mountain Bike Center, P.O. Box 430, Nederland, CO 80466 * Private trails open 9–5 daily. Guides, rentals, overnight trips available.

Elk River Touring Center, Slatyfork, WV 26291, 304/536–1944 * Has trails, rental, and B & B.

Gnaw Bone Camp, R.R. 2, Box 91, Nashville, IN 47448, 812/988–4852 * Private mountain bike area.

Mammouth Adventure Connection, Box 353, Mammouth Lakes, CA 93546, 800/228–4947, 619/934–2581 * Mountain bike park. Also has tours.

Wapahini Mountain Bike Park, 349 S. Walnut, Bloomington, IN 47401, 812/332–9668
* City park open to mountain bikers exclusively.

NORTH AMERICAN
TOURIST INFORMATION

If you are planning a bicycle trip, a good place to start is the tourism division of the state or country you will be visiting. Many such agencies—those of California, Maryland, Oregon, and Utah, to name a few—offer maps and other detailed material useful for cyclists. Call or write these tourism departments for up-to-date information. For more information on bicycling abroad (and for access to a wide variety of maps both abroad and in the U.S.) contact Bikecentennial, P.O. Box 8308, Missoula, MT 59807, 406/721–1776.

United States

Alabama Bureau of Tourism and Travel, 532 S. Perry St., Montgomery, AL 36104, 800/ALABAMA.

Alaska Division of Tourism, Department of Commerce and Economic Development, P.O. Box E, Juneau, AK 99811, 907/455–6299.

Arizona Office of Tourism, 1100 W. Washington, Phoenix, AZ 85077, 602/542–TOUR.

Arkansas Department of Parks and Tourism, 1 Capitol Mall, Little Rock, AR 72201, 800/643–8383 (outside AR); 800/482–8999 (inside AR).

California Office of Tourism, 1121 L St., Suite 103, Sacramento, CA 95814, 916/322–1397.

Colorado Tourism Board, 1625 Broadway, Suite 1700, Denver, CO 80202, 800/433–2656, 303/592–5510.

Connecticut Department of Economic Development, 865 Brook St., Rocky Hill, CT 06067, 800/262–6863, 203/258–4290. Try also the Office of State Parks and Recreation, 165 Capitol Ave., Hartford, CT 06106, 203/566–2304, 800/282–6863.

Delaware Tourism Office, 99 Kings Hwy., Box 1401, Dover, DE 19903, 800/441–8846 (outside DE); 800/282–8667 (inside DE).

Florida Division of Tourism, Visitor Inquiry, 126 Van Buren St., Tallahassee, FL 32304, 904/487–1465.

Georgia Department of Industry, Trade and Tourism, 230 Peachtree St. NW, Atlanta, GA 30303, 404/656–0577.

Hawaii Visitors Bureau, 2270 Kalakaua Ave., Suite 801, Honolulu, HI 96815, 808/923–1811.

Idaho Travel Council, Capitol Building, Rm. 108, 700 W. State St., Boise, ID 83720, 800/635–7820, 208/334–2470.

Illinois Bureau of Tourism, Travel Information Center, 310 S. Michigan Ave., Suite 108, Chicago, IL 60604, 312/793–2094.

Indiana Division of Tourism, Department of Commerce, One N. Capitol Ave., Suite 700, Indianapolis, IN 46204, 317/232–8860.

Iowa Department of Economic Development, Division of Tourism, 200 E. Grand, Des Moines, IA 50309, 800/345–IOWA, 515/281–3100.

Kansas Department of Economic Development, Travel and Tourism Division, 400 W. Eighth, Fifth Fl., Topeka, KS 66603, 800/252–6727, 913/296–2009.

Kentucky Travel, Capitol Plaza Tower, Frankfort, KY 40601, 800/225–TRIP, 502/564–4930.

Louisiana Office of Tourism, Department of Culture, Recreation, and Tourism, P.O. Box 94291, Baton Rouge, LA 70804–9291, 800/33–GUMBO, 504/342–8119.

Maine Publicity Bureau, 97 Winthrop St., Hallowell, ME 04347, 800/533–9595, 207/289–6070.

Maryland Office of Tourism Development, 217 E. Redwood St., Baltimore, MD 21202, 301/333–6611.

Massachusetts Division of Tourism, 100 Cambridge St., 13th Fl., Boston, MA 02202, 800/343–9072, 617/727–3201.

Michigan Department of Commerce, Travel Bureau, P.O. Box 30226, Lansing, MI 48909, 800/5432–YES.

Minnesota Office of Tourism, 375 Jackson St., St. Paul, MN 55101, 800/657–3700, 612/296–5029.

Mississippi Division of Tourism Development, P.O. Box 22825, Jackson, MS 39205, 800/647–2290, 601/359–3297.

Missouri Division of Tourism, P.O. Box 1055, Jefferson City, MO 65102, 800/877–1234, 314/751–4133.

Montana Travel Promotion Division, Department of Commerce, 1424 Ninth Ave., Helena, MT 59620, 800/548–3390, 406/444–2654.

Nebraska Division of Travel and Tourism, P.O. Box 94666, 301 Centennial Mall S., Lincoln, NE 68509, 800/228–4307, 402/471–3796.

Nevada Commission on Tourism, Capitol Complex, Carson City, NV 89710, 800/237–0774, 702/687–4322.

New Hampshire Department of Resources and Economic Development, Office of Vacation Travel, 105 Loudon Rd., P.O. Box 856, Concord, NH 03301, 603/271–2666.

New Jersey Division of Travel and Tourism, CN826, Trenton, NJ 08625, 800/JERSEY–7, 609/292–2470.

New Mexico Tourism and Travel Division, 7533 Joseph M. Montoya Bldg., 1100 St. Francis Dr., Santa Fe, NM 87503, 800/545–2040, 505/827–0291.

New York Department of Economic Development, Tourism Division, 1 Commerce Plaza, Albany, NY 12245, 800/225–5697, 518/474–4116.

North Carolina Division of Travel and Tourism, Department of Economic Development and Cultural Resources, 430 N. Salisbury St., Raleigh, NC 27611, 800/VISIT NC.

North Dakota Tourism Promotion, 604 East Blvd., Bismark, ND 58505, 800/437–2077 (outside ND); 800/472–2100 (in ND).

Ohio Division of Travel and Tourism, P.O. Box 1001, Columbus, OH 43266, 800/BUCKEYE.

Oklahoma Tourism and Recreation Department, 500 Will Rogers Bldg., Oklahoma City, OK 73105, 800/652–6552, 405/521–2586.

Oregon Tourism Division, Economic Development Department, 595 Cottage St. NE, Salem, OR 97310, 800/547–7842 (outside OR); 800/543–8838, 503/378–3451 (inside OR).

Pennsylvania Bureau of Travel Marketing, 453 Forum Bldg., Harrisburg, PA 17120, 800/VISIT–PA.

Rhode Island Tourism Division, 7 Jackson Walkway, Providence, RI 02903, 800/556–2484 (in the Northeast); 401/277–2601.

South Carolina Department of Parks, Recreation, and Tourism, P.O. Box 71, Columbia, SC 29202, 803/734–0235.

South Dakota Division of Tourism, 711 Wells, Pierre, SD 57501, 800/843–1930 (outside SD); 800/952–2217 (inside SD).

Tennessee Department of Tourist Development, P.O. Box 23170, Nashville, TN 37302, 615/741–2158.

Texas Travel and Information Division, P.O. Box 5064, Austin, TX 78763, 800/888–8839.

Utah Travel Council, Council Hall/Capitol Hill, Salt Lake City, UT 84114, 801/538–1030.

Vermont Travel Division, 134 State St., Montpelier, VT 05062, 802/828–3236.

Virginia Division of Tourism, 1021 E. Cary St., Richmond, VA 23219, 800/248–4833, 804/786–4484.

Washington Department of Trade and Economic Development, Tourism Development Division, 101 General Administration Bldg. AX–13, Olympia, WA 98504, 800/544–1800, 800/321–2808.

Washington, D.C. Convention and Visitor Association, 1212 New York Ave. NW, Washington, DC 20005, 202/789–7000.

West Virginia Department of Parks and Tourism, Capitol Complex, Charleston, WV 25305, 800/CALL–WVA.

Wisconsin Division of Tourism, P.O. Box 7606, Madison, WI 53707, 800/ESCAPES (for WI and adjacent states); 608/266–2161.

Wyoming Travel Commission, Frank Norris Jr. Travel Center, Cheyenne, WY 82002, 800/225–5996, 307/777–7777.

Canada

Alberta Tourism, Vacation Counseling, 10155–102 St., Edmonton, Alberta T5J 4L6, Canada, 800/661–8888.

Tourism British Columbia, Parliament Bldg., Victoria, British Columbia V8V 1X4, Canada, 800/663–6000.

Tourism New Brunswick, Box 12345, Fredericton, New Brunswick E2L 4R7, Canada, 800/561–0123.

Newfoundland and Labrador, Department of Development, Tourism Branch, P.O. Box 8730, St. John's Newfoundland A1B 4K2, Canada, 800/563–6353, 709/576–2830.

Nova Scotia Department of Tourism and Culture, P.O. Box 130, Halifax, Nova Scotia B3J 2M7, Canada, 800/341–6096.

Ontario Travel, Queens Park, Toronto, Ontario M7A 2E5, Canada, 800/ONTARIO, 800/668–2746.

Prince Edward Island Visitor Information Center, Box 940, Charlottetown, PEI C1A 7M5, Canada, 800/565–0267.

Tourism Quebec, P.O. Box 2000, Quebec, Quebec G1K 7X2, Canada, 800/363–7777.

Tourism Victoria, 612 View St., 6th Fl., Victoria, British Columbia V8W 1J5, Canada, 800/663–3883.

Tourism Yukon, P.O. Box 2703, Whitehorse, Yukon Y1A 2C6, Canada, 403/667–5340.

Mexico

Mexican Government Tourism Office, 70 E. Lake St., Suite 1413, Chicago, IL 60601, 800/262–8900, 312/565–2786.

Mexico Government Tourism Office, 1911 Pennsylvania NW, Washington, DC 20006, 800/262–8900, 202/728–1750.

Mexico Government Tourism Office, 405 Park Ave., Suite 1002, New York, NY 10022, 800/262–8900, 212/755–7261.

Mexican Consulate, 1019 19th St. NW, Washington, DC 20036, 202/293–1710, 1711, 1712.

seventeen

BIKING: EVERYONE CAN DO IT

TAKING THE FAMILY ALONG

According to the Bicycle Federation of America in Washington, D.C., more than 90 million Americans bicycle. They pedal alone, join clubs, and venture out with their family. On tandems, single bikes, recumbents, tricycles, and in trailers, families of all sizes have embraced bicycling as a sport that almost any age can enjoy and participate in. Bicycling with the family provides an opportunity for exercise and quality time. Parents and children get to share the outdoors and each is able to contribute in his or her own way. If you love cycling and want to encourage the rest of your family to join in, consider the following suggestions.

First, make sure everyone's bicycle is in good shape. If you're the only one on a comfortable, well-maintained bicycle, that's not exactly fair. And, you're less likely to have converts to the sport if the folks you hope to convince are squirming on uncomfortable saddles or having to stop every block to retrieve a chain that falls off.

Charles Dukes and his daughter Carolyn, 8, bicycled across America on Bikecentennial's TransAmerica Bicycle Trail. They were accompanied by two other tandems ridden by Jean Dukes, wife and mother, with daughter Sara Beth, and son Joe with a family friend. (Bikecentennial Photo by Greg Siple)

Pick a great route. Beginning cyclists are usually loathe to ride alongside traffic. They enjoy quiet streets, far from the madding crowd. If there are uncrowded bicycle trails nearby, consider taking your family there. Make it a short route, perhaps one that conveniently stops at an ice cream shop.

Give instructions and a pep talk at the beginning. Let your family know a bit about the route and what they can expect. Some instruction on safe bicycling is appropriate. It's a given that everyone, from the adults down to the toddler you've safely fastened in the child carrier, should wear a helmet. If you are going to be sharing a path or trail, tell your family how best to do this. For example, on trails that walkers, strollers, hikers, and cyclists of all skills use, cycle single file. If you are planning to pass, check to make sure you have ample space to do so safely and always pass to the individual's left. Courteously warn the user with a friendly "On your left" or a ring of a bell. Be sure to demonstrate all the bicycling skills you use when you ride by yourself or with others.

Aim for a day when the weather is superb. You want to bias your potential converts. Surely, few things can compare with a gentle ride on a warm day. Perhaps springtime in your part of the country comes with magnolia blossoms or daffodils. Combine a ride with a little botany—point out the flowers. The sun and a refreshing breeze, along with a great route, can combine to make your first ride as a family memorable, one that everyone clamors to repeat.

If you're successful, and you've begun to create a family activity, there are several ways to continue the relationship. Take a tour with your family. Go explore New England in the fall or the California wine country, either with a professional touring company or other experts. Take bicycles on your summer vacation. If you have young children who can't keep up with you on single bikes, consider buying a tandem, a trailer, or a child carrier to mount on your bike (check out "Young Children and Biking" in this section).

For more information on family cycling, contact your local bicycle club or write, enclosing a self-addressed, stamped envelope, to the Family Cycling Club, FCC RR8, Box 319E, Glenwood Dr., Bridgeton, NJ 08302.

YOUNG CHILDREN AND BIKING

It's a natural. The bicycle can be a child's first vehicle—a means to explore, discover, acquire physical and social skills, become independent, and have fun. By starting a child young, either as a passenger in a child carrier mounted on the bicycle or as a passenger in a trailer, you can begin to get your child involved in cycling, a great habit.

If you are introducing a child to the pleasures of bicycling, you can start as soon as the child's neck becomes strong enough to support the weight of a helmet. Most experts believe this happens at eight to twelve months of age.

You may choose to purchase a child carrier or a trailer for your beginning cyclist. Both purchases have their pros and cons; it's best to talk to other cyclists and your local bicycle store to decide what's best for you. Whichever you buy, remember that bicycles handle differently with weight. Practice cycling with weight in the child carrier or trailer before placing your child in it. A child shifting in a child carrier can shift your center of balance suddenly. You must be prepared for that possibility.

In general, child carriers can handle a child up to forty pounds. The carrier should fasten securely to the bicycle and be equipped with straps and a cushion. It's especially crucial that the carrier protect your child's feet so that they cannot poke their way into the spokes. Make sure your child is firmly and comfortably settled in the child carrier. Encourage him or her not to move around too much, but be prepared for squirming. Remember, any shift of weight affects your bicycle's handling.

Some parents enjoy the child carrier because its position allows them to converse with their child. There's also a bit more physical contact; a youngster riding in a child carrier has a great view of the parent's back and could touch him or her for reassurance (or to give a child's version of a back massage).

Another option for young children is a trailer. These fasten to the bicycle, either on the rear triangle or just below the seat. They tend to be eight to ten times more expensive than a good bike-mounted carrier, but they have some advantages that longtime cyclists, especially those with more than one child, swear by. First, because the center of gravity is lower, trailers are more stable. This means your child can move around a bit without disrupting the bicycle. Second, because a trailer is closer to the ground than a bike-mounted carrier, the child will not fall as far if there is an accident. And third, a trailer protects the child from tip-over accidents. For added safety, some parents place their young child in an approved infant car seat and strap that into the trailer. Several trailer users advise using pillows to help keep youngsters cozy and to prop them up.

(Burley Design Cooperative)

Trailers can portage more than one child, easily carrying up to a hundred or more pounds. Some can carry more. This means if you're willing to carry them, you can take two small children and their collection of toys. (Note: some trailer users report that their passengers sometimes lighten the load by tossing out everything not strapped in.)

Trailers are considerably more expensive than child carriers, but if you plan on using one for many years, it may be worth the initial outlay. Often local bike clubs have members whose children have outgrown the need for a trailer. Perhaps you can pick one up used.

Don't plan on long rides with your new passengers at first. Acquaint them with cycling gradually, stopping often to check on their comfort. Encourage them to help with the route choice or play word games to keep their attention.

Introducing your child to cycling is far from drudgery: many parents claim that doing so doubles their cycling pleasure. Phil Miller, the Bicycle Coordinator for King County, Washington, loves taking nine-month old Ryan along. Says Miller, "It's great training for me, and it gives me a chance to get out in the sunshine and share cycling at an early age with my guy. He does seem to like it."

CYCLING FOR SENIORS

By Gordy Shields

Don't sit there thinking cycling is for younger people. If you've done it all your life, it can always be a part of your plans. If you're thinking about taking up cycling late in life, that too is possible.

Most of us cycled as kids. It's good to know that once learned, it's a skill that is never lost. If you've been away from it for a while, the hiatus may have damaged your confidence, but the ability to balance and steer is still there. You may wish to start off slowly, in quiet flat places, and build up your confidence. Although there have been some changes in bikes—now there are off-road machines, beach bikes, commuter bikes, "funny" bikes with one big and one little wheel, and racing bikes—basically it comes down to two wheels on a triangular frame with you supplying the power to the pedals. Some of you may find a mixte or drop frame bicycle more appealing—even an adult tricycle if your balance needs some support—but the dynamics are still the same.

Whatever you decide to ride, there are important things to know. First, realize that you come under the vehicle code in all states and, with few exceptions, you have all the rights and responsibilities of a motorist. That means stop at stop signs. Obey the traffic lights and ride responsibly. Join a local bicycling club, learn the rules of the road, and ride with a group to get some helpful pointers and a feeling for safety. Almost all cities and towns have clubs.

For those of you who think that all you can do is play golf or bowl, think again. In this sport you will enjoy the best of companionship while burning off fat, lowering your blood pressure, strengthening your heart, dropping your cholesterol level, and feeling great doing it. One of the most important things to remember is that older folks have a need for healthy, purposeful recreation. For many reasons, cycling is simply the best answer. (But remember, as the saying goes, to consult your physician before embarking on a program of physical exercise.)

One older cyclist for whom age is no barrier is Jim Kehew. No stranger to cycling, Kehew celebrated his seventy-fourth birthday by riding from Maine to Virginia. Kehew has cycled 40,000 miles in 30 years, pedaling coast to coast and from Southern England to Northern Scotland. Says Kehew, "Biking is perfect for seniors of all ages and either sex. You don't need a partner, although that's a nice way to go." Like many men and

Robert C. Hammersmith, a retired engineer from Rocklin, California, is the oldest known rider to have ridden Bikecentennial's 4300-mile TransAmerica Trail. He made his 78-day crossing at age 79. (Bikecentennial Photo by Greg Siple)

women who are over sixty, Kehew claims cycling is "easy to learn, and it's never too late to start."

Thousands of older folks find cycling is perfect for their exercise needs. It keeps you in shape, and as Kehew aptly says, "You can't beat it for enjoying nature or the outdoors; you're helping the environment and traffic problems, and best of all—it's fun!"

While gently cycling down a local path might be fun, there are options for those who want to push the pedals competitively. Does the competitive spirit still burn after 60? You bet. Today, under the banner of the U.S. Cycling Federation (USCF), there are bicycle racing events for every age. The Masters events, for cyclists 30 to 35, 36 to 40, 41 to 45, etc., now draw about 8,000 riders in the USCF. In fact, racing events continue to attract cyclists in their seventies and eighties. Older cyclists can look to the World Senior Games in Utah, the U.S. National Senior Olympics every two years, the World Cup Races in Austria, and the record challenge time trials in New Mexico.

Gordy Shields began cycling at age fifty. He lives and cycles in Southern California, where he's diligently working on keeping the U.S. National Senior Cycling Federation's time trial record for age group 70 to 74. For more information, contact the Record Challenge Time Trial, P.O. Box 40235, Albuquerque, NM 87198, 505/884–1880, and Langshaw's Sports Competition Management, Inc., 12812 Ocean Gateway, Queen Anne, MD 21657, 301/822–8060, which sponsors trips for all ages to the Master World Cup and Master World Bike Race in Austria.

THE PHYSIOLOGICAL BENEFITS OF BIKING

By Julie Ridge

Beyond the simple pleasures of taking in the country, sharing good times with good friends, or getting where you need to go in an environmentally responsible fashion, biking offers a slew of physiological benefits. Here are some.

Burning Calories

Depending on the intensity of the terrain and the pedaling power exerted, you'll burn anywhere from 500 to 1,000 calories per hour of bicycling. That's between ½ and ¾ of a pint of macadamia brittle Hagen Daz.

Muscle Firming

Provided your seat height is set properly and your biking form is clean, you'll be firming, toning, and building a *lot* of muscles. The most obvious muscle groups that benefit are quadriceps and back muscles. The less obvious, but just as efficiently exercised, are calves, gluteus, and those tough-to-reach abdominals.

Rehabilitating Stressed Knees

Biking is the first piece of aerobic equipment a good sports rehab facility will prescribe to anyone recovering from a knee injury. Why? Because the even circular motion required to move the wheels round and round strengthens all of the muscles surrounding the knee, without stressing the joint.

There is no pounding or jarring. If you apply as much effort to pulling on the up-stroke as you do to pushing on the down-stroke, you strengthen *all* of the muscles around the knee.

Nothing keeps a healthy knee healthier, or strengthens a stressed, strained, or recovering knee more than strong muscles all around it.

Sweating

Simple formula—bike hard (enough to burn calories and raise your heart rate into your training zone), and you will sweat. Perspiration brought on through effort expended (as opposed to a steam room or sauna) is cleansing for the body and just feels good.

Whether the benefits are something you can see on the outside, like firmer and shapelier legs, or feel on the inside, like a stronger and younger heart, biking will provide them for you.

Julie Ridge is a freelance writer living in New York. She was entered in the *Guinness Book of World Records* for swimming one 28.5 mile lap around Manhattan each day for five consecutive days in 1985. In 1990 she bicycled across America with her 67–year-old father.

TWO FOR THE ROAD

. . . .

Faster than a speeding bullet? More powerful than a locomotive? Is it a super hero, or could it just be two cyclists whizzing by on a long bicycle? Bicycles built for two, tandems, long bikes, or "twicers," as enthusiasts affectionately call them, are designed for taking along company and also happen to be quite speedy. You may have seen them swooping down hills and seemingly effortlessly eating up the miles on the flats.

This is something of which Jack Goetz speaks. An avid tandem rider of some twenty years, Jack likes to go fast. "This way I can keep up with my wife," he emphasizes, adding somewhat mischievously, "It's probably the best way two people can do things together on a bicycle."

In many ways, Jack and his wife, Susan, a tandem rider with ten years of experience, typify why two cyclists join up

(Burley Design Cooperative)

on one bicycle. For both Jack and Susan, cycling together is pleasurable and their tandem equalizes cycling partners with unequal strengths. When one cyclist is stronger than another, a tandem can provide the "bridge" to enjoying cycling at the same speed. While Jack Goetz captains, or has the front position, and Susan is the stoker, pedaling in the rear and giving directions, things move smoothly. Says Susan, "I enjoy riding a tandem because it's fun to be cycling together. Sometimes you realize you're clicking along and it doesn't feel like you're working."

Bruce Johnson is mostly a single bike rider, but he enjoys getting on a tandem when he can. Bruce often captains for a cycling friend who is blind, providing an opportunity for her to enjoy cycling. A strong cyclist who's usually challenging Virginia's hills, Bruce enjoys the efficiency of a tandem and being able to "talk to the person you're riding with."

Bonnie and Chuck Dye, parents who take their children on tandem rides, are active long-bike riders. Because they are the same height, either Bonnie or Chuck can be the captain or stoker on their tandem. While one of them captains the front, the other can read the map, talk the whole time, or even give the other a back massage. They've adapted their tandem for their children, ages seven and four. Since Bonnie and Chuck don't get to ride the tandem together much anymore, Chuck declares, "We're thinking of getting another tandem." That way, with one child on the back of each tandem, they'll be able to talk to each other. Both Bonnie and Chuck recommend the Eastern Tandem Rally, an event just for long bikes. The Tandem Club of America, 2220 Vanessa Dr., Birmingham, AL 35242, has information available on that yearly happening for a self-addressed, stamped envelope (SASE).

CYCLING WITH A DISABILITY

It's a given that people of various skills and abilities enjoy cycling. Bicycling provides mobility, access to the outdoors, and, of course, hours of pleasure. Over the years, designers and others have worked to enable individuals with partial use of their arms or legs to pursue cycling. Now there's a selection of specially adapted bicycles to meet almost any cyclist's needs, enabling him or her to participate fully. The following builders, organizations, individuals, and companies are resources for cyclists with special needs. Feel free to contact them for information on specially designed bicycles, tours oriented for cyclists with a disability, or other contacts.

Cyclists with visual impairments often pair up with tandem riders, acting as a stoker. They should check with their local bicycle club or send a self-addressed and stamped envelope to the Tandem Club of America, P.O. Box 83, Palo Alto, CA 94302 or Bicycles Built for One World, listed below.

Builders

Access Designs Inc., 627 SE 53rd, Portland, OR 97215, 503/238–0049 * Manufactures the Cycl-one.

Angle Lake Cyclery, 20840 Pacific Highway South, Seattle, WA 98188, 206/878–7457 * Makes the Counterpoint, a tandem with a forward-mounted stoker. Offers special adapter pedals for children and a hand crank system.

Cadet (Cumnock and Doon Enterprise Trust), Caponacre Industrial Estate, Cumnock, Ayrshire, KA18 1SH, Scotland, 0290–21159/25203; fax: 0290–25533 * Produces the Howie Dual Cycle, which is two cycles joined together enabling an able-bodied person to ride beside a less able cyclist. Can be used by one blind and one sighted cyclist.

Magic in Motion, 20604 84th Ave. South, Kent, WA 98032, 800/342–1579, 206/872–0722 * Has a three-wheel racer and equipment for other sports.

Matthews Cycles, 20 Russell Blvd., Bradford, PA 16701, 800/525–4444, 814/368–4773 * Since 1956, Bill Matthews's company has specialized in tricycles, bicycles, industrial tricycles, unicycles, trailers, baskets, and tote boxes. Their Leisure Line features tricycles for children (with an inseam of 20" or more) and adults with disabilities.

New England Handcycles, 48 Bogle St., Weston, MA 02193, 617/237–7720 * One of the oldest manufacturers of handcycles. They also offer a racing version for triathlon athletes.

Palmer Industries, P.O. Box 707, Endicott, NY 13760, 800/847–1304, 607/754–1954 * Manufactures a hand-pedaled tricycle called the Handcycle for large children or adults.

WR Pashley Ltd., Masons Rd., Stratford-upon-Avon, Warwickshire CV37 9NL, England, 0789/292263 * Makes a range of adult tricycles.

Paterek Frames, Rt. 2, Box 234, River Falls, WI 54022, 715/386–7661 (day) * Builds custom tandems, frames, and hand-pedaled bicycles. Can do any number of variations on frames to suit client's needs. See also "Schools" in the *Tools* section.

Rifton, Rte. 213, Rifton, NY 12471, 914/658–3141 * Specializes in products for people of all ages with disabilities. Offers tricycles with additional support for children; both small and medium hand-driven tricycles; and small and large chain tricycles that allow pedalling below the seat and steering independent of foot control.

Chris Schwandt, 90127 West Demming Rd., Elmira, OR 97347, 503/935–2828 * Designer of various alternative cycles.

Doug Schwandt, Biomedical Engineer, Rehabilitation Research and Development Center (640/153), Veterans Administration Medical Center, 3801 Miranda Ave., Palo Alto, CA 94303, 415/493–5000 x 4473 * Designer of hand-"pedaled" bicycles and of the Sunburst Tandem.

Serotta Cycles, Inc., P.O. Box 106, Middle Grove, NY 12850, 800/338–0998, 518/587–9085 * Designer and builder who will adapt a frame to suit needs.

Harper Zarker, 4065 Fountain Plaza Dr., Brookfield, WI 53005, 414/781–0170 * Designer and builder of hand-pedaled bicycles.

Touring, Racing, and Other Contacts

Gary Bertelsen, 6054 Sunwood Pl., Westerville, OH 43081, 614/625–6136 (day) * Coach and contact for disabled racing.

A Bicycle Built for One World, P.O. Box 460697, San Francisco, CA 94124, 415/378–5973 * Organization of blind and sighted people who promote peace, cycling, and tandems.

International Bicycle Tours, 12 Mid Place, Chappaqua, NY 10514, 914/238–4576 * Offers tandem touring in Holland for visually impaired cyclists.

International Human Powered Vehicle Association, P.O. Box 51255, Indianapolis, IN 46251, 317/876–9478 * A non-profit organization which promotes human-powered vehicle use.

Ross Jantz, Coordinator for New Directions, 2172 Temple Cir., Eureka, CA 95501, 707/444–8510 * Coordinates and leads bike tours for people with disabilities for New Directions. Can be contacted directly.

Klein Bicycle Corporation, 118 Klein Rd., Chehalis, WA 98532, 206/262–3305 * Designer and builder who can adapt frames to suit any cyclist's needs. See also *Custom-built Frames.*

National Amputee Summer Sports Association, 215 W. 92nd St., New York, NY, 212/874–4138.

National Handicapped Sports and Recreation Association, 1145 Nineteenth St. NW, Suite 717, Washington, DC 20036, 202/393–7505 * Promotes all sports for people with a disability. Jan Wilson is their coordinator for bicycling.

New Directions, 5276 Hollister Ave., #207, Santa Barbara, CA 93111, 805/967–2841 * Works with people with disabilities; sponsors bike tours through Ross Jantz.

Overland Expeditions, 1773 11th St., Los Osos, CA 93402, 805/528–6381 * Designs specialty tours for those with a disability.

Paralyzed Veterans of America, 801 Eighteenth St. NW, Washington, DC 20006, 202/USA–1300 * Publishes *Sports and Spokes,* a bi-monthly magazine available by subscription. Offers information on all sorts of recreational activities and builders of specialized equipment.

Rail Riders, P.O. Box 1480, Hillsboro, NH 03244, 603/927–4690 * Organizes rides for people with disabilities and manufactures bikes for use on the more than 45,000 miles of abandoned railroad tracks.

The Royal Association for Disability and Rehabilitation (RADAR), 25 Mortimer St., London W1N 8AB, England, 01–637–5400 * Formed in 1977, RADAR provides supports and information. RADAR has an extensive list of builders for people with disabilities. Its mission is "to remove architectural, economic and attitudinal/social barriers which impose restrictions on disabled people, and to ensure that disabled people are able to play their full role in the community."

P eighteen

THE HISTORY OF CYCLING

THE MECHANICS OF BICYCLE HISTORY

It's been said that the first dream of a bicycle came from the pen of a student of Leonardo da Vinci. This student's drawing shows a vehicle with two wheels, a bar, and no method of steering. It does, however, have a bicycle-like quality about it. Although hints of other bicycle-type contraptions appear on three-thousand-year-old Egyptian tombs, most historians date the emergence of the first bicycle to the late 1700s and early 1800s.

It was around 1790 when the "bicycle" that some consider the progenitor of all bicycles came along. The celerifere, developed by Comte de Sivrac in France, was a sort of "hobbyhorse" on wheels. It was a simple frame mounted on two wheels, made of wood, and it lacked the capacity for steering. A rider sat astride the celerifere, propelling it forward, scooter-style, with his feet. (It would be decades before the Ladies' Hobby Horse, a paddled contraption women could call their own, would permit women to enjoy the sport.) There were no handlebars, seat, pedals, or measure of comfort as we know it.

Some twenty-five years later, German Baron Karl von Drais created the Draisienne, which had a rudder for directing the front wheel and a padded seat. Dubbed the dandy horse, the swiftwalker, the velocipede, hobby, and the running machine, von Drais's invention took off. Despite the rough ride it offered, thousands found it useful. Writer Jim McGurn notes in his illustrated history of cycling, *On Your Bicycle,* "It seems that Draisiennes were closely associated with places of entertainment such as fairgrounds, amusement parks and theatres; and they were ridden in a corresponding spirit of fun" (McGurn, p. 17). Unfortunately for von Drais, although he patented his machine, other inventors adapted his basic form as their own, preventing him from receiving financial compensation.

The following years brought many modifications to the Draisienne, adding wheels, levers, and other whistles and bells. This bicycle in its early stages excited the imagina-

(Schwinn History Center)

tion, attracting inventors and tinkerers. Here was a human-powered vehicle: no one seemed content to let it stay in the form von Drais had left it in. Although not yet comfortable or practical, the draisienne was evolving and, for the most part, was called a velocipede.

In late 1839, a Scottish blacksmith named Kirkpatrick Macmillan made a machine which was treadle operated with a rear-driving wheel. This permutation of the velocipede didn't attract a good deal of attention, but it did win the inventor a fine for knocking over (but not injuring) a child. Many bicycle historians consider Macmillan's addition crucial to the development of the bicycle of today.

In 1861, the first direct-action pedal was produced by the Frenchman Pierre Michauex and his son. Soon riders could be seen propelling themselves along the Champs Elysees in Paris by means of pedals attached to the front wheel of the velocipede. With a frame and tires made of iron, Michauex's velocipede featured a seat attached to a spring. Most important, this version of the velocipede kept the rider's feet off the ground. This pedal-driven vehicle also had a slightly bigger front wheel and a handlebar that was held by both hands. Later on the velocipede would have solid rubber tires, but for a while its heaviness and teeth-battering ride earned it the moniker "boneshaker."

Velocipede riding and racing was not solely confined to Europe. Brought to the states in the late 1860s, velocipedes became quite popular in gymnastic exhibitions. Schools were even set up to teach riding skills.

Around 1869, the heavy boneshaker gave way to the high wheeler or penny farthing, a lighter bicycle with one huge front wheel and a smaller back wheel. It, too was a challenge to ride, although for different reasons than the boneshaker. The high wheeler, which came to be known as the "ordinary" because of its commonness and popularity, typically had a 50–inch front wheel. It was anywhere from forty to fifty pounds lighter than its predecessor, the boneshaker. The ordinary, however, demanded that its rider be a bit of an acrobat. Ascending the ordinary or high wheeler meant putting a foot on a side step, getting the bike rolling, and then extending yourself up to a saddle that was five feet above the ground. This was definitely not for children, non-athletic men, or women in long skirts.

Stopping an ordinary was difficult too. If not done correctly, the unfortunate rider would take a "header" off the bike, falling a dangerous distance. Imagine riding one of these on the unpaved, rough surfaces of the 1880s and 1890s. Obviously, the bicycle's evolution could not stop here: its potential as a mode of transportation and recreation had not yet been reached.

St. Louis Cycling Club tour, spring 1892. (Schwinn History Center)

Some manufacturers filled this need by producing tricycles, a machine appropriate for those of more cautious spirit. Tricycles could also carry packages and anything else an ordinary rider, concerned with balance, wouldn't dream of taking.

It makes sense that the ordinary, a somewhat dangerous bicycle given the roads and the balancing act required, would evolve into the "safety." Aptly named, the safety reflected the fact that disfigurement and injury were less likely on this machine. The safety arrived on the scene sometime between 1885 and 1891. The first safeties had small wheels, were turned by a pedal-chain system, and had no front wheel pedals.

In general, bicycles have changed very little since the safety. The small wheels of the safety, a welcome change from the ordinary's huge front wheel, allowed riders to get on and off easily. The safety weighed approximately thirty pounds less than both the ordinary and the tricycle. Pneumatic tires came into being in 1888, making the safety even more comfortable and lighter. Women could easily ride the safety too; many models had drop frames. It's little wonder that the basic design of the safety has persisted some 110 years.

The Bicycle and Society

It's impossible to separate the bicycle's mechanical evolution from the changes it spawned in society. In many respects, the history of the bicycle is as much social as it is technological. From its first appearance to its current diverse standing in the world, the bicycle has been a vehicle for change. Cycling's initial converts were varied: many loved the athletic aspect of cycling; others enjoyed the long-distance travel it enabled. Still others were attracted by the freedom it brought. For example, Frenchwomen of the 1870s who raced on velocipedes could wear practical clothing instead of the girdle-confining fashions of the times. Disparate as these cyclists riding high wheelers, or ordinaries, were, many were drawn together by a common cause: the need to improve cycling conditions by getting irregularly surfaced roads repaired.

Roads at that time were nothing like they are now. Back then, they were unpredictable quagmires, distinguished by deep ruts. Wheeling the hard-to-balance ordinary or any other kind of bicycle down them was a delicate enterprise at best. In the latter part of the 1870s in England, the Bicycling Touring Club, which evolved into the contemporary Cyclists Touring Club (CTC), began. Attracting a membership of three thousand, it disseminated information on dangerous bicycling conditions and also acquainted a group of visiting cyclists from the U.S. with their organization and structure.

These cyclists started the League of American Wheelmen, now considered the nation's oldest bicycle advocacy group. Members of the League of American Wheelmen (L.A.W. for short because they followed the law of the road) fought for all cyclists' rights, and are recognized for their Good Roads Campaign, instrumental in improving the roads for all users.

In addition to making the road surfaces better, cyclists were expanding their horizons. Even before the roads were improved, the intrepid Karl Kron related his journeys in his 1887 book, *Ten Thousand Miles on a Bicycle*. Thomas Stevens rode around the world in the 1880s, chronicling his adventures in *Around the World on a Bicycle*.

Women cyclists expanded their horizons in other ways. Drawn by the independence the bicycle offered, women in England and the U.S. took to the sport in droves. Riding a bicycle was difficult in the typical garb of that time; long, bulky dresses were confining and caught in the wheels. Women adopted, in some folks' perspective, "scandalous" practices: they took to bloomers and other practical clothing more suited for bicycling. The bicycle engendered a

Tillie Anderson, USA's ladies champion, 1897.
(Schwinn History Center)

clothing revolution for women, in addition to offering them the opportunity to get around on their own.

In the 1890s, cycling had what many considered a golden age. Thousands of Americans came to watch six-day bicycle races on wooden tracks. The League of American Wheelmen's membership was at its peak—its magazine boasting of nearly 100,000 members. Cyclists such as Major Taylor, the first black professional cyclist, won the World's Professional Sprint Championship in 1899 in Montreal. (This one-mile sprint has only been won by three Americans.) Taylor further established his place in history by winning the U.S. National Championship in 1900 and competing widely in Europe and Australia until his retirement in 1910.

Cycling attracted national attention at this time. In New York City, four patrolmen "walked" their beat on bikes, and Charles "Mile-a-Minute" Murphy rode behind a Long Island Railroad train. He astonished everyone, cycling a mile in less than one minute. Although John D. Rockefeller was not as swift as "Mile-a-Minute" Murphy, he too was one of thousands of bicycle enthusiasts.

Cycling was also a part of the romantic fabric. Strains of that bicycle song, "Daisy, Daisy," were heard by courting cyclists. In fact, there were more than 150 songs relating to cycling. Americans went bicycling with their sweeties and took them to bike races. Some of them even made romantic overtures at the bicycle races. (See "A Romantic Moment in Cycling History" in this section.)

With the advent of automobiles and trolleys, bicycling lost its popularity. Fewer adults rode them, and they became the province of children. Paper boys spun out on their morning routes, while adults and families went for drives in the family car. Fortunately, the balloon tire bicycle, introduced by Schwinn in 1933, helped the bike industry ride out the Depression. Kids really took to this bike, much the way people now take to its descendant—the mountain bike. Their enthusiasm for the bicycle helped establish its status as a toy.

Then, in the late 1930s, bicycling both abroad and in the U.S. experienced a resurgence as transportation. The bicycle was the way to get around during World War II. Patriotic Americans pedaled to work, to school, and to shop; gas rationing was a way of life. Soon, however, the car again caught popular consciousness. Americans shined, waxed, courted, and practically memorialized their automobiles while bicycles languished in garages. Teenagers seemed particularly susceptible to the lure of the automobile. And thus the car culture temporarily dampened the bicycle's popularity.

Although cycling hasn't returned to its heyday of the 1890s, it is making a comeback. In 1991 the Bicycle Federation of America estimates that more than 90 million Americans cycle. That is up from 72 million in 1983. Nearly 26 million Americans cycle regularly, at least once a week. There are 3 million participants in recreational events and 3.5 million bicycle commuters. Children pedal to school and recreational activities; adults integrate bicycling into their routine, using it for errands and fitness, in addition to commuting. Mountain bikes are drawing more converts than ever since they came down from Mt. Tamelpais in California. And the ever-increasing number of tour operators offering bicycle-oriented vacations further speaks to the bicycle's growing popularity. In fact, more than 1.3 million Americans take bicycles on vacations.

Writer Peter Nye, author of *Hearts of Lions: The Story of American Bicycle Racing,* is pleased about this trend. "I'm happy to see cycling come back, because long ago it was an inherent part of our American popular culture." The next decade promises to revive bicycling in the mainstream. With additional government, grassroots, and organizational encouragement, the numbers of people bicycling regularly could increase exponentially.

A ROMANTIC MOMENT IN CYCLING HISTORY

By John Lucas

Impossible as it may seem to us on the edge of the twenty-first century, the most important spectator sport in New York City from 1875 to 1890 was indoor ultra-marathon running, or, as it was called, Six-Day, Go-As-You-Please Pedestrianism. On Thanksgiving Day 1888, Englishman George Littlewood alternately fast-walked and ran for six days and six nights on a tight little sawdust-tanbark track in Madison Square Garden (MSG), outdistancing his international opponents and winning $9,000 for his 142 hours of voluntary ultra-agony. It was the last big race of its kind. The public had grown weary of pedestrian plods and had fallen in love with a new amusement—indoor six-day bicycle marathons.

The action was four times faster, the thrills and spills (many of both) of the highest magnitude for the urban working classes who had no visible forms of recreation—and, of course, no motion pictures, radio, or television. Just as Littlewood had been the darling of the Big Apple MSG, so Chicago-born Charlie Miller was the super star of the new sport, Six-Day Bicycle Racing. The craze began in 1891, rose in interest like a rocket, and ended in 1898 (on the edge of the 20th-century technological leisure revolution) with Charlie Miller's ultimate world record of bicycling 2,007.20 miles on a tiny squirrel-cage wooden track inside the same MSG. Like his running predecessor, Charlie Miller won a great sack full of money for his labors. He captured a place in the *Guinness Book of Records* . . . and he won a wife.

Racing on Sunday, the Lord's Day, was forbidden, so thirty-two riders gathered on the starting line a few moments after midnight of December 5, 1898, the brand new ten-laps-to-the-mile track awaiting the mesmeric hum of bicycle tires. Incongruously, at this be-witching hour, thousands of fans crowded the Garden shouting for peanuts, popcorn, candy, lemonade, and their favorite cyclist, "the whole scene looking like a miniature country fair." Whirling, whirling, thousands of laps, day and night, with almost no respite for sleep and food, the powerfully built defending world's champion, Charlie Miller, finished the first day's grind in third place (461 miles) behind Waller, the "Flying Dutchman" (471 miles), and "Plucky" Pierce, with 478 miles. The leader must have needed food more than rest, and consumed in the next twenty-four hours, "four eggs, two chops, two quarts of milk, four quarts of beef tea, four ounces of calf's foot jelly, a half-pound of crackers, one pound of steak, two apples, a half-pound of grapes, four ounces of beef extract, four slices of toast, and two siphons of Vichy mineral water." It didn't help, because by midnight Thursday, Miller had taken the lead with 1,473 miles. Waller (1,463 miles) and Pierce (1,455 miles) were still in hot pursuit. Seventeen cyclists had logged over a thousand miles each in four days and nights of numbing riding.

The attractive Genevieve Hanson of Chicago had resisted all offers of marriage from Charlie Miller, until this critical fifth day of the championship, when "she relinquished her coyness and agreed to marry Miller if he could win this race." In a burst of riding skill and endurance, probably not a coincidence, Miller began lapping his opponents. He opened a twenty-mile gap between himself and Waller, and the race was essentially "in the bag." He coasted the last 24 hours, waved continuously to Miss Hanson, and defeated Waller 2,007 ⅕ miles to 1,985 ¼ miles. Genevieve retired from her seat in order to prepare for the wedding on Saturday afternoon, the 10th of December.

At 4:40 p.m. the band started to play the Wedding March and the Garden fans shouted, "They're coming," for it seemed that the blissful couple had decided to marry at center stage. The bride's costume was a dove-colored broadcloth dress with a small hat and gloves to match. She carried a bouquet of bride's roses. The crowd cheered as Charlie Miller appeared, clad in an orange and white bathrobe and accompanied by his trainer. The self-possessed Miller reached Genevieve's side, threw off his bathrobe, and "displayed a wonderful costume." He was clad in gorgeous new racing tights, one leg pink and the other white. His sweater was blue and white and over this he wore a shirt colored like his tights, only the colors were reversed so that the pink half of the shirt came over the white leg of the tights. Around his waist was a silk American flag, and on the back of the shirt was embroidered an eagle and shield. Miller was eager and remarkably "fresh" at the wedding, his wallet filled with the $3,800 in victor's spoils—more money than he could have made in two years as a Chicago laborer.

Following the ceremony, Charlie kissed his bride, then got on his wheel for several spins around the Garden track. The fans cheered and the band played "Auld Lang Syne." Miller and his wife slipped out the side door, returning to Chicago to a comfortable life . . . and obscurity. The drum beat of indoor cycling continued the next winter, this time to the new and titillating 142–hour cycling racing, with alternating riders. Mr. and Mrs. Miller probably watched with the greatest interest as it all unfolded.

John Lucas is a professor at Penn State University, where he has been a senior sports historian since 1962. He was a finalist in the USA Olympic Trials 10,000 meters in 1952 and was recently featured in *Runner's World* for having run 80,000 miles in his life. *The Future of the Olympic,* the most recent of Professor Lucas's four books, is forthcoming from Human Kinetics Publishing Company.

COLLECTING THE PAST

You are at a garage sale, poking among pots and planters, when you spot a bicycle that looks old and beat reclining against a rickety bookcase. On closer inspection, you see that the bicycle is merely caked with dust and has flat tires. It is also somewhat reminiscent of one you owned when you were nine, with the same balloon tires and even a spring above the front fender. Memories pop out unbidden: your sister and you spinning down to the local lake for a forbidden swim or racing to the candy store. You can't resist. Before anyone can utter "bicycle rack," you've plunked down a few dollars, and the memory—plus the bicycle—is yours.

This is the way many a new bicycle collector gets started. According to T.A. Gordon, managing editor of *Antique/Classic Bicycle News,* many collectors get drawn to the hobby because they stumble across a bicycle from their childhood days. Gordon recalls that the first bicycle that prompted her interest was a J.C. Higgins. "It had more glass reflectors than anything I had ever seen. The colors were so much richer, and they didn't scratch." To Ms. Gordon, the reflectors on that older 1950s Sears bicycle were lovely. Not only was there a totally different look to the way they showed off the light, but the bicycle had a Batwing headlight and other features not found on contemporary bicycles.

New collectors are also attracted to the pinstripes, chrome, Donald Duck horn, or other characteristics that distinguish those classic bicycles of the thirties, forties, and fifties from those manufactured today. Some cyclists seek out high-wheel bicycles, acquiring the hundred-year-old originals or quality reproductions of them. And then there are the collectors who delight not only in acquiring classic bicycles but in restoring them to their former glory.

Whatever compels you to collect old bicycles, you can locate many of these beauties at auctions, garage sales, flea markets, antique shops, and even bicycle shops that have been in business for generations. Your friends and neighbors, even a relative in Idaho, may have a basement which holds several old bikes, more untapped collecting potential. For many hobbyists, sleuthing is an art and as much appreciated as the catch itself. Attics, estate sales, country sales: all of these can yield a classic bicycle. The trick, according to many collectors, is to always be on the prowl for a prize in every part of the country.

What should you look for? In general, whatever attracts you and makes you happy to take the time to restore it, says Gordon. Some collectors go for the design appeal of a bicycle. Schwinn's Black Phantom, for example, produced in the fifties, attracts hobbyists because it is shiny and flashy with lots of chrome. This popular bicycle reminds Gordon of

*Schwinn Black
Phantom*
(Schwinn History
Center)

a 1956 Buick, and indeed many of the popular classic bicycles take their cue from the automotive industry. After all, for many, the bicycle was the first form of transportation, a lead-in, if you will, to driving a car. Other classic bicycles, such as the 1968 Schwinn Run-A-Bout or the Whizzer WZ, have their own appeal. Cyclists might remember the 1955 Schwinn Hornet, with a horn tank and built in headlight and enameled wheel rims.

Before you buy your first classic bicycle, there are several things to consider. First, look for a complete bicycle. It can cost more to buy parts for the bicycle than to pay a fair price for one that is whole. Second, if you are interested in a particular model, bring photos of the desired bicycle along with you. These can help you easily identify someone's long-stored bicycle as what you want. Books such as James L. Hurd's and Don A. Henning's *Introductory Guide to Collecting the Classics* (available for $11.95 postpaid from *Antique/Classic Bicycle News,* P.O. Box 1049, Ann Arbor, MI 48106) can get you started. You may also want to tap into the friendly and helpful network of bicycle collecting enthusiasts. Contact the Classic Bicycle & Whizzer Club of America, 35769 Simon, Fraser, MI 48026, 313/791–5594.

After you find your treasure, there's the question of restoration. Do you want to have everything as it once was? Are you interested in using the bicycle on the road? Do you just want to clean it up so it can be displayed and appreciated? Whatever you decide will determine your next step.

Although a bicycle restoration can have many steps—as detailed in the introductory guide listed above—a few tips will keep you from inadvertently damaging your new purchase. Restoring expert Art Bransky writes that collectors should refrain from wiping off dirt because of all the abrasives. Instead, after covering the saddle with a plastic bag and pumping up the tires, the bicycle should be washed with a mixture of soap and water and allowed to dry quickly. Delicate decals, which add to the bike's authenticity, should be treated with care. Bransky cautions against the use of tape, because it removes paint, and recommends using wax to preserve decals, not polish.

Whether you uncover a Roadmaster or a sleek Airflo built by Shelby, bicycle collecting is a hobby that may grow on you. It's also a fun pastime to share. Several national bicycle shows and swaps can whet your appetite, introducing you to a wonderful variety of classics. In addition to meets listed in the newsletter *Antique/Classic Bicycle News,* P.O. Box 1049, Ann Arbor, MI 48106, enthusiasts can attend the Indian Summer Bicycle & Wheel Goods Show and Swap Meet. Held annually in late September or early October in Macungie, Pennsylvania, this meet is organized by Art Bransky, RD 2, Box 558, Breiningsville, PA 18031. Dorothy and Toto are obviously not the only things Kansas has: the Kansas State Fairgrounds (316/662–0887) offers an annual Swap Meet and Bicycle Show in Hutchinson, Kansas. Maybe you'll even locate the Wicked Witch of the West's heavy black bicycle, a classic in its own right.

CYCLING MUSEUMS AROUND THE WORLD

Located throughout the United States, Europe, and elsewhere are museums and libraries that either focus on bicycling exclusively or contain bicycle memorabilia and literature. If you're passing near or pedaling through these areas, check out their displays. You may also encounter private collectors through clubs such as the Classic Bicycle and Whizzer Club of America (see "Collecting the Past").

United States

Carillon Park, 2001 S. Patterson Blvd., Dayton, OH 513/293–2841 * Has a reproduction of the Wright Cycle Shop.

Columbia Historical Society, 1307 New Hampshire Ave. NW, Washington, D.C. 20036, 202/785–2068 * Has research library with bicycle literature.

On display at the Henry Ford Museum & Greenfield Village is this ten person bicycle, made in 1896 by the Orient Bicycle Company of Waltham, Massachusetts. This 23-foot long, 305-pound bicycle could reach speeds of 45 mph. (From the Collections of Henry Ford Museum & Greenfield Village)

Crawford Museum, Western Reserve Historical Society, 10825 E. Blvd., Cleveland, OH 44106, 216/721–5722.

Henry Ford Museum, 20900 Oakwood Blvd., Dearborn, MI 48121, 393/271–1620.

The Franklin Institute Science Museum and Planetarium, 20th and Ben Franklin Pkwy., Philadelphia, PA 19103, 215/448–1200.

Library of Congress, 10 First St. SE, Washington, DC 20540, 202/707–5522 * Has literature from the nineteenth century relating to bicycles.

Mountain Bike Hall of Fame and Museum, P.O. Box 1961, Crested Butte, CO 81224, 303/349–7280.

Museum of Science and Industry, 57th St. and Lakeshore Dr., Chicago, IL 60637, 312/684–1414.

Museum of Transportation, 15 Newton, Brookline, MA 02146, 617/522–6140.

New York Museum of Transportation, Box 136, West Henrietta, NY 14586, 716/533–1113.

Schwinn History Center, 312/454–7471 * The Schwinn History Center is not open to the public yet, but will respond to calls.

Smithsonian's National Museum of American History, 14th & Constitution Ave. NW, Washington, DC 202/352–2700 * In the Road Transportation Hall, there are seventeen bicycles on exhibit, dating from 1819–1989.

Sports Museum of New England, 1175 Soldiers Field Rd., Boston, MA 02134, 617/787–7678.

Texas Transportation Museum, 11731 Wetmore Rd., McAllister Park, San Antonio, TX 78247, 512/490–3554.

U.S. Bicycling Hall of Fame, 34 E. Main St., Somerville, NJ 08876, 908/725–0461 * Has memorabilia and information on inductees in the Hall.

European and International

Australian Gallery of Sport, P.O. Box 175, E. Melbourne, Australia 3002, 036–54–8922.

Canberra Bicycle Museum, 2 Badham St., Dickson, ACT, Australia, 062–48–0999 * Located in a tradesman's club and pub, the Canberra Bicycle Museum has an assortment of old bicycles, including a clunky 40–passenger model which spans an entire wall.

Denmark's Cykel (cycle) Museum, Borgergade 10, DK–9620, Aalestrup, Denmark, 1–45–9864–1960.

Deutsches Museum, Museumsinsel 1, 8000 Munchen 22, Munich, Germany, 89–21791.

Deutsches Zweirad-Museum, Urbanstrasse 11, 7107 Neckarsulum, Germany, 07132–35271 * Museum of bicycles only.

London Science Museum, Exhibition Rd., South Kensington, London SW7 2OD, 71–938–8000.

Museum of Gianthood, Palms, 20 Palmerston Park, Rathmines, Dublin 6, Ireland, 01–973–223 * Children's memorabilia from 1730 to 1940s. Said to include some bicycles.

Museum of the Little Queen, 152, rue de la Draisienne, 5511 Falmignoul, Nanur, Belgium * Bicycles and motorcycles from 1818 and later.

Museum of Sport and Bicycling, 118 President Kennedy Ave., 75775 Paris, CEDEX 16 France.

National Museum of Scotland, Royal Museum of Scotland, Chambers St., Edinburgh, Scotland EH1 1JF, 031–226–7534, ext. 219 * Has a bicycle collection started in 1810. Includes everything from a hobby horse once owned by Earl of Eglinton to a mountain bike make in Edinburgh in 1989.

Old Mill Folk and Transport Museum, Slane, County Meath, Ireland, 041–51827 * Display of transport items and memorabilia.

Sport Australia Hall of Fame, 76 Jolimont St., Jolimont, Victoria, Australia, 613/654–7633.

Transport Museum, Howth Castle, Dublin Rd. Howth, County Dublin, Ireland, 01353–1475623.

Velorama, Waackade 107, 65 11 XR Nijmegen, Netherlands, 080–225 851 * Rumored to house one of the best collections in Europe.

HUMAN-POWERED VEHICLES: PEDALLING ACROSS AIR, LAND, AND SEA

By Marti Daily

They set records for speed, in addition to recording human cleverness. Sometimes they have low-slung frames with a clear cover, sometimes they've got more than two wheels and they ride . . . on water. You've probably seen them—if not on a local bike ride then at least on television. You may have even tried one at some point, or even been tempted to own one. It's easy to surmise that they're from the bicycle family, but are they a distant cousin or an odd offspring? Although individual differences abound, they quite obviously fit into the catch-all category of "funny bikes." To enthusiasts of transportation alternatives, however, they fall into the classification of human-powered vehicles (HPVs).

Yes, of course, a traditional bicycle is indeed a human-powered vehicle, but there is a difference. The Draisienne, considered by many to be the first bicycle, was developed in 1818, less than two centuries ago. The bicycle underwent several evolutions, and its present incarnation began as the "safety"— essentially characterized as a bicycle with two wheels of the same size, a crank, and pedals. (The safety evolved from the highwheeler or "ordinary," a tricky contraption with one huge wheel, typically 48 to 50 inches, and a smaller one of 14 to 18 inches.) But human-powered vehicles today have another dimension. They take off, literally and figuratively, from what's considered the standard, the safety bicycle first developed around 1885.

Browsing through any of several museum displays tracing the early development of the bicycle, it's easy to see the wide variety of design and implementation. However, the safety bicycle looks very much like the standard diamond-frame bicycles of today. What happened? Why, after such a brief flurry of experimentation, did one design come to be accepted as the ultimate in perfection?

One easy answer is that the automobile was also developed in the late 1800s, and energy which had been channeled into bicycle design was then focused on motorcars. That's a definite possibility, but other factors seemed to have a more direct influence.

As early as 1933, a bicycle with a radically new design, the Velocar, was raced by a non-champion racer and demolished existing records for several distance events. The International Cycling Union (UCI), which had by this time established itself as the sanctioning and record-certifying body for bicycle racing, debated for days in Paris over whether or not to recognize this new challenger. The final decision was that this new design was not a bicycle, even though it had two wheels and was powered only by a human being. At that time, this decision effectively halted the further development of the bicycle in its tracks. What was the point of further innovation, if the "powers that be" would only outlaw their implementation?

Although it did not directly involve bicycles, a prize offered in 1959 by the British industrialist Henry Kremer for the first human-powered aircraft that could navigate a one-mile figure eight course initiated a flurry of activity around the world. Inventors, tinkerers, and creative thinkers of all kinds responded with new designs and creations. This motivated Dr. David Gordon Wilson, a professor at Massachusetts Institute of Technology (MIT), to offer a similar prize for developments in human-powered land transportation in 1967. Seventy-three entries from six countries were received; some were actually built, and the resultant publicity inspired Dr. Chester Kyle to work with his students at the University of California-Long Beach in streamlining traditional bicycles as well as in creating new designs. The test runs of these vehicles resulted in speeds that well exceeded existing bicycle records, but again, the UCI refused to recognize these records.

In typical California fashion, Dr. Kyle and other enthusiasts decided to establish a new organization to recognize and to keep track of these records: thus was born the International Human Powered Vehicle Association (IHPVA), and the annual International Human Powered Speed Championships began in 1974.

Gold Rush Team; from left: Gardner Martin, Nathan Dean, Fred Markhan, Allan Osterbauer. (IHPVA)

In contrast to the UCI, the IHPVA requires that vehicles competing under its auspices comply with only two rules: they must be propelled by human power only, and no energy storage is allowed. Articles of understanding were established with the United States Cycling Federation (USCF) to recognize that a bicycle was a bicycle and that anything else was a "human powered vehicle," allowing licensed racers to compete in non-USCF-sanctioned IHPVA competitions; a similar agreement was later reached with the UCI.

So, when you see a vehicle on two or three or more wheels being pedalled down the road, or through the water, or in the air, technically you are not witnessing a bicycle ride: you are watching an HPV in action. Some human-powered vehicle accomplishments include the establishment of a land speed record of 65.48 mph; an air distance record of nearly 74 miles achieved by Greek cyclist Kannelos Kannelopolus; and speeds on water approaching 20 knots (approximately 23 mph).

But far more significant than the higher speeds is the philosophy that designs are limited only by the imagination. The human-powered vehicle builds on the principles of the bicycle and the courage and skills of the inventor. It is human nature to continually strive for something better: only when artificial constraints are accepted is this trait stifled. Will we ever see a commuting vehicle that enables its rider/driver to replace his or her automobile with a non-polluting, self-sustained, healthy alternative?

Why not? Right now teams of inventors and cyclists have risen to this challenge. Past inspirations include the *Gold Rush,* powered by "Fast Freddy" Markhan; a hydrofoil with the moniker of the *Flying Fish;* the *Daedalus,* a pedal-powered airplane; and hordes of other successful creations which prove that our only limitations are those of the imagination.

Marti Daily is the President of the International Human Powered Vehicle Association, P.O. Box 51255, Indianapolis, IN 46251. From August 14 to 18, 1991, she will be at the 17th Annual International Human Powered Speed Championships in Milwaukee, Wisconsin.

Appendix

Tips on Effective Cycling

Cycling Techniques

Wear gloves. Cycling gloves prevent numbness, provide crash protection, and improve grip. The following technique and position tips can also help your hands:

1. Take the load off. Support some of your torso weight with your back and abdominal muscles instead of resting it all on your arms and hands.

2. Relax your arms. Rigid arms transmit road shock to your hands and torso. Loosely flexed arms absorb shock for more comfort and control.

3. Raise your handlebar stem to shift weight from your hands to your seat.

For a smoother ride over bumps, relax your elbows and shoulders and bend both knees as you lift 1" to 3" off the seat. Keep pedaling so your weight isn't "dead," and as bumps or holes go under each wheel, absorb the shock with flexed elbows and knees.

Stay loose and agile. You'll take less pounding and maintain better speed and control.

Tune up your pedaling technique:

1. Climbing a hill: Alternate spinning in a low gear while seated with standing and pedaling in a higher gear.

2. On flat roads: Work on a smooth power stroke. Instead of an up-and-down "stair climb" movement, imagine pedaling through a complete circle. You'll be amazed at how efficient you become.

3. Higher rpms: Try turning the cranks faster (85–95 rpm) in an easier gear. This faster cadence is easier on your knees, allows you to ride longer, and promotes better cardiovascular fitness.

4. The increased efficiency of cycling shoes helps you deliver power from the 2 o'clock position all the way through to 9 o'clock.

Drinking and riding DO mix. Keep up your body's fluid level for maximum alertness and performance. It's easy to become dehydrated because you're losing water through perspiration and respiration.

When? Always drink before you're thirsty. Once you're thirsty, your fluid level is already low. Have a long pre-ride drink and refill your bottle for the ride.

How much? About a pint an hour depending on your size and the heat. This is about one large bottle every two hours.

ADJUSTING YOUR BIKE

Get the right fit for comfort.

1. Saddle height is correct when your leg is fully extended with your heel on the pedal. When the ball of your foot is over the pedal axle, your knee should be slightly bent at the bottom of the stroke and your hips shouldn't rock as you pedal.

2. Saddle tilt is correct when a yardstick on the saddle, pointing front-to-rear, is close to level. Tipping the nose down makes you slide forward, putting more weight on your hands.

3. Your reach to the bars can be easily changed. Stiff arms or sore shoulders, back, or hands can mean a stem that's too long or too low. Even ½" makes a

noticeable comfort difference. If you have a shorter or longer torso, you may need a different length stem. Bring your bike in for a free check.

Handlebar height. High is more comfortable, but slower. You're less aerodynamic, and less able to use your back muscles to pedal. Start with the bars at, or 1" below, seat level and experiment up or down in ¼" increments. Never raise the stem above the seat level indicator line. Tighten it snugly.

CLOTHES
· ·

Look for these features in your riding apparel:

Jerseys:

1. Stand-up collar seals in body heat.

2. Neck zipper for ventilation control.

3. Cut wider across the back for arms-forward comfort.

4. Sleeves shaped and set for unrestricted forward lean.

5. Conveniently placed pockets.

6. Stretchy, highly breathable fabric.

7. Form-fitted to avoid flapping and binding.

8. Cut longer in back.

Shorts:

Riding shorts are so popular because they feel good and make riding easier and more fun.

9. Extremely stretchy material for total freedom of motion.

10. Multi-panel construction for comfortable fit in the riding position.

11. Lower-cut front won't constrict abdomen.

12. Smooth, soft saddle pad minimizes friction and absorbs shock.

13. Longer legs protect from saddle chafing.

14. Gentle grip-strips in leg hems hold shorts in place.

Knees freeze. Cover your knees in cool weather. Cycling coaches insist that the tights go on below 65 degrees.

Why cycling shoes?

1. Stiff soles. So your feet won't flex and fatigue. This rigidity means more comfort and better transfer of your leg power to the crank.

2. Better fit. They slip easily into toe clips and fit precisely onto narrower pedals. Specially placed padding protects your toes from clip and strap pressure.

3. Pedal grip. Firm shoe-to-pedal connection gives you steady leg power throughout the pedal stroke. You'll go faster with less energy.

Why cycling socks?

Because your foot is a critical link to your pedals, your socks should fit snugly to allow the best connection to your pedals and keep your feet comfortable. Now available are fast-drying socks with excellent moisture transmission. They're shorter for better training.

Before washing cycling garments, close Velcro™ and zippers to avoid snagging. Whenever possible, line-dry your cycling apparel. Check the label for special care instructions.

Wash your gloves by soaking them in mild soap and gently squeezing to release the sweat and dirt (tight wringing may tear or distort them). Synthetic gloves may be machine washable. Always close the Velcro™ to avoid snagging. Carefully slip your hands into the damp gloves so they'll dry in a comfortable shape.

Cycling eyewear protects you from bugs, dust, and harmful radiation. Consider these factors.

1. Temple length: If too long, the glasses will slide down your nose. Too short and they'll dig into the back of your ears. Adjustable temples offer the perfect fit.

2. Ventilation: If you perspire heavily, you'll need air-flow space between the glasses and your forehead. Contact lens wearers may want a tight seal to keep out dust.

3. UV Protection: Your lenses should block out harmful ultraviolet and blue light rays. Interchangeable lenses allow you to adapt to varying light levels.

HELMETS

. . . .

For a secure stay-on-your-head helmet fit, use these three tests:

1. The Shake Test: Shake your helmeted head from side to side. The fit pads should hold the helmet snugly in place.

2. The Open Mouth Test: Buckle the chin strap and open your mouth. You should feel the helmet press firmly against the top of your head when your mouth is halfway open.

3. The Peel-Off Test: With chin-strap tightened, if you can "peel" the helmet off your head to the front or rear, the straps need adjusting.

For maximum protection, your helmet should be level on your head.

Look for the certificate stickers on helmets that meet these standards: ANSI (American National Standards Institute), and the more rigorous Snell Memorial Foundation, are the independent test standards for judging bicycle helmet safety.

MOUNTAIN BIKES

. . . .

Toe clips are even more valuable for ATBs than road bikes. Here's why:

1. Stay attached on bumpy descents. Toe clips are like stirrups for a cowboy on a bucking bronco.

2. Climbing efficiency. Why waste your strength? In those super-low gears, toe clips give you more power.

3. Power for the road. High rpm stretches of pavement are easier with firm foot attachment.

Still clip-phobic? Try 'em without the toe straps.

On steep descents, use your quick release to lower your seat 2" to 4". Your center of gravity is lower and you can get further back for increased anti-flip stability.

On bumpy descents, try deflating your tires slightly for a softer ride. You'll decrease pounding on your body and your bike, plus your steering will improve—your tires absorb the bumps instead of bouncing off them. Re-inflate for better rolling on smooth roads.

You stop faster using the front brake because the weight shifts forward as you stop. Use both brakes to avoid skidding or somersaulting. Keep your brakes well-adjusted and develop a feel for the range of pressure you must apply to stop quickly. Avoid panic stops by watching traffic and the road ahead.

TIRES

Just in Case

1. Gashed tires must have the slit reinforced with rugged tape from the inside or the inflated tube will burst through. Use handlebar tape or carry duct tape wrapped around a tire lever. (Or use a section from an old tire.)

2. Scraped skin should be immediately and thoroughly rinsed of grit. Don't delay. The longer you wait, the more it hurts.

3. Carry identification, your insurance card, emergency phone numbers, and a quarter for a call.

Correct tire inflation improves performance and safety. Because high-pressure tires lose air over several days, you should check them before every ride. Under-inflated tires roll slower, wear out faster, create dangerous handling conditions, and you risk expensive rim damage. A gauged floor pump is an essential cycling investment.

Rub talc on the tube and the bead edge of the tire you're mounting. A light powdering reduces friction to help the tube and tire "seat" well for easier mounting. Talc your spare tube and carry it in a sealed plastic bag.

Don't park your bike in the hot sun for very long. The heat can raise the tire pressure to the point of explosion.

If you ride over broken glass, avoid a puncture by lightly brushing the rotating tire with your gloved palm. This keeps small bits of glass from working into the tire.

Prevent flats by inspecting your tires regularly. Look for cuts, broken cords, and thinning tread. Replace worn tires before you start to get punctures.

What do those numbers on the tire mean?

1. The first number (700c, 27", 26") is the approximate diameter of your wheel.

2. The second number (25, 28, 1", 1¼") is the approximate width of the tire.
This measurement varies among manufacturers so it's best used as a guide.

Your bike has more than 1,000 moving parts, most of them in the chain. Chains are extremely reliable but when worn, dry, or dirty, friction increases, performance declines, shifting is slower, and damage to the gears can occur. Clean and lubricate your chain at the beginning of the season and then every 300 miles—more often if your rides are dusty or wet.

Chains last as long as tires (1,000 miles or so), so replace them together.

RACKS AND PACKS

. . . .

Don't rack your bike so that:

It obscures your tail lights

It's near your exhaust

Seat pack checklist:

Tire levers

Spare inner tube

patch kit (also great for carrying safety pins, an emergency $5, and a quarter for a phone call.)

Allen wrenches

Y-wrenches

Spoke wrench

Small screwdriver

ATB: Chain tool, tire gauge

Cycle Wipes™

Sunscreen for lips and skin

PowerBars™/Body fuel

Remember to leave space in your seat pack for arm and leg warmers and/or a jacket.

A book to read if you get stuck

Adapted with permission from Catalyst Communications, 1515 Walnut St., Boulder, CO 80302. Catalyst produced many of these tips for the Bicycle Exchange, a chain of stores in the Washington, D.C., area.

Glossary

Many of these terms appear frequently in this book.

Aero-bars. Handlebars that allow the rider to stretch forward to assume a more aerodynamic profile while cycling.

ANSI. *See* Helmet.

ATB. *See* Mountain Bike

Biathlon. A two-sport event featuring bicycling and running.

Bicycle Federation of America (BFA). A national, non-profit organization promoting the increased, safe use of bicycles.

Bicycle-friendly. Used to describe human-made environments designed to accommodate bicycles and facilitate their use.

Bicycle Institute of America (BIA). An international, nonprofit organization promoting bicycle sales and use through increased media coverage.

Bike-a-thon. An event held to raise money for a cause, with teams or individuals collecting contributions based on the distance they ride.

Bike-hiking. A new, fast-growing recreational activity which involves using a mountain bike for "hiking." Trails and dirt "fire-roads" are the most popular facilities.

Bikecentennial. This national, non-profit membership organization maps long-distance bicycle routes, provides information for touring bicyclists, and supports cycling advocacy.

BMX. Bicycle motocross (BMX) is a sport for young riders racing on short dirt tracks, using sturdy, single-speed bicycles.

Bonk. Also, "hitting the wall"; sudden exhaustion caused by the depletion of glycogen from muscles. Can be prevented by eating and drinking sensibly during rides.

Bottom bracket. The bottom of the frame; the place where the pedals and crank go.

Butted tube. An expensive frame material, thin throughout except where tubes are welded together.

Century. A 100–mile bicycle ride. The term is also used for bicycle rides of 25 miles (quarter century), 50 miles (half century), and 100 kilometers (metric century). Most recreational bicycle clubs sponsor at least one century a year. September is National Century Month (sponsored by the League of American Wheelmen).

Chromoly. Chrome-molybdenum, a common metal used in steel-frame alloys.

Clinchers. Tires with a beaded edge and a tube. Standard-issue for all but racing bikes. *See* Sew-up.

Criterium. A competitive cycling event held on a short road course, generally one mile or less per lap.

Cycle computer. A bicycle-mounted electronic accessory used to measure distance covered, time-elapsed, pace maintained, and with some models, elevation climbed.

Diamond-frame. Bicycle frame with high cross-bar (top tube). Also called "men's frame."

Facilities. Capital improvements designed to accommodate bicycles. Examples include bike paths, bike lanes, bikeways, shared roadways (when designed for shared use), and bicycle parking.

Freestyle. A type of bicycling that involves cycling acrobatics (e.g., on ramps) on modified BMX-style bikes. Popular among young riders.

Helmet. Helmets meeting standards set by American National Standards Institute (ANSI) or the Snell Memorial Foundation provide proven protection for bicyclists of all ages.

International Mountain Bicycle Association (IMBA). An advocacy organization concerned with off-road access for bicycles.

Invitational Ride. A recreational cycling event, often a century ride or multi-day tour, advertised and promoted by a club, business, or organization, which "invites" other riders to participate.

Kilometer. A competitive time trial event of 1,000 meters held on a bicycle-racing track (velodrome) in which the rider posting the lowest time wins.

League of American Wheelmen (LAW—the initials L.A.W. are always pronounced individually). Founded in 1880, the LAW is a national organization of bicyclists and bicycle clubs. It promotes cyclists' rights, sponsors rallies, and provides members with touring information. Also called "the League."

Mountain Bike. Also called all-terrain bike, city bike, or fat tire bike. Characterized by upright handlebars, heavy-duty brakes, wide tires, and low gearing. Mountain bikes are used for on-road riding even more than off-road, but bike-hiking is rapidly gaining in popularity.

National Bike Ride. A non-competitive national event, generally held in May, designed to encourage bike riders everywhere to ride their bikes.

Ordinary. *See* Safety.

Panniers. Literally "bread-baskets." Bicycle saddlebags.

Pro-Am. A competitive event in which professional and amateur cyclists race together.

Pursuit. A competitive track event in which individual or team competitors start on opposite sides and try to catch each other.

RAAM. The Race Across AMerica, a transcontinental ultra-marathon bicycle race from the West to the East Coast with both men and women competing.

Road Race. This competitive event, held on roadways, may be run several times around a single circuit, from point to point, or out and back on the same course.

Safety, Safeties. Equal-sized-wheel bicycle(s) of the 1890s. The term was used to distinguish these bicycles (which were safer to ride) from the more dangerous to ride "ordinary" high-wheel cycles of the 1880s.

Sag Wagon. A support vehicle that might accompany a race or tour to provide mechanical or personal assistance. Also called a "broom wagon" because such vehicles usually follow, or sweep, a race or tour.

Sanctioned Event. A recreational or racing event conforming to the rules of the appropriate governing organization.

Sew-up. Racing tires, with tube sewn into the belt, that are glued to the rim. Formerly puncture-prone, now available in relatively bulletproof versions.

Snell. *See* Helmet.

Sprint. A high-speed finish. Always occurs at the end of a race and may occur in the middle of a race to win a prime (pronounced "preem," points or prizes awarded within a race). Also, a competitive track event matching two to four riders over 1,000 meters.

Stage Race. A multi-day competitive event composed of several legs, or stages, such as road races and time trials. The Tour de France is a famous example.

Team Time Trial (TTT). Held on highways, where teams of four riders work together to race against the clock. Usually 50 km long for women's teams, 100 km for men's teams.

Time Trial. A competitive event where teams or individuals race against the clock. Held on roads or tracks.

Tour. A general term for a long recreational ride or vacation by bicycle. Also used for some shorter invitational rides and some races.

Track Race. Any competitive event held on a bicycle track. (*See* Velodrome.)

Triathlon. A three-sport event featuring swimming, running, and bicycling.

UCI. The Union Cycliste Internationale, the international governing body of bicycle racing.

UMCA. The Ultra Marathon Cycling Association sanctions the Race Across AMerica and other long-distance bicycle racing events in the U.S.

USCF. The United States Cycling Federation governs amateur bicycle racing in the U.S., selects the U.S. Olympic Cycling team, and organizes off-road bicycle racing events.

US Pro. The U.S. Professional Cycling Federation governs U.S. professional bicycle racing.

Velodrome. A bicycle racing track with banked turns. There are about 15 permanent velodromes in the U.S. See section on *Racing*.

Adapted and expanded from the Bicycle Institute of America's *Bicycling Reference Book*, 1990–91.

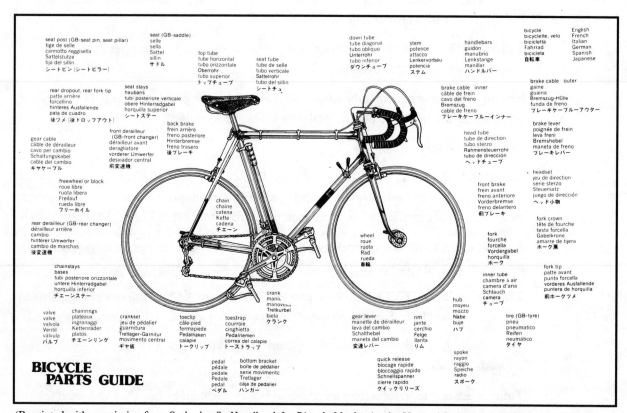

(Reprinted with permission from *Sutherland's Handbook for Bicycle Mechanics,* by Howard Sutherland, Sutherland Publications.)

Corporate Index

Subject Index

About the Authors:

A dedicated rider who has toured much of the U.S. and Europe by bicycle, Michael Leccese is a senior editor for *Landscape Architecture* and the author of the bestselling *Short Bike Rides in and around Washington, D.C.*(Globe Pequot, 1990). Arlene Plevin, also an avid cyclist, is the former editor of *Bicycle USA* and the former director of publications for the League of American Wheelmen. Currently, she's a freelance writer who makes her home in Washington, D.C.